For general information on our other products and services or for technical support, please contact our Customer Care Department within the United States at (800) 762-2974, outside the United States at (317) 572-3993 or fax (317) 572-4002.

Wiley also publishes its books in a variety of electronic formats. Some content that appears in print may not be available in electronic formats. For more information about Wiley products, visit our web site at www.wiley.com.

Library of Congress Cataloging-in-Publication Data:

Minoli, Daniel, 1952–
   Building the internet of things (IoT) with IPv6 and MIPv6 / Daniel Minoli.
     pages cm
   ISBN 978-1-118-47347-4 (hardback)
  1. Embedded Internet devices.   2. Internet of things.   3. TCP/IP (Computer network protocol)
4. Mobile computing.   I. Title.
   TK7895.E43M56 2013
   004.6'2–dc23

                                                                2012049072

10 9 8 7 6 5 4 3 2 1

BUILDING THE INTERNET OF THINGS WITH IPv6 AND MIPv6
The Evolving World of M2M Communications

DANIEL MINOLI

WILEY

BUILDING THE INTERNET OF THINGS WITH IPv6 AND MIPv6

For Anna

CONTENTS

PREFACE

The proliferation of an enlarged gamut of devices able to be directly connected to the Internet is leading to a new ubiquitous-computing paradigm: the Internet of Things (IoT). The IoT is a new type of Internet application that endeavors to make the thing's information (whatever that may be) available on a global scale. It has two attributes: (i) being an Internet application, and (ii) dealing with thing's information. The IoT is predicated on the expansion of the scope, network reach, and possibly even architecture of Internet through the inclusion of physical, instrumented objects. IoT aims at providing smarter services to the environment or the end-user as more *in situ*, transferable data becomes available. Thus, the IoT is seen as a new-generation information network that realizes machine-to-machine communication. The IoT eliminates time and space isolation between geographical space and virtual space, forming what proponents label as "smart geographical space," and creating new human–environment relationships. The latter implies that the IoT can advance the goal of integration of human beings and their surroundings. Applications range from energy efficiency to logistics, and many more.

At the "low end" of the spectrum, the thing's information is typically coded by the Unique Identification (UID) and/or Electronic Product Code (EPC); the information is (typically) stored in a Radio Frequency Identification (RFID) electronic tag; and, the information is uploaded by noncontact reading using an RFID reader. More generally, smart cards (SCs) will also play an important role in IoT; SCs typically incorporate a microprocessor and storage. At the mid-range of the spectrum one finds devices with embedded intelligence (microprocessors) and embedded active wireless capabilities to perform a variety of data gathering and possibly control functions. On-body biomedical sensors (supporting body area networks), home appliance and power management, and industrial control are some examples of these applications. At the other end of the spectrum, more sophisticated sensors can be employed in the IoT: some of these sensor approaches use distributed wireless sensor networks (WSNs) systems that can collect, process, and forward a wide variety of environmental data such as temperature, atmospheric and environmental chemical content, or even low or high resolution ambient video images from geographic dispersed locations; these objects may span a city, region, or large distribution grid.

The IoT is receiving a large amount of interest on the part of researchers, with thousands of papers published on this topic in the recent past. While specific applications have existed for several years, perhaps supported on private enterprise networks, Internet-based systems along with system supporting a broader application scope are now beginning to be deployed. *The capabilities offered by IP Version 6 (IPv6) are critical to the wide-spread deployment of the technology.*

This text aims at exploring these evolving trends and offering practical suggestions of how these technologies can be implemented in the service provider networks to support cost-effective applications, and how new revenue-generating services could be brought to the market. All the latest physical layer, MAC layer, and upper layer IoT and Machine to Machine (M2M) protocols are discussed.

Planners are asking questions such as: What is the Internet of Things? How does M2M apply? How can it help my specific operation? What is the cost of deploying such a system? Will standardization help? What are the security implications? This text addresses the following IoT aspects: evolving wireless standards, especially low energy and medical applications; IPv6 technologies; Mobile IPv6 (MIPv6) technologies; applications; key underlying technologies for IoT applications; implementation approaches; implementation challenges; and mid-range and long-range opportunities.

More specifically, the text reviews the latest technologies, the emerging commercial applications (especially health care), and the recently evolving standards, including all layers of the protocol stack applicable to IoT/M2M. The text focuses on extensively IPv6, MIPv6, and 6LowPAN/RPL and argues that the IoT/M2M may be the killer app for IPv6. It covers the latest standards supporting the IoT and the M2M applications, including home area networking (HAN), AMI, IEEE 802.15.4, 6LowPAN/RPL, Smart Energy 2.0, ETSI M2M, ZigBee IP (ZIP); ZigBee Personal Home and Hospital Care (PHHC) Profile; IP in Smart Objects (IPSO); BLE; IEEE 802.15.6 wireless body area networks (WBAN); IEEE 802.15 WPAN Task Group 4j (TG4j) medical body area networks; ETSI TR 101 557; near field communication (NFC); dedicated short-range communications (DSRC)/WAVE and related protocols; the Internet Engineering Task Force (IETF) IPv6 Routing Protocol for Low power and lossy networks (RPL)/Routing Over Low power and Lossy networks (ROLL); IETF Constrained Application Protocol (CoAP); IETF Constrained RESTful environments (CoRE); 3rd Generation Partnership Project (3GPP) Machine-Type Communications (MTC); long term evolution (LTE) cellular systems; and IEEE 1901.

This text covers the latest standards supporting IoT/M2M from the perspective of Body Area Network/E-health/Assistive Technologies; it also covers over-the-air surveillance, object tracking, smart grid, smart cards, and home automation.

This is believed to be the first book on MIPv6 with applications to the IoT, especially in a mobile context. This work will be of interest to technology investors; planners with carriers and service providers; CTOs; logistics professionals; engineers at equipment developers; technology integrators; Internet and Internet Service Providers (ISP); and telcos, and wireless providers, both domestically and in the rest of the world.

ABOUT THE AUTHOR

Among other activities, Mr. Minoli has done extensive work in Internet engineering, design, and implementation over the years. The results presented in this book are based on the foundation work done while at *Telcordia, NYU, Stevens Institute of Technology, Rutgers University, AT&T,* and other engineering firms, starting in the early 1990s and continuing to the present. Some of his Internet- and wireless-related work that plays a role in the deployment of the Internet of Things has been documented in books he has authored, including:

- *Internet and Intranet Engineering* (McGraw-Hill, 1997)
- *Internet Architectures* (co-authored) (Wiley, 1999)
- *Hotspot Networks: Wi-Fi for Public Access Locations* (McGraw-Hill, 2002)
- *Wireless Sensor Networks* (co-authored) (Wiley 2007)
- *Handbook of IPv4 to IPv6 Transition Methodologies For Institutional & Corporate Networks* (co-authored) (Auerbach, 2008)
- *Satellite Systems Engineering in an IPv6 Environment* (Francis and Taylor 2009)
- *Mobile Video with Mobile IPv6* (Wiley 2012)

Mr. Minoli has many years of technical hands-on and managerial experience in planning, designing, deploying, and operating IP/IPv6, telecom, wireless, satellite, and video networks, and Data Center systems and subsystems for global Best-In-Class carriers and financial companies. He has worked on advanced network deployments at financial firms such as *AIG, Prudential Securities, Capital One Financial*, and service provider firms such as *Network Analysis Corporation, Bell Telephone Laboratories,*

ITT DTS/Worldcom, Bell Communications Research (now Telcordia), AT&T, Leading Edge Networks Inc., SES, and other institutions. In the recent past, Mr. Minoli has been responsible for (i) the development and deployment of IPTV systems, (ii) the development and deployment of terrestrial and mobile IP-based networking services; (iii) deployments of large aperture antenna at teleports in the United States and abroad; (iv) deployment of satellite monitoring services worldwide using IP/MPLS services; and (v) IPv6 services. He also played a founding role in the launching of two companies through the high tech incubator Leading Edge Networks Inc., which he ran in the early 2000s: *Global Wireless Services,* a provider of secure broadband hotspot mobile Internet and hotspot VoIP services; and, *InfoPort Communications Group,* an optical and Gigabit Ethernet metropolitan carrier supporting Data Center/SAN/channel extension and cloud network access services. For several years, he has been Session, Tutorial, and more recently overall Technical Program Chair for the IEEE ENTNET (Enterprise Networking) conference; ENTNET focuses on enterprise networking and security requirements for large financial firms and other corporate institutions.

Mr. Minoli has also written columns for *ComputerWorld, NetworkWorld,* and *Network Computing* (1985–2006). He has taught at *New York University* (Information Technology Institute), *Rutgers University,* and *Stevens Institute of Technology* (1984–2006). Also, he was a Technology Analyst At-Large, for Gartner/DataPro (1985–2001); based on extensive hand-on work at financial firms and carriers, he tracked technologies and wrote CTO/CIO-level technical scans in the area of telephony and data systems, including topics on security, disaster recovery, network management, LANs, WANs (ATM and MPLS), wireless (LAN and public hotspot), VoIP, network design/economics, carrier networks (such as metro Ethernet and CWDM/DWDM), and e-commerce. Over the years, he has advised Venture Capitals for investments of $150M in a dozen high tech companies.

Mr. Minoli has also acted as Expert Witness in a (won) $11B lawsuit regarding a VoIP-based wireless Air-to-Ground radio communication system for airplane in-cabin services, as well as for a large lawsuit related to digital scanning and transmission of bank documents/instruments (such as checks). He has also been engaged as a technical expert in a number of patent infringement proceedings in the digital imaging and VoIP space supporting law firms such as *Schiff Hardin LLP, Fulbright & Jaworski LLP, Dimock Stratton LLP/Smart & Biggar LLP,* and *Baker & McKenzie LLP,* among others.

CHAPTER 1

WHAT IS THE INTERNET OF THINGS?

1.1 OVERVIEW AND MOTIVATIONS

The proliferation of an ever-growing set of devices able to be directly connected to the Internet is leading to a new ubiquitous-computing paradigm. Indeed, the Internet—its deployment and its use—has experienced significant growth in the past four decades, evolving from a network of a few hundred hosts (in its ARPAnet form) to a platform capable of linking billions of entities globally. Initially, the Internet connected institutional hosts and accredited terminals via specially developed gateways (routers). More recently, the Internet has connected servers of all kinds to users of all kinds seeking access to information and applications of all kinds. Now, with social media, it intuitively and effectively connects all sorts of people to people, and to virtual communities. The growth of the Internet shows no signs of slowing down, and it is steadily becoming the infrastructure fabric of choice for a new paradigm for all-inclusive pervasive computing and communications. The next evolution is to connect all "things" and objects that have (or will soon have) embedded wireless (or wireline) connectivity to control systems that support data collection, data analysis, decision-making, and (remote) actuation. "Things" include, but are not limited to, machinery, home appliances, vehicles, individual persons, pets, cattle, animals, habitats, habitat occupants, as well as enterprises. Interactions are achieved utilizing a plethora of possibly different networks; computerized devices of various functions, form factors,

Building the Internet of Things with IPv6 and MIPv6: The Evolving World of M2M Communications,
First Edition. Daniel Minoli.
© 2013 John Wiley & Sons, Inc. Published 2013 by John Wiley & Sons, Inc.

sizes, and capabilities such as iPads, smartphones, monitoring nodes, sensors, and tags; and a gamut of host application servers.

This new paradigm seeks to enhance the traditional Internet into a smart *Internet of Things* (IoT) created around intelligent interconnections of diverse objects in the physical world. In the IoT, commonly deployed devices and objects contain an embedded device or microprocessor that can be accessed by some communication mechanism, typically utilizing wireless links. The IoT aims at closing the gap between objects in the material world, the "things," and their logical representation in information systems. It is perceived by proponents as the "next-generation network (NGN) of the Internet." Thus, the IoT is a new type of Internet *application* that endeavors to make the thing's information (whatever that may be) available on a global scale using the Internet as the underlying connecting fabric (although other interconnection data networks, besides the Internet, can also be used such as private local area networks and/or wide area networks). The IoT has two attributes: (i) being an Internet application and (ii) dealing with the thing's information. The term *Internet of Things* was coined and first used by Kevin Ashton over a decade ago[1] (1). The "things" are also variously known as "objects," "devices," "end nodes," "remotes," or "remote sensors," to list just a few commonly used terms.

The IoT generally utilizes low cost information gathering and dissemination devices—such as sensors and tags—that facilitate fast-paced interactions in any place and at any time, among the objects themselves, as well as among objects and people. Actuators are also part of the IoT. Hence, the IoT can be described as a new-generation information network that enables seamless and continuous machine-to-machine (M2M)[2] and/or human-to-machine (H2M) communication. One of the initial goals of the IoT is to enable connectivity for the various "things"; a next goal is to be able to have the "thing" provide back appropriate, application-specific telemetry; an intermediary next step is to provide a web-based interface to the "thing" (especially when human access is needed); the final step is to permit actuation by the "thing" (i.e., to cause a function or functions to take place). Certain "things" are stationary, such as an appliance in a home; other "things" may be in motion, such as a car or a carton (or even an item within the carton) in a supply chain environment (either end-to-end, or while in an intermediary warehouse).

At the "low end" of the spectrum, the thing's information is typically coded by the unique identification (UID) and/or electronic product code (EPC); the information is (typically) stored in a radio frequency identification (RFID) electronic tag; and, the information is uploaded by noncontact reading using an RFID reader. In fact, UID and RFID have been mandated by the Department of Defense (DoD) for all their suppliers to modernize their global supply chain; RFID and EPC were also mandated

---

[1] Synonym key words are: "Ubiquitous computing (Ubi-comp), pervasive computing, ambient intelligence, sentient computing, and internet of objects." Multiple terminology terms should not confuse the reader, because, as a side note, often industry players redefine terms just to give the concept some cachet. For example, what some in the late 1960s called "time-sharing," others in the 1980s called it "utility computing." Then in the 1990s, people called it "grid computing." And now in the 2000s–2010s all the rage is "cloud." Same concepts, just new names.

[2] Some (e.g., 3GPP) also use the term machine-type communications (MTC) to describe M2M systems.

by Wal-Mart to all their suppliers as of January 1, 2006, and many other commercial establishments have followed suit since then. More generally, smart cards (SCs) will also play an important role in IoT; SCs typically incorporate a microprocessor and storage.

At the "mid range" of the spectrum, one finds devices with embedded intelligence (microprocessors) and embedded active wireless capabilities to perform a variety of data gathering and possibly control functions. On-body biomedical sensors, home appliance and power management, and industrial control are some examples of these applications.

At the other end of the spectrum, more sophisticated sensors can also be employed in the IoT: some of these sensor approaches use distributed wireless sensor network (WSN) systems that (i) can collect a wide variety of environmental data such as temperature, atmospheric and environmental chemical content, or even low- or high resolution ambient video images from geographically dispersed locations; (ii) can optionally pre-process some or all of the data; and (iii) can forward all these information to a centralized (or distributed/virtualized) site for advanced processing. These objects may span a city, region, or large distribution grid.

Other "things" may be associated with personal area networks (PANs), vehicular networks (VNs), or delay tolerant networks (DTNs).

The IoT is seen by many as a comprehensive extension of the Internet and/or Internet services that can establish and support pervasive connections between objects (things) (and their underlying intrinsic information) and data collection and management centers located in the network's "core" (possibly even in a distributed "cloud") (2, 3). The IoT operates in conjunction with real-time processing and ubiquitous computing. The IoT is also perceived as a global network that connects physical objects with virtual objects through the combination of data capture techniques and communication networks. As such, the IoT is predicated on the expansion of the scope, network reach, and possibly even the architecture of the Internet through the inclusion of physical instrumented objects, such expansion fused with the ability to provide smarter services to the environment or to the end user, as more *in situ* transferable data become available. Some see the IoT in the context of ambient intelligence; namely, a vision where environment becomes smart, friendly, context aware, and responsive to many types of human needs. In such a world, computing and networking technology coexist with people in a ubiquitous, friendly, and pervasive way: numerous miniature and interconnected smart devices create a new intelligence and interact with each other seamlessly (4).

The IoT effectively eliminates time and space isolation between geographical space and virtual space, forming what proponents label as "smart geographical space" and creating new human-to-environment (and/or H2M) relationships. The latter implies that the IoT can advance the goal of integration of human beings with their surroundings. A smart environment can be defined as consisting of networks of federated sensors and actuators and can be designed to encompass homes, offices, buildings, and civil infrastructure; from this granular foundation, large-scale end-to-end services supporting smart cities, smart transportation, and smart grids (SGs), among others, can be contemplated. Recently, the IEEE Computer Society stated that

"...The Internet of Things (IoT) promises to be the most disruptive technology since the advent of the World Wide Web. Projections indicate that up to 100 billion uniquely identifiable objects will be connected to the Internet by 2020, but human understanding of the underlying technologies has not kept pace. This creates a fundamental challenge to researchers, with enormous technical, socioeconomic, political, and even spiritual, consequences. IoT is just one of the most significant emerging trends in technology . . ." (5).

Figure 1.1 depicts the high level logical partitioning of the interaction space, showing where the IoT applies for the purpose of this text; the figure illustrates human-to-human (H2H) communication, M2M communication, H2M communications, and machine in (or on) humans (MiH) communications (MiH devices may include human embedded chips, medical monitoring probes, global positioning system (GPS) bracelets, and so on). The focus of the IoT is on M2M, H2M, and MiH applications; this range of applicability is the theme captured in this text.

Top left: Interaction space partitioning showing humans and machines
Top right: The target machine is shown explicitly to be embedded in the "thing"
Bottom left: Interaction space showing icons
Bottom right: Embedded machine, icon view

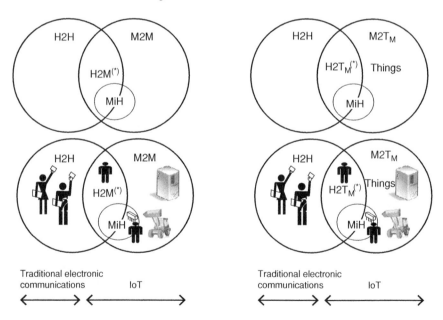

H2H: Human to Human
H2M: Human to Machine = H2T$_M$: Human to Thing with Microprocessor/Machine
M2M: Machine to Machine = M2T$_M$: Machine to Thing with Microprocessor/Machine
MiH: Machine in Humans
    (e.g., medical sensors)
    (also includes chips in animals/pets)

(*) People have been communicating with computers for over half-a-century, but in this context "machine" means a microprocessor embedded in some objects (other than a traditional computer)

FIGURE 1.1   H2H, H2M, and M2M environment.

Recently, the IoT has been seen as an emerging "paradigm of building smart communities" through the networking of various devices enabled by M2M technologies (but not excluding H2M), for which standards are now emerging (e.g., from European Telecommunications Standards Institute [ETSI]). *M2M services* aim at automating decision and communication processes and support consistent, cost-effective interaction for ubiquitous applications (e.g., fleet management, smart metering, home automation, and e-health). *M2M communications* per se is the communication between two or more entities that do not necessarily need direct human intervention: it is the communication between remotely deployed devices with specific roles and requiring little or no human intervention. M2M communication modules are usually integrated directly into target devices, such as automated meter readers (AMRs), vending machines, alarm systems, surveillance cameras, and automotive equipment, to list a few. These devices span an array of domains including (among others) industrial, trucking/transportation, financial, retail point of sales (POS), energy/utilities, smart appliances, and healthcare. The emerging standards allow both wireless and wired systems to communicate with other devices of similar capabilities; M2M devices, however, are typically connected to an application server via a mobile data communication network.

IoT applications range widely from energy efficiency to logistics, from appliance control to "smart" electric grids. Indeed, there is increasing interest in connecting and controlling in real time all sorts of devices for personal healthcare (patient monitoring and fitness monitoring), building automation (also known as building automation and control (BA&C)—for example, security devices/cameras; heating, ventilation, and air-conditioning (HVAC); AMRs), residential/commercial control (e.g., security HVAC, lighting control, access control, lawn and garden irrigation), consumer electronics (e.g., TV, DVRs); PC and peripherals (e.g., mouse, keyboard, joystick, wearable computers), industrial control (e.g., asset management, process control, environmental, energy management), and supermarket/supply chain management (this being just a partial list). Figures 1.2–1.5 provide some pictorial views of actual IoT applications; these figures only depict illustrative cases and are not exhaustive or normative. As it can be inferred, however, in an IoT environment there are a multitude of applications and players that need to be managed across multiple platforms (6). Some see IoT in the context of the "Web 3.0" (a name/concept advanced by John Markoff of *The New York Times* in 2006), although this term has not yet gained industry-wide, consistent support (7). The proposed essence of the term implies "an intelligent Web," such as supporting natural language search, artificial intelligence/machine learning, and machine-facilitated understanding of information, with the goal of providing a more intuitive user experience. IoT might fit such paradigm, but does not depend on it.

The initial vision of the IoT in the mid-2000s was of a world where physical objects are tagged and uniquely identified by RFID transponders; however, the concept has recently grown in multiple dimensions, encompassing dispersed sensors that are able to provide real-world intelligence and goal-oriented collaboration of distributed smart objects via local interconnections (such as through wireless LANs, WSNs, and so on), or global interconnections (such as through the Internet). The

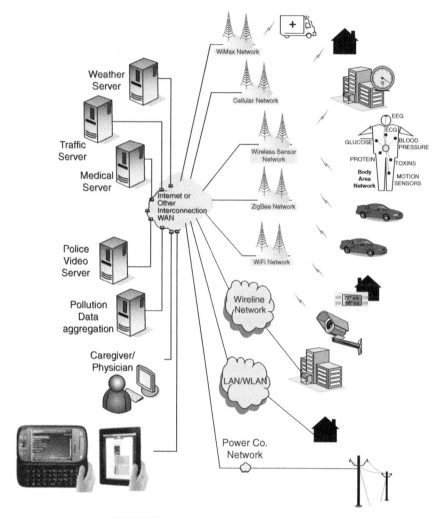

FIGURE 1.2   Illustrative example of the IoT.

seamless integration of communication capabilities between RFID tags, sensors, and actuators is seen as an important area of development. WSNs are likely the "outer tier" communication apparatus of the IoT. Thus, the IoT is not just an extension of today's Internet: it represents an aggregate of intelligent end-to-end systems that enable smart solutions, and, as such, it covers a diverse range of technologies, including sensing, communications, networking, computing, information processing, and intelligent control technologies, some of which are covered in this text.

As stated above, we take the IoT to encompass the M2M, H2M, and MiH space. It has been estimated that in 2011, there were 7 billion people on earth and 60 billion machines worldwide. Market research firm Frost & Sullivan recently forecasted that

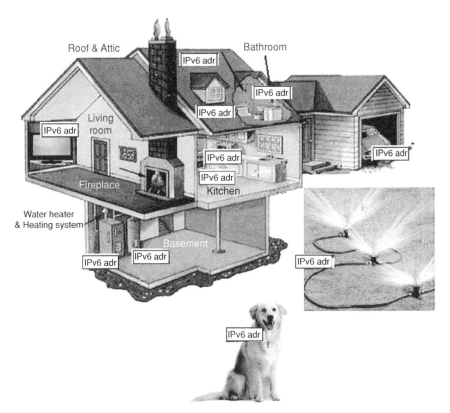

FIGURE 1.3   Another illustrative example of the IoT.

mobile computing devices, such as connected laptops, netbooks, tablets, and MiFi nodes, will increase to 50 million units by 2017 in the United States, while total cellular M2M connections are expected to increase from around 24 million in 2010 to more than 75 million over the same period; worldwide, the expectation is that the number of M2M device connections will grow from around 60 million in 2010 to over 2 billion in 2020 (8). Other market research puts the worldwide M2M revenues at over \$38 billion in 2012 (9). Yet other market research companies project 15 billion connected devices moving 35 trillion gigabytes of data at a cost of \$3 trillion annually by 2015 (10). These market data point to major development and deployment of the IoT technology in the next few years. Note that personal communication devices (smartphones, pads, and so on) can be viewed as machines or just simply as end nodes; when personal communication devices are used for H2M devices where the human employs the smartphone to communicate with a machine (such as a thermostat or a home appliance), then we consider the personal communication devices part of the IoT (otherwise we do not).

The definition of "IoT" has still some variability and can encompass different aspects depending on the researcher and/or the field in question. The European

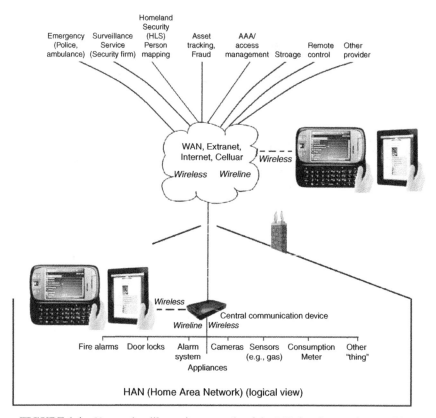

FIGURE 1.4   Yet another illustrative example of the IoT showing service providers.

Commission recently made these observations, which we can employ in our discussion of the IoT (11):

> "... Considering the functionality and identity as central it is reasonable to define the IoT as *"Things having identities and virtual personalities operating in smart spaces using intelligent interfaces to connect and communicate within social, environmental, and user contexts."* A different definition, that puts the focus on the seamless integration, could be formulated as "Interconnected objects having an active role in what might be called the Future Internet." The semantic origin of the expression is composed by two words and concepts: "Internet" and "Thing," where "Internet" can be defined as *"The world-wide network of interconnected computer networks, based on a standard communication protocol, the Internet suite (TCP/IP),"* while "Thing" is *"an object not precisely identifiable."* Therefore, semantically, "Internet of Things" means "a world-wide network of interconnected objects uniquely addressable, based on standard communication protocols ..."

Some see IoT as an environment where "things talk" and/or "things talk back" (7); effectively this simply means that devices have communication capabilities. The set of

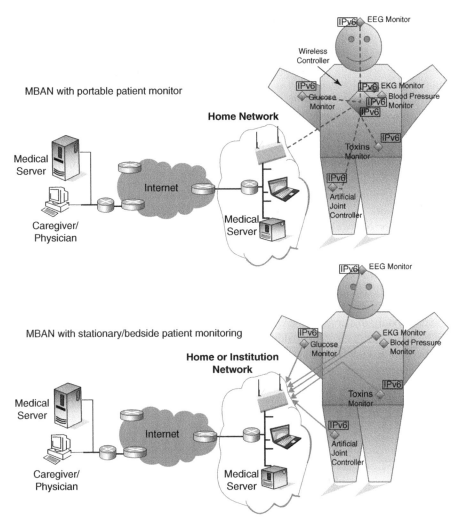

FIGURE 1.5 Yet another illustrative example of the IoT (body area network (BAN) application).

data and environmental awareness that objects should have depends on the application in question. Researchers are suggesting that objects should have the capability to be aware of such data as, but not limited to, its creation, transformation, ownership change, and physical-world parameters. Also, in some applications, objects should be able to interact actively with the environment, operating as actuators.

At a macro level, an IoT comprises a remote set of assets (a sensing domain), a network domain, and an applications domain. We define the data processing thing, also known as data integration point or person (DIPP), as the point (entity, person) where the administrative decisioning and/or the data accumulation takes place. We define the "remote things," also known as data end points (DEPs), as the devices where events are sensed, data are collected, and/or an actuation takes place. Table 1.1 provides a working taxonomy of "things" in the IoT universe, as perceived in this text. There are interactions of interest between a DIPP being a human (H) and a "remote thing" being a machine/device (e.g., a thermostat) (such as a person changing the setting of the thermostat while away from home) or between two machines (M) (such as a server handling the usage reading from a residential electric meter). A person/human may use a PC or laptop, but increasingly a person may be using an iPad/tablet or a smartphone. The DIPP could be accessing the IoT system from a stationary location (e.g., a PC or server), from a wireless local environment (e.g., a fixed home hotspot), or from a completely mobile venue (e.g., using a smartphone). The "remote thing" could be stationary (e.g., a thermostat), on a wireless LAN or sensor network (but be relatively stationary), or be completely mobile (e.g., on a mobile ad hoc Network (MANET)—a self-configuring infrastructureless network of mobile devices connected by wireless links—or on a 3G/4G cellular network).

IoT is not seen by advocates as a future thing, but a set of capabilities that are already available at this time. Proponents and developers are endeavoring to reuse what is already available by way of the Internet suite of protocols, although there may be a need for some more research and/or standards, especially for large-scale, low power, broadly dispersed (where sensors are broadly dispersed in the environment) applications. An overriding goal is not to redesign the Internet (12); many researches position the IoT and work in support of the IoT simply as the (normal) "Evolution of the Internet" (what might be called by analogy with cellular networks, the long-term evolution of the Internet (LTEI)). A key observation is that if each of the large multitude of things in the IoT is to be addressed directly and individually, then a large address space is needed.

Cost as well as energy requirements of embedded devices require the use of efficient protocols and efficient communication architectures for the IoT. Standardization of IoT elements also becomes critical: the benefits of standardization include reduced complexity of IoT deployments, reduced deployment time for new services, lower capital requirements (CAPEX), and lower operating expense (OPEX). The IoT requires robust "last-yard," "last-mile," and "core" network technologies to make it a commercial reality.

Various technologies have indeed emerged in the past two decades that can be utilized for implementations, including PANs, such as IEEE 802.15.4; wireless local area networks (WLANs); WSNs; 3G/4G cellular networks; metro-Ethernet networks; multiprotocol label switching (MPLS); and virtual private network (VPN) systems. Wireless access and/or wireless ad hoc mesh systems reduce the "last-mile" cost of IoT applications, such as for distributed monitoring and control applications. However, we believe that the fundamental technical advancement that will foster the deployment of the IoT is IP Version 6 (IPv6). *In fact, IoT may well become the "killer-app" for IPv6.* IoT is deployable using IP Version 4 (IPv4) as has been the case in the recent past, but only IPv6 provides the proper scalability and functionality to make it economical, ubiquitous, and pervasive. There are many advantages in using IP for IoT, but we have to ascertain that the infrastructure and the supporting

TABLE 1.1 Taxonomy of "Things" in IoT

H2M

DIPP "thing"	H	Stationary access/connectivity			Local mobility access/connectivity			Full mobility access/connectivity		
Remote "thing" (DEP)	M	Target device is stationary	Target device has local mobility	Target device has full mobility	Target device is stationary	Target device has local mobility	Target device has full mobility	Target device is stationary	Target device has local mobility	Target device has full mobility
Example		Access a home thermostat from an office PC	Access a monitor on a home-bound pet from an office PC	Access a GPS device on a teenager's car from an office PC	Access a home thermostat from a home, office, or hotspot wireless PC	Access a monitor on a home-bound pet from a home, office, or hotspot wireless PC	Access a GPS device on a teenager's car from a home, office, or hotspot wireless PC	Access a home thermostat from a smartphone	Access a monitor on a home-bound pet from a smartphone	Access a GPS device on a teenager's car from a smartphone

M2M

DIPP "thing"	M1	Stationary access/connectivity			Local mobility access/connectivity			Full mobility access/connectivity		
Remote "thing" (DEP)	M2	Target device is stationary	Target device has local mobility	Target device has full mobility	Target device is stationary	Target device has local mobility	Target device has full mobility	Target device is stationary	Target device has local mobility	Target device has full mobility
Example		Access a home electrical meter from an office/provider server	Access a monitor on a home-bound pet from an office/provider server	Access a GPS device on a person's car from an office/provider server	Access a home electrical meter from a WLAN-based office/provider server	Access a monitor on a home-bound pet from a WLAN-based office/provider server	Access a GPS device on a person's car from a WLAN-based office/provider server	Access a home electrical meter from a roaming-3G/4G based provider server	Access a monitor on a home-bound pet from a roaming-3G/4G-based provider server	Access a GPS device on a person's car from a roaming-3G/4G-based provider server

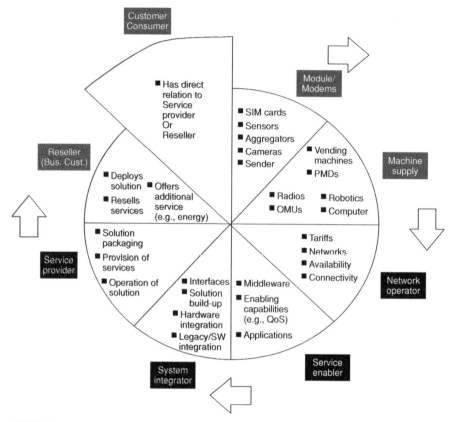

FIGURE 1.6 Stakeholder universe in the IoT/M2M world (representative, not complete view).

technology scale to meet the challenges. This is why there is a broad agreement that IPv6 is critical for the deployment of the IoT.

IoT stakeholders include technology investors, technology developers, planners with carriers and service providers, chief technical officers (CTOs), logistics professionals, engineers at equipment developers, technology integrators, Internet-backbone and ISP providers, cloud service providers, and telcos and wireless providers, both domestically and in the rest of the world. See Figure 1.6.

1.2 EXAMPLES OF APPLICATIONS

Vertical industries in arenas such as automotive and fleet management, telehealth (also called telecare by some) and Mobile Health (m-Health—when mobile communications are used), energy and utilities, public infrastructure, telecommunications, security and defense, consumer telematics, automated teller machines (ATMs)/kiosk/POS, and digital signage are in the process of deploying IoT services and capabilities. Proponents make the claim that IoT will usher in a wide range of smart applications and services to cope with many of the challenges individuals and organizations face in their everyday lives. For example, remote healthcare monitoring systems could aid in managing costs and alleviating the shortage of healthcare personnel; intelligent transportation systems could aid in reducing traffic congestion and the issues caused by congestion such as air pollution; smart distribution systems from utility grids to supply chains could aid in improving the quality and reducing the cost of their respective goods and services; and, tagged objects could result in more systematic recycling and effective waste disposal (13). These applications may change the way societies function and, thus, have a major impact on many aspects of people's lives in the years to come. Many of today's home entertainment and monitoring systems often offer a web interface to the end user; the IoT aims at greatly extending those capabilities to many other devices and many other applications.

A short list of (early) applications includes the following (also see Table 1.2):

- Things on the move
    Retail
    Logistics
    Pharmaceutical
    Food
- Ubiquitous intelligent devices
- Ambient and assisted living
    Health
    Intelligent Home
    Transportation
- Education and Information
- Environmental aspects/Resource Efficiency
    Pollution and disaster avoidance

A longer, but far from complete, list of applications includes the following:

- Smart appliances
- Efficient appliances via the use of eco-aware/ambient-aware things
- Interaction of physical and virtual worlds; executable tags, intelligent tags, autonomous tags, collaborative tags
- Intelligent devices cooperation
- Ubiquitous readers
- Smart transportation
- Smart living
- *In vivo* health

TABLE 1.2   The Scope of IoT

Service Sector	Application Group	Location (Partial List)	Devices ("Things") of Interest (Partial List)
Real estate (industrial)	Commercial/ institutional	Office complex, school, retail space, hospitality space, hospital, medical site, airport, stadium	UPS, generator, HVAC, fire and safety (EHS), lighting, security monitoring, security control/access
	Industrial	Factory, processing site, inventory room, clean room, campus	
Energy	Supply providers/ consumers	Power generation, power transmission, power distribution, energy management, AMI	Turbine, windmills, UPS, batteries, generators, fuel cells
	Alternative energy systems	Solar systems, wind system, cogeneration systems	
	Oil/gas operations	Rigs, well heads, pumps, pipelines, refineries	
Consumer and home	Infrastructure	Home wiring/routers, home network access, home energy management	Power systems, HVAC/thermostats, sprinklers, MID, dishwashers,
	Safety	Home fire safety system, home environmental safety system (e.g., CO_2), home security/intrusion detection system, home power protection system, remote telemetry/video into home, oversight of home children, oversight of home based babysitters, oversight of home-bound elderly	refrigerators, ovens, eReaders, washer/dryers, computers, digital videocameras, meters, lights, computers, game consoles, TVs, PDRs
	Environmentals	Home HVAC, home lighting, home sprinklers, home appliance control, home pools and jacuzzis	
	Entertainment	TVs, PDRs	

TABLE 1.2 (*Continued*)

Service Sector	Application Group	Location (Partial List)	Devices ("Things") of Interest (Partial List)
Healthcare	Care	Hospitals, ERs, mobile POC, clinic, laboratories, doctor's office	MRIs, PDAs, implants, surgical equipment, BAN devices, power systems
	In vivo/home	Implants, home monitoring systems, body area networks (BANs)	
	Research	Diagnostic laboratory, pharmaceutical research site	
Industrial	Resource automation	Mining sites, irrigation sites, agricultural sites, monitored environments (wetlands, woodlands, etc.)	Pumps, valves, vets, conveyors, pipelines, tanks, motors, drives, converters, packaging systems, power systems
	Fluids management	Petrochemical sites, chemical sites, food preparation site, bottling sites, wineries, breweries	
	Converting operations	Metal processing sites, paper processing sites, rubber/plastic processing sites, metalworking site, electronics assembly site	
	Distribution	Pipelines, conveyor belts	
Transportation	Nonvehicular	Airplanes, trains, busses, ships/boats, ferries	Vehicles, ships, planes, traffic lights, dynamic signage, toll gates, tags
	Vehicles	Consumer and commercial vehicle (car, motorcycle, etc.), construction vehicle (e.g., crane)	
	Transportation subsystems	Toll booths, traffic lights and traffic management, navigation signs, bridge/tunnel status sensors	

(*continued*)

TABLE 1.2 (*Continued*)

Service Sector	Application Group	Location (Partial List)	Devices ("Things") of Interest (Partial List)
Retail	Stores	Supermarkets, shopping centers, small stores, distribution centers	POS terminals, cash registers, vending machines, ATMs, parking meters
	Hospitality	Hotel, restaurants, café', banquet halls, shopping malls	
	Specialty	Banks, gas stations, bowling, movie theaters	
Public safety and security	Surveillance	Radars, military security, speed monitoring systems, security monitoring systems	Vehicles, ferries, subway trains, helicopters, airplanes, video cameras, ambulances, police cars, fire trucks, chemical/radiological monitors, triangulation systems, UAVs
	Equipment	Vehicles, ferries, subway trains, helicopters, airplanes	
	Tracking	Commercial trucks, postal trucks, ambulances, police cars	
	Public infrastructure	Water treatment sites, sewer systems, bridges, tunnels	
	Emergency services	First responders	
IT systems and networks	Public networks	Network facilities, central offices, data centers, submarine cable, cable TV headends, telco hotels, cellular towers, poles, teleports, ISP centers, lights-off sites, NOCs	Network elements, switches, core routers, antenna towers, poles, servers, power systems, backup generators
	Enterprise networks	Data centers, network equipment (e.g., routers)	

- Security-based living
- Energy and resource conservation
- Advanced metering infrastructure (AMI)
- Energy harvesting (biology, chemistry, induction)
- Power generation in hash environments
- Energy recycling
- Ambient intelligence
- Authentication, trust, and verification

- Search the physical world ("Google of things")
- Virtual worlds
- Web of things (WoT) which aims for direct web connectivity by pushing its technology down to devices

Regarding **retail**, the first large-scale application of the IoT technologies will be to replace the bar code in retail environments. The challenge so far has been the (i) higher cost of the tag over the bar code, (ii) some needed technology improvement for transportation of metals and liquid items, and (iii) privacy concerns. Nonetheless, the replacement has already started in some pilot projects. Although one may expect to see the coexistence of the two identification mechanisms for many years into the future, advances in the electronics industry will make the RFID tag more affordable and, thus, more attractive and accessible to the retailers. **Logistics** aims at improving efficiency of processes or enables new value-added features. The warehouses of the future will likely become completely automated, with items being checked in and out and orders automatically passed to the suppliers. For example, with IoT techniques foods may be transported without human intervention from producer to consumer, and the manufacturers will have a direct feedback on the market's needs. **Health** logistics is one of the near-term applications of IoT, noting, for example, that reportedly more than 7000 people lose their lives in US hospitals every year because of the errors in medication delivery to the patient. *Health logistics, the flow of drugs and patients, requires one to design systems that can be supported by the healthcare workers and that can be integrated from the supply chain to the bedside, and even before the patient is admitted to a hospital (11)*. The cost of healthcare is rising every year, having reached 16% to 17% of the US gross domestic product (GDP), with the trend to add at least 1% each year. Wide utilization of wireless communications in conjunction with mobile monitoring devices can reduce healthcare costs by billions of dollars on an annual basis, with much of that savings derived by reducing hospitalizations and extending independent living for seniors (14). These observations are but a small sample of the applications and scope of IoT. The evolution to a connected world spans the arena of measurement, data collection, state inference, and reaction. Some researchers also see a convergence of utility computing (cloud computing) with the IoT (15). These and other practical applications will be discussed in the chapters that follow, particularly in Chapter 3.

1.3   IPv6 ROLE

We retain the position that *IoT may well become the "killer-app" for IPv6.* Using IPv6 with its abundant address spaces, globally unique object (thing) identification and connectivity can be provided in a standardized manner without additional status or address (re)processing—hence, its intrinsic advantage over IPv4 or other schemes.

It is both desirable as well as feasible for all physical (and even virtual or logical) objects to have a permanent unique identifier, an object ID (OID). It is also desirable as well as feasible for all end-point network locations and/or intermediary-point network locations to have a durable unique network address (NAdr); the IPv6 address space enables the concrete realization of these goals. When objects that have enough intelligence to (run a communication protocol stack so that they can) communicate are placed on a network, these objects can be tagged with an NAdr. Every object then has a tuple (OID, NAdr) that is always unique, although the second entry of the tuple may change with time, location, or situation. In a stationary, nonvariable, or mostly static environment, one could opt, if one so chose, to assign the OID to be identical to the NAdr where the object is expected to attach to the network; that is, the object inherits the tuple (NAdr, NAdr). In the rare case where the object moved, the OID could then be refreshed to the address of the new location; that is, the object then inherits the tuple (NAdr', NAdr'). However, there is a general trend toward object mobility, giving rise to a dynamic environment (e.g., for mobile or variable case); hence, to retain maximal flexibility it is best to separate, in principle, the OID from the NAdr and thus assign a general (OID, NAdr) tuple where the OID is completely invariant; however, the OID can still be drawn from the NAdr space, that is from the IPv6 address space.

What was described above is not feasible in an IPv4 world, because in the 32-bit address space, only $2^{32} \sim 10^{10}$ NAdr location can be identified uniquely. IPv6 offers a much larger 2^{128} space; hence, the number of available unique node addressees is $2^{128} \sim 10^{39}$. IPv6 has more than 340 undecillion (340,282,366,920,938,463,463,374, 607,431,768,211,456) addresses, grouped into blocks of 18 quintillion addresses. Already today many tags operate with a 128-bit OID field that allows $2^{128} \sim 10^{39}$ ($\approx 3.4 \times 10^{38}$) unique identifiers, but the tuple (OID, NAdr = OID) could not be defined uniquely in the IPv4 world.

IPv6 was originally defined in 1995 in request for comments (RFC) 1883 and then further refined by RFC 2460, "Internet Protocol, Version 6 (IPv6) Specification," authored by S. Deering and R. Hinden (December 1998). A large body of additional RFCs has emerged in recent years to add capabilities and refine the IPv6 concept. IPv6 embodies IPv4 best practices but removes unused or obsolete IPv4 characteristics; this results in a better-optimized Internet protocol. Some of the advantages of IPv6 include the following:

- Scalability and expanded addressing capabilities: as noted, IPv6 has 128-bit addresses versus 32-bit IPv4 addresses. With IPv4, the theoretical number of available IP addresses is $2^{32} \sim 10^{10}$. IPv6 offers a much larger 2^{128} space. Hence, the number of available unique node addressees is $2^{128} \sim 10^{39}$.

- "Plug-and-play": IPv6 includes a "plug-and-play" mechanism that facilitates the connection of equipment to the network. The requisite configuration is automatic; it is a serverless mechanism.

- Security: IPv6 includes and requires security in its specifications such as payload encryption and authentication of the source of the communication. End-to-end security, with built-in strong IP-layer encryption and authentication (embedded security support with mandatory IP security (IPsec) implementation), is supported.

- Mobility: IPv6 includes an efficient and robust mobility mechanism namely an enhanced support for mobile IP, specifically, the set of mobile IPv6 (MIPv6) protocols, including the base protocol defined in RFC 3775.

For the IoT as well as for other applications for smartphones and similar devices, there is a desire to support direct communication between mobile nodes (MNs) and far-end destinations, whether such far-ends are themselves a stationary node or another MN. Such far-end destination could be, for example, a roving sensor collecting environmental or other data. In order to efficiently maintain reacheability, thus supporting flexible mobility, the goal is to retain the same explicit IP address regardless of the real-time location or specific network elements and/or networks used to support connectivity. This is not easily achievable with IPv4 for a number of reasons; however, MIPv6 described in RFC 3775, "Mobility Support in IPv6" (June 2004), among others, facilitates this task. RFC 3775 is known as the "MIPv6 base specification." RFCs are specifications and related materials published by the Internet Engineering Task Force (IETF). IPv6 mobility, specifically MIPv6, relies on IPv6 capabilities.

RFC 3775 notes that without specific support for mobility in IPv6, packets destined to an MN would not be able to reach it while the MN is away from its home network. In order to continue communication in spite of its movement, an MN could change its IP address each time it moves to a new link, *but the MN would then not be able to maintain transport and higher-layer connections when it changes location.* Mobility support in IPv6 is particularly important, as mobile users are likely to account for a majority, or at least a substantial fraction, of the population of the Internet during the lifetime of IPv6, including instrumented objects, which is the topic of this text. MIPv6 allows nodes to remain reachable while moving around in the IPv6 Internet: it enables a device (an MN) to change its attachment point to the Internet without losing higher-layer functionality through the use of tunneling between it and a designated home agent (HA). Stated another way, MIPv6 enables an MN to maintain its connectivity to the Internet when moving from one AR to another, a process referred to as handover. See Figure 1.7.

Two fundamental questions are: (1) how to deliver and/or receive information from an instrumented object and (2) how to do so in the presence of mobility. It is to be understood that mobility management (items 1 and 2 just listed) can be handled, to some (considerable) degree, by acquiring new physical links at the physical layer, namely, via a new channel acquisition at the PHY layer as supported by a cellular-level cell handoff (or a WiFi, WiMAX, or ZigBee handoff), in a transparent manner to the upper layers (which include IP and higher layers supporting the video stream). However, there are situations where an IP-level handoff is desirable; MIPv6 addresses the latter case. Figure 1.8 depicts the protocol stacks at a generic level supporting these two modes.

These (IPv6) mechanisms, which give objects the ability of addressing each other and of verifying their respective identities, enable all the objects to exchange information, if they so choose and/or if it is necessary. This enables one to create a highly woven fabric of processing hosts, communication nodes and relays, sensors, and actuators.

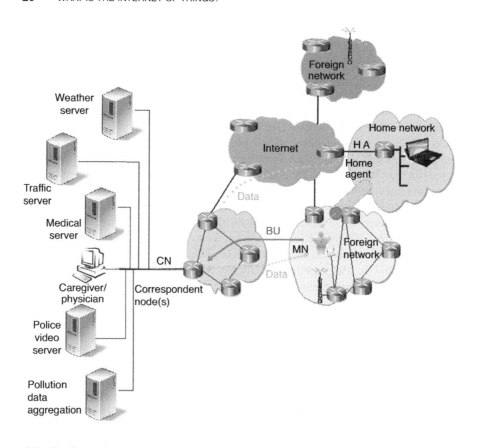

BU = Binding updates
MN = Mobile node
CN = Correspondent note

FIGURE 1.7   Communication supported in MIPv6 through the HA.

1.4   AREAS OF DEVELOPMENT AND STANDARDIZATION

Despite significant technological advances in many subtending disciplines, difficulties associated with the evaluation of IoT solutions under realistic conditions in real-world experimental deployments still hamper their maturation and significant rollout. Obviously, with limited standardization, there are capability mismatches between different devices; also, there are mismatches between communication and processing bandwidth. While IoT systems can utilize existing Internet protocols, as mentioned earlier, in a number of cases the power-, processing-, and capabilities-constrained IoT environments can benefit from additional protocols that help optimize the communications and lower the computational requirements. The M2M environment

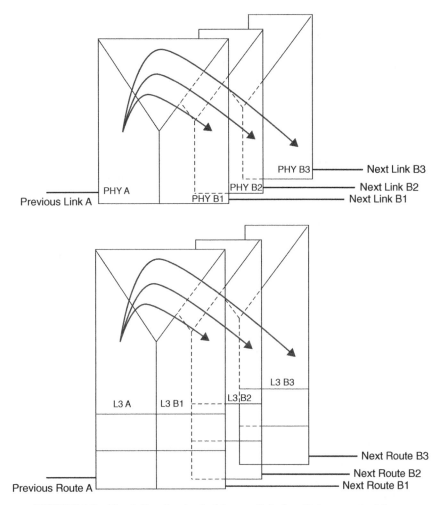

FIGURE 1.8   Handoff at the physical (e.g., cellular) or IP (e.g., routing) layer.

has been a fragmented space, but recent standardization efforts are beginning to show results.

Some see the four "pillars" supporting or defining the IoT: (i) M2M/MTC as the "Internet of devices"; (ii) RFID as the "Internet of objects"; (iii) WSN as the "Internet of transducers"; and (iv) supervisory control and data acquisition (SCADA) as the "Internet of controllers" (7). Certainly, these are the constituent elements of the IoT ecosystems, but they do not uniquely define the space, especially since WSNs are not uniquely well defined, and SCADA and RFIDs are legacy technologies. We see the IoT mostly, but not exclusively, as a new generation of collaborative, ubiquitous-computing entities that have significant embedded computing/communication capabilities, by and large using wireless links at the physical/media access layer and migrating (or natively using) IPv6 at the networking layer; while not aiming at excluding any subsegment of the space, a forward-looking environment is assumed and predicated in our discussion.

Standards covering many of the underlying technologies are critical because proprietary solutions fragment the industry. Standards are particularly important when there is a requirement to physically or logically connect entities across an interface. Device-, network-, and application standards can enable global solutions for seamless operations at reduced costs. The focus of this text is to make the case that IPv6 is the fundamental optimal network communication technology to deploy IoT in a robust, commercial manner rather than just a preliminary desktop "science experiment" in some academic researcher's laboratory. (Layer 2 wireless technologies are also critical to IoT's end-to-end connectivity.)

IoT standardization spans several domains, including physical interfaces, access connectivity (e.g., low power IEEE802.15.4-based wireless standards such as IEC62591, 6LoWPAN, and ZigBee Smart Energy (SE) 2.0, DASH7, ETSI M2M), networking (such as IPv6), and applications. Some studies have shown that for the home two wireless physical layer communication technologies that best meet the overall performance and cost requirements are Wi-Fi (802.11/n) and ZigBee (802.15.4) (16). Examples of standardization efforts targeted for these environments include the initiatives known as "constrained RESTful environments (CoRE)," "IPv6 over low power WPAN (6LoWPAN)," and "routing over low power and lossy networks (ROLL)," which have been (and are being) studied by appropriate working groups of the IETF (12).

Some specific considerations need to be taken when designing protocols and architectures for interconnecting smart objects to the Internet, including scalability, power efficiency, interworking between different technologies and network domains, usability and manageability, and security and privacy (12). To make the IoT a practical pervasive reality, significant research needs to be conducted within and across these technological aspects of IoT. This has recently motivated a voluminous amount of research activities in the field. Some areas of active research include but are not limited to the following (13–15):

- Standardization at all layers/domains
- Architectures and middlewares for IoT integration
- Protocols for smart things: end-to-end/M2M protocols and standardization
- Mobility management
- Cloud computing and things internetworking
- Lightweight implementations of cryptographic stacks
- End-to-end security capabilities for the things
- Bootstrapping techniques
- Routing protocols for the IoT
- Global connectivity

1.5 SCOPE OF THE PRESENT INVESTIGATION

Given potential benefit of the technology, corporate and technical planners may be asking questions such as, but not limited to, "What is the IoT?", "How can it help my specific operation?", "What is the cost of deploying such a system?", and "What are the security implications?". This text addresses the following IoT aspects: IPv6 technologies, MIPv6 technologies, applications, key technologies for the IoT applications, implementation approaches, implementation challenges, and mid-range and long-range opportunities.

Observations such as these give impetus to the investigation in this text (11):

" . . . RFID and related identification technologies will be the cornerstone of the upcoming Internet of Things . . . While RFID was initially developed with retail and logistics applications in mind in order to replace the bar code, developments of active components will make this technology much more than a simple identification scheme. In the not too distant future, it can be expected that a single numbering scheme, such as IPv6, will make every single object identifiable and addressable. Smart components will be able to execute different set of actions, according to their surroundings and the tasks they are designed for. There will be no limit to the actions and operations these smart "things" will be able to perform: for instance, devices will be able to direct their transport, adapt to their respective environments, self-configure, self-maintain, self-repair, and eventually even play an active role in their own disposal. To reach such a level of ambient intelligence, however, major technological innovations and developments will need to take place. Governance, standardization and interoperability are absolute necessities on the path towards the vision of things able to communicate with each other . . . "

and (8):

"The M2M Evolution: In a "Perfect Storm" of technology adoption, M2M is leveraging modern Internet technologies and infrastructures with mature IT middleware and solutions to address the Enterprise's desire for better utilizing operational assets and their associated information."

and (9):

"M2M is poised to become an integral part of the telecoms landscape with a potentially transformative impact on a vast number of industries—with an equally vast number of services and applications to monetize. As operators struggle to gain market share in a time of subscriber saturation, M2M represents an opportunity to transform revenue streams, ARPU and churn rates . . . M2M is already being successfully utilized in several industries, with impressive results . . . With other industries as diverse as automotive and e-health . . . smart services, smart metering and the connected home promise a future of eco-friendly energy use, technologically advanced living spaces and machine to machine connectivity. M2M seeks to improve the lives of subscribers, the success of enterprises and the operations of service providers . . . "

and (17):

"After years of anticipation, the M2M era has finally arrived. A new Yankee Group forecast predicts enterprise cellular M2M connections worldwide will surge from 81.8 million in 2011 to nearly 217.5 million in 2015. In the same time frame, connectivity revenue will more than double from U.S. $3.1 billion to U.S. $6.7 billion, making the M2M market one of the highest growth areas in the wireless arena during the next decade... Falling hardware prices and the increased availability of end-to-end solutions have established a more accessible M2M market for enterprises around the world."

and (18):

"The IoT makes possible for virtually any object around us to exchange information and work in synergy to increase quality of our life. There are smart clothes which will interact intelligently with climate control of car and home to select the most suitable temperature and humidity for the person. Smart book interacts with entertainment devices such as TV in order to elaborate the topic we are reading..."

and (19):

"... the possibilities and opportunities are endless..."

and (20):

The IoT is a key enabler for the realization of M2M, as it allows for the pervasive interaction with/between smart things leading to a effective integration of information into the digital world. These smart (mobile) things – which are instrumented with sensing, actuation, and interaction capabilities – have the means to exchange information and influence the real world entities and other actors of a smart city eco-system in real time, forming a smart pervasive computing environment. The objective is to reach a global access to the services and information through the so-called Web of Things and efficient support for global communications, in order to embrace the M2M communications in the future IoT composed of IPv6 network and various smart things... issues such as the adaptation of legacy technologies and RFID to IPv6 and the Future IoT, security and privacy requirements in Smart Cities and the design of a secure and privacy-aware IoT, as well as the definition of new advanced architectures and models for the Internet and its application to smart livable Cities, [are important].

After the introductory chapter, Chapter 2 provides a formal framework for the IoT. Chapter 3 identifies a number of practical IoT applications, including BANs and over-the-air-passive surveillance (such as the Ring of Steel in London and now in many US cities). Chapter 4 looks at fundamental IoT mechanisms, for example, addressing, followed by a survey of key technologies to support the IoT applications. Emerging and applicable standards are discussed in Chapter 5. Chapter 6 discusses wireless connectivity at Layer 1 and Layer 2. Chapter 7 discusses connectivity at Layer 3, specifically IPv6 mechanisms, which are critical to the large-scale deployment of the IoT. Chapter 8 reviews MIPv6 technologies for possible mobile applications while Chapter 9 provides an overview of 6LoWPAN which is ideally suited to IoT environments.

Interested readers include technology investors, researchers and academics, technology developers, planners with carriers and service providers, technology integrators, Internet-backbone and ISP providers, cloud service providers, and telcos and wireless providers.

This text is one in a series of texts by the author on the topic of IPv6. We are not implying in this text that IPv6 and/or MIPv6 is *strictly and uniquely required* to support IoT developments—early deployments are, in fact, using IPv4. We are advocating, however, that platforms based on these protocols provide an ideal, future-proof, scalable, and ubiquitous environment for such evolving services and capabilities. Appendix 1.A identifies some related books, a number of which are edited monographs; our treatise endeavors to put emphasis on the use of IPv6.

APPENDIX 1.A: SOME RELATED LITERATURE

This appendix contains some related literature. As it can be seen, most of this IoT literature is fairly recent and, therefore, does not uniquely cover the focus of this text, which is related to IPv6 being the fundamental optimal communication technology to deploy IoT in a robust commercial manner rather than just a desktop "science experiment" in some academic researcher's laboratory.

Here are some related books, a number of which are edited monographs:

- (Edited text) Giusto D, Iera A, Morabito G, Atzori L, editors, *The Internet of Things: 20th Tyrrhenian Workshop on Digital Communications.*1st ed. Springer; 2010.
- (Edited text) Uckelmann D, Harrison M, Michahelles F, editors, *Architecting the Internet of Things*, Springer; 2011.
- (Edited text) Chaouchi H, editor, *The Internet of Things: Connecting Objects*, Wiley; 2012.
- (Edited text) Chabanne H, Urien P, Susini J-F, editors, *RFID and the Internet of Things*, Wiley-ISTE; 2011.
- Lu Yan, Yan Zhang, Laurence T. Yang, *The Internet of Things: from RFID to the Next-generation Pervasive Networked Systems*, Wireless Networks and Mobile Communications Series, CRC Press, Taylor and Francis Group; 2008.
- Evdokimov S, Fabian B, Günther O, Ivantysynova L, Ziekow H, *RFID and the Internet of Things: Technology, Applications, and Security Challenges*, Hanover, Mass.: Now Publishers Inc.; 2011.
- Hazenberg W, Huisman M, *Meta Products: Building the Internet of Things,*Amsterdam, NL: BIS Publishers; 2011.

- Hersent O, Boswarthick D, Elloumi O, *The Internet of Things: Key Applications and Protocols.* New York: Wiley; 2012.
- Zhou H, *The Internet of Things in the Cloud: A Middleware Perspective*, New York, NY: CRC Press; 2013.

REFERENCES

1. Ashton K. That 'Internet of things' thing. RFID Journal, 2009.
2. Ping L, Quan L, Zude Z, Wang H. Agile supply chain management over the Internet of Things. 2011 International Conference on Management and Service Science (MASS), 2011 Aug, 1–4; Wuhan, China.
3. Zheng J, Simplot-Ryl D, et al. The Internet of Things. IEEE Communications Magazine, November 2011;49(11):30–31.
4. Practel, Inc., Role of Wireless ICT in Health Care and Wellness – Standards, Technologies and Markets, May, 2012. CT: Published by Global Information, Inc. (GII).
5. IEEE Computer. The Internet of Things: The Next Technological Revolution. Special Issue, February 2013.
6. Schlautmann A. Embedded Networking Systems in the Smart Home & Office. *M2M Zone Conference* at the International CTIA Wireless 2011; 2011 Mar 22–24; Orange County Convention Center, Orlando Florida.
7. Zhou H. *The Internet of Things in the Cloud: A Middleware Perspective.* New York: CRC Press; 2013.
8. Duke-Woolley R. Wireless Enterprise, Industry & Consumer Apps for the Automation Age. *M2M Zone Conference* at the International CTIA Wireless 2011; 2011 Mar 22–24; Orange County Convention Center, Orlando Florida.
9. Peerun S. Machine to Machine (M2M) Revenues Will Reach $38.1bn in 2012. Visiongain Report, United Kingdom; 2012.
10. Kreisher K. Intel: M2M data tsunami begs for analytics, security. Online Magazine, (Oct 8), 2012. Available at http://www.telecomengine.com.
11. *Internet of Things in 2020 – Roadmap For The Future,* INFSO D.4 Networked Enterprise & RFID, INFSO G.2 Micro & Nanosystems in co-operation with the Working Group RFID Of The ETP EPOSS. (European Commission – Information Society and Media.) Version 1.1–27, May, 2008.
12. Internet Architecture Board, Interconnecting Smart Objects with the Internet Workshop 2011, 25th March 2011, Prague.
13. Gluhak A, Krco S, et al. A Survey on Facilities for Experimental Internet of Things research. Communications Magazine, IEEE, 2011;49(11):58–67.
14. Staff. Smart networked objects and Internet of Things. White paper, January 2011, Association Instituts Carnot, 120 avenue du Général Leclerc, 75014 Paris, France.
15. Ladid L. Keynote Speech, International Workshop on Extending Seamlessly to the Internet of Things (esloT-2012), in conjunction with IMIS-2012 International Conference; 2012 July 4–6; Palermo, Italy.
16. Drake J, Najewicz D, Watts W. Energy Efficiency Comparisons of Wireless Communication Technology Options for Smart Grid Enabled Devices. White Paper, General Electric Company, GE Appliances & Lighting, December 9, 2010.

17. Yankee Group. *Global Enterprise Cellular M2M Forecast*, April 2011, Boston, MA. Available at www.yankeegroup.com.

18. Lee GM, Park J, Kong N, Crespi N. The Internet of Things – Concept and Problem Statement. July 2011. Internet Research Task Force, July 11, 2011, draft-lee-iot-problem-statement-02.txt.

19. Principi B. CTIA: Global M2M deployments becoming a reality. Telecom Engine Online Magazine, (May 9) 2012. Available at www.telecomengine.com.

20. Ladid L, Skarmeta A, Ziegler S. Symposium On Selected Areas In Communications: Internet Of Things Track, IEEE 2013 Globecom, December 9–13, Atlanta, GA, U.S.A.

CHAPTER 2

INTERNET OF THINGS DEFINITIONS AND FRAMEWORKS

This chapter elaborates on the concept, definition, and a usable framework of the Internet of Things (IoT).

2.1 IoT DEFINITIONS

We noted in Chapter 1 that the IoT is an evolving type of Internet *application* that endeavors to make a thing's information (whatever that may be) securely available on a global scale if/when such information is needed by an aggregation point or points. Since the definition of the IoT is still evolving, the material that follows provides illustrative concept definitions rather than a tightly worded definition; nonetheless, a provisional "working definition" is in fact provided in order to baseline our discussion.

2.1.1 General Observations

Some applicable observations related to the definition of the IoT include the following:

> "Internet of Things is a twenty-first century phenomenon in which physical consumer products (meta products) connect to the web and start communicating with each other by means of sensors and actuators . . . " (1).

Building the Internet of Things with IPv6 and MIPv6: The Evolving World of M2M Communications, First Edition. Daniel Minoli.
© 2013 John Wiley & Sons, Inc. Published 2013 by John Wiley & Sons, Inc.

"Today's Internet is experienced by users as a set of applications, such as email, instant messaging, and social networks. While these applications do not require users to be present at the time of service execution, in many cases they are. There are also substantial differences in performance between the various end devices, but in general end devices participating in the Internet are considered to have high performance. As we move forward with the interconnection of all kinds of devices via the Internet, these characteristics will change. The term "Internet of Things" denotes a trend where a large number of devices benefit from communication services that use Internet protocols. Many of these devices are not directly operated by humans, but exist as components in buildings, vehicles, and the environment. There will be a lot of variation in the computing power, available memory, and communications bandwidth between different types of devices. Many of these devices provide new services or provide more value for previously unconnected devices. Some devices have been connected in various legacy ways in the past but are now migrating to the use of the Internet Protocol, sharing the same communications medium between all applications and enabling rich communications services . . ." (2).

"The M2M . . . term is used to refer to machine-to-machine communication, i.e., automated data exchange between machines. ("Machine" may also refer to virtual machines such as software applications.) Viewed from the perspective of its functions and potential uses, M2M is causing an entire "Internet of Things", or internet of intelligent objects, to emerge . . . On closer inspection, however, M2M has merely become a new buzzword for demanding applications involving telemetry (automatic remote transmission of any measured data) and SCADA (Supervisory, Control and Data Acquisition). In contrast to telemetry and SCADA-based projects, the majority of M2M applications are broadly based on established standards, particularly where communication protocols and transmission methods currently in use are concerned. Telemetry applications involve completely proprietary solutions that, in some cases, have even been developed with a specific customer or application in mind. M2M concepts, meanwhile, use open protocols such as TCP/IP, which are also found on Internet and local company networks. The data formats in each case are similar in appearance . . ." (3).

"IoT spans a great range of applications. People bring varied assumptions about what devices are 'things'. Most IoT devices have constraints but the nature of constraints varies. IoT needs to be divided into manageable topic areas . . ." (4).

"Information Communications Technology (ITC) evolution has led to wireless personal devices such as smart phones, personal computers and PDAs. These devices have in common that they are designed to operate over IP networks. Hence, the number of devices that are connected to the Internet is growing exponentially. This has led to define a new concept of Internet, the commonly called Future Internet and Internet of Things (IoT). The objective of IoT is the integration and unification of all communication systems located surrounds us. Thereby, the systems can get control and total access of the other systems for leading to provide ubiquitous communication and computing with the purpose of defining a new generation of services . . ." (5).

"The vision of the internet of things is to attach tiny devices to every single object to make it identifiable by its own unique IP address. These devices can then autonomously communicate with one another. The success of the internet of things relies on overcoming the following technical challenges: (1) The current manner of using IP addresses must change to a system that provides an IP address to every possible object that may need one in the future. (2) The power behind the embedded chips on such devices will need to be smaller and more efficient. And, (3) The software applications must be developed that can communicate with and manage the stream of data from hundreds of interconnected non-computing devices that comprise a 'smart' system which can adapt and respond to changes..." (6).

"... Order(s) of magnitude bigger than the Internet, no computers or humans at end-point, inherently mobile, disconnected, unattended... IoT is going to be an advanced network including normal physical objects together with computers and other advanced electronic appliances. Instead of forming ad hoc network, normal objects will be a part of whole network so that they can collaborate, understand real time environmental data and react accordingly in need... The basic idea is that IoT will connect objects around us (electronic, electrical, non electrical) to provide seamless communication and contextual services provided by them. Development of RFID (radio-frequency identification) tags, sensors, actuators, mobile phones make it possible to materialize IoT which interact and co-operate each other to make the service better and accessible anytime, from anywhere... The 'Internet of Things (IoT)' refers to the networked interconnection of everyday objects. An 'IoT' means 'a world-wide network of interconnected objects uniquely addressable, based on standard communication protocols'... In the IoT, 'things' are very various such as computers, sensors, people, actuators, refrigerators, TVs, vehicles, mobile phones, clothes, food, medicines, books, etc. These things are classified as three scopes: people, machine (for example, sensor, actuator, etc) and information (for example clothes, food, medicine, books and so on). These 'things' should be identified at least by one unique way of identification for the capability of addressing and communicating with each other and verifying their identities... if the 'thing' is identified, we call it the 'object'..." (7, 8).

"... Commonly we focus on the deployment of a new generation of networked objects with communication, sensory and action capabilities for numerous applications with a vision 'from simple connected objects as sensor networks to more complex and smarter communicated objects as in the envisioned IoT'... In the IETF/IRTF perspective, one of our visions is to provide global interoperability via IP for making heterogeneous/constraint objects very smart..." (8, 9).

"... M2M describes devices that are connected to the Internet, using a variety of fixed and wireless networks and communicate with each other and the wider world. They are active communication devices. The term embedded wireless has been coined, for a variety of applications where wireless cellular communication is used to connect any device that is not a phone. This term is widely used by the GSM Association (GSMA)..." (10).

Originally the term "Internet of Things" was invented by the MIT Auto-ID Center in 2001 and referred to an architecture that comprises four elements, as follows (11):

- Passive radio frequency identification (RFIDs), such as Class-1 Generation-2 UHF RFIDs, introduced by the electronic product code (EPC) Global Consortium and operating in the 860–960 MHz range[1]
- Readers plugged to a local (computing) system, which read the EPC
- A local system offering IP connectivity that collects information pointed by the EPC, thanks to a protocol called object naming service (ONS)
- EPCIS (EPC Information Services) servers that process incoming ONS requests and returns physical markup language (PML) files, for example, XML documents carrying meaningful information linked to RFIDs

However, as noted in the discussion so far, the term is now much more encompassing. A short, incomplete bibliography of articles describing the IoT includes the references at the end of this chapter in general and the following in particular: (7–9, 12–19).

2.1.2 ITU-T Views

The ITU-T is in the process of identifying a common way to define/describe the IoT. So far, the ITU-T has not found "*a good definition to cover all aspects of IoT as the IoT has quite big scope not only the technological viewpoints but also other views . . . We recognized whatever we define, everyone cannot be happy*" (20).

One can view the Internet as an *infrastructure* providing a number of technological capabilities or as a *concept* to provide an array of data exchange and linkage services. The infrastructure perspective describes the Internet as a global system of interconnected computer networks (of many conceivable technologies) that use the TCP/IP Internet Protocol Suite to communicate; the networks comprise millions of private, public, business, academic, and governmental servers, computers, and nodes. The concept perspective sees the Internet as a worldwide logical interconnection of computers and networks that support the exchange of information among users, including but not limited to interlinked hypertext documents of the World Wide Web (WWW). Similarly, at the current time different experts can define the IoT differently, the conceptual way or the infrastructural way as follows (20):

View A: IoT is just a concept (conceptual aspects of definition): the IoT does not refer to a network infrastructure; the IoT is not a technical term but a concept (or a phenomenon).

View B: IoT is an infrastructure: The IoT refers to an infrastructure.

As shown in Figure 2.1, if defined as an infrastructure, IoT should be identified for all aspects of infrastructure such as service and functional requirements, architectures,

---

[1](also known as the "Gen 2" standard) this standard defines the physical and logical requirements for a passive-backscatter, interrogator-talks-first (ITF), RFID system operating in the 860–960 MHz frequency range; the system comprises interrogators (also known as readers), and tags (also known as labels).

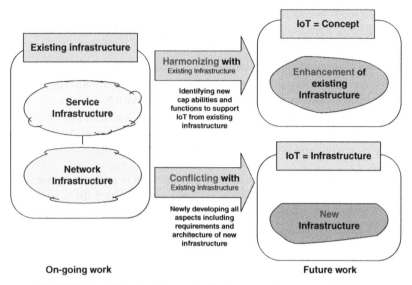

FIGURE 2.1   Direction for standardization according to IoT definition.

and so on. If defined as a concept, all relevant capabilities and specific functions to support (or realize) that concept of IoT will need to be identified for each technical area.

When ITU-T SG13 had developed Y.2002 ("*Overview of ubiquitous networking and of its support in NGN*"), the study group (SG) noted that ubiquitous networking is not a new network; the IoT is a conceptual design goal, which one has to consider for developing standards. Based on this conceptual goal (a simple definition), each SG can define detailed concepts with its own view. From SG13's perspective, next-generation network (NGN), smart ubiquitous network (SUN), and the future network (FN) should support key characteristics for realizing IoT. The main role of SG13 is to focus on the enhancement of networking technologies based on the NGN, the SUN, and the FN, rather than creating a new network.

The ITU-T is suggesting to define the IoT as a short definition with more general concept rather than as a technical definition; this should be done, in their view, in order for the IoT to be easily incorporated into various areas from technology, as well as accepted to all other interested SGs. After that, one can concentrate on defining the scope for IoT (e.g., service, network, control, security, quality, billing/charging aspects, and others) and finding related technological issues for further standardization work. ITU-T "*strongly insists on a short definition as concept instead of a technical definition (long or detailed description of technology)*" (20). Tables 2.1 and 2.2 from TD27 (IoT-GSI) show a representative set of working definitions.

Some see machine-to-machine (M2M) deployments into four domains: sensors and controllers; "the edge," where data from these devices are gathered; the cloud, where the data are stored and managed; and the client, where that data are ultimately evaluated (21).

TABLE 2.1 Examples of Definitions for Case A (IoT is Just a Concept)

Candidate Definition	Reference
A *technological revolution* that represents the future of computing and communications, and its development depends on dynamic technical innovation in a number of important fields, from wireless sensors to nanotechnology	Source: ITU Internet Reports 2005: The Internet of Things, Executive Summary
The networked interconnection of objects—from the sophisticated to the mundane—through identifiers such as sensors, RFID tags, and IP addresses	Margery Conner, Technical Editor of EDN Magazine, "Sensors empower the 'Internet of Things' ", May 2010
The Internet of things *links the objects of the real world with the virtual world*, thus enabling anytime, anyplace connectivity for anything and not only for anyone. It refers to a world where physical objects and beings, as well as virtual data and environments, all interact with each other in the same space and time	Cluster of European Research Projects on the Internet of Things, "Vision and Challenges for Realizing the Internet of Things", March 2010
The IoT refers to as *ubiquitous networking or pervasive computing environments*, is *a vision* where all manufactured things can be network enabled, that is connected to each other via wireless or wired communication networks	European Network and Information Security Agency (ENISA)
The IoT is *a world where physical objects are seamlessly integrated into the information network*, and where the physical objects can become active participants in business processes. Services are available to interact with these "smart objects" over the Internet, query and change their state and any information associated with them, taking into account security and privacy issues. RFID, sensor networks, and so on are just enabling technologies	SAS
IoT is a [*high-level service concept* based on] existing and evolving global ICT (Information and Communication Technology) infrastructures that provide information services by interconnecting things	

2.1.3 Working Definition

Generalizing from the published literature and the observations made thus far in this text, we characterize the IoT with a "working definition" as follows:

Definition: *A broadly-deployed aggregate computing/communication application and/or application-consumption system, that is deployed over a local (L-IoT),*

TABLE 2.2 Examples of Definitions for Case B (Infrastructural Aspects of Definition)

Candidate Definition	Reference
A *global network infrastructure*, linking physical and virtual objects through the exploitation of data capture and communication capabilities. This infrastructure includes existing and evolving Internet and network developments. It will offer specific object identification, sensor and connection capability as the basis for the development of independent federated services and applications. These will be characterized by a high degree of autonomous data capture, event transfer, network connectivity, and interoperability	Coordination and Support Action (CSA) for Global RFID-related Activities and Standardization (CASAGRAS)
A *global information and communication infrastructure* enabling automated chains of actions (not requiring explicit human intervention) facilitating information assembly and knowledge production and contributing to enrichment of human life by interconnecting physical and logical objects based on standard and interoperable communication protocols and through the exploitation of data capture and communication capabilities supported by existing and evolving information and communication technologies NOTE: Physical objects may include sensors, devices, machines, and so on. Logical objects may include contents and so on	Originally produced by the discussion among China-Japan-Korea. ITU Q3/13 has made some modifications
A *global ICT infrastructure* linking physical objects and virtual objects (as the informational counterparts of physical objects) through the exploitation of sensor and actuator data capture, processing and transmission capabilities. As such, the IoT is an overlay above the "generic" Internet, offering federated physical-object-related services (including, if relevant, identification, monitoring, and control of these objects) to all kinds of applications.	Proposed by France Telecom on the IoT definition mailing list.
IoT is (*a global ICT infrastructure*) which provides information services by interconnecting things NOTE: Infrastructure should not be interpreted only as a network	
A more prescriptive definition follows:	
The Internet of Things consists *of networks of sensors attached to objects and communication devices*, providing data that can be analyzed and used to initiate automated actions. The data also generate vital intelligence for planning, management, policy, and decision-making	Proposed by Cisco

metropolitan (M-IoT), regional (R-IoT), national (N-IoT), or global (G-IoT) geogra-
phy, consisting of (i) dispersed instrumented objects ("things") with embedded one-
or two-way communications and some (or, at times, no) computing capabilities, (ii)
where objects are reachable over a variety of wireless or wired local area and/or
wide area networks, and, (iii) whose inbound data and/or outbound commands are
pipelined to or issued by a(n application) system with a (high) degree of (human or
computer-based) intelligence.

In this definition, things are generally objects, tags, sensors, or actuators in the environment, but not typically business/personal PCs, laptops, smartphones, or tablets.
We posit that this definition looks at the IoT as both a concept and an infrastructure, from a hybrid perspective. Unless there is a specific need to clarify the nature
of the geographic scope, we use the generic term IoT to cover all instances of the
technology.

Note that a variety of definitions could be formulated; the above formulation is not
offered to be exclusive of other definitions offered by other researchers, but simply
to be a useful reference baseline for the present discussion.

Two other related "working definitions" are as follows:

Definition: *Sensors are active devices that measure some variable of the natural or*
man-made environment (e.g., a building, an assembly line, an industrial assemblage
supporting a process).

The technology for sensing and control includes electric and magnetic field sensors; radiowave frequency sensors; optical-, electro-optic-, and infrared sensors;
radars; lasers; location/navigation sensors; seismic and pressure-wave sensors; environmental parameter sensors (e.g., wind, humidity, heat, and so on); and, biochemical
Homeland Security-oriented sensors.

Sensor networks usually consider remote devices as belonging to two classes,
based on device capabilities: Full-function devices (FFDs) and reduced function
devices (RFDs). Sensors and actuators are part of a larger universe of objects. Objects
in the IoT context can also be classified from a functionality perspective.

Definition: *An actuator is a mechanized device of various sizes (from ultra-small to*
very large) that accomplishes a specified physical action, for example, controlling a
mechanism or system, opening or closing a valve, starting some kind or rotary or
linear motion, or initiating physical locomotion. An actuator is the mechanism by
which an entity acts upon an environment.

The actuator embodies a source of energy, such as an electric current (battery,
solar, motion), and a source of physical interaction such as a hydraulic fluid pressure
or a pneumatic pressure; the device converts that energy into some kind of action or
motion upon receipt of an external command or stimulus.

An object is a model of an entity. An object is distinct from any other object and
is characterized by its behavior. An object is informally said to perform functions
and offer services (an object that performs a function available to other entities
and/or objects is said to offer a service). For modeling purposes, these functions

and services are specified in terms of the behavior of the object and of its interfaces (18, 22). An object can, as needed, perform more than one function and a function can be performed by the cooperation of several objects. Objects are also called "smart/connected objects" by some. In the definition of the ITU (18), objects include terminal devices (e.g., used by a person to access the network such as mobile phones, personal computers, and so on), remote monitoring devices (e.g., cameras, sensors, and so on), information devices (e.g., content delivery server), products, contents, and resources. We stated in Chapter 1, however, that for the purpose of our discussion, personal communication devices (smartphones, pads, and so on) can be viewed as machines or just simply as end nodes: when personal communication devices are used for H2M devices where the human employs the smartphone to communicate with a machine (e.g., a thermostat or a home appliance), then we consider the personal communication devices as part of the IoT; otherwise, we do not. Smart/connected objects are heterogeneous with different sizes, mobility capabilities, power sources, connectivity mechanisms, and protocols. A physical object interacts with several entities, performs various functionalities, and generates data that might be used by other entities. Usually, the resources of these objects are limited. Furthermore, there are various types of networking interfaces that have different coverage and data rates. These environments have the characteristics of low power and lossy networks such as Bluetooth, IEEE 802.15.4 (6LoWPAN, ZigBee), near field communication (NFC), and so on (8). Things (objects) can be classified as shown in Figure 2.2. Objects have the following characteristics, among others, (8):

- have the ability to sense and/or actuate
- are generally small (but not always)
- have limited computing capabilities (but not always)
- are energy/power limited
- are connected to the physical world
- sometimes have intermittent connectivity
- are mobile (but not always)
- of interest to people
- managed by devices, not people (but not always)

While the IoT can in principle be seen as a more encompassing concept than what is captured under the ETSI M2M standards and definitions, nonetheless the M2M definitions can serve the purpose adding some structure to the discussion. We noted in Figure 1.1 a high level logical partitioning of the entity-to-entity interaction space that included human to human (H2H) communication, M2M communication, human to machine (H2M) communications, and machine in (or on) human (MiH) communications. (MiH devices may include medical monitoring probes, global positioning system (GPS) bracelets, and so on.) For the present discussion, the focus of the IoT is on M2M, H2M, and MiH applications; this range of applicability is the theme captured in this text, also as depicted in Figure 2.3. Figure 2.4 illustrates classes of generic IoT arrangements that are included in our discussion.

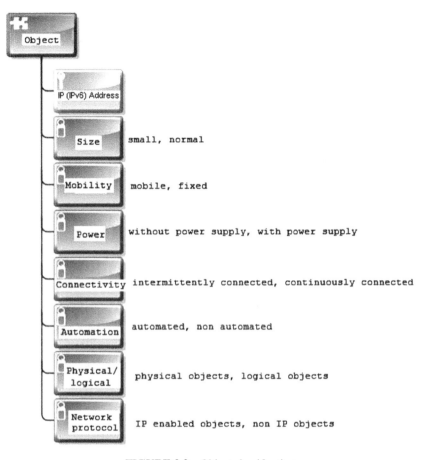

FIGURE 2.2   Object classification.

Intuitively, an M2M/H2M environment comprises three basic elements: (i) the data integration point (DIP)[2]; (ii) the communication network; and; (iii) the data end point (DEP) (again, a machine M). See Figure 2.5, where the process (X) and application (Y) form the actual functional end points. Typically, a DEP refers to a microcomputer system, one end of which is connected to a process or to a higher level subsystem via special interfaces; the other end is connected to a communication network. However, the DEP can also be a machine M in a human H, as is the case in the MiH environment. Many applications have a large base of dispersed DEPs (3). A DIP can be an Internet server, a software application running on a firm-resident host, or an application implemented as a cloud service. As previously mentioned,

---

[2]In Chapter 1, we also called the DIP a "data integration point or person (DIPP)" because the DIP corresponds with a point (P, that is a machine M) or with a person (P).

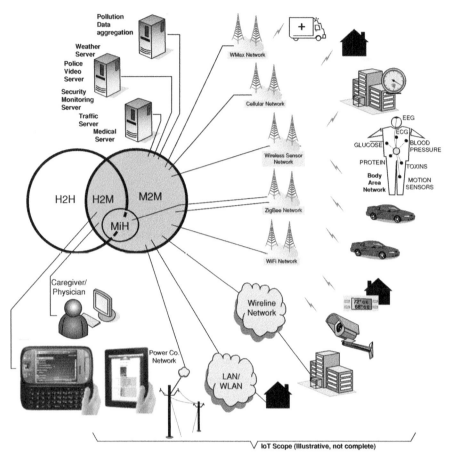

FIGURE 2.3   Scope of IoT by way of illustration.

basic applications include, but are not limited to, smart meters, e-health, track-and-trace, monitoring, transaction, control, home automation, city automation, connected consumers, and automotive.

As noted in Chapter 1, at a macro level, an IoT comprises a remote set of sensing assets (sensing domain, also known as M2M domain in an M2M environment), a network domain, and an applications domain. Figures 2.6 and 2.7 provide illustrative pictorial view of the domains.

2.2 IoT FRAMEWORKS

A high level M2M system architecture (HLSA) (see Figure 2.8) is defined in the ETSI TS 102 690 V1.1.1 (2011–10) specification that is useful to the present discussion. We describe the HLSA next, summarized from Reference 23. The HLSA comprises the device and gateway domain, the network domain, and the applications domain.

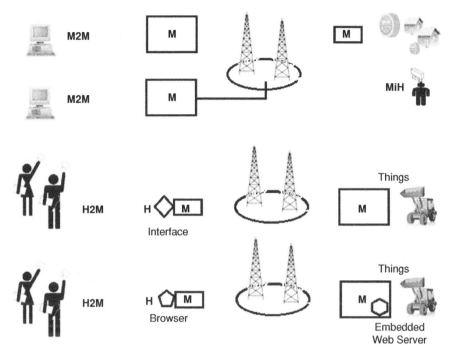

FIGURE 2.4   Classes of generic IoT arrangements.

The **device and gateway domain** is composed of the following elements:

1. **M2M device:** A device that runs M2M application(s) using M2M service capabilities. M2M devices connect to network domain in the following manners:
   - **Case 1 "Direct Connectivity":** M2M devices connect to the network domain via the access network. The M2M device performs the procedures such as

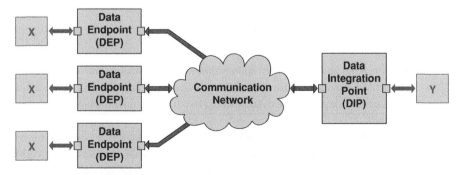

FIGURE 2.5   Basic elements of an M2M application.

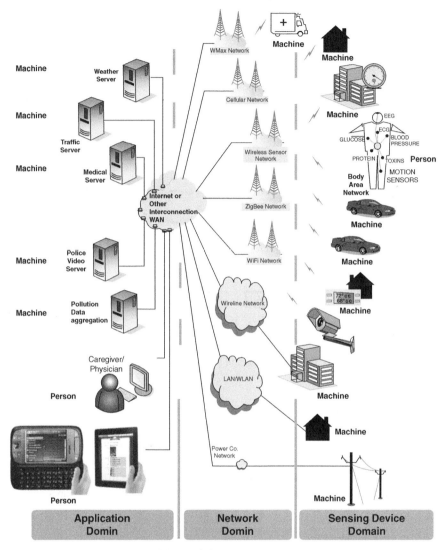

FIGURE 2.6 M2M domains.

registration, authentication, authorization, management, and provisioning with the network domain. The M2M device may provide service to other devices (e.g., legacy devices) connected to it that are hidden from the network domain.

- Case 2 "Gateway as a Network Proxy": The M2M device connects to the network domain via an M2M gateway. M2M devices connect to the M2M gateway using the M2M area network. The M2M gateway acts as a proxy for the network domain toward the M2M devices that are connected to it.

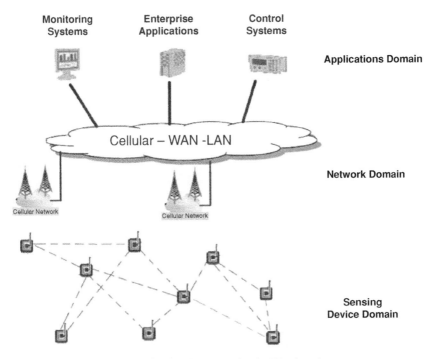

FIGURE 2.7 Other example of M2M domains.

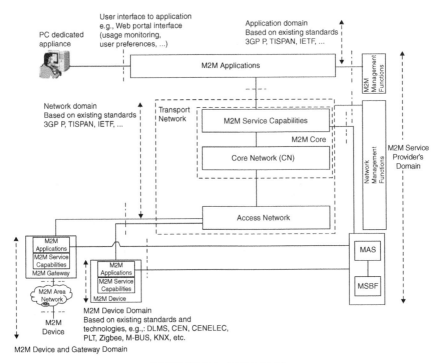

FIGURE 2.8 M2M HLSA.

Examples of procedures that are proxied include authentication, authorization, management, and provisioning.

(M2M devices may be connected to the network domain via multiple M2M gateways.)

2. **M2M area network:** It provides connectivity between M2M devices and M2M gateways. Examples of M2M area networks include personal area network (PAN) technologies such as IEEE 802.15.1, Zigbee, Bluetooth, IETF ROLL, ISA100.11a, among others, or local networks such as power line communication (PLC), M-BUS, Wireless M-BUS, and KNX.[3]

3. **M2M gateway:** A gateway that runs M2M application(s) using M2M service capabilities. The gateway acts as a proxy between M2M devices and the network domain. The M2M gateway may provide service to other devices (e.g., legacy devices) connected to it that are hidden from the network domain. As an example, an M2M gateway may run an application that collects and treats various information (e.g., from sensors and contextual parameters).

The **network domain** is composed of the following elements:

1. **Access network:** A network that allows the M2M device and gateway domain to communicate with the core network. Access networks include (but are not limited to) digital subscriber line (xDSL), hybrid fiber coax (HFC), satellite, GSM/EDGE radio access network (GERAN), UMTS terrestrial radio access network (UTRAN), evolved UMTS terrestrial radio access network (eUTRAN), W-LAN, and worldwide interoperability for microwave access (WiMAX).

2. **Core network:** A network that provides the following capabilities (different core networks offer different features sets):
   - IP connectivity at a minimum, and possibly other connectivity means
   - Service and network control functions
   - Interconnection (with other networks)
   - Roaming

---

[3]KNX (administered by the KNX Association) is an OSI-based network communications protocol for intelligent buildings defined in standards CEN EN 50090 and ISO/IEC 14543. KNX is the follow-on standard built on the European Home Systems (EHS) Protocol, BatiBUS, and the European Installation Bus (EIB or Instabus). Effectively, KNX uses the communication stack of EIB but augmented with the physical layers and configuration modes BatiBUS and EHS; thus, KNX includes the following PHYs:

- Twisted pair wiring (inherited from the BatiBUS and EIB Instabus standards). This approach uses differential signaling with a signaling speed of 9.6 Kbps. Media access control is controlled with the CSMA/CA method
- Powerline networking (inherited from EIB and EHS)
- Radio (KNX-RF)
- Infrared
- Ethernet (also known as EIBnet/IP or KNXnet/IP)

- Core networks (CoNs) include (but are not limited to) 3GPP CoNs, ETSI TISPAN CoN, and 3GPP2 CoN

3. **M2M service capabilities:**
   - Provide M2M functions that are to be shared by different applications
   - Expose functions through a set of open interfaces
   - Use CoN functionalities
   - Simplify and optimize application development and deployment through hiding of network specificities

The "M2M service capabilities" along with the "core network" is known collectively as the "M2M core."

The **applications domain** is composed of the following elements:

1. **M2M applications:** Applications that run the service logic and use M2M service capabilities accessible via an open interface.

There are also management functions within an overall M2M service provider domain, as follows:

1. **Network management functions:** Consists of all the functions required to manage the access and core networks; these functions include provisioning, supervision, fault management.
2. **M2M management functions:** Consists of all the functions required to manage M2M service capabilities in the network domain. The management of the M2M devices and gateways uses a specific M2M service capability.
   - The set of M2M management functions include a function for M2M service bootstrap. This function is called M2M service bootstrap function (MSBF) and is realized within an appropriate server. The role of MSBF is to facilitate the bootstrapping of permanent M2M service layer security credentials in the M2M device (or M2M gateway) and the M2M service capabilities in the network domain.
   - Permanent security credentials that are bootstrapped using MSBF are stored in a safe location, which is called M2M authentication server (MAS). Such a server can be an AAA server. MSBF can be included within MAS, or may communicate the bootstrapped security credentials to MAS, through an appropriate interface (e.g., the DIAMETER protocol defined in IETF RFC 3588) for the case where MAS is an AAA server.

The H2M portion of the IoT could theoretically make use of these same mechanisms and capabilities, but the information flow would likely need to be front-ended by an access layer (which can also be seen as an application in the sense described above) that allows the human user to interact with the machine using an intuitive interface. One such mechanism can be an HTML/HTTP-based browser that interacts with a suitable software peer in the machine (naturally this requires some higher level capabilities to be supported by the DEP/machine in order to be able to run an embedded web server software module). (When used in embedded devices or applications, web servers must assume they are secondary to the essential functions the device or application must perform; as such, the web server must minimize its resource demands and should be deterministic in the load it places on a system.[4])

2.3 BASIC NODAL CAPABILITIES

Consistent with the HLSA, a remote device generally needs to have a basic protocol stack that supports as a minimum local connectivity and networking connectivity (we include the transport layer in our terminology here, whether this is TCP, UDP, or some other protocol); in addition, some higher layer application support protocols are generally needed, with varying degrees of computational/functional sophistication. See Figure 2.9. IoT devices may have capability differences, such as but not limited to the following (25): maximum transmission unit (MTU) differences, simplified versus full-blown web protocol stack (COAP/UDP versus HTTP/TCP), single stack versus dual stack, sleep schedule, security protocols, processing and communication bandwidth. The networking technologies listed above, including 3GPP, 3GPP2, ETSI TISPAN, eUTRAN, GERAN, HFC, IETF ROLL, ISA100.11a, KNX, M-BUS, PLC, Satellite, SCADA (Supervisory Control And Data Acquisition), UTRAN, WiMAX, Wireless M-BUS, W-LAN, and xDSL, are discussed in more detail in the chapters that follow.

Distributed control/M2M typically entails continuously changing variables to control the behavior of an application. Typical requirements include the following capabilities (26):

- Retransmission
  - Network recovers from packet loss or informs application
  - Recovery is immediate: on the order of RTTs, not seconds

---

[4]As an illustrative example of an embedded web server, Oracle's GoAhead WebServer is a simple, portable, and compact web server for embedded devices and applications; it runs on dozens of operating environments and can be easily ported and adapted. The GoAhead WebServer is a simple, compact web server that has been widely ported to many embedded operating systems. Appweb is faster and more powerful—but requires more memory. If a device requires a simple, low end web server and has little memory available, the GoAhead WebServer is ideal; if the device needs higher performance and extended security, then Appweb is the right choice. As one of the most widely deployed embedded web servers, Appweb is being used in networking equipment, telephony, mobile devices, consumer and office equipment as well as hosting for enterprise web applications and frameworks. It is embedded in hundreds of millions of devices. The server runs equally well stand-alone or in a web farm behind a reverse proxy such as Apache (24).

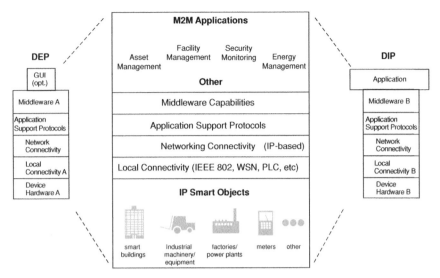

FIGURE 2.9   Protocol stack, general view.

- Network independent of MAC/PHY
- Scale
  - Thousands of nodes
  - Multiple link speeds
- Multicast
  - Throughout network
  - Reliable (positive Ack)
- Duplicate suppression
- Emergency messages
  - Routed and/or queued around other traffic
  - Other traffic slushed as delivered
- Routine traffic delivered in sequence
- Separate timers by peer/message
- Polling of nodes
  - Sequential
  - Independent of responses
- Paradigm supports peer-to-peer
  - Not everything is client/server
- Capabilities
  - Discover nodes
  - Discover node capabilities
  - Deliver multisegment records (files)

- Exchange of multisegment records
- Network and application versioning
- Simple publish/subscribe parsers
- Security
  - Strong encryption
  - Mutual authentication
  - Protection against record/playback attacks
  - Suite B ciphers

Related to the last item, Suite B security is a National Security Agency (NSA) directive that requires that key establishment and authentication algorithms be based on elliptic curve cryptography, and that the encryption algorithm be AES. Suite B defines two security levels, of 128 and 192 bits (see Glossary for additional information).

REFERENCES

1. Hazenberg W, Huisman M. *Meta Products: Building the Internet of Things*. Amsterdam, NL: BIS Publishers; 2011.
2. Internet Architecture Board. Interconnecting Smart Objects with the Internet Workshop 2011, 25th March 2011, Prague.
3. Walter K-D. Implementing M2M applications via GPRS, EDGE and UMTS. Online Article, August 2007, http://m2m.com. M2M Alliance e.V., Aachen, Germany.
4. Nordman B. Building Networks. Interconnecting Smart Objects with the Internet Workshop 2011, 25th March 2011, Prague.
5. Ladid L. Keynote Speech, International Workshop on Extending Seamlessly to the Internet of Things (esIoT-2012), in conjunction with IMIS-2012 International Conference; 2012 Jul 4–6; 2012, Palermo, Italy.
6. Financial Times Lexicon, London, U.K. Available at http://lexicon.ft.com.
7. Botterman M. Internet of Things: an early reality of the Future Internet. Workshop Report, European Commission Information Society and Media, May 2009.
8. Lee GM, Park J, Kong N, Crespi N. The Internet of Things – Concept and Problem Statement, July 2011. Internet Research Task Force, July 11, 2011, draft-lee-iot-problem-statement-02.txt.
9. Staff. Smart networked objects and Internet of Things. White paper, January 2011, Association Instituts Carnot, 120 avenue du Général Leclerc, 75014 Paris, France.
10. OECD. Machine-to-Machine Communications: Connecting Billions of Devices. *OECD Digital Economy Papers*, No. 192, 2012, *OECD Publishing*. doi:10.1787/5k9gsh2gp043-en
11. Urien P, Lee GM, Pujolle G. HIP support for RFIDs. HIP Research Group, Internet Draft, draft-irtf-hiprg-rfid-03, July 2011.
12. Atzori L, Iera A, Morabito G. The internet of things: a survey. Computer Networks, October 2010;54 (15):2787–2805.

13. Guinard D, Trifa V, Karnouskos S, Spiess P, Savio D. Interacting with the SOA-based Internet of things: discovery, query, selection, and on-demand provisioning of web services. IEEE Services Computing, IEEE Transactions, July–September 2010;3 (3).

14. ITU-T Internet Reports. Internet of Things. November 2005.

15. Malatras A, Asgari A, Bauge T. Web enabled wireless sensor networks for facilities management. IEEE Systems Journal, 2008;2 (4).

16. Sarma A, Girao Joao. Identities in the Future Internet of Things. Wireless Pers Comm., 2009.

17. Sundmaeker H, Guilemin P, Friess P, Woelffle S, editors. *Vision and Challenges for Realizing the Internet of Things*. European Commission, Information Society and Media, March 2010.

18. ITU-T Y. 2002. Overview of ubiquitous networking and of its support in NGN. November 2009.

19. Zouganeli E, Svinnset IE. Connected objects and the Internet of things-a paradigm shift. Photonics in Switching 2009, September 2009.

20. International Telecommunications Union, Telecommunication Standardization Sector Study Period 2009–2012. IoT-GSI – C 44 – E. August 2011.

21. Kreisher K. Intel: M2M data tsunami begs for analytics, security. Online Magazine, October 8, 2012. Available at http://www.telecomengine.com.

22. Lee GM, Choi JK, et al. Naming architecture for object to object communications. HIP Working Group, Internet Draft, March 8, 2010, draft-lee-object-naming-02.txt

23. Machine-to-Machine Communications (M2M); Functional Architecture Technical Specification, ETSI TS 102 690 V1.1.1 (2011-10), ETSI, 650 Route des Lucioles F-06921 Sophia Antipolis Cedex – France.

24. Embedthis Inc. Promotional Materials, Embedthis Software, LLC, 4616 25th Ave NE, Seattle, WA 98105. Available at http://embedthis.com.

25. Arkko J. Interoperability Challenges in the Internet of Things. Interconnecting Smart Objects with the Internet Workshop 2011, 25th March 2011, Prague.

26. Dolan B, Baker F. Distributed Control: Echelon's view of the Internet of Things. Interconnecting Smart Objects with the Internet Workshop 2011, 25th March 2011, Prague.

CHAPTER 3

INTERNET OF THINGS
APPLICATION EXAMPLES

This chapter provides a sample of applications than can be provided with/by the Internet of Things (IoT), although any such survey is invariably incomplete and is limited in the temporal domain (with new applications being added on an ongoing basis). We look at applications that are already emerging and/or have a lot of current industry interest. Related to IoT applications, proponents make the observation that (1)

> "... there are so many applications that are possible because of IoT. For individual users, IoT brings useful applications like home automation, security, automated devices monitoring, and management of daily tasks. For professionals, automated applications provide useful contextual information all the time to help on their works and decision making. Industries, with sensors and actuators operations can be rapid, efficient and more economic. Managers who need to keep eye on many things can automate tasks connection digital and physical objects together. Every sectors energy, computing, management, security, transportation are going to be benefitted with this new paradigm. Development of several technologies made it possible to achieve the vision of Internet of things. Identification technology such as RFID allows each object to represent uniquely by having unique identifier. Identity reader can read any time the object allows real time identification and tracking. Wireless sensor technology allows objects to provide real time environmental condition and context. Smart technologies allow objects to become more intelligent which can think and communicate. Nanotechnologies are helping to reduce the size of the chip incorporating more processing power and communication capabilities in a very small chip.

Building the Internet of Things with IPv6 and MIPv6: The Evolving World of M2M Communications, First Edition. Daniel Minoli.
© 2013 John Wiley & Sons, Inc. Published 2013 by John Wiley & Sons, Inc.

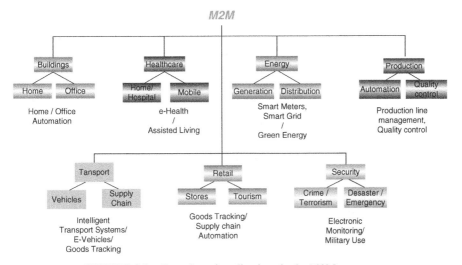

FIGURE 3.1   Grouping of applications in the M2M context.

3.1 OVERVIEW

Table 1.2 offered a taxonomy of applications, although no claim is made here that this taxonomy is complete or fully normative; in the same vein, Figure 3.1, partially inspired by Reference 2, depicts a grouping of applications, particularly in the machine-to-machine (M2M) context. As should be clear by now, some of the possible short-term applications include the following: building automation and remote control (facilitating efficient commercial spaces); smart energy (supporting office building/home energy management); healthcare (providing health and fitness monitoring); home automation (giving rise to smart homes); and retail services (enabling smart shopping). A longer list of applications includes, but is not limited to, the following:

- Public services and smart cities:
  - Telemetry: for example, smart metering, parking metering, and vending machines
  - Intelligent transportation systems (ITSs) and traffic management
  - Connecting consumer and citizens to public infrastructure (such as public transportation)
  - In-building automation, municipal, and regional infrastructure
  - Metropolitan operations (traffic, automatic tolls, fire, and so on)
  - Electrical grid management at a global level; smart grids (SGs)
  - Electrical demand response (DR) at a global level
- Automotive, fleet management, asset tracking:
  - e-Vehicle: for example, navigation, road safety, and traffic control

- ○ Driver safety and emergency services
- ○ Fleet management systems: hired-car monitoring, goods vehicle management
- ○ Back-seat infotainment device integration
- ○ Next-generation global positioning system (GPS) services
- ○ Tracking: asset tracking, cargo tracking, and order tracking
- Commercial markets:
  - ○ Industrial monitoring and control, for example, industrial machines, and elevator monitoring
  - ○ Commercial building and control
  - ○ Process control
  - ○ Maintenance automation
  - ○ Home automation
  - ○ Wireless automated meter reading (AMR)/load management (LM)
  - ○ Homeland security applications: chemical, biological, radiological, and nuclear wireless sensors
  - ○ Military sensors
  - ○ Environmental (land, air, sea) and agricultural wireless sensors
  - ○ Finance: Point-of-sale (POS) terminals, ticketing
  - ○ Security: Public surveillance, personal security
- Embedded networking systems in the smart home and smart office:
  - ○ Smart appliances: for example, AC-power control, lighting control, heating control, and low power management
  - ○ Automated home: remote media control
  - ○ Smart meters and energy efficiency: efficiencies obtained by exploiting the potential of the SG
  - ○ Telehealth (e-health): Assisted Living and in-home m-health services (including remote monitoring, remote diagnostic)
  - ○ Security and emergency services: integrated remote services

Table 3.1 provides some examples by category as defined in 3GPP machine-type communication (MTC) documentation (3). MTC is the term used in 3GPP to describe M2M systems.

In recent years, ETSI has published a number of use cases for IoT (specifically for M2M) applications in the following documents:

- ETSI TR 102 691: *"Machine-to-Machine Communications (M2M); Smart Metering Use Cases."*
- ETSI TR 102 732: *"Machine-to-Machine Communications (M2M); Use Cases of M2M Applications for eHealth."*

TABLE 3.1   Examples of MTC Applications as Defined in 3GPP TS 22.368 Release 10

Category	Specific Example
Consumer devices	Digital camera
	Digital photo frame
	eBook
Health monitoring vital signs	Remote diagnostics
	Supporting the aged or handicapped
	Web access telemedicine points
Metering	Gas
	Grid control
	Heating
	Industrial metering
	Power
	Water
Payment	Gaming machines
	POS
	Vending machines
Remote maintenance/control sensors	Elevator control
	Lighting
	Pumps
	Valves
	Vehicle diagnostics
	Vending machine control
Service area MTC applications	Backup for landline
	Car/driver security
	Control of physical access (e.g., to buildings)
	Security surveillance systems
Tracking and tracing fleet management	Asset tracking
	Navigation
	Order management
	Pay as you drive
	Road tolling
	Road traffic optimization/steering
	Traffic information

- ETSI TR 102 897: *"Machine-to-Machine Communications (M2M); Use Cases of M2M Applications for City Automation."*
- ETSI TR 102 875: *"Access, Terminals, Transmission, and Multiplexing (ATTM); Study of European Requirements for Virtual Noise for ADSL2, ADSL2plus, and VDSL2."*
- ETSI TR 102 898: *"Machine-to-Machine Communications (M2M); Use Cases of Automotive Applications in M2M Capable Networks."*
- ETSI TS 102 412: *"Smart Cards; Smart Card Platform Requirements Stage 1 (Release 8)."*

The International Organization for Standardization (ISO) has published the following relevant document, among others:

- ISO 16750: *"Road Vehicles—Environmental Conditions and Testing for Electrical and Electronic Equipment."*

Some of these (ETSI-covered) applications are discussed in the sections that follow.

3.2 SMART METERING/ADVANCED METERING INFRASTRUCTURE

The European Technology Platform for Electricity Networks for the Future defines an SG as: "an electricity network that can intelligently integrate the actions of all users connected to it—the consumers, the power generators, and those that do both—in order to efficiently deliver sustainable, economic, and secure electricity supplies." A key element of an SG is a smart metering network that enables automated metering capabilities on the customer side (downstream). On the upstream, the utility acquires the capability for real-time grid monitoring and for information processing of significant network events; this includes fault detection, isolation, and resolution. Specifically, a smart metering network enables a utility company to (i) remotely connect or disconnect power to individual customers, (ii) remotely or automatically update the grid configuration, (iii) collect power consumption data in variable time intervals, and (iv) modulate customer loads automatically during critical demand periods. The SG is also able to automatically detect theft and is able to notify the utility if a meter is tampered with. Smart appliances and SG devices are often referred to being as "DR-enabled." Some of the consumer benefits of smart metering include the elimination of domicile/site access issues, improved billing accuracy, and cost savings derived from DR/demand management in conjunction with incentivized tariffs (4).

The general goal is to monitor and control the consumption of utilities-supplied consumable assets, such as electricity, gas, and water. Utility companies deploy intelligent metering services by incorporating M2M communication modules into metering devices ("the thing"); these intelligent meters are able to send information automatically (or on demand) to a server application that can directly bill or control the metered resource. The ultimate objective is to improve energy distribution performance and efficiency by utilizing accurate real-time information on endpoint consumption. A variation of this application for metering of gas, electricity, and water is a pre-payment arrangement: here a consumer can purchase a specific volume of gas, electricity, water, and so on by pre-payment; the information about the purchased volume is securely transmitted to the metering device and then securely stored on the M2M modules. During use, the actual information about the consumed volume is transmitted to the M2M module, and when the purchased volume has been consumed, the supply can be stopped (via a secure actuation capability) (5, 37). See Figure 3.2 for an example of a smart flowmeter for a water utility application; similar concepts apply to natural gas or electric power.

FIGURE 3.2   Example of an instrumented flowmeter.

The advanced metering infrastructure (AMI) is the electric information service infrastructure that is put in place between the end-user (or end device) and the power utility. AMI is a system for implementing the SG, and it is the principal means for realizing DR. According to press time market forecasts, shipments of smart meter units were expected to continue to grow at a 15% annual rate, with a total of about half-a-billion meters shipped by 2015.

Proponents expect that the use of smart appliances and energy management systems will allow consumers to manage and reduce their energy bills and overall consumption. The combination of the AMI meter and an appropriate home area network (HAN) enables consumers to become aware of electricity consumption costs on a near real-time basis; to be able to monitor their energy usage; and to manage their usage based on their financial metrics. To assist consumers in managing their energy use, manufacturers are designing products that contain built-in communication systems that communicate with the HAN (and the AMI meter). Having knowledge of the cost of electricity and of the consumer preferences, these smart devices are able to manage appliances to either defer operation or adjust the operating condition to reduce peak energy demand. Thus, this intelligent management has the potential to reduce the consumer's energy bills and also reduce the peak demand for the utility. Peak reduction can save utilities money by helping them avoid the construction of new peaking power plants[1] that exist only to handle peak loads; peak load may occur only a few hours per day, or, in some cases, for only a few hours per year. Utilities can

---

[1]Peaking power plants are power plants that operate only when there is a high peak demand for electric power.

also avoid (or defer) the cost of upgrading their infrastructure to meet these infrequent peak loads (6).

The AMI environment is fairly complex. The underlying technology that enables these benefits to the consumer and the utility company is the availability of an AMI and HAN communication system. To be effective and easily deployed, the HAN communication network should preferably be based on a network technology that (i) utilizes open standards, (ii) is low cost, (iii) consumes a minimum amount of energy, and (iv) does not require extensive new infrastructure. Metering devices are typically monitored and controlled by a centralized entity outside or inside the network operator system. Due to the need for centralized control, the centralized entity will inform or poll the metering device when it needs measurement information rather than the metering device autonomously sending measurements. Depending on the nature of the metering application, low latency responses are sometimes required (metering for high pressure pipelines, for example). To accomplish this, the centralized entity will need to inform the metering device when it needs a measurement. Typically, due to the limitation of IPv4 address space, the metering terminal is behind a network address translator (NAT) where it is not assigned a routable IPv4 address (3). This predicament is one of the reasons why it is desirable to utilize IPv6 for IoT devices/things.

AMI can utilize a number of methods and communication standards to connect the end device to the applications of the utility company. To communicate between physical service layers, some combinations and/or refinements of existing communication protocols are required. See Figure 3.3, loosely modeled after reference (37). While a number of power line carrier (PLC)-based communication approaches are technically feasible, at the current time none of these technologies and protocols have reached the level of technical maturity and cost competitiveness to enable one

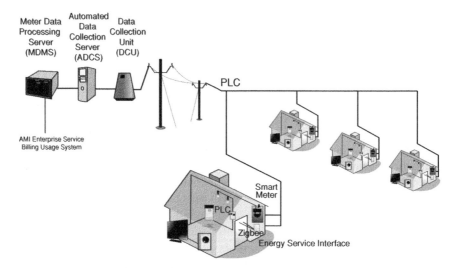

FIGURE 3.3 Advanced Metering Infrastructure.

to institutionalize a viable solution. However, there is work underway by several industry and/or standards organizations to develop standards for devices supporting these applications; for example, the European Commission (EC) has given support to the following initiatives:

- EC's M/411 Smart Metering Mandate: EC mandate issued in March 2009 by the Directorate-General for Transport and Energy (DG TREN) and sent to the three ESOs (European Standards Organizations)—CEN, CENELEC, and ETSI. The objective is to build standards for European smart meters, allowing interoperability and consumer actual consumption awareness.
- EC's M/490 SG Mandate: EC mandate issued in March 2011 by DG TREN and sent to the three ESOs—CEN, CENELEC, and ETSI. The objective is to build standards for European SGs.

3.3 e-HEALTH/BODY AREA NETWORKS

e-Health applications include health and fitness. Advocates envisage an environment where mobile health monitoring systems interoperate seamlessly and cohesively to reduce the lag time between the onset of medical symptoms in an individual and the diagnosis of the underlying condition. These applications make use of one or more biosensors placed on, or in, the human body, enabling the collection of a specified set of body's parameters to be transmitted and then monitored remotely. These sensors free patients from the set of wires that would otherwise tie the patients to a specific site at home or to a hospital bed; the on-body sensors are generally light and the links are wireless in nature, allowing the patient to enjoy a high degree of mobility (7). Sensors may consist of several wearable body sensor units, each containing a biosensor, a radio, an antenna, and some on-board control and computation. When multiple sensors are used by a patient, they are typically homed to a central unit also on the body. These on-body sensor systems—the sensors and the connectivity—are called wireless body area networks (WBANs), or alternatively, medical body area networks (MBANs), or alternatively medical body area network system (MBANS), although in the latter case the term does not necessarily mean a wireless system (8). Figure 3.4 provides a pictorial view of a WBAN.

MBAN technology consists of small, low powered sensors on the body that capture clinical information, such as temperature and respiratory function. Sensors are used for monitoring and trending for disease detection, progression, remission, and fitness. As patients recover, MBANs allow them to move about the healthcare facility, while still being monitored for any health issues that might develop. MBANs consist of two paired devices—one that is worn on the body (sensor) and another that is located either on the body or in close proximity to it (hub) (9). Some of these devices are disposable and are similar to a band-aid in size and shape; the disposable sensors include a low power radio transmitter. Sensors typically register patient's temperature, pulse, blood glucose level, blood pressure (BP), and respiratory health; the benefits

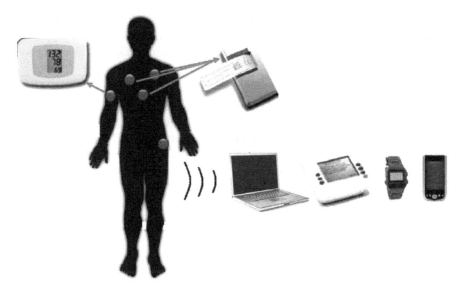

FIGURE 3.4 Wireless body area network/Medical body area network.

include increased mobility, better care, and lower costs. Examples of healthcare-related sensors include, but are not limited to:

- Glucose meter: A device that measures the approximate concentration of glucose in the blood; it is used by chronic disease (e.g., diabetes) management applications.
- Pulse oximeter: A device that indirectly measures the amount of oxygen in a patient's blood (oxygen saturation (SpO_2)).
- Electrocardiograph (ECG): A device that records and measures the electrical activity of the heart over time.
- Social alarm devices: Devices that allow individuals to raise an alarm and communicate with a caretaker when an emergency situation occurs; the caretaker may be a monitoring center, a medical care team, or a family member; these include devices fall detector and panic pendant/wrist transmitters.

The development activities related to WBANs/MBANs/MBANSs pertain to the formalization and standardization of wireless on-body monitoring technology entailing low power radio system used for the transmission of non-voice data to and from medical devices, especially in terms of frequency bands and communications at the higher layers (PHY, MAC, IP). A WBANs/MBANs consists of one or more on-body wireless sensors to simultaneously collect multiple vital sign parameters and/or medical actuator devices that can communicate with a monitoring device placed on/around (up to 10 m from) the human body. Today, existing technologies allow for *wired* solutions for monitoring patient vital signs as well as controlling actuators such as ventilators and infusion pumps. On-body sensors—measuring vital signs of a patient—and actuators are typically wired up to a bedside patient monitor. This bundle-of-wires situation limits the mobility of patients and reduces their comfort, adversely affecting their recovery times. Workflow delays are also introduced due to caregivers moving tethered patients. In Europe, the first wireless patient monitoring solutions operating in the generic short-range device (SRD) band from 2400 MHz to 2483.5 MHz have recently been introduced by vendors to overcome the disadvantages of wired solutions. However, the increasingly intensive use of this band by other applications (such as WiFi®, Bluetooth®, and ISM equipment) will tend to prevent such systems from offering the required reliability as their use increases within healthcare facilities (8). Hence the need for a standardized dedicated approach for MBANs, preferably with a worldwide and/or multiregion standard. There is movement to that effect in the United States (see below) and in Europe (with ETSI TR 101 557 as discussed in Chapter 6).

WBANs/MBANs are considered to be an assistive technology (AT). AT can be defined as "any device or system that allows an individual to perform a task that they would otherwise be unable to do, or increases the ease and safety with which the task can be performed" (according to the United Kingdom Royal Commission on Long-term Care). Another definition is "any product or service designed to enable independence for disabled or older people" (according to the European Union SOPRANO Review State-of-the-Art and Market Analysis Deliverable D1.1.2 published in 2007) (10). Table 3.2 depicts some of the benefits of (and/or motivations for) MBAN technology (9).

Standards drive economy-of-scale benefits for components; standards also simplify the control and monitoring of patients in hospitals, in care facilities, and in homes. e-Health and m-health rely on groups of connected devices, including devices communicating with classic smartphones using near field communication (NFC) technology, or with other nodes using low power, short-range radio communication technology such as Bluetooth low energy (BLE), or ZigBee (10), Kingsley (39).

- ZigBee aims at enabling the deployment of reliable, cost-effective, low power, wireless monitoring and control products based on an open IEEE standard; it was designed with simplicity in mind and is efficient in the use of power, allowing monitoring devices to operate on commonly available batteries for years.
- BLE is a low power version of Bluetooth capable of reporting data from a sensor for up to a year from a small button battery; although the BLE data rate and radio range is lower than that of classic Bluetooth, also an IEEE standard, the low power and long battery life make it suitable for short-range monitoring applications in medicine.
- NFC is a form of contactless communication between devices such as smartphones or tablets and readers. Contactless communication allows a user to wave the smartphone over an NFC-compatible device to send information without requiring the devices to touch or to use a cable.

TABLE 3.2   Benefits of (and/or Motivations for) MBAN Technology

Benefit	Description
Transforming Patient Care, Saving Lives	• Almost 50% of all patients in US hospitals are not monitored. MBANs provide a cost-effective way to monitor patients in a healthcare institution, so clinicians *can provide real-time and accurate data*, allowing them to intervene and save lives • MBANs allow for ubiquitous and reliable monitoring and give healthcare providers the chance to identify life-threatening problems or events before they occur. According to a study by the Institute for Healthcare Improvement, a monitored hospital patient has a 48% chance of surviving a cardiac arrest—this number plummets as low as 6% without monitoring • Portions of MBAN spectrum can also be used outside the hospital and in patients' homes. Monitoring a patient at home saves money by reducing readmission rates • MBAN-equipped devices allow patients *greater independence and mobility*, both in the hospital and in the home, implying a higher level of comfort and care
Driving Down Costs	• With MBAN technology, physicians can intervene before a patient's condition seriously deteriorates—resulting in less time spent in the intensive care unit—and can reduce costly follow-up visits. One healthcare company estimates it could save *$1.5 million per month* if unplanned (emergency) transfers could be prevented by early detection and treatment • Disposable wireless sensors can also help decrease hospital-acquired infections. The industry estimates that disposable sensors could help to *save an estimated $2000 to $12,000 per patient*—more than $11 billion nationwide • As one example, remote monitoring of patients with congestive heart failure would create an annual savings of *over $10 billion a year*
Spurring Innovation in Mobile Health	• The m-health industry consists of mobile applications, cloud-based data management, wireless medical devices, and other solutions to increase patient engagement and improve the delivery of healthcare services • Almost 17 million people are accessing health data on their mobile phones in the United States, a 125% increase since 2010 • m-health is expected to be *a $2 to 6 billion industry* by 2015 • About 88% of doctors support patients monitoring their health at home, especially weight, blood sugar, and vital signs • Early detection allows earlier treatment and better outcomes. For example, after an initial hospitalization for heart failure, 60% of patients are readmitted at least once within 6–9 months. Industry estimates indicate that remote monitoring could *generate net savings of $197 billion* over 25 years from just four chronic conditions

These wireless technologies are discussed in more detail in Chapter 6.

In mid-2012, the US Federal Communications Commission (FCC) announced it was planning to allocate spectrum bandwidth in the United States for use of body sensors to monitor wirelessly a variety of patient's vital signs using MBANSs. The FCC was planning to adopt new rules to permit more intensive use of spectrum for wireless medical devices, making the United States the first country in the world to dedicate spectrum for MBANs in hospitals, clinics, and doctors' offices (9). Using the newly allocated spectrum bandwidth, the sensors on a patient's body wirelessly form a network to a designated control node that aggregates the results and transmits that data to centralized computer systems. The FCC's MBAN proposal is a multi-industry effort to foster innovation in this spectrum band (2360–2400 MHz) by allowing distinct but compatible users to share. This proposed use of spectrum provides wireless health manufacturers with *increased spectrum capacity and reliability*, giving them the certainty they need to streamline their product development, which for many years operated on a variety of frequencies. The proposed new spectrum allocation can:

- Provide more reliable service and increased capacity for the use of MBANs in hospital waiting rooms, elevator lobbies, preparatory areas, and other high density settings.
- Greatly improve the quality of patient care with more effective monitoring, catching patients before critical stages, improving patient outcomes, and ultimately saving lives.
- Decrease expenses while increasing competition and innovation, easing entry for companies that are developing new wireless medical devices.

Healthcare monitoring applications include chronic disease monitoring, personal wellness monitoring, and personal fitness. Chronic diseases include diabetes, asthma, heart diseases, and sleep disorders. Chronic diseases typically require some kind of health monitoring, especially in advanced stages of the disease progression. Chronic disease monitoring encompasses the following, as described in Reference 10 (on which the next few paragraphs are based):

- *Episodic patient monitoring*; this is utilized in noncritical patients to track specific indicators and identify the progress of the disease or recovery. In this use case, the patient's vital signs (e.g., heart rate, temperature) and disease-specific indicators (e.g., BP, blood glucose level, EKG) are monitored to determine anomalies and identify trends. The monitoring is done periodically, and all the information collected by the medical sensors is time-stamped and then securely forwarded to a gateway that functions as a patient monitoring system. Additionally, the gateway forwards the aggregated information in a secure way to a database server. Medical personnel and family caregivers can access the information stored in the database server to monitor the progress of the disease.
- *Continuous patient monitoring*; this is associated with acute conditions that require constant or frequent measurement of health status. In this case, the

vital signs (e.g., heart rate, temperature, pulse oximeter) are monitored on a constant basis to allow continuous measurement of patients' health status at rest or during mild exercise for purpose of treatment adjustment, recovery, or diagnosis. The vital signs measurements waveforms (e.g., pulse pleth wave or heart rate) are securely streamed to an on-body data collection unit for data fusion and/or sequential storage. The data is securely forwarded from the data collection unit to an off-body gateway (e.g., PC/laptop, PDA or mobile phone) for storage and data analysis; alternatively, the data can be sent directly to a mobile terminal. The patient or the care provider remotely activates the on-body sensors via the off-body unit; the measurement data from the body sensors is securely transmitted continuously to the on-body unit, where it is temporarily stored. Subsequently, the recorded measurement data is securely sent to the off-body unit via batch transmission for persistent storage and further analysis by the healthcare provider. Optionally, an off-body unit can also be used for secure waveform viewing during the measurement. The healthcare professional uses the captured data to provide the appropriate diagnosis or to adjust the treatment level.

- *Patient alarm monitoring*: this entails the triggering of alarms based on preset conditions that are specific to the patient and the disease. In this use case, the patient's vital signs (e.g., heart rate, temperature) and disease-specific indicators (e.g., BP, EKG, EEG) are monitored on a continuous basis. The data collected by the sensors is time-stamped and securely forwarded to a gateway that acts as a patient monitoring system. The gateway securely forwards the aggregated information to a database server. Additionally, at predetermined settings, alarms are issued and responses/actions could be triggered automatically. For example, if during the monitoring of a diabetic patient the blood glucose level falls below a certain threshold, an alert can be sent to the patient, physician(s), and/or medical personnel. Increasing the sampling rate of a given monitor can also be triggered once an alarm has been asserted. The alarm can be issued either by the medical device or by the gateway.

Personal wellness monitoring concerns a person's activity and safety (especially for the elderly). Applications include but are not limited to smoke alarms, panic buttons, motion sensors, home sensors (e.g., bed, door, window, shower), and other monitors for assisted living facilities. The information collected by these devices is securely transmitted to a central location for decision-making, analysis, trending, and storage. Personal wellness monitoring includes the following:

- *Senior activity monitoring scenario* focuses on monitoring an elderly person's daily activity. Besides a wearable medical sensors/devices that monitor the vital signs (e.g., heartbeat, body temperature), this application involves monitoring other nonmedical sensors such as environmental sensors. If an elderly person has to follow a certain daily schedule, for example, taking a weight measurement in the morning, obtaining glucose level readings at 11 AM and at 5 PM, and so on, the caregiver can monitor the daily activity status of the person. If certain routine activities are not completed, the person can be sent a reminder.

- *Safety monitoring scenario* deals with monitoring the safety of the home environment. The home environment is monitored for safety hazards including toxic gases, water, and fire. Additionally, the vital signs (e.g., heartbeat, temperature) of the persons in the home are also monitored.

Personal fitness monitoring includes (i) monitoring and tracking fitness level and (ii) personalized fitness schedule scenario:

- The *monitoring and tracking fitness level* use case focuses on tracking the fitness level or progress made by an individual. A number of parameters that the individual wishes to monitor are recorded as that individual performs his/her workout routine (e.g., while running on a treadmill, the individual monitors his/her heart rate, temperature, and blood oxygen level). This information, obtained from medical sensors that are worn by the individual, is securely streamed to a gateway or a collection data unit and displayed on the treadmill's console in real time, along with other performance information provided by the treadmill. Additionally, the gateway sends the information to a database server for recordkeeping.
- The *personalized fitness schedule* use case focuses on personalization of the fitness schedule of an individual. The schedule to be followed by that individual can be entered by a trainer or the individual. For example, training for a marathon could include running on a treadmill according to a schedule designed by his/her trainer. For each training day, the trainer schedules the distance, the pace, and the maximum heart rate at which the individual is to train. The trainer would also like to monitor the individual's respiration pattern. While the distance and the pace are provided by the treadmill, the heart rate and the respiration are monitored by wireless medical devices worn by the individual.

Some press time demonstrations of MBAN technology included the following:

- *Fetal telemetry*: A small, lightweight, and noninvasive way to continuously monitor a baby's health, while allowing the mother to move freely.
- *LifeLine home care pendants*: A device that collects health information for the elderly or those with chronic diseases—allowing them to live independently with the security and peace of mind that they are being monitored.
- *Predictive and early warning systems*: Provides continuous monitoring to help prevent sudden and acute deterioration of a patient's condition.
- A greatly abbreviated press time list of specific illustrative *examples* in this arena includes the following.[2]

---

[2]Companies named in this text are simply illustrative examples of entities that may offer technologies and services under discussion at point in the text; named companies are generally not the only suppliers that

Sierra Wireless has developed Positive ID secure modules to provide support for diabetics through monitoring levels of glucose in the blood. Cinterion/Gemalto has developed Aerotel, a system capable of modulating in real time the flow of air sent to people suffering from sleep apnea; the company has also developed M2M modules to remotely monitor problems of cardiac arrhythmia in real time. The first applications of NFC technology appeared recently in the United States with the launch by the company iMPack of a system "tracking" the quality of sleep, allowing a clock to transmit data collected during the night to the Nokia C7 NFC smartphone. It uses an embedded application to generate an initial result, which can then be transmitted to a physician (11).

Press time research issues for WBANs include but are not limited to the following:

- Antenna design for in- and on-body networks
- Channel modeling radio propagation issues for WBAN
- Electromagnetic radiation and human tissues
- Interference management and mitigation
- Coexistence of WBAN with other wireless technologies
- Protocols and algorithms for the PHY, MAC, and network layer
- End-to-end quality of service (QoS) provision for WBAN
- Energy-efficient and low power consumption protocols
- Power management for WBAN
- Integration of WBAN with heterogeneous networks
- (Lightweight) security, authentication, and cryptography solutions for WBAN
- Standardization activities

3.4 CITY AUTOMATION

Some applications in this domain include but are not limited to the following:

- Traffic flow management system in combination with dynamic traffic light control
- Street light control
- Passenger information system for public transportation
- Passive surveillance (see Section 3.9)

Generic city sensors include environmental sensors and activity sensors. Environmental sensors include:

- thermal
- hygrometric

---

may provide such services, and mention of a company and/or service does not imply that such entities or capabilities are recommended herewith, or considered in any way better than others.

- anemometric
- sound
- gas
- particles
- light, other EM spectrum
- seismic

Activity sensors include:

- pavement/roadway pressure
- vehicle and pedestrian detection
- parking space occupancy

ETSI TR 102 897: "*Machine-to-Machine Communications (M2M); Use Cases of M2M Applications for City Automation*" provides the following description of these applications (12):

Use Case 1: Traffic Flow Management System in Combination with Dynamic Traffic Light Control. The flow of road traffic within cities depends on a number of factors such as the number of vehicles on the road, the time and the day, the current or expected weather, current traffic issues and accidents, as well as road construction work. Traffic flow sensors provide key traffic flow information to a central traffic flow management system; the traffic flow management system can develop a real-time traffic optimization strategy and, thus, endeavor to control the traffic flow. The traffic control can be achieved by dynamic information displays informing the driver about traffic jams and congested roads; traffic signs can direct the traffic to utilize less used roads. The traffic flow management system can also interact with controllable traffic lights to extend or to reduce the green light period to increase the vehicle throughput on heavy used roads; dynamically changeable traffic signs can lead to an environment where the vehicular traffic is managed more efficiently, thus enabling cities to reduce fuel consumption, air pollution, congestions, and the time spent on the road.

Use Case 2: Street Light Control. Street lights are not required to shine at the same intensity to accomplish the intended safety goal. The intensity may depend on conditions such as moonlight or weather. Adjusting the intensity helps to reduce the energy consumption and the expenditures incurred by a municipality. The street light controller of each street light segment is connected (often wirelessly) with the central street light managing and control system. Based on local information measured by local sensors, the control system can dim the corresponding street lights of a segment remotely or is able to switch street lights on and off.

Use Case 3: Passenger Information System for Public Transportation. Public transportation vehicles, such as busses, subways, and commuter trains, operate on a schedule that may be impacted by external variables and, thus, have a degree of variability compared with a baseline formal schedule. Passengers need to know when their next connection is available; this information also allows passengers to select alternative connections in the case of longer delays. In this application, the current locations of the various public transport vehicles are provided to the central system that is able to match the current location with the forecasted location at each time or at specific checkpoints. Based on the time difference, the system is able to calculate the current delay and the expected arrival time at the upcoming stops. The vehicle location can be captured via checkpoints on the regular track or via GPS/general packet radio service (GPRS) tracking devices that provide the position information in regular intervals. Two approaches are possible:

- With a checkpoint-based approach, the line number (of the bus or the street car) is captured at each station where the vehicle stops regularly, or at defined checkpoint in between. Because of the fact that the sensor at a specific station is able to provide the data to the central system, the expected delay can be calculated by comparing the information of the scheduled arrival time and the actual arrival time. This change can be added to the arrival time displayed at each following station. Each vehicle must be equipped with a transponder (variously based on infrared, radio frequency identification (RFID), short-range communication, or optical recognition). In addition, each station has to be equipped with one or more checkpoint systems that are able to readout or to receive the line number information of the vehicle. In case of larger stations with several platforms, multiple systems are needed.
- With a GPS/GPRS-based approach, each vehicle has to be equipped with a GPS/GPRS tracking device that provide, besides the current position, the information that can be directly or indirectly matched to the serviced line number. Based on the "regular" position/time pattern, the system is able to calculate the actual time difference and provide the expected time on the passenger display.

A combination of checkpoint- and GPS/GPRS-based solution can be used to integrate railed vehicles (such as subways and street cars) and road vehicles (such as busses).

3.5 AUTOMOTIVE APPLICATIONS

IoT/M2M automotive and transportation applications focus on safety, security, connected navigation, and other vehicle services such as, but not limited to, insurance or road pricing, emergency assistance, fleet management, electric car charging management, and traffic optimization. These applications typically entail IoT/M2M communication modules that are embedded into the car or the transportation equipment. Some of the technical challenges relate to mobility management and environmental hardware considerations. A brief description of applications follows from Reference 13 (on which the next few paragraphs are based).

- *bCall (breakdown call):* A bCall sends the current vehicle position to a roadside assistance organization and initiates a voice call. The bCall trigger is usually a switch that is manually pushed by the user in order to activate the service. An "enhanced" bCall service allows current vehicle diagnostic information to be transmitted in addition to the vehicle position.

- *Stolen vehicle tracking (SVT):* A basic application for automotive M2M communications is tracking of mobile assets—either for purposes of managing a fleet of vehicles or to determine the location of stolen property. The goal of a SVT system is to facilitate the recovery of a vehicle in case of theft. The SVT service provider periodically requests location data from the Telematics Control Unit (TCU) in the vehicle and interacts with the police. The TCU may also be capable of sending out automatic theft alerts based on vehicle intrusion or illegal movement. The TCU may also be linked to the Engine Management System (EMS) to enable immobilization or speed degradation by remote command. Vehicles contain embedded M2M devices that can interface with location-determination technology and can communicate via a mobile cellular network to an entity (server) in the M2M core. The M2M devices will communicate directly with the telecommunication network; the M2M devices will interface with location-determination technology such as standalone GPS, or network-based mechanisms such as assisted GPS, Cell-ID, and so on. For theft-tracking applications, the M2M device is typically embedded in an inaccessible or inconspicuous place so that it may not be easily disabled by a thief. The tracking server is an entity located in the M2M core and owned or operated by the asset owner or service provider to receive, process, and render location and velocity information provided by the deployed assets. The tracking server may trigger a particular M2M device to provide a location/velocity update, or the M2M devices may be configured to autonomously provide updates on a schedule or upon an event-based trigger.

- *Remote diagnostics*: Remote diagnostic services can broadly be grouped into the following categories:

  - Maintenance minder—when the vehicle reaches a certain mileage (e.g., 90% of the manufacturer's recommended service interval since the previous service), the TCU sends a message to the owner or the owner's named dealership, advising the owner (or the dealership) that the vehicle is due for service.

  - Health check—Either on a periodic basis or triggered by a request from the owner, the TCU compiles the vehicle's general status using inbuilt diagnostic reporting functions and transmits a diagnostic report to the owner, the owner's preferred dealership, or to the vehicle manufacturer.

  - Fault triggered—When a fault (a diagnostic trouble code [DTC]) is detected with one of the vehicle systems, this triggers the TCU to send the DTC code and any related information to the owner's preferred dealer, or to the vehicle manufacturer.

  - Enhanced bCall—When a manual breakdown call is initiated by the owner, the TCU sends both position data and DTC status information to the roadside assistance service or to the vehicle manufacturer.

- *Fleet management:* The fleet owner wishes to track the vehicles—that is, to know, over time, the location and velocity of each vehicle—in order to plan and optimize business operations. A fleet management application assumes that a fleet of vehicles have been deployed with M2M devices installed that are able to:
  - Interface with sensors on the vehicle that measure velocity
  - Interface with devices that can detect position
  - Establish a link with a mobile telecommunication network using appropriate network access credentials, such as a USIM (universal subscriber identity module)

A server in the fleet owner's employ receives, aggregates, and processes the tracking data from the fleet and provides this information to the fleet owner. Devices could be configured to autonomously establish communication with the server via a cellular network either at regular intervals, at prescheduled times, or based on some event such as crossing a geographic threshold. Alternatively, the M2M devices could be commanded by the M2M server to report their location/velocity data. See Figure 3.5 for an illustrative example.

- *Vehicle-to-infrastructure communications.* A European Intelligent Transport Systems Directive[3] seeks the implementation of eSafety applications in vehicles. Some vehicle manufacturers have begun to deploy vehicle-to-vehicle communication, for example, in the context of wireless access in vehicular environments (WAVE). On the other hand, vehicle to roadside applications are less well-developed; in this case, vehicles have embedded M2M devices that can interface with location-determination technology and can communicate via a mobile telecommunication network to an entity (server). This application assumes that vehicles have been deployed with M2M devices installed that are able to:
  - Interface with sensors on the vehicle that measure velocity, external impacts
  - Interface with devices that can detect position
  - Establish a link with a mobile telecommunication network using appropriate network access credentials, such as a USIM
  - Upload or download traffic and safety information to a traffic information server

Devices could be configured to establish communication with the server via the cellular network based on some event triggered by a vehicle sensor such as external impact, motor failure, and so on. For example, the traffic information server pushes roadside or emergency information out to vehicles based on location (cell location or actual location). Or, vehicle information is pushed to the traffic information server

---

[3] A directive is a legislative act of the European Union requiring member states to achieve a stated result but without mandating the means of achieving that result.

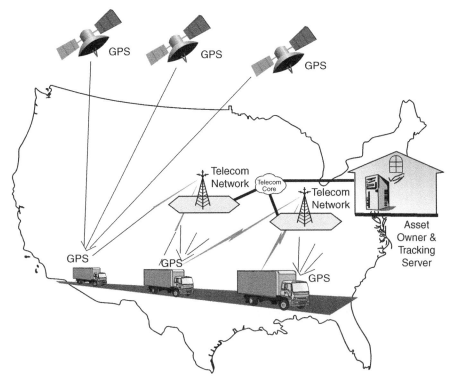

FIGURE 3.5   Vehicular asset tracking.

based on external sensor information, internal sensor information, or subscription basis. See Figure 3.6.

- *Insurance services:* Pay-as-you-drive (PAYD) schemes offer insurers the opportunity to reduce costs based on actual risk and provide more competitive products to the end-user based on getting feedback from the vehicle as to when, where, how, or how far the vehicle is being driven (or a combination of these factors).

3.6 HOME AUTOMATION

Home automation has received a lot of attention of late in the IoT/M2M context. Basic applications of the automated home include remote media control, heating control, lighting control (including low power landscape lighting control), and appliance control. Sensed homes, as examples of smart space, are seen as "next-step/next-generation" applications. Smart meters and energy efficiency (making use of the potential of SG), discussed above, also fit this category. Telehealth (e.g., assisted living and in-home m-health services) also can be captured under this set of applications; security and emergency services also can be included here.

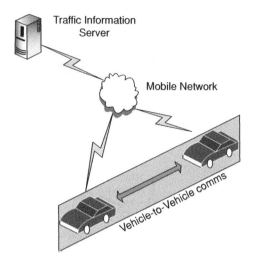

FIGURE 3.6   Vehicle-to-infrastructure communications.

M2M communications is expected to play a major role in residences, where instrumentation of elements supporting daily living (e.g., appliances), comfort, health, security, and energy efficiency can improve the quality of life and the quality of experience. Home control applications include but are not limited to:

- Lighting control
- Thermostat/HVAC
- White goods/
- Appliance control
- In-home displays

Home security applications include but are not limited to:

- Door access phone
- Window locks
- Motion detector
- Smoke/fire alert
- Baby monitors
- Medical pendant

See Figure 3.7 for an illustrative example.

Energy efficiency at home is a key application of interest because of the possibility of monetary saving for the consumer. Occupancy sensors can be used to establish whether there is somebody in a room or not and when the room becomes unoccupied the lights are automatically switched off; other types of sensors can be used to control

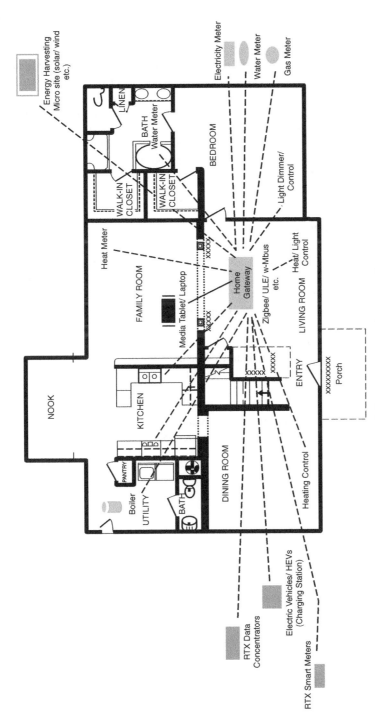

FIGURE 3.7 Home automation example.

Energy Harvesting Micro site (solar/ wind etc.)

Electricity Meter

Water Meter

Gas Meter

LINEN

BATH
Water Meter

WALK-IN CLOSET

WALK-IN CLOSET

BEDROOM

Light Dimmer/ Control

Heat Meter

FAMILY ROOM

Media Tablet/ Laptop

Home Gateway

Zigbee/ ULE/ w-Mbus etc.

Heat/ Light Control

LIVING ROOM

NOOK

KITCHEN

PANTRY

ENTRY

Porch

Boiler

UTILITY

BATH

DINING ROOM

Heating Control

RTX Data Concentrators

Electric Vehicles/ HEVs (Charging Station)

RTX Smart Meters

the energy consumption from different equipments (e.g., temperature, TVs, and so on). The sensors and actuators can be autonomous (as in the case of light sensors), or can be connected to an M2M gateway control node (wirelessly or using wires, e.g., via PLC). By integrating the data from a plethora of sensors (e.g., outside temperature, multizone heating status), the gateway can dispatch the appropriate commands to the relevant actuators (e.g., to switch off the heater in a room or zone, or in the entire house). The M2M system allows reducing energy consumption by automatically adapting the use of the house equipment to various short-term situations (people moving in and out of rooms, people going to work and retuning later) or long-term situations (people taking vacations or long weekends or managing a second/vacation home) (5).

3.7 SMART CARDS

Smart cards (SCs) in general, and M2M-based systems in particular, enable wired and wireless communication for a large set of commercial and industrial applications. SCs are now routinely accepted as credentials for controlling secure physical access. The purpose of an SC is to safeguard user identities and secret keys and to perform requisite cryptographic computations (an SC is a tamper-resistant device). SC technology includes contact and contactless systems. A terminal is the entity with which the SC can establish a secure channel. Examples include generic card acceptance devices (CADs), a CAD on a mobile handset, a Set-top box, a laptop/PC/tablet. See Figure 3.8.

Applications include utility monitoring, vending machines, security systems, industrial machines, automotive, traffic management, speed cameras, and medical equipment. A more inclusive list of SC applications is as follows:

- Biometrics
- Cybersecurity
- Enterprise ID
- Government ID
    ePassport
    FIPS 201
    Real ID
    Passport Card/WHTI
- Healthcare
- Identity
- Logical access
- Market research
- Mobile telecommunications
- Network security

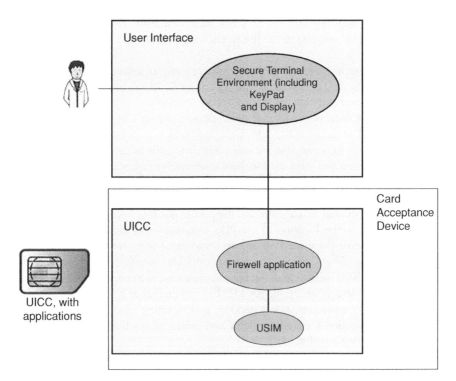

FIGURE 3.8   UICC environment, including user interfaces.

- Payments
    POS
    Contactless payments
    EMV payments
    Mobile payments/NFC
    Transportation payments
- Physical access
- Privacy
- RF/RFID tags
- Security
    ePassport security
    Contactless payments security
    Transit fare payment system security
- Transportation (toll tags, speed-of-vehicle readers)

These applications require advanced, durable USIM cards. SCs are resource-limited devices because they are designed to be economic and portable (small and light).

In recent years, memory size on SCs has increased from KBs up to MBs; this trend is expected to continue in the future allowing operators to offer enhanced new services.

Applications such as electronic payment, electronic ticketing, and transit can be combined with physical access to provide a multiapplication and multitechnology ID credential; the issuer can also record and update appropriate privileges from a single central location. Contactless SCs can authenticate a person's identity, determine the appropriate level of access, and admit the cardholder to a facility, all from data stored on the card; SCs can also include additional authentication factors (such as biometric templates) and other card technologies (such as an SC chip) (14). Another application example is POS use. Currently, most POS terminals are connected using a wired connection; as a consequence, the terminals are placed at a fixed position within the establishment in question, and the person needing to perform a transaction is required to go to the location of the POS terminal—this may be inconvenience or restrict commerce (in some fashion). In some cases (e.g., remotely located POS terminals, parking meters, garage checkout booths, and so on), a wired connection is difficult and costly to be installed. An option, therefore, is to connect POS terminals via a secure wireless connection. As M2M communication modules are installed into wireless POS terminals, street parking, and ticketing machines, and so on to provide communication for credit or debit card online transactions, new commercial applications become a reality (5).

Contactless cards use NFC to communicate and receive power over short distances; since these devices do not need physical contact with a reader, they simplify operation and increases transaction speeds. For transponders to work they require power, although the levels are very small. Passive devices operate without an internal battery source, deriving the power to operate from the field generated by the reader; this implies that passive devices offer an unlimited operational lifetime but have shorter read ranges and require a higher-powered reader (15). There are three basic contactless technologies considered for physical access control applications: 125 kHz, ISO/IEC 14443, and ISO/IEC 15693 technologies.

- 125 kHz read-only technology is used by many of today's RFID access control systems and is based on de facto industry standards rather than international standards. 125 kHz technology allows for a secure, uniquely coded number to be transmitted and processed by a back-end system. The back-end system then determines the rights and privileges associated with that card.
- Contactless SC technology based on ISO/IEC 14443 and ISO/IEC 15693 standards are intelligent, read/write devices capable of storing different kinds of data and operating at different ranges. Contactless SCs operate at 13.56 MHz and are further divided into proximity (ISO 14443) and vicinity (ISO 15693) devices with nominal operating ranges of up to 10 cm and 1 m, respectively. ISO 14443 specifies A and B operation modes that use different communication and card selection procedures. The ISO 14443A standard is used with most contactless cards and is compatible with the lower layers of popular commercial products. The standard specifies the operating frequency, modulation and coding schemes

(ISO 14443-2), anti-collision routines (ISO 14443-3), and communication protocols (ISO 14443-4). It uses amplitude shift keying (ASK) modulation with modified miller coding (106 Kbps) in reader to card communication (15).

NFC setups allow a device (known as a *reader*, *interrogator*, or *active device*) to create a radio frequency current that enables communication with another NFC-compatible device or a small NFC tag holding the information the reader wants. Passive devices, such as the NFC tag in smart posters, store information and communicate with the reader, but do not actively read other devices. Peer-to-peer communication through two active devices is also a possibility with NFC, allowing both devices to send and receive information. NFC maintains interoperability between different wireless communication methods such as Bluetooth and other NFC standards including FeliCa—popular in Japan—through the NFC Forum. Founded in 2004 by Sony, Nokia, and Philips, the NFC Forum enforces standards that manufacturers must meet when designing NFC-compatible devices. This ensures that NFC is secure and remains easy to use with different versions of the technology. Compatibility is the key to the growth of NFC as a popular payment and data communication method. It must be able to communicate with other wireless technologies and be able to interact with different types of NFC transmissions. For example, by integrating credit cards, subway tickets, and paper coupons all into one device, a customer can board a train, pay for groceries, redeem coupons or store loyalty points, and even exchange contact information all with the wave of a smartphone. NFC technology is popular in parts of Europe and Asia and is also being deployed in the United States. As an illustrative example, Google launched Google Wallet that supports MasterCard Pay-Pass, PayPal offers money transfers between smartphones, and other companies are expected to follow suit. The expectation is that as the technology is deployed, more NFC-compatible smartphones will be available, and more stores will offer NFC card readers for customer convenience (16). This topic is revisited later in the text.

SC use depends on the environment in which they are deployed. For example, in banking, user information includes identity, account information, and possibly information on recent transactions made and secret keys used in security functions; the operations allowed encompass card holder authentication, automatic transaction registration, and transaction nonrepudiation. In mobile communications, user information includes identity, personal information such as address book, operator-related information, and again secret keys used in security functions. Functions executed include user authentication, voice encryption, as well as data access to user's private information. There are no peripherals that allow user direct access, such as a keyboard or a screen: SC access must go through a terminal, and, unless the communication is secure end-to-end, this may constitute a security weakness. System security is determined at the weakest link and, unless strengthened, attackers may target the terminal or the data exchange with the terminal, to get round the robustness of the tamper-resistant device (17). For example, a UICC (Universal Integrated Circuit Card) is the SC used in mobile terminals in GSM and UMTS networks. A UICC typically contains several applications, and the same SC provides access to both GSM and UMTS networks. The UICC also provides storage (e.g., for a directory). In a GSM network, the UICC contains a subscriber identification module (SIM) application; in a UMTS network it is the USIM application. It is a new-generation SIM included in cell phones or laptops using high speed 3G cellular networks. The UICC SC typically has a CPU, ROM, RAM, EEPROM, and I/O circuits.

Occupational use of health cards still lags behind that of credit cards and mobile phone SIM/USIM cards, but they are finding applications in countries where the health system is subject to extensive major fraud and where the costs of conventional treatment of medical data are becoming difficult to manage. The Health Information Technology for Economic and Clinical Health (HITECH) Act, signed in the United States in February 2009, encourages stakeholders in the health ecosystem to work toward the creation of a network (protected health infrastructure) for the collection and exchange of standardized medical data (electronic health record) using "certified technology" capable of simultaneously ensuring the availability, sharing, security, accuracy, and confidentiality of such data. Although not explicitly named, smart security technologies are at the forefront of this trend: any candidate technology must be able to handle the rights of all stakeholders (patients, doctors, nurses, specialists, pharmacists, and so on), keys and certificates, means of encryption, and strong authentication (in some cases, biometric). The American Medical Association (AMA) has stressed the benefits offered by the use of an SC that stores personal medical information (allergies, blood type, current treatment, and so on), especially in emergency situations. The Secure ID Coalition, which also campaigns in the United States for the generalization of personal health cards, observed recently that SCs could be employed to reduce fraud in health spending of around $370 billion over a period of just 10 years. Several health SCs have already emerged in the United States as of press time. For example, LifeNexus[4] launched a health card that also serves as a personal credit card. A bracelet containing a contactless chip (MasterCard PayPass) has also been issued; the bracelet contains a unique number (VITAnumber[5]), providing access in emergencies to the bearer's personal medical data. Germany was preparing to launch a new generation of health cards (eGK Generation 1plus) designed in conjunction with insurance companies for online use. In France, the new CPS3 card for health professionals entered circulation earlier this year; this contactless card is now in line with the European IAS ECC standard (signature, identification, and authentication) (11).

Other examples of SC/UICC applications include the following as described in Reference 17 (some of these applications require a high speed dedicated channel between UICC and terminal):

- The UICC is a control point for device management (DM). DM aims to provide the protocols and mechanisms to achieve remote management of devices. DM includes: (a) setting initial configuration information in devices; (b) subsequent installation and updates of persistent information in devices (firmware update);

---

[4]See previous footnote.

[5]VITA Products Incorporated's VITAnumber is a unique numerical identifier printed on a VITAband that is individually assigned to each user. The VITAnumber links the user to his/her Emergency Response Profile (ERP). Unlike other ID bracelets, which print all the personal information on the band, the VITAnumber anonymizes the personal information until it is needed.

(c) retrieval of management information from devices; and (d) processing events and alarms generated by devices. In this application, the SC inserted in the device is expected to: (i) support dynamic provisioning of the device with up-to-date information and (ii) handle a part of the security during the update of device firmware (service access controlled by the operator, authentication of the origin, and so on). To achieve this, the SC must store DM objects accessible by the device through the SC to device interface and also manageable by a remote server (through the device).

- Digital rights management (DRM) and distributed applications. DRM is used to secure media content owned by a service provider; the end-user has a limited set of rights to use the content. Usually, media content is supposed to be rendered on any type of compatible terminal (e.g., CD audio on any CD player) so that the user can transport his/her content wherever he/she wants. Adding security should not change this user experience. When the user is a mobile network operator (MNO) subscriber, the rights are bound to a device, not to a user. This implies that when the user needs to change the player (i.e., the handset), the rights have to be downloaded onto the new device and the certificates are to be recalculated with the new terminal ID. This scheme works well as long as a network connection is available and/or the terminal belongs to the same user domain.

- Multimedia file management. As the UICC will be able to store and encrypt/decrypt multimedia files (such as multimedia message service [MMS], pictures, MP3 files, video clips), customer's usability and quality user experience cannot be compromised by a too long wait for the data download/upload. For example, it could be of interest to associate an image, a sound, and eventually a short video with the information relative to each contact in order to display all the images and video when accessing the phonebook.

- Man–machine interface (MMI) on UICC. Large-sized SCs offer the possibility to store card issuer's MMI in the UICC. During initialization process, the terminal can detect the type of UICC (which operator, which service providers, which features) and upload the whole MMI that the card issuer has defined for its purposes and its services.

- Real-time multimedia data encryption/decryption. UICC can be used to directly encrypt/decrypt data stream (such as protected voice communications or streamed video and music). For example, the user should be able to receive multimedia files encrypted using rights stored inside the UICC. Both the content and its decryption key should be stored in the UICC and also the decryption process could be executed inside the card. The decrypted content could be offered via a streaming protocol in order to increase the level of security. In addition, the user could also store personal contents in the UICC and send them after having protected them through encryption features of the UICC.

- Storage of terminal applications on the UICC. UICC could be used to store and distribute applications that could be uploaded by the terminal during the initialization phase or later. The uploading from the UICC to the terminal (or vice versa) of the applications should happen dynamically according to user rights purchased from the operator. This enables efficient management of operator-related applications on the terminal and easy deployment of innovative services on the field.

- Direct and indirect UICC connection to a PC. As it is now possible for some devices, it should be possible either to insert a UICC directly into a PC laptop or to connect the handset to PC laptop in order to download/retrieve some personal data (MMS, pictures, movies, applications, and so on) to/from the card in a very quick time but also to easily execute cryptographic operations for accessing a secure environment (e.g., PKI for e-commerce). The user should consider the UICC as his/her trusted storage device, ensuring acceptable performances for the targeted use.

- Web server on SC. UICC can be considered similar to a web server, to which an Internet connection can be established with a usual Internet browser. Such a solution removes the needs of deployment of middleware to interface the functionality of the UICC as standard browsers and protocols would be used to access UICC contents and applications. Contents will be both stored and dynamically generated on the SC and then transferred to the terminal: the aim is to reuse standard graphic features of handsets to allow mobile operators to offer attractive and secure services. An effective communication interface between the terminal and the UICC will enhance the web server performances; TCP/IP-based communication allows internal pages (in the UICC) to be served locally and remotely using standard protocols and methods.

- Antivirus on UICC. The usage of the UICC as a storage device or the downloading on it of new applications and services leads to the need of antivirus running on the UICC itself, as is the case in a PC environment. The UICC could be able to perform auto-scan, to update virus signature or manage user rights.

- High priced ticketing scenario. Tickets can be purchased and stored securely on the UICC. In view of the (medium to) high value of the tickets, the UICC-based implementation must provide adequate protection mechanisms (e.g., to make it useless to steal someone's phone to enter an event). The UICC-based ticket may need the system to authenticate itself before each ticket can be viewed, used, or deleted. The ability to view and legitimately and securely transfer tickets is potentially an added benefit for tickets stored in a UICC (as compared with a "classical" contactless card). For this type of application, UICC-based ticketing offers the issuers of these tickets a cheaper way of implementing a contactless ticketing system. For the user, UICC-based ticketing should offer a more convenient and secure way to carry ticket and more flexible purchase experience.

- Payment application. Here the UICC contains the application and data required for contactless payment application. The terminal containing the UICC in this scenario has two possibilities: (i) it can act like a contactless payment application to pay at a contactless-enabled POS; (ii) it can act as a proxy for a payment account in which a third party performs a debit transaction, passing the payment to the merchant.

- Loyalty application. Here the UICC contains the application and data required for loyalty application. The terminal containing the UICC can act like a contactless loyalty application at a contactless-enabled POS.
- Healthcare application. Here the UICC contains the application and data required for a healthcare application. The terminal containing this UICC is used to store medical and health insurance data. These essential data would be available whatever the powering mode of the UICC. The use of the contactless interface may occur in places where strict security or safety rules apply (e.g., regulations requiring a terminal to be switched off in a hospital).

The SC Alliance is an advocate for a multitude of applications of SC technology; it is a not-for-profit, multi-industry association of member firms working to accelerate the widespread acceptance of multiple applications for SC technology—the Alliance membership includes leading companies in banking, financial services, computer, telecommunications, technology, healthcare, retail and entertainment industries, as well as a number of government agencies.

3.8 TRACKING (FOLLOWING AND MONITORING MOBILE OBJECTS)

Track and trace applications are typical of automotive environments as well as of goods movement in production environments, distribution, and retail; in the latter case RFID tags are often utilized. Automotive applications are focused on (i) physical security for people such as emergency situations, (ii) asset tracking for theft or law enforcement applications, and (iii) fleet management to achieve increased operational efficiency. Other facets of these services include remote diagnostics, navigation systems, PAYD (insurance, in-car services), and so on. See Table 3.3, loosely based on references (5, 13). In these applications, the M2M modules will have to function in an extended temperature and humidity range; in addition, the connection with the M2M communication module will have to withstand the vibration produced by the engine of a car, truck, or construction machinery, as well as by the movement of the vehicle on the road. Tracking devices are often placed in harsh environments; this means that may experience strong vibrations or shocks. The space is often very limited, implying that the size of the M2M communication module needs to be kept to a minimum.

Tracking (such as vehicles of any kind, containers, people, pets, and so on) is a common application implemented in conjunction with GPS; it can also be implemented using cellular technology. GPS is based on a cluster of satellites that continually send out signals. The satellites orbit the earth approximately every 12 h; the height of the orbits is about 20,183 km in the MEO (medium earth orbit). See Figure 3.9. GPS receivers can determine their position based on the time delay between transmission and reception of the signals transmitted by the satellites. The satellites are arranged on six planes, each of them containing at least four slots where satellites can be arranged equidistantly. Typically more than 24 GPS satellites orbit the earth (Russia and Europe are also planning to deploy their own GPS systems). In theory,

TABLE 3.3 Track and Trace Application Examples

Example	Description
Emergency call	The in-vehicle emergency call system can automatically or manually send location and driver information to an emergency center. The in-vehicle M2M communication module supports the transfer of emergency call data between the vehicle and the emergency service center. The on-board M2M communication module is connected to sensors that can identify an accident event and in such case set up a connection to an emergency center forwarding information about the location, an indication about the level of the accident, and possibly other additional information. A key requirement for this application is that the M2M module and its sensors/interfaces are able to survive and operate after a shock caused by an accident
Fleet management	For this application, a vehicle has a built-in M2M communication module (typically owned by the service provider not the driver) that collects information, such as location, timings, traffic jams, maintenance data, and travel location environmental conditions at any point along the way. This information is transmitted by the module via a mobile network to a server application where it is used to track the vehicle and deliveries. Using real-time information (such as traffic conditions), a logistics application can optimize the delivery plan and route; the updated delivery plan is then sent to the vehicle's driver. Using maintenance-related information, maintenance can be planned or remote emergency maintenance can be performed. In addition, environmental sensors can be used to retrieve information on the storage environment and condition of product being transported
Theft tracking	In this application, the use of M2M capabilities allows the recovery of a stolen vehicle. The M2M module supports secure communication over the network to a third-party entity. The M2M module needs to be protected against theft and misuse; another factor in this environment is the often limited space available to conceal or secure the system from theft and misuse, implying that the size of M2M modules should be kept small
Person/animal protection/ tracking	In this application, humans (e.g., workers, healthcare, elderly, or children) and/or animals are equipped with portable and/or wearable devices incorporating an M2M communication module that transmits information (automatically or on demand) to a server application used to monitor the status and positioning of the subject. Cellular and/or GPS-based triangularization functions are used. These services may be implemented via applications residing inside the M2M module/ UICC
Object protection/ tracking	The purpose of this application is to track and trace. In this application, objects (e.g., containers, construction equipment, and so on) are equipped with portable devices containing an M2M communication module, and optionally a GPS function, which forward location/status information either automatically or on demand to a server application; the server can monitor the status and location of those objects

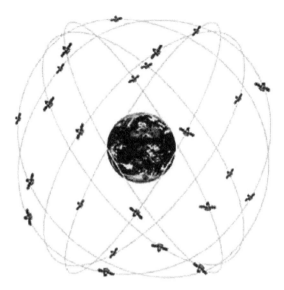

FIGURE 3.9   GPS satellites.

three satellites emitting signals are sufficient to determine the precise position and height; in practice additional satellites are utilized. GPS allows one to establish the receiver's position as well as the receiver's speed and direction (this is done by measuring the Doppler effect or the numerical differentiation of a location according to time). Figure 3.10 shows a basic service arrangement: the DEP is comprised of a GPS sensor and a cellular modem; the GPS sensor transfers the position data to the cell modem and the modem transmits the position data to the DIP via a cellular network. The positioning data is then manipulated, displayed (e.g., using a map or GIS—geographic information system), and/or stored as needed.

3.9 OVER-THE-AIR-PASSIVE SURVEILLANCE/RING OF STEEL

Integrated open-air surveillance (IOS) technologies such as high resolution digital video surveillance (DVS), license plate recognition technology, facial recognition systems, traffic light cameras, gunshot detection systems (GDSs), aerial surveillance with drones (UAVs—unmanned aerial vehicles), and other related technologies are increasingly being put to use to support public safety mandates at a reduced surveillance/interdiction costs for those jurisdictions that deploy the infrastructure, while at the same time generating revenues for service providers and system integrators. *Open air* refers to the fact that the surveillance is done in the public domain; this type of surveillance can be done, for example, with (i) high resolution (even low light level) digital video cameras (which can be wired and/or wireless); (ii) license plate/face recognition technology; (iii) GDSs; and (iv) other related technologies or sensors. *Integrated* refers to the internetworking of multiple geographically dispersed

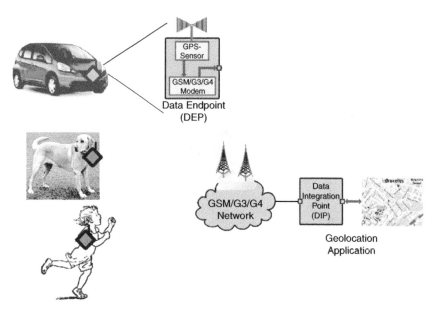

FIGURE 3.10   Geolocation/tracking application.

systems and multiple technologies with database systems that may archive a variety of pertinent background data or metadata. IOS technologies make use of both of these capabilities. Many of these applications can be seen as IoT applications, where the "things" are the sensors, the cameras, and other related instrumentation.

IOS enables the collection, aggregation, and analysis of factors in physical public view. This is not identical to the term *mass surveillance.* Mass surveillance is used to describe the pervasive surveillance of an entire (or large fraction of the) population.[6,7]

---

[6]*Mass surveillance* could be done, say, with wiretapping of voice and data communications, metadata collection, or with other means. We are not covering this topic because different technologies are in play compared with those used for integrated open-air surveillance: We only make passing mention of this by noting that recent surveys in about 50 countries suggest that there has been an increase in recent years in surveillance. For example, there are already mass surveillance (and open-air surveillance) in Taiwan, Thailand, the United States, Singapore, the United Kingdom, China, Malaysia and Russia, and others. In 2006, the European Union passed and adopted the Data Retention Directive (Directive 2006/24/EC), which requires telecommunication companies to retain metadata on telecommunications (e.g., who called whom, when, how often, etc.) and to keep the collected data at the disposal of governmental agencies for up to two years. Under this directive, access to the information is not required to be limited to investigation of serious crimes nor is a warrant required for access.

[7]The directive requires member states to ensure that communication providers must retain necessary data as specified in the directive

- to trace and identify the source of a communication;
- to trace and identify the destination of a communication;
- to identify the date, time, and duration of a communication;
- to identify the type of communication;

We focus in this section only on open-air surveillance and not other areas (e.g., wiretapping of voice and data communications). Open-air surveillance may be done either with or without the consent of those under surveillance; it may or may not serve their interests. The focus of this section, however, is on legitimate law enforcement applications. There are legitimate legal law enforcement uses of the technology, but also there are other uses of the technology. Considerations and issues related to possible surveillance abuse and privacy concerns are not addressed herewith, although these should not be ignored outright.[8]

As a backdrop, note that during the 1990s, the City of London, England, deployed for a security and surveillance an electronic cordon surrounding the city. The popular name of the system was and remains *Ring of Steel*. In 2005, the Ring of Steel was widened to include more businesses in the City. In 2007, New York City announced plans to install an array of cameras and roadblocks designed to detect, track, and deter terrorists; this effort is known as the *Lower Manhattan Security Initiative*, which is similar to the "Ring of Steel." The Lower Manhattan Security Initiative aims at hardening a number of physical "high value target" areas. The New York Police Department also deployed a system to track every car, truck, or other vehicle entering Manhattan and screen it for radiation or other terror threats; this proposal is called *Operation Sentinel* and is being developed alongside the Security Initiative to tighten security throughout lower Manhattan. As of early 2013 Lower Manhattan reportedly had 3,000 publicly deployed monitoring video cameras. These cameras are integrated via a system known as Domain Awareness System, that provides data mining using artificial intelligence techniques. In the recent past, many other cities in the United States have made similar announcements. In recent years, the federal budget sought to increase the amount of money spent on surveillance technology and programs; the money is being used by state and local governments to create networks of surveillance cameras to watch over the public in the streets, shopping centers, at airports, and elsewhere (18–20). At the private level, many universities are now using camera surveillance systems, including the University of Nevada at Reno, the University of Texas at Austin, and the University of Pennsylvania (18).

Figure 3.11 depicts a generalized scenario of dispersed equipment such as video cameras, triangularization devices, and wireless sensors connected over a (multitechnology) network to a control/operations center. Connectivity services may include traditional telephone company facilities, including T1 lines, fiberoptic links, metro

---

- to identify the communication device;
- to identify the location of mobile communication equipment.

The data is required to be available to competent national authorities in specific cases, "for the purpose of the investigation, detection and prosecution of serious crime, as defined by each Member State in its national law."

[8] There are advocates that are (strongly) opposed to the idea of surveillance. The reader may wish to consult the Electronic Privacy Information Center, Spotlight on Surveillance, http://epic.org/, and/or Privacy International, http://www.privacyinternational.org, for such advocacy.

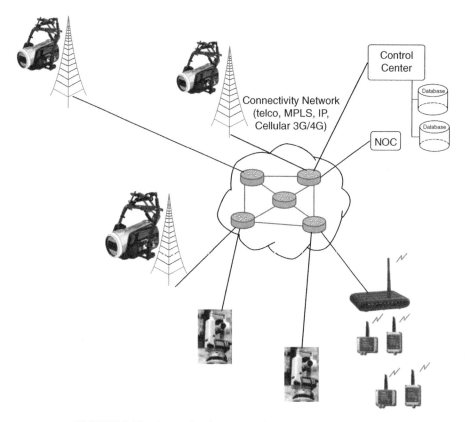

FIGURE 3.11 Generalized scenario of dispersed IOS equipment.

Ethernet services, MultiProtocol label switching, Internet services, and wireless links, including cellular 3G/4G, WiMax, WiFi links, point-to-point microwave, and other wireless technologies.

IOS' baseline objective is to create and maintain (through a combination of technologies and analysis tools) a "crime-free zone" within an urban or suburban environment by securing a perimeter both physically and electronically. At this time, cameras are found in stores, streets, parks, and intersections where police seek to ticket drivers for running red lights; cameras installed at intersections monitor every vehicle coming into the city—the cameras capture all license plate numbers.

The recent Law Enforcement success in using video imaging to identify suspects the Boston Marathon bombing will give further impetus to sustained additional deployment of IOS-based technologies in general, and video monitoring in particular, in major U.S. cities and abroad. While the data fusion and data mining will require large computational (and human) capabilities, the utility of having these data is self-evident. Face recognition technology will become widespread in the future.

Deployments of IOS-like services have seen quantifiable success in high crime areas. IOS proponents and law enforcement personnel often feel that the benefits "outweigh concern over privacy." Basic open-air surveillance is increasingly being undertaken by metropolitan (law enforcement) jurisdictions and by homeland security agencies: IOS systems are now being deployed in various forms in the United States and abroad. Cities such as Baltimore, Chicago, and New Orleans have installed camera surveillance networks with financing from the federal government; during the 2010s, many additional agencies and municipalities have deployed these IOS capabilities.

IOS functionality, however, can go beyond routine law enforcement and can provide sensor-based capabilities for toxic chemicals, explosives, and biological agents; applications include anti-terrorist detection, for example, with a chemical sensing overlay. Furthermore, with every telephone call, swipe of a card, and click of a mouse that an individual may make, information is being recorded, compiled, and stored, and this data is generally available for mining by authorities; while the latter is not exactly "open air," it is still affords a somewhat "passive" form of monitoring.

IOS approaches can be taxonomized as follows:

- Public space open-air surveillance: Methods of collecting (any type of) information about individuals when they are in any public environment (whether indoors or outdoors). Examples are people in a crowd, people in the street, cars with toll tags, and so on.
- Private space open-air surveillance: Methods of collecting (any type of) information about individuals when they are in a private environment, typically indoors. Examples are people in a doctor's office, people at work, and so on.
- Hybrid public/private space open-air surveillance: Methods of collecting (any type of) information about individuals that crosses both boundaries. Examples include using cell phones to track movements.

At the macro level, three drivers have been offered for IOS services:

- Detection/prevention of crimes
- Anti-terrorism
- Increased municipal revenue collection via remote monitoring of infractions

Recent events in Boston, Massachusetts, will further fuel sales growth in the \$3.2 billion video U.S. surveillance industry, as assessed in 2013; the U.S. market was projected to grow to \$4.1 billion by 2016.

Looking at the first driver, for example, some US cities have a high rate of violent crime, with 2332.6 violent crimes per 100,000 population, compared with a national average of 454.5 (2008 statistics) (21). Some claim that studies have found that surveillance systems have limited effect on crime, and that it is more effective to place more officers on the streets and improve lighting in high crime areas (18); law enforcement entities tend to take the view that services such as the IOS services described here can be very helpful. San Francisco has given license plate readers to police as well as to parking control officers, allowing them to track cars parked for too long in one spot; some cities use the cameras to assess anti-congestion tolls on motorists, while casino bosses get an alert when a high roller—or a cheater—arrives at the establishment (22).

At this juncture, the apparent goal of metropolitan (law enforcement) jurisdictions and homeland security agencies is to have a capability to support quick turnkey installations for IOS services. The deployment can be motivated and "sold" to the appropriate governmental funding agency on the idea that recurring revenue stream generated by IOS enablement (parking tickets (38), expired registration, suspended license, bail jumpers) will pay for itself in a matter of months. Most importantly, criminal activity detection coupled with rapid interdiction can result in the reduction, migration, and cessation of the same. IOS systems are being positioned by advocates for Homeland Security grant money similar to the approach used for Public Safety Interoperable Communications (PSIC) grants for state, municipal, and local jurisdictions.

As noted, the basic model for IOS is based on the concept of *Ring of Steel*. During the 1990s, the City of London, England, deployed for a security and surveillance cordon surrounding the city to deter identifiable threats; the popular name of the system was and remains *Ring of Steel*. Under this arrangement, roads entering the city are narrowed and have small chicanes to force drivers to slow down and be recorded by interconnected video cameras. A chicane is an obstacle on a racecourse or a series of tight serpentine curves in a roadway (opposite directions in an otherwise straight stretch—usually an S-shape curve), used on city streets to slow down traffic. These roads typically have a concrete median with a sentry box where police can stand guard and monitor traffic.[9] Since February 2003, the London congestion charging zone contains the *Ring of Steel* and also records all traffic on closed-circuit TV (CCTV). These measures were introduced following an IRA bombing campaign in the city; during the 1990s, the sentry posts were guarded by armed police continuously. Following the September 11, 2001, terrorist attacks, and other terrorist threats, security has been stepped up again. In 2005, the *Ring of Steel* was widened to include more businesses in the City. London had 200,000 cameras in 2005, and more than 4.3 million cameras have been deployed throughout the country. (Britain now has a fifth of the cameras in use around the world—and around 8000 speed cameras.) It is estimated that there is one camera for every 14 citizens and the typical Briton is seen by 300 cameras per day—some say the average Briton is being recorded 3,254 times a week inclusively using a variety of means (the average person living in Britain has that many pieces of personal information stored about him or her—details about shopping habits, mobile phone use, emails, locations during the day, journeys and Internet searches—most of which is kept in databases for years and in some cases indefinitely) (23).

Video surveillance is only one of several technologies and techniques used for IOS. Much of the technology needed to implement IOS is off-the-shelf; however

---

[9]Notwithstanding the term "Ring of Steel," the roadblocks and chicanes are actually created with concrete blocks that are wedged together.

the integration is novel. Sensor technologies can be upgraded as new and/or afford-able developments emerge (e.g., EM detection of IEDs, microwave bombardment using ultra wide band (UWB) methods at stationary and moving structures, etc.). The potential enhancements to visual detection are numerous (including night vision/IR sensors, gait analysis, etc.). Constituent technologies that can be deployed in inte-grated open-air surveillance consist of:

- **High resolution (low light level) DVS (wired & wireless).** Cameras can be indoor/outdoor, PTZ (pan, tilt, zoom) and configured in covert or exposed modes depending upon deterrent philosophy, field conditions, and field of view considerations.
  - Outdoor cameras will be physically hardened, vandal–proof and pole, wall and surface mountable.
  - Transport media (copper, fiber, wireless) and camera power (wired, solar, bat-tery) will depend upon physical constraints. Dozens to hundreds of cameras will be deployed in a scalable architecture.
  - Recording can be selective or under all conditions at all times for a given view.
  - These cameras can be remotely controlled by police to PTZ and rotate; have day and night vision capabilities, and wireless technologies. The cost can be as high as $60,000 per unit for some complex systems.
- **Image processing systems (at the command center)** to analyze the video streams in real time, alert law-enforcement personnel, and detect aberrant behav-ior (individuals walking erratically, lying prone), imagery of interest (e.g., crowd gathering, individuals running, etc.) as well as simple motion detection and if possible facial recognition of "persons of interest."
- **License plate recognition** of both parked and moving vehicles (within the field of view) at speeds up to 60 MPH moving past certain checkpoints. This can be augmented with UPC handheld scanners of registration stickers by roving patrols.
- **GDSs** using acoustic triangulation technology (pioneered with great success in Iraq to ferret out night snipers). GDS will be integrated with DVS so that after detecting gunfire, DVS will "train" on specific areas viewing in zoom for low light conditions and initiating event recording.
- **Moveable barrier technology** to inhibit selectively the movement of people and vehicle and/or people at designated checkpoints.
- **Real-time position reporting system** for vehicles, personnel, assets (VPA) using a combination of GPS, radio triangulation, and other automated vehi-cle locator (AVL) technologies (sign post transponders/checkpoints); per-sonnel can be equipped with either or both active transponders/vehicles also. The tracking can start with inexpensive techniques (available from cell phone or other portable radio systems) and evolve to military-style resolution (+/−1 m).

- **Computer-aided dispatch** will direct VPA to events, targets based on prede-fined and/or user-defined threat categories/priorities. This can be augmented of course with AI techniques working off a predefined knowledge base.
- **GIS** will be overlaid and integrated with photogrammetry and remote sensing (PRS), as appropriate to identify building structures, natural resources, and known hazardous materials.
- **Interoperability** may be needed between different systems to extend coverage and surveillance area as well as among types of personnel (local police, state authorities, law enforcement, Office of Domestic Preparedness (ODP), and intelligence types) as well as in some cases the Feds (FEMA, FBI, DEA, ATF, etc.).
- **Traditional covert alarms** alerting personnel to events of interest.
- **Wireless sensors** for detection of toxic chemicals, explosives, and biological agents, along with sensor networking systems to support a city-wide distributed environment.

The surveillance ring provided by IOS can be tightened or loosened dynamically by enabling different regional cameras and/or "illuminating" areas of interest. Table 3.4 (based partially on Reference 23) provides a perspective on data collection, including "over-the-air" information.

Table 3.5 lists a number of recent examples to illustrate some of the approaches, issues, and perspectives; this appendix is only illustrative of some announcements in the past few years; of late, there has been an acceleration in the deployment of IOS systems across the United States, also including the use of domestic drones.

3.10 CONTROL APPLICATION EXAMPLES

Some other possible examples are discussed below, as described in Reference 5.

Controlling vending machines. Vending machines can be found in a variety of locations, for example inside office or public buildings, outdoors in public places, and gas stations. The re-stocking and maintenance of vending machines is typically done manually by staffers that visit the vending machines at regular intervals to check the re-stock levels, re-stock the machines, and perform any requisite maintenance functions. The introduction of M2M technology automates vending machine man-agement: by having access to a (mobile) telecommunication network, the built-in M2M communication module provides information to the operator about the current status of the vending machine (e.g., current fill-levels, maintenance status, possible damages, malfunctions, and so on); as a consequence, the vending machines need only to be visited when absolutely required.

Controlling production machines. Various industrial processes make use of dispersed production devices (including but not limited to construction machines, manufacturing machines, food production machines, and so on). These machines may be exposed to harsh environments driving repair and maintenance requirements. This

TABLE 3.4   A Perspective on Data Collection

Mobile phones	Every day the average person makes three mobile phone calls and sends at least two text messages. Each time the network provider logs information about who was called as well as the caller's location and direction of travel, worked out by triangulation from phone towers. Customers can also have their locations tracked even when they are not using their phones, as the devices send out unique identifying signals at regular intervals. All of this information can be accessed by police and other public authorities investigating crimes
The Internet	Internet service providers (ISPs) compile information about their customers when they go online, including name, address, the unique identification number for the connection, known as an IP address, any browser used, and location. They also keep details of emails, such as whom they were sent to, together with the date and time they were sent. In 2008, an average of 50 websites are visited and 32 emails sent per person in Britain every day; very likely these numbers are higher today (23). Privacy campaigners have expressed concern that the country's three biggest ISPs—BT, Virgin Media, and TalkTalk—now provide this data to a digital advertising company called Phorm so that it can analyze web surfing habits. ISPs are already voluntarily providing information they hold about their customers if requested by law-enforcement agencies and public authorities. A total of 520,000 requests were made in the United Kingdom by public officials for telephone and Internet details last year, an increase from around 350,000 the previous year. Internet search engines also compile data about their users, including the IP address and what was searched for. Google receives around 68 searches from the average person each day and stores this data for 18 months. Companies such as Google and ISPs are building up huge databases of data about Internet users. These companies may be compelled, through a legal action, to hand over this information to third parties or the Government, or the companies may lose the data and it can then be misused
Loyalty cards	Store "loyalty" cards also retain large amounts of information about individuals who have signed up to use them. They link a person's personal details to the outlets used, the transaction times, and how much is spent. In the case of Nectar cards, which are used by more than 10 million people in Britain once a week, information from dozens of shops is compiled, giving a detailed picture of a cardholder's shopping habits
Banks	Banks can also be required to hand over personal account information to the authorities if requested as part of an investigation. They also provide personal data to credit reference agencies, debt collectors, and fraud prevention organizations. Debit and credit card transactions can give information about where and on what people are spending their money

(*continued*)

TABLE 3.4   (*Continued*)

CCTV	The biggest source of surveillance in Britain is through the network of CCTV (closed-circuit television) cameras. On average, an individual will appear on 300 CCTV cameras during a day and those tapes are kept by many organizations for indefinite lengths of time. On the London Underground network, Transport for London (TfL) keeps footage for a minimum of 14 days. TfL operates more than 8500 CCTV cameras in its underground stations, 1550 cameras on tube trains, and up to 60,000 cameras on buses. Britain now has more CCTV cameras in public spaces than any other country in the world. A study in 2002 estimated that there were around 4.2 million cameras, but that number is likely to now be far higher
Number plate recognition	The latest development in CCTV is the increased use of automatic number plate recognition systems, which read number plates and search databases for signs that a vehicle has been used in crime. A national automatic number plate recognition system is maintained by the Association of Chief Police Officers along motorways and main roads. Every number plate picked up by the system is stored in a database with date, time, and location for two years
Public transport and car toll cards	Travel passes such as the Oyster Card used in London and the Key card, in Oxford, can also reveal remarkable amounts of information about an individual. When they are registered to a person's name, they record journey history, dates, times, and fares. The same can be said about EasyPass (toll) cards for cars
The workplace	Employers are increasingly using radio-tagged security passes for employees, providing them with information about when staff enter and leave the office
On the street	Car-mounted video-camera passby to record pictures of the street for Google's StreetView website
Airports	Miami International Airport is one of a dozen airports in the United States that have begun pilot-testing whole-body imaging machines, which reveal weapons and explosives concealed under layers of clothing. It allows authorities to detect threat objects that are not metallic and that cannot be detected by metal detectors, and items that are sometimes missed even in a physical pat-down, in a nonintrusive manner using millimeter wave technology to create an image. This technology is being discontinued in some locations due to privacy concerns (24).

maintenance is typically done by dedicated personnel who have to visit the production machines at regular intervals to repair, perform maintenance, and identify damages or malfunction. M2M technologies improve the efficiency and optimization of the operation by allowing access to a mobile telecommunication network to forward information about the current status of the production machine (e.g., the current maintenance status, possible damages which may lead to malfunctions, and so on; additionally it is possible to transmit updates of updated software or perform remote maintenance).

TABLE 3.5 Recent Examples of IOS Systems; for Illustrative Purposes

New York City, New York	The New York Police Department is working on a plan to track every car, truck, or other vehicle entering Manhattan and screen it for radiation or other terror threats; the proposal, called *Operation Sentinel*, is being developed alongside a separate $90 million security initiative to tighten security throughout lower Manhattan in New York City. Police officials say *Operation Sentinel* would rely on license plate readers, radiation detectors, and closed-circuit cameras installed at the 16 bridges and four tunnels serving Manhattan, including the Brooklyn and George Washington bridges and the Lincoln Tunnel. About a million vehicles drive into Manhattan every day. The vehicle data—license plate numbers, radiological readings, and photos—would be automatically analyzed by computers programmed with information about suspicious vehicles. Vehicle data deemed innocent would be purged from police records after 30 days. The plan calls for 116 fixed and mobile license plate readers and 3000 closed-circuit cameras monitored by officers assigned to a command center on Broadway (this goal was reportedly achieved as of early 2013). The plan was modeled in part after the *Ring of Steel* surveillance measures in London's financial district. There is no estimate yet for the cost of *Operation Sentinel* since it was only in the planning phase at press time. The proposal has raised red flags for civil rights advocates, as one might expect (25)
Washington D.C.	For public health and safety reasons D.C. officials were planning in 2008 to give police access to more than 5260 CCTV cameras citywide that monitor traffic, schools, and public housing; this makes D.C. one of the largest surveillance networks in the country. The Video Interoperability for Public Safety (VIPS) program aims at consolidating more than 5200 cameras operated by D.C. agencies—including D.C. Public Schools and the D.C. Housing Authority—into one network managed by the city's Homeland Security and Emergency Management Agency. The program will allow agencies to share camera video feeds and provide the city with a network that is actively monitored and that will operate 24×365 days a year. The initiative was expected to enhance the District's counter-surveillance and public safety capabilities by increasing the number of cameras available for authorities to monitor. For example, 225 surveillance cameras in high crime neighborhoods will become available to police, and other agencies also will have access to 1388 outside cameras and 3874 cameras inside buildings throughout the city. Nearly 3500 of the cameras are operated by D.C. Public Schools. The city's transportation department operates 131 of the devices, which are normally trained on streets but can swivel (26). The Police Chief testified in 2008 that the department's cameras have resulted in a 19% reduction in violent crime within 250 feet of the devices, and a 4% violent crime reduction within 1000 feet. The District expected to spend an estimated $900,000 in recent years to operate and staff the consolidated monitoring network

(continued)

TABLE 3.5 *(Continued)*

	In the recent past, D.C. officials have placed cameras on light poles, police cars, and government buildings. But now, they are planning to put them on street-sweepers in the latest example of increasing surveillance of city residents. Officials will equip the District's street-sweeping machines with cameras that can scan license plates and photograph vehicles illegally parked in a street-sweeping zone. The cameras will cost approximately $40,000 each and will be placed initially on two street-sweepers. The city also operates 74 surveillance cameras affixed to light poles and buildings in neighborhoods as part of an effort to deter crime. Officials say that if 20% of motorists violate regulations against parking in blocks marked for street sweeping in a given month, the city will collect over $200,000 in additional monthly revenue
Boston	As of mid-2013 the Boston Financial District had about 250 public and private cameras and dvs to terrorist events that number is expected to increase over time.
Medina, Washington	In Medina, a new sign bears this warning: "You Are Entering a 24 Hour Video Surveillance Area." Cameras have recently been installed at intersections to monitor every vehicle coming into the city. Under the "automatic license plate recognition" project, once a car enters Medina, a camera captures its license plate number. Within seconds, the number is run through a database. If a hit comes up for a felony—say, the vehicle was reported stolen or is being driven by a homicide suspect—the information is transmitted instantaneously to police, who can "leap into action." All captured information is stored for 60 days—even if nothing negative turns up, he said. That allows police to mine data if a crime occurs later. The Police Chief has stated that "These cameras provide us with intelligence; they gets us in front of criminals." Medina had discussed the idea for years as a way to discourage crime (in 2008 there were 11 burglaries). Spokesmen for the American Civil Liberties Union of Washington argue that such a system raises the issue of privacy violations but Medina City Council members state that crime prevention "outweighs concern over privacy" (27)
Hunts Point, Washington	Hunts Point has been using a video-camera setup to record a continuous loop of car traffic in and out of town since 2006. There are eight cameras in all; pairs of cameras point in four directions. No residents have ever complained about it. The town has used it for evidence in a couple of traffic accident cases (27)
Michigan and New York Borders	The US Border Patrol is erecting 16 more video surveillance towers in Michigan and New York as part of its plans to use technology to help secure parts of the United States' 4000-mile northern border with Canada. The government awarded the $20 million project to Boeing Co., the same company responsible for the so-called virtual fence along the United States–Mexico border that has come under criticism for faulty technology. Eleven of the towers are being installed in Detroit and five in Buffalo, N.Y., to help monitor water traffic between Canada and the United States along Lake St. Clair and the Niagara River. At present, Border Patrol agents are posted along the river to keep an eye on water traffic (28)

TABLE 3.5 *(Continued)*

	Also in Michigan, the City of Flint was looking for sponsors for surveillance cameras that will be mounted around the city to keep a watch out for criminals. In exchange for cash, the city will show the business names next to police logos on the pole-mounted camera boxes that sport a blue police light that flashes 24 h a day. These systems are known as PODDS (portable overt digital surveillance system). The 14 cameras being planned cost around half-a-million dollars (29)
Illinois, Arizona, Maryland	Chicago is the US city that has made the most aggressive use of surveillance technology, has installed more than 2250 cameras in its "Homeland Security Grid," which DHS helped finance, and began linking the devices into a single network over a 900-mile fiber-optic grid (26). The cameras are linked to an operations center constantly monitored by police officers. Additionally, the State of Illinois has reportedly considered installing speed cameras in each direction of every interstate in the 20 State Police districts across the state to raise $50 million a year in revenue. Currently, camera-equipped vans nab speeders in construction zones, but state law does not allow speed cameras on interstates. As of 2013 Chicago authorities had access to our 10,000 public and private video surveillance cameras. Also, Cicero, Ill., was planning to install several surveillance cameras with a grant from Homeland Security
	In Arizona, 100 speed cameras were planned to be deployed on highways at a cost of about $20 million. The state was planning to raise $90 million a year by imposing $165 fines on vehicles going 10 mph over the speed limit
	Baltimore has used federal grants to finance its camera system and a "Watch Center." The cameras are connected to the state's existing highway monitoring cameras, and the plan is for five counties in Maryland—Anne Arundel, Baltimore, Carroll, Hartford, and Howard—to connect with the city's surveillance system
Florida	A surveillance video program is being implemented in Orlando called Innovative Response to Improve Safety (IRIS) aimed at detecting crimes or other incidents and send alerts to law enforcement. High-tech cameras similar to those used in London will be installed in busy sections of Orlando to help curb crime. The IRIS cams are also known as "intelligent cameras." The first 18 of 60 motion-detecting cameras installed around Orlando will cost about $1.3 million. Orlando is one of the first US cities in the nation to get the high-tech cameras that provide real-time data enabling the police to send officers as soon as they see some activity and we send officers to that activity in a "hot zone"—the legacy technology that is in stores employs offline recording (typically for evidence for future use, for future follow-up, and future investigative purposes); these systems do all that, but also allow real-time video collection (30)
	As of 2013 Orlando police had 138 cameras scattered throughout the city with more on the way. Police stated that in 2012 the cameras were used in nearly 800 criminal investigations, leading to more than 100 arrests.

(continued)

TABLE 3.5 *(Continued)*

	The Miami Police Department could soon be the first in the United States to use cutting-edge, spy-in-the-sky technology to beef up their fight against crime. A small pilotless drone manufactured by Honeywell International, capable of hovering and "staring" using electro-optic or infrared sensors, is expected to make its debut soon in the skies over the Florida Everglades. If use of the drone wins Federal Aviation Administration approval after tests, the Miami-Dade Police Department will start flying the 14-pound (6.3 kg) drone over urban areas with an eye toward full-fledged employment in crime fighting. It is intended to be used in tactical situations as an extra set of eyes. The wingless Honeywell aircraft fits into a backpack and is capable of vertical takeoff and landing. Government agencies acknowledge the development of a dragonfly-sized unmanned aerial vehicle (UAV) known as the "Insectohopter" for laser-guided spy operations as long ago as the 1970s. There is reportedly strong interest from law-enforcement agencies in getting UAVs up and running and smaller aircrafts are possibly having a "huge economic impact" over the next 10 years (31). (Reportedly there are around 100 different designs of flying drones currently in use by the US Government.)
Other localities	Tiburon, a town that juts into San Francisco Bay, is planning to use cameras to record the license plate number of every vehicle that crosses city limits. Some residents describe the plan as a commonsense way to thwart thieves, most of whom come from out of town. The readers, which use character recognition software, can compare plates to databases of cars that have been stolen or linked to crimes, then immediately notify police of matches. The project has an expected price tag of $100,000. Once the street cameras are installed, hunting a burglary suspect could be easier: officials will look for a plate that came and went and detectives could then check to see if any of the cars has been linked with crimes in the past. Information on which cars enter and leave town will be erased within 60 days and police officers will be granted access to the information only during an investigation. License plate readers have exploded in popularity in recent years, but Tiburon would be one of the first to mount them at fixed locations—and perhaps the very first to record exhaustively *every* car coming or going. California Highway Patrol (CHP) officials have put the readers on 18 cruisers and at four fixed locations. CHP officers have seen an increase in recoveries of stolen cars since the devices were installed, starting in August 2005. Through December 2008, CHP had used the devices to recover 1739 cars and arrest 675 people (22)
	In New Orleans, digital camera images are sent to a main server archive for monitoring, and the Internet-based archive can be accessed from any location, including police vehicles. Paramus, N.J., is launching a pilot camera surveillance system at shopping malls that will be partially financed by federal grants. A federal grant was expected to help Newport, R.I. pay for the installation of surveillance cameras. St. Bernard Parish, La., has used federal funds for surveillance cameras

TABLE 3.5   (*Continued*)

England	Local newspapers read: "Now snooping on the public has reached new heights with local authorities putting spy planes in the air to snoop on homeowners who are wasting too much energy" (32). Thermal imaging cameras are being used to create color-coded maps that will enable council officers to identify offenders. The aircraft takes images of homes and businesses, with those losing the most heat showing up as red, while better insulated properties appear blue. The City Council has spent £30,000 using a plane carrying a thermal camera to determine which homes are wasting energy. A scheme is already underway in Broadland District Council in Norfolk, which has spent £30,000 hiring a plane with a thermal imaging camera. The exercise has been so successful that other local authorities are planning to follow suit. In England, police could soon use unmanned spyplanes like those used to track enemy troops in Iraq and Afghanistan for surveillance operations on British homes. Plans to introduce the UAVs are outlined in the Home Office's Science and Innovation Strategy. The Home Office has suggested that the remote-controlled drones could be used to help police gather evidence and track criminals without putting officers at risk. The miniature aircraft could be fitted with cameras and heat-seeking equipment, allowing police to carry out aerial reconnaissance from a control room. They also have the benefit of being quieter than conventional helicopters or spotter planes and are much cheaper to run due to their fuel economy. Home Office's Science and Innovation Strategy states that "UAVs are likely to become an increasingly useful tool for police in the future, potentially reducing the number of dangerous situations the police may have to enter and also providing evidence for prosecutions and support police operations in real time" (33) In one week, the average person living in Britain has 3254 pieces of personal information stored about him or her, most of which is kept in databases for years and in some cases indefinitely. The data include details about shopping habits, mobile phone use, emails, locations during the day, journeys, and Internet searches. In many cases, this information is kept by companies such as banks and shops, but in certain circumstances they can be asked to hand it over to a range of legal authorities. The U.K. Government has published plans to grant local authorities and other public bodies access to the email and Internet records of millions. Phone companies already retain data about their customers and (in the United Kingdom, for example) give it to 650 public bodies on request

3.11 MYRIAD OTHER APPLICATIONS

Many other examples of IoT applications can be cited and many more will evolve in the future. For example, M2M and SCADA applications are now also being extended to support over satellite links. Satellite service providers perceive M2M communications as an approach the global demand for uninterrupted and seamless data connectivity across a mixture of urban, suburban, exurban, rural, and oceanic environments: satellite-based M2M can facilitate the delivery of small quantities of information to and from anywhere in the world. Applications include civil government, environmental monitoring and climate analysis, police and coast guard, off-shore oil drilling, and mining. Observers are noticing an increased demand for satellite services from several companies associated with finance, energy, and maritime industries. Although at press time, satellite-based services were only a small share of the M2M market which is largely dominated by cellular systems (around 2% in terms of volume and 6% of revenue in 2011), M2M is a growing segment for the satellite industry: forecasts say the global satellite M2M market will reach 2.3 billion EUR by 2016. The region with the highest rate of progress will be the Asia-Pacific with developments in countries such as China, Indonesia, Vietnam, and India (34). Proponents make the case that "M2M market represents an interesting and potentially huge revenue stream for the satellite industry with opportunities in many markets, particularly vertical ones." (35).

As another application, Bank of America Corp has been testing a technology that allows a customer to pay at a store register by simply scanning an image with a smartphone, such as Apple Inc's iPhone or Google Inc's Android devices. This is similar but not identical to the SC concept described earlier in the chapter. Companies such as, but not limited to, Google and eBay Inc's PayPal are investigating ways to turn phones into digital wallets that house credit and debit cards, coupons and store loyalty program details. The market for global mobile payments was over $170 billion at press time. Initially Bank of America experimented with NFC technology, in which a chip installed in a phone transmits a radio signal when it is waved or tapped at a device at the cash register; newer approaches entail the use of iPhones and phones that implement the Android operating system (iPhone 5 does not embed NFC chips). In the bank's NFC trials, customers stored their payment information digitally in a secure area on their phone and then paid at a merchant who kept a device to read the signal from the phone (36). In the latest test, customers store their payment cards on a computer server and when they pay, they use an application on their phone that scans a Quick Response code displayed at the register.

REFERENCES

1. Lee GM, Park J, Kong N, Crespi N. The Internet of Things – Concept and Problem Statement. July 2011. Internet Research Task Force, July 11, 2011, draft-lee-iot-problem-statement-02.txt.

2. Scarrone E, Boswarthick D. Overview of ETSI TC M2M Activities, March 2012, ETSI, 650 Route des Lucioles F-06921 Sophia Antipolis Cedex – France.

3. 3rd Generation Partnership Project, Technical Specification Group Services and System Aspects; Service Requirements for Machine Type Communications (MTC); Stage 1 (Release 10); Technical Specification 3GPP TS 22.368 V10.1.0 (2010–06).

4. African Utility Week Conference: 22–23 May 2012, Nasrec Expo Centre, Johannesburg. Available at www.african-utility-week.com.

5. Machine-to-Machine communications (M2M); M2M Service Requirements. ETSI TS 102 689 V1.1.1 (2010–08). ETSI, 650 Route des Lucioles F-06921 Sophia Antipolis Cedex – France.

6. Drake J, Najewicz D, Watts W. Energy Efficiency Comparisons of Wireless Communication Technology Options for Smart Grid Enabled Devices. White Paper, General Electric Company, GE Appliances & Lighting, December 9, 2010.

7. ETSI TR 102 732: Machine to Machine Communications (M2M); Use Cases of M2M Applications for eHealth. (2011–03). ETSI, 650 Route des Lucioles F-06921 Sophia Antipolis Cedex – France.

8. ETSI TR 101 557 V1.1.1 (2012–02), Electromagnetic Compatibility and Radio Spectrum Matters (ERM); System Reference document (SRdoc); Medical Body Area Network Systems (MBANSs) in the 1785 MHz to 2500 MHz range.

9. Staff. FCC Chairman Unveils Proposal to Spur Innovation in Medical Body Area Networks, to Transform Patient Care, and Lower Health Care Costs. May 17, 2012, Federal Communications Commission, 445 12th Street SW, Washington, DC 20554.

10. ZigBee Wireless Sensor Applications for Health, Wellness and Fitness, March 2009, ZigBee Alliance. Available at www.zigbee.org.

11. Staff. Smart Cards, Mobile Telephony and M2M at the Heart of e-health Services. CARTES & IDentification Conference, Parc des Expositions Paris-Nord Villepinte, November, 2011.

12. ETSI TR 102 897: Machine to Machine Communications (M2M); Use Cases of M2M Applications for City Automation. (2010-01). ETSI, 650 Route des Lucioles F-06921 Sophia Antipolis Cedex – France.

13. ETSI TR 102 898: Machine to Machine Communications (M2M); Use Cases of Automotive Applications in M2M Capable Networks. (2010-09). ETSI, 650 Route des Lucioles F-06921 Sophia Antipolis Cedex – France.

14. Smart Card Alliance. Contactless Technology for Secure Physical Access: Technology and Standards Choices. Smart Card Alliance Report, October 2002, Publication Number: ID-02002, Princeton Junction, New Jersey.

15. Hancke G. A Practical Relay Attack on ISO 14443 Proximity Cards. White Paper, July 2008, University of Cambridge, Computer Laboratory JJ Thomson Avenue, Cambridge, CB3 0FD, UK.

16. Promotional Material of NearFieldCommunication.org. Available at www.nearfield communication.org.

17. ETSI TS 102 412: Smart Cards; Smart Card Platform Requirements Stage 1 (Release 8). (2007-07). ETSI, 650 Route des Lucioles F-06921 Sophia Antipolis Cedex – France.

18. Electronic Privacy Information Center, Spotlight on Surveillance, More Cities Deploy Camera Surveillance Systems with Federal Grant Money, May 2005, Washington, D.C. Available at http://epic.org/.

19. Department of Homeland Security, *Budget-in-Brief Fiscal Year 2006,* at 81-82 (Feb. 7, 2005).Available at http://www.epic.org/privacy/surveillance/spotlight/0505/dhsb06.pdf.

20. Rotenberg M, Laurant C. *Privacy and Human Rights: An International Survey of Privacy Laws and Developments*, EPIC and Privacy International 2004 (EPIC 2004).

21. O'Leary-Morgan K, Morgan S, Boba R, editors, *City Crime Rankings 2009—2010.* Washington, DC: CQ Press, A Division of SAGE; November 23, 2009.

22. Bulwa D. *Tiburon May Install License Plate Cameras*. San Francisco Chronicle; July 10, 2009.

23. Gray R. How big brother watches your every move. The Sunday Telegraph, 16 Aug 2008.

24. Cordle IP. Miami Airport Security Cameras see Through Clothing. Miami Herald, July 22, 2008.

25. AP/Crain's New York, NYPD Planning to Track Every Vehicle in Manhattan. August 18, 2008.

26. Washington Times. D.C. Police Set to Monitor 5,000 Cameras. April 9, 2008.

27. Krishnan S. Cameras Keep Track of all Cars Entering Medina. Seattle Times, September 16, 2009.

28. Sullivan E. Surveillance Towers Planned for Detroit, Buffalo, AP, March 31, 2009.

29. Foren J. Flint seeks sponsors for police surveillance cameras. Flint Journal, July 30, 2008.

30. Local6.com. Orlando Surveillance Cams Will Detect Motion, Alert In Real-Time. June 23, 2008.

31. Brown T. Spy-in-the-sky Drone Sets Sights on Miami. Reuters, March 26, 2008.

32. Levy A. Council Uses Spy Plane with Thermal Imaging Camera to Snoop on Homes Wasting Energy. Daily Mail, 24th March 2009.

33. Wardrop M. Remote-controlled Planes Could Spy on British Homes. The Sunday Telegraph, 24 Feb 2009.

34. IDATE. The Satellite M2M Market 2012–2016. Report, IDATE Consulting & Research, April 23, 2012, London, UK.

35. Staff. Satellite M2M: An Emerging Revenue Stream, September/October 2010. Available at www.satellite-evolution.com.

36. Rothacker R. Bank of America Tests Technology to Pay with Phones. Reuters, October 1, 2012.

37. Jung N-J, Yang I-K, Park S-W, Lee S-Y. "A design of AMI protocols for two way communication in K-AMI", Control, Automation and Systems (ICCAS), Conference Proceedings 2011 11th international Conference on, Date of Conference: 26-29 Oct. 2011, S/W Center, KEPCO Res. Inst., Daejeon, South Korea, Page(s): 1011–1016.

38. Washington Times. Street-sweeper Cameras Eye Illegal Parking. April 2, 2008.

39. Kingsley S, "Personal body networks go wireless at 2.4GHZ", ElectronicsWeekly Online Magazine, 16 May 2012, http://www.electronicsweekly.com.

CHAPTER 4

FUNDAMENTAL IoT MECHANISMS AND KEY TECHNOLOGIES

This chapter looks briefly at some fundamental issues and technologies that have to be considered in the context of Internet of things (IoT) design and deployment. In fact, there are indeed many issues that have to be considered; only a small set of such issues are covered here as a way to highlight some of the underlying logical and technological infrastructure needed. A hybrid view of the IoT both as a service (application) concept and as an infrastructure is utilized in this discussion.

4.1 IDENTIFICATION OF IoT OBJECTS AND SERVICES

There are a number of key underpinning issues that come into play in the (architectural) design and field deployment of IoT applications. The discussion that follows is synthesized from a number of published documents including References 1–3 among others.

An important first issue is the identification of objects and services. There are various types of identifiers with different purposes and practicality. Globally unique identifiers are highly desirable. Identification codes can be classified as (i) object IDs (OIDs) and (ii) communication IDs. Examples of the former include but are not limited to radio frequency identification (RFID)/electronic product code (EPC),

Building the Internet of Things with IPv6 and MIPv6: The Evolving World of M2M Communications,
First Edition. Daniel Minoli.
© 2013 John Wiley & Sons, Inc. Published 2013 by John Wiley & Sons, Inc.

content ID,[1] telephone number, and uniform resource identifier (URI)/uniform resource locator (URL); examples of the latter include media access control (MAC) address, network layer/IP address, and session/protocol ID. A number of researchers advocate defining an identity layer for objects that is logically independent of the networking addresses; according to these proponents, the IoT should be identity oriented. One such practical, but not necessarily elegant, approach might be to use RFIDs physically attached to the objects in question that would act as electronic ID for objects to which they are linked.

Among other identification approaches, one can use the general approach briefly described in Chapter 1. There we noted that it is both desirable and feasible for all objects to have a permanent unique identifier, an OID. It is also desirable as well as feasible for all end-point network locations and/or intermediary-point network locations to have a durable, unique network address (NAdr); the IPv6 address space enables the concrete realization of these location identification goals. When objects that have enough intelligence to run a communications protocol stack (so that they can communicate), are placed on a network, these objects can be tagged with a NAdr.

Every object then has a tuple (OID, NAdr) that is always unique, although the second entry of the tuple may change with time, location, or situation. In a stationary, non-variable, or mostly static environment, one could opt, if one so chose, to assign the OID to be identical to the NAdr where the object is expected to attach to the network; that is, the object inherits the tuple (NAdr, NAdr). In the rare case where the object moved, the OID could then be refreshed to the address of the new location; that is, the object then inherits the tuple (NAdr', NAdr'). However, there is a general trend toward object mobility, giving rise to a dynamic environment; hence, to retain maximal flexibility, it is best to separate, in principle, the OID from the NAdr and thus assign a general (OID, NAdr) tuple where the OID is completely invariant; however, the OID can still be drawn from the NAdr space, that is, from the IPv6 address space.

The basic requirement for an identification scheme is that it affords global uniqueness. Additionally, it is useful to have mechanisms for hierarchical grouping to deal with large populations. The aggregation feature of IPv6 address provides such hierarchical grouping. For a number of applications, there is a need to map/bind IP addresses (communications IDs) with other relevant OIDs. Additionally, modern layered communication architectures also require addressing and processing capabilities at several layers, for example, at the Data Link Layer, at the Network Layer, at the Transport (Protocol ID), and at the session/application layer. Naturally, there is also a desire for simplicity. Some argue that different identification schemes are required for different applications. For example, the information related to things such as books, medicine, and clothes may not require global identification because revocation lists are required (e.g., some objects may eventually be consumed and/or destroyed).

---

[1] The content ID, defined by the Content ID Forum, is an identifier that is typically attached to a content-based object. It can specify and distinguish digital content, being a complete set of attribute information about a content object stored as metadata including, among other aspects, the nature of the contents, rights-related information, and information about distribution.

An example of IDs for objects is the above-mentioned EPC used in the RFID/sensor context. An EPC is a number assigned to an RFID tag representative of an actual EPC. Their value is that they have been carefully characterized and categorized to embed certain meanings within their structure. Each number is encoded with a header, identifying the particular EPC version used for coding the entire EPC number. An EPC manager number is defined, allowing individual companies or organizations to be uniquely identified; an object class number is present, identifying objects used within this organization, such as product types. Finally, a serial number is characterized, allowing the unique identification of each individual object tagged by the organization (4). An EPC is a unique identification code that is generally thought of as the next generation of the traditional bar code. Like the bar code, EPC uses a numerical system for product identification, but its capabilities are much greater. An EPC is actually a number that can be associated with specific product information, such as date of manufacture and origin and destination of shipment. This provides significant advantages for businesses and consumers. The EPC is stored on an RFID tag, which transmits data when prompted by a signal emitted by a special reader. Note that EPC and RFID are not interchangeable—there are numerous RFID applications that have nothing to do with the EPC, such as E-Z Pass use at tollbooths (5).

In addition to OID, there may be a need for object naming. Domain name system (DNS) is one example of a mechanism for Internet-based naming; however, currently one only identifies the specific server in which the contents are stored; the data itself is not named. In the IoT context, some proponents have argued for the advantages of identifying information by name, not by node address. DNS is used to map the "human-friendly" host names of computers to their corresponding "machine-friendly" IP addresses. Hence, one is able, for example, to access the server (or large farm of servers) of CNN, Google, and so on, simply by the term www.cnn.com and so on. To some large degree, object name service (ONS) will also be important in the IoT to map the "thing-friendly" names of object which may belong to heterogeneous name spaces (e.g., EPC, uCode, and any other self-defined code) on different networks (e.g., TCP/IP network) into their corresponding "machine-friendly" addresses or other related information of another TCP/IP network (1). However, a "thing" or an object in an IoT world may be a lot more mundane and modest in scope/function (say, than CNN, Citibank, United Airlines, Ford), such that it does not need to have its own name, since very few people may be interested in that specific thing. For example, a large villa may have, for argument's safe, a dozen security sensors. While it is true that they could be named "Smith-villa-front-door sensor," "Smith-villa-front-gate sensor," "Smith-villa-back-door sensor," "Smith-villa-garage-door sensor," very few people besides Mr. Smith or Mr. Smith's security company will ever want to specifically identify these objects by name. Nonetheless, object naming service for IoT applications needs to be developed, at least for a set of applications.

For some applications, especially where there is a need for simple end-user visibility of a small set of objects (i.e., where the objects are few and discretely identifiable – a home's thermostat, a home's refrigerator, a home's lighting system, a pet of the owner), the object may be identified through Web Services (WSs). WSs provide standard infrastructure for data exchange between two different distributed applications. Lightweight WS protocols are of interest; for example, the representational state transfer (REST) interface may be useful in this context. REST is a software architecture for distributed systems to implement WSs. REST is gaining popularity compared with more classical protocols such as simple object access protocol (SOAP) and web services description language (WSDL) due to its relative simplicity.

Given the potential pervasive nature of IoT objects and IoT applications (e.g., grid control, home control, traffic control, and medical monitoring), security and privacy in communications and services become absolutely critical. Security needs to be intrinsically included in protocol development, and not just be a catch-up afterthought. The plethora of heterogeneous devices now connected to the Internet, from traditional PCs and laptops, to smartphones and Bluetooth-enabled devices, to name just a few, aggravates the risk. Strong authentication, encryption while transmitting, and also encryptions for data at rest is ideal; however, the computational requirements for encryption can be significant. Furthermore, at the central/authenticating site, rapid authentication support is desirable; otherwise objects would not be able to authenticate in large-population environments.

In some IoT applications, as discussed in Chapter 3, there is a need to know the precise physical location of objects; thus, the challenge is how to cost-effectively obtain location information; methods that rely on GPS or cellular services may be too expensive for some applications. In some cases, objects move independently; in other cases, the objects move as the one group. Different tracking methods may be required to achieve efficient handling of tracking information. That is, if a group of objects is known to move as an ensemble (say, a myriad of sensors on a cruise ship; or, multiple medical monitors on an individual, as part of a medical body area network (MBAN) with one gateway controller), then one needs only to figure out where one object is, and the rest of the objects is then in the same relative position. Typically, there is a need to maintain ubiquitous and seamless communication while tracking the location of objects.

Capabilities for scalability are important in order to be able to support an IoT environment where there is a large population that is highly distributed. Solutions are necessary in the arena of distributed networking. For example, the IAB's October 2006 Routing and Addressing Workshop (RFC 4984) refocused interest in scalable routing and addressing architectures for the Internet. Among the many issues driving this renewed interest are concerns about the scalability of the routing system. Proposals have been made recently based on the "locator/identifier separation." The basic idea behind the separation is that the Internet architecture combines two functions, routing locators (where one is attached to the network) and identifiers (where one is located), in one number space: the IP address. Proponents of the separation architecture postulate that splitting these functions apart will yield several advantages, including improved scalability for the routing system. The separation aims to decouple locators and identifiers, thus allowing for efficient aggregation of the routing locator space and providing persistent identifiers in the identifier space. The locator/ID separation protocol (LISP) IETF Working Group (WG) has completed the first set of experimental RFCs describing the LISP. LISP requires no changes to end-systems or to routers that do not directly participate in the LISP deployment. LISP aims for an incrementally deployable protocol. The LISP WG is working on deliverables for the 2012/2013 time frame that include (i) an architecture description, (ii) deployment models, (iii) a description of the impacts of LISP, (iv) LISP security threats and solutions, (v) allocation of end-point identifier (EID) space, (vi) alternate mapping system designs, and (vii) data models for management of LISP. The first three items (architecture, deployment models, and impacts) need to be completed first before other items can be submitted as RFCs (2). Shim6 (RFCs 5533 through 5535) is another example of possible interest. This protocol is a layer 3 shim for providing locator agility with failover capabilities for IPv6 nodes. Hosts that employ Shim6 use multiple IPv6 address prefixes and setup state with peer hosts. This state can later be used to failover to a different set of locators, should the original locators stop working. The Shim6 approach has a number of advantages, such as enabling small sites to be multihomed without requiring a provider-independent IPv6 address prefix for the site. However, the approach has also been criticized, for example, for the operational impacts that the use of multiple prefixes causes; at this time, there is no clear view on how well Shim6 works in practice, and implementation and deployment in select networks is needed to determine its true characteristics (3).

4.2 STRUCTURAL ASPECTS OF THE IoT

Some key structural related desiderata are highlighted in this section; these issues ultimately may determine the extent and/or rapidity of deployment of IoT services and technologies. This list is not exhaustive.

4.2.1 Environment Characteristics

As we have seen at various points in this text, most (but certainly not all) IoT/machine-to-machine (M2M) nodes have noteworthy design constraints, such as but not limited to the following (6):

- Low power (with the requirement that they will run potentially for years on batteries)
- Low cost (total device cost in single-digit dollars)
- Significantly more devices than in a LAN environment
- Severely limited code and RAM space (e.g., generally desirable to fit the required code—MAC, IP, and anything else needed to execute the embedded application—in, for example, 32K of flash memory, using 8-bit microprocessors)
- Unobtrusive but very different user interface for configuration (e.g., using gestures or interactions involving the physical world)
- Requirement for simple wireless communication technology. In particular, the IEEE 802.15.4 standard is very promising for the lower (physical and link) layers

TABLE 4.1 Properties and Requirements of M2M Applications

	ITS	e-Health	Surveillance	Smart Meters
Mobility	Vehicular	Pedestrian/ vehicular	None	None
Message size	Medium	Medium?	Large	Small (few kB)
Traffic pattern	Regular/ irregular	Regular/ irregular	Regular	Regular
Device density	High	Medium	Low	Very high (up to 10,000 per cell)
Latency requirements	Very high (few milliseconds)	Medium (seconds)	Medium (<200 ms)	Low (up to hours)
Power efficiency requirements	Low	High (battery power devices)	Low	High (battery-powered meters)
Reliability	High	High	Medium	High
Security requirements	Very high	Very high	Medium	High

Courtesy: A. Maeder, NEC Laboratories Europe.

4.2.2 Traffic Characteristics

The characteristics of IoT/M2M communication is different from other types of networks or applications. For example, cellular mobile networks are designed for human communication and communication is connection centric; it entails interactive communication between humans (voice, video), or data communication involving humans (web browsing, file downloads, and so on). It follows that cellular mobile networks are optimized for traffic characteristics of human-based communication and applications. Specifically, communication takes place with a certain length (sessions) and data volume; furthermore, communication takes place with a certain interaction frequency and patterns (talk-listen, download-reading, and so on) (7). On the other hand, in M2M the expectation is that there are many devices, there will be long idle intervals, transmission entails small messages, there may be relaxed delay requirements, and device energy efficiency is paramount. Table 4.1 depicts some key properties and requirements of M2M applications.

4.2.3 Scalability

While some applications (e.g., smart grid, home automation, and so on) may start out covering a small geographic area or a small community of users, as noted above, there invariably will be a desire over time for the service to expand, in order to make such service more cost-effective on a per-unit basis, or to have sufficient critical mass for developers to be motivated to invest resources to add capabilities to the service. When contemplating expansion, one wants to be able to build on previously deployed technology (systems, protocols), without having to scrap the system and start from scratch. Also, the efficiency of a larger system should be better than the efficiency of a smaller system. This is what is meant by scalability. The goal is to make sure that capabilities such as addressing, communication, and service discovery, among others, are delivered efficiently in both small and large scale. There is a need for enough name space to support increasing populations of devices and new applications. In particular, note that IPv6 is an ideal component (but not the only one) to be employed to support scalability, both for a given application as it reaches more users and for use for a wide class of applications spanning many fields (as described in Chapter 3).

4.2.4 Interoperability

Because of the plethora of applications, technology suppliers, and stakeholders, it is desirable to develop and/or re-use a core set of common standards. To the degree possible, existing standards may prove advantageous to a rapid and cost-effective deployment of the technology. Product and service interoperability is of interest.

4.2.5 Security and Privacy

Unfortunately, security is chronically an after-thought when it comes to protocol development: almost invariably a protocol spec will have many pages of data format and operation procedures and only a short paragraph or two on security considerations. When IoT relates to electric power distribution, goods distribution, transport and traffic management, e-health, and other key applications, as noted earlier, it is critical to maintain system-wide confidentiality, identity integrity, and trustworthiness.

4.2.6 Open Architecture

The goal is to support a wide range of applications using a common infrastructure, preferably based on a service-oriented architecture (SOA) over an open service plat-form, and utilizing overly networks (these being logical networks defined on top of a physical infrastructure). In an SOA environment, objects expose their functionalities using a protocol such as SOAP or REST application programming interface (API). These devices may provide their functionality as a WS that can in turn be used by other entities (other devices or other business applications).

4.3 KEY IoT TECHNOLOGIES

There are a number of key supportive technologies that are needed for wide-scale deployment of IoT applications. This list is not exhaustive.

4.3.1 Device Intelligence

A key consideration relates to on-board intelligence. In order for the IoT to become a reality, the objects should be able to intelligently sense and interact with the envi-ronment, possibly store some passive or acquired data, and communicate with the world around them. Object-to-gateway device communication, or even direct object-to-object communication, is desirable. These intelligent capabilities are necessary to support the ubiquitous networking to provide seamlessly interconnection between humans and objects. Some have called this mode of communication *Any Services, Any Time, Any Where, Any Devices, and Any Networks* (also known as "5-Any") (1). Pervasive computing (also known as ubiquitous computing) deals with the embedded ability to support logical processing as well with the ability to be in continuous range of a wireless gateway peer.

4.3.2 Communication Capabilities

As just noted, it is highly desirable for objects to support ubiquitous end-to-end communications; hence, another technological consideration relates to communication mechanisms. To achieve ubiquitous connectivity human-to-object and object-to-object communications, networking capabilities will need to be implemented in the objects ("things"). In particular, IP is considered to be key capability for IoT objects; furthermore, the entire TCP/IP Internet Suite is generally desirable. Self-configuring capabilities, especially how an IoT device can establish its connectivity automatically without human intervention, are also of interest. IPv6 auto-configuration and multihoming features are useful in this context, particularly the scope-based IPv6 addressing features.

While we have discussed objects that have sophisticated capabilities (IP support, IPv6 support, Web server capabilities, and so on) in the past few paragraphs, some applications, especially those using simple sensors and/or where is there a very large number of dispersed sensors and/or where there is limited remote energizing power, may have a need to support leaner protocols both at the network layer (e.g., route and/or topology management) and at the transport layer (e.g., using UDP). This may entail some extensions of existing networking protocols to achieve a level of simplicity and minimize power consumption. For constrained objects that do not have high levels of energizing power, memory, and/or computing, lightweight protocols that minimize energy consumption is a desiderata; however, one needs to keep in mind that these protocols may not have enough capabilities to support advanced applications. It should be noted that some existing applications may not even support the IP protocol (even IPv4) and the IP addressing scheme. Hence, there is a need to support heterogeneous (IP and non-IP) networking interfaces, at least in the short term. There may be a need for proxy gateways; such gateways would support multiple interfaces that have evolved from different heterogeneous networks. Interoperability among heterogeneous interfaces can facilitate commercial deployment.

4.3.3 Mobility Support

Yet another consideration relates to tracking and mobility support of mobile object (1). Mobility-enabled architectures and protocols are required. Some objects move independently, while others will move as one of group. Therefore, according to the moving feature, different tracking methods are required. It is important to provide ubiquitous and seamless communication among objects while tracking the location of objects. Mobile IPv6 (MIPv6) offers several capabilities that can address this requirement.

4.3.4 Device Power

A key consideration relates to the powering of the "thing," especially for mobile devices or for devices that otherwise would not have intrinsic power. M2M/IoT applications are almost invariably constrained by the following factors: devices have ultra-low-power capabilities, devices must be of low cost, and devices generally must have small physical size and be light. Specifically, efficient communication mechanisms are needed. A number of devices operate with a small battery, while other devices use a self-energizing energy source, for example a small solar cell array. Yet other devises are passive (e.g., passive RFID) and, thus, need to derive energy indirectly from the environment, such as an intercepting electric/magnetic field. The power requirement is driven by the need to operate for extended periods of time from small batteries or from energy-scavenger mechanisms. In general, wireless technologies require significant amounts of power; hence, the need for low energy (LE) wireless technologies, as discussed in Chapter 6. Batteries are critical to all sorts of products including laptops, pads, smartphones, and IoT objects. The so-called "coin batteries," also known as "button batteries," are typical in many IoT applications.

In recent years, battery technology has seen a doubling in performance approximately every 10 (some say 15) years. Unfortunately, battery technology does not follow Moore's Law which observes empirically that computer chips double in performance and drop their price 50% every 18 to 24 months.

Batteries convert chemical energy released in particular chemical reactions into electrical energy. Batteries have a positive and a negative electrode (the cathode and the anode), separated by an electrolyte. When the electrodes are connected to a closed circuit, a series of chemical reactions occurs such that at one end charged particles (ions) from the electrolyte flow to the anode, react, and free up electrons; at the other end, reactions at the cathode attract free electrons. Thus, electrons at the anode move to the cathode and the flow of electrons through the electric circuit creates an electric current—the electrolyte also prevents the electrons from taking the shortest direct path, instead forcing them through the attached circuit. In rechargeable batteries, the reactions are reversible, with the ions and electrons flowing back in the opposite direction during charging. Batteries can be classified into primary and secondary systems (8). Primary batteries are disposable batteries, that is, batteries that cannot be recharged, and their conversion of chemical energy into electrical energy is irreversible (the chemicals are consumed while the battery discharges). Secondary batteries can be recharged, and the electrode material is reconstituted using an electric charge, so that discharge process can be repeated a number of times during the lifecycle of the battery.

The most common primary systems are alkaline, lithium, and metal/air batteries. Among secondary batteries, lead acid, nickel/cadmium (NiCd), nickel/metal hybrid (NiMH), and lithium-ion (Liion)/lithium-polymer (Li-polymer) batteries dominate the market, but efforts are constantly being made to find new systems that can match or exceed the performance of existing systems, improve their safety, and reduce their cost.

Rechargeable Liion batteries have an anode comprising carbon (e.g., graphite), a metal oxide cathode, and an electrolyte containing lithium salt. It is relatively easy to peel ions from lithium metal. The widespread deployment of this battery technology is due to the fact that the resulting batteries are lightweight, have a high energy density, hold their charge better than other batteries, and they do not suffer from the "memory effect," where batteries hold less and less charge over time if they are not drained and then recharged completely. The technology became popular in the early 1990s, replacing the nickel cadmium predecessors. In recent years, manufacturers have improved battery performance by applying enhanced engineering, optimizing the structures, and/or adding new materials inside the battery to make them more efficient. While battery technology is evolving, Liion batteries will continue to be important for the foreseeable future.

Materials such as silicon and others are being studied as possible replacement of the graphite anodes in Liion batteries. Silicon is of interest because it is inexpensive, it is abundant, and, by weight, it can store 10 times more lithium ions than graphite; this implies that it could theoretically allow a 10-fold increase in performance. However, to be useful, researchers must overcome a problem: while graphite anodes hold their shape when they soak up lithium ions, silicon swells, causing silicon particles to become separated, quickly reducing the performance of the battery. There is work underway to address this challenge, for example, by developing rubbery conductive binders that stick to the silicon particles within the anode, stretching and shrinking as the battery is charged and discharged. Others are looking to develop Liion batteries with anodes containing silicon nanowires. We are also starting to see a research on totally different chemistries. One example is lithium–air batteries with anodes made of lightweight porous carbon. Oxygen from the air enters the porous carbon and reacts with the lithium ions in the electrolyte and electrons in the external circuit to form solid lithium oxide. Recharging causes the lithium compound to decompose, releasing the lithium ions and releasing the oxygen; calculations of the amount of energy involved in the chemical reactions involved suggest it could produce batteries that last three to five times as long as existing Liion batteries. Other researchers are also investigating lightweight lithium–sulfur packs, which have a life span of three times that of current Liion batteries. Research work is proceeding on these and other technologies (9). However, these advances represent only incremental improvements in performance. New materials may be needed to make a quantum leap forward. MIT's Materials Project has already identified four new materials with the potential to be used in batteries. For example, the use of magnesium metal anode could result into a three-fold energy density compared with the best Liion batteries; furthermore these magnesium-ion batteries hold the majority of their charge over 3000 charge cycles. The technology, however, is not ready for widespread commercialization.

Another approach is the fuel cell, which is a proven technology since they were used to power electronics of the Gemini and Apollo space missions. Fuel cells convert chemical energy into electricity by converting the chemical energy from a fuel (e.g., alcohol) into electricity through a chemical reaction with oxygen. Fuel cells have a high energy density: hydrogen contains nearly 150 times the energy of an equivalent weight of lithium. However, to be practical, they need to be small and have an easily rechargeable reservoir for fuel. Microelectromechanical system (MEMS) technology is being investigated for this purpose. MEMSs are miniaturized mechanical devices that are already used in solar cells and flat-screen TVs. Currently, the technology is expensive because precious metals such as platinum and palladium are used; companies such as, but not limited to, NEC, Toshiba, and Apple are continuing substantive research in the field.

Some evolving technologies use small solar panels embedded in the screen of a smartphone or object; other systems may use kinetic devices that translate movement of objects into an electric current. Solar cells are an example of an energy harvester, but they are for low efficiency when converting ambient light into useful electrical energy. A 3 cm^2 solar cell (dimensions similar to the common CR2032 coin cell) yields only 12 µW.

There are a number of factors that must be considered in selecting the most suitable battery for a particular application; key considerations include (8):

- Operating voltage level
- Load current and profile
- Duty cycle—continuous or intermittent
- Service life
- Physical requirement
  - Size
  - Shape
  - Weight
- Environmental conditions
  - Temperature
  - Pressure
  - Humidity
  - Vibration
  - Shock
  - Pressure
- Safety and reliability
- Shelf life
- Maintenance and replacement
- Environmental impact and recycling capability
- Cost

4.3.5 Sensor Technology

A sensor network is an infrastructure comprising sensing (measuring), computing, and communication elements that gives the administrator the ability to instrument, observe, and react to events and phenomena in a specified environment. The administrator typically is some civil, government, commercial, or industrial entity.

Network(ed) sensor systems support a plethora of applications, not the least being Homeland Security. Typical applications include, but are not limited to, data collection, monitoring, surveillance, and medical telemetry. Sensors facilitate the instrumenting and controlling of factories, offices, homes, vehicles, cities, and the ambiance, especially as commercial off-the-shelf technology becomes available. With sensor network technology, specifically, with embedded networked sensing, ships, aircrafts, and buildings can "self-detect" structural faults (e.g., fatigue-induced cracks). Places of public assembly can be instrumented to detect airborne agents such as toxins and to trace the source of the contamination, should any be present (this also can be done for ground/underground situations). Earthquake-oriented sensors in buildings can locate potential survivors and can help assess structural damage; tsunami-alerting sensors can certainly prove useful for nations with extensive coastlines. Sensors also find extensive applicability in battlefield for reconnaissance and surveillance. In addition to sensing, one is often also interested in control and activation (13).

There are four basic components in a sensor network: (i) an assembly of distributed or localized sensors; (ii) an interconnecting network (usually, but not always, wireless-based); (iii) a central point of information clustering; and (iv) a set of computing resources at the central point (or beyond) to handle data correlation, event-trending, querying, and data mining. Because the interconnecting network is generally wireless, these systems are known as wireless sensor networks (WSNs).

In this context, the sensing and computation nodes are considered part of the sensor network; in fact, some of the computing may be done in the network itself. Because of the potentially large quantity of data collected, algorithmic methods for data management play an important role in sensor networks. The computation and communication infrastructure associated with sensor networks is often specific to this environment and rooted in the device- and application-based nature of these networks. For example, unlike most other settings, in-network processing is desirable in sensor networks; furthermore, node power (and/or battery life) is a key design consideration.

Sensors, the things or objects in this discussion, are active devices that measure some variable of the natural or man-made environment (e.g., a building, an assembly line, an industrial assemblage). Sensors in a WSN have a variety of purposes, functions, and capabilities. The radar networks used in air traffic control, the national electrical power grid, and the nation-wide weather stations deployed over a regular topographic mesh are all examples of early-deployment sensor networks. All of these systems, however, use specialized computers and communication protocols and are very expensive. Less expensive WSNs are now being planned for novel applications in physical security, healthcare, and commerce. The technology for sensing and control includes electric and magnetic field sensors; radio-wave frequency sensors; optical, electro-optic, and infrared sensors; radars; lasers; location/navigation sensors; seismic and pressure-wave sensors; environmental parameter sensors (e.g., wind, humidity, heat, and so on); and biochemical Homeland Security-oriented sensors.

Sensors can be described as "smart" inexpensive devices equipped with multiple on-board sensing elements: they are low cost, low power, untethered multifunctional nodes that are logically homed to a central sink node. Sensors are typically internetworked via a series of multihop short-distance low power wireless links (particularly within a defined "sensor field"); they typically utilize the Internet or some other network for long-haul delivery of information to a point (or points) of final data aggregation and analysis. In general, within the "sensor field," WSNs employ contention-oriented random access channel sharing/transmission techniques that are now incorporated in the IEEE 802 family of standards; indeed, these techniques were developed in the late 1960s and 1970s expressly for wireless (not cabled) environments, and for large sets of dispersed nodes with limited channel-management intelligence. However, other channel management techniques are also available. Sensors are typically deployed in a high density manner and in large quantities: a WSN consists of densely distributed nodes that support sensing, signal processing, embedded computing, and connectivity; sensors are logically linked by self-organizing means (sensors that are deployed in short-hop point-to-point master-slave pair arrangements are also of interest). Wireless sensors typically transmit information to collecting (monitoring) stations that aggregate some or all of the information. WSNs have unique characteristics, such as, but not limited to, power constraints/limited battery life for the wireless sensors, redundant data, low duty cycle, and many-to-one flows. Consequently, new design methodologies are needed across a set of disciplines, including, but not limited to, information transport, network and operational management, confidentiality, integrity, availability, and in-network/local processing. In some cases, it is challenging to collect (extract) data from wireless nodes (WNs) because connectivity to/from the WNs may be intermittent due to a low battery status (e.g., if these are dependent on sun light to recharge), or other wireless sensor malfunction. Furthermore, a lightweight protocol stack is desired. Often, a very large number of client units (say 64K or more) need to be supported by the system and by the addressing apparatus.

Sensors span several orders of magnitude in physical size; they (or, at least some of their components) range from nanoscopic-scale devices to mesoscopic-scale devices at one end; and, from microscopic-scale devices to macroscopic-scale devices at the other end. Nanoscopic (also known as nanoscale) refers to objects or devices in the order of 1–100 nm in diameter; mesoscopic scale refers to objects between 100 and 10,000 nm in diameter; the microscopic scale ranges from 10 to 1000 microns; and the macroscopic scale is at the millimeter-to-meter range. At the low end of the scale, one finds, among others, biological sensors, small passive microsensors (such as "smart dust"), and "lab-on-a-chip" assemblies. At the other end of the scale, one finds platforms such as, but not limited to, identity tags, toll collection devices, controllable weather data collection sensors, bioterrorism sensors, radars, and undersea submarine traffic sensors based on sonars.[2] Some refer to the latest generation of sensors, especially the miniaturized ones that are directly embedded in some physical infrastructure, as "microsensors." Microsensors with on-board processing and wireless interfaces can be utilized to study and monitor a variety of phenomena and environments at close proximity.

Sensors may be passive and/or be self-powered; further along in the power-consumption chain, some sensors may require relatively low power from a battery

---

[2]While satellites can be used to support sensing, this book does not explicitly include them in the technical discussion.

or line feed. At the high end of the power-consumption chain, some sensors may require very high power feeds (e.g., for radars). Chemical-, physical-, acoustic-, and image-based sensors can be utilized to study ecosystems (e.g., in support of global parameters such as temperature, microorganism populations, and so on). Near-term commercial applications include, but are not limited to, industrial/building WSNs, appliance control (lighting and heating, ventilation, and air conditioning (HVAC)), automotive sensors and actuators, home automation and networking, automatic meter reading/load management (LM), consumer electronics/entertainment, and asset management. Commercial market segments include the following:

- Industrial monitoring and control
- Commercial building and control
- Process control
- Home automation
- Wireless automated meter reading (AMR)/ LM
- Metropolitan operations (traffic, automatic tolls, fire, and so on)
- Homeland Security applications: chemical, biological, radiological, and nuclear wireless sensors
- Military sensors
- Environmental (land, air, sea)/agricultural wireless sensors

Suppliers and products tend to cluster according to these categories.

Implementations of WSNs have to address a set of technical challenges; however, the move toward standardization will, in due course, minimize a number of these challenges by addressing the issues once and then resulting in off-the-shelf chipsets and components. One of the challenges of WSNs is the need for extended temporal operation of the sensing node in spite of a (typically) limited power supply (and/or battery life). In particular, the architecture of the radio, including the use of low power circuitry, must be properly selected. In practical terms, this implies low power consumption for transmission over low bandwidth channels and low power-consumption logic to pre-process and/or compress data. Energy-efficient wireless communications systems are being sought and are typical of WSNs. Low power consumption is a key factor in ensuring long operating horizons for non-power-fed systems (some systems can indeed be power-fed and/or relay on other power sources). Power efficiency in WSNs is generally accomplished in three ways:

(i) Low duty cycle operation

(ii) Local/in-network processing to reduce data volume (and, hence, transmission time)

(iii) Multihop networking (this reduces the requirement for long-range transmission since signal path loss is an inverse power with range/distance (e.g., 4)—each node in the sensor network can act as a repeater, thereby reducing the link range coverage required, and, in turn, the transmission power

Conventional wireless networks are generally designed with link ranges of the order of tens, hundreds, or thousands of miles. The reduced link range and the compressed data payload in WSNs result in characteristic link budgets that differ from conventional systems.

4.3.6 RFID Technology

RFIDs are electronic devices associated with objects ("things") that transmit their identity (usually a serial number) via radio links. The RFID space is large and well documented. Our discussion here is very limited by choice; the reader requiring more details is encouraged to seek out the literature on the topic.

RFID tags are devices that typically have a read-only chip that stores a unique number but has no processing capability. RFID tags have broad applications, including the rapid collection of data in commercial environments. For example, RFID and bar coding are nearly ubiquitous in the inventory process, providing both accuracy and speed of data collection. These technologies facilitate the global supply chain and impact all subsystems within that overall process, including material requirement planning (MRP), just in time (JIT), electronic data interchange (EDI), and electronic commerce (EC). RFIDs are also used in industrial environments, such as but not limited to dirty, wet, or harsh environments. The technology can also be used for identification of people or assets. Figure 4.1 depicts two illustrative examples of RFIDs. Figure 4.2 depicts the basic operation of an RFID system.

Contactless smart cards (SCs) are more sophisticated than RFID tags, being that they contain a microprocessor that enables (i) on-board computing, (ii) two-way

FIGURE 4.1   Illustrative examples of RFIDs.

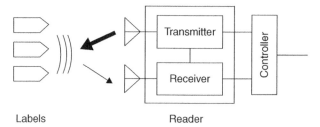

FIGURE 4.2 RFID reader operation.

communication including encryption, and (iii) storage of predefined and newly acquired information. Because of their more restricted capabilities, RFID tags are typically less expensive than SCs. When an RFID tag or contactless SC passes within a defined range, a reader generates electromagnetic waves; the tag's integrated antenna receives the signal and activates the chip in the tag/SC, and a wireless communications channel is set up between the reader and the tag enabling the transfer of pertinent data. Figure 4.3 provides a comparison between SCs and RFID tags.

RFID examples applicable to IoT include but are not limited to the following:

- Warehouse retailer automotive
- Grocery chain transportation
- Distribution center asset management
- Manufacturing
- Inventory management
- Warehousing and distribution
- Shop floor (production)
- Document tracking and asset management
- Industrial applications (e.g., time and attendance, shipping document tracking, receiving fixed assets)
- Retail applications

There are a number of standards for RFIDs. Some of the key ones include the following:

- The ISO 14443 standard describes components operating at 13.56 MHz frequency that embed a CPU; power consumption is about 10mW; data throughput is about 100 Kbps and the maximum working distance (from the reader) is around 10 cm.
- The ISO 15693 standard also describes components operating at 13.56 MHz frequency, but it enables working distances as high as 1 m, with a data throughput of a few Kbps.

Overview: what happens in RF (radio frequency) communication

❶ When a contactless smart card or an RFID tag passes within range, a reader sends out radio frequency electromagnetic waves.

❷ The antenna, tuned to receive these waves, wakes up the chip in the smart card or tag.

❸ A wireless communications channel is set up between the reader and the smart card or tag.

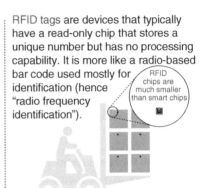

The contactless smart card contains a microprocessor, a small but real computer that makes calculations, communicates both ways, remembers new information, and actively uses these capabilities for security and many other applications.

RFID tags are devices that typically have a read-only chip that stores a unique number but has no processing capability. It is more like a radio-based bar code used mostly for identification (hence "radio frequency identification").

RFID chips are much smaller than smart chips

Characteristics of a contactless card

● Strong security capacities:
  ● mutual authentication before providing access to information
  ● access can be further protected via PIN or biometric
  ● encryption to protect data on card during exchange
  ● hardware and software protection to combat attacks or counterfeiting

● Hundreds of security features mean an individual's personal ID, financial details, payment transactions, transit fares or physical access privileges can be safely stored, managed, and exchanged

● Read and write memory capacity of 512 bytes and up, with very large memory storage possible

● Short-distance data exchange, typically two inches

Characteristics of an RFID tag

● Minimal security:
  ● one-way authentication; card cannot protect itself
  ● insufficient storage for biometrics
  ● no on-chip calculations of new information
  ● relies on static keys

● Single function; used to help machines identify objects to increase efficiency. Example: inventory control

● Small memory (92 bytes); often read-only

● Larger distance data exchange, typically several yards

Because of their more restricted capabilities, RFID tags are generally cheaper.

FIGURE 4.3   Comparison between contactless SCs and RFID tags. *Source:* Gemalto (used with Permission).

- The ISO 18000 standard defines parameters for air interface communications associated with frequency such as 135 KHz, 13.56 MHz, 2.45 GHz, 5.8 GHz, 860–960 MHz, and 433 MHz. The ISO 18000–6 standard uses the 860–960 MHz range and is the basis for the Class-1 Generation-2 UHF RFID, introduced by the EPCglobal Consortium.

As a side note, EPCglobal Inc. was created as a joint venture between GS1 (formerly EAN International) and GS1 US (formerly the Uniform Code Council, Inc.)—the same organizations entrusted to drive adoption of the barcode—to develop standards and to create a "visible" global supply chain. EPCglobal is a neutral, not-for-profit standards organization consisting of manufacturers, technology solution providers, and retailers. Many industries participate in the EPCglobal standards development process such as aerospace, apparel, chemical, consumer electronics, consumer goods, healthcare and life sciences, and transportation and logistics.

Typically, EPC codes used for active RFIDs or IP addresses are transmitted in clear form; however, some new protocols are now emerging that can provide strong privacy for the IoT. The host identity protocol (HIP) is one example; with this protocol, active RFIDs do not expose their identity in clear text, but protect the identity value (e.g., an EPC) using cryptographic procedures (10).

Table 4.2 based on material from Reference 11 provides a very basic listing of RFID concepts. An RFID system is logically comprising several layers, as follows: the tag layer, the air interface (also called media interface) layer, and the reader layer; additionally there are network, middleware, and application aspects. Some of the key aspects of the basic layers are as follows:

- Tag (device) layer: Architecture and EPCglobal Gen2 tag finite state machine
- Media interface layer: Frequency bands, antennas, read range, modulation, encoding, data rates
- Reader layer: Architecture, antenna configurations, Gen2 sessions, Gen2

The following is a list of key specifications supporting basic RFID operations:

- EPCglobal™: *EPC™ Tag Data Standards*
- EPCglobal™ (2004): *FMCG RFID Physical Requirements Document*
- EPCglobal™ (2004): *Class-1 Generation-2 UHF RFID Implementation Reference*
- EPCglobal™ (2005): *Radio-Frequency Identity Protocols, Class-1 Generation-2 UHF RFID, Protocol for Communications at 860 MHz–960 MHz*
- European Telecommunications Standards Institute (ETSI), EN 302 208: *Electromagnetic Compatibility and Radio Spectrum Matters (ERM)—Radio-Frequency Identification Equipment Operating in the Band 865 MHz to 868 MHz with Power Levels up to 2 W, Part 1 – Technical Characteristics and Test Methods*

TABLE 4.2   Basic RFID Concepts

Concept	Definition
Air interface	The complete communication link between an interrogator and a tag including the physical layer, collision arbitration algorithm, command and response structure, and data-coding methodology
Continuous wave (CW)	Typically a sinusoid at a given frequency, but more generally any interrogator waveform suitable for powering a passive tag without amplitude and/or phase modulation of sufficient magnitude to be interpreted by a tag as transmitted data
Cover-coding	A method by which an interrogator obscures information that it is transmitting to a tag. To cover-code data or a password, an interrogator first requests a random number from the tag. The interrogator then performs a bit-wise EXOR of the data or password with this random number and transmits the cover-coded (also called ciphertext) string to the tag. The tag uncovers the data or password by performing a bit-wise EXOR of the received cover-coded string with the original random number
EPC	A unique identifier for a physical object, unit load, location, or other identifiable entity playing a role in business operations. EPCs are assigned following rules designed to ensure uniqueness despite decentralized administration of code space, and to accommodate legacy coding schemes in common use. EPCs have multiple representations, including binary forms suitable for use on RFID tags, and text forms suitable for data exchange among enterprise information systems
EPCglobal architecture framework	A collection of interrelated standards ("EPCglobal Standards"), together with services operated by EPCglobal, its delegates, and others ("EPC Network Services"), all in service of a common goal of enhancing business flows and computer applications through the use of EPCs
Interrogator	A device that modulates/transmits and receives/demodulates a sufficient set of the electrical signals defined in the signaling layer to communicate with conformant tags, while conforming to all local radio regulations. A typical interrogator is a passive-backscatter, interrogator-talks-first (ITF), RFID system operating in the 860–960 MHz frequency range. An interrogator transmits information to a Tag by modulating an RF signal in the 860 MHz–960 MHz frequency range. The tag receives both information and operating energy from this RF signal. Tags are passive, meaning that they receive all of their operating energy from the interrogator's RF waveform. An interrogator receives information from a tag by transmitting a continuous-wave (CW) RF signal to the tag; the Tag responds by modulating the reflection coefficient of its antenna, thereby backscattering an information signal to the interrogator. The system is ITF, meaning that a tag modulates its antenna reflection coefficient with an information signal only after being directed to do so by an interrogator. Interrogators and tags are not required to talk simultaneously; rather, communications are half-duplex, meaning that interrogators talk and tags listen, or vice versa

(continued)

TABLE 4.2 *(Continued)*

Concept	Definition
Operating environment	A region within which an interrogator's RF transmissions are attenuated by less than 90dB. In free space, the operating environment is a sphere whose radius is approximately 1000 m, with the interrogator located at the center. In a building or other enclosure, the size and shape of the operating environment depends on factors such as the material properties and shape of the building and may be less than 1000 m in certain directions and greater than 1000 m in other directions
Operating procedure	Collectively, the set of functions and commands used by an interrogator to identify and modify tags (also known as the *tag-identification layer*)
Passive tag (or passive label)	A tag (or label) whose transceiver is powered by the RF field
Physical layer	The data coding and modulation waveforms used in interrogator-to-tag and tag-to-interrogator signaling
Singulation	Identifying an individual tag in a multiple-tag environment
Slotted random anticollision	An anticollision algorithm where tags load a random (or pseudo-random) number into a slot counter, decrement this slot counter based on interrogator commands, and reply to the interrogator when their slot counter reaches zero
Tag air interface	As defined in ISO 19762–3, a conductor-free medium, usually air, between a transponder and a reader/interrogator through which data communication is achieved by means of a modulated inductive or propagated electromagnetic field
Tag-identification layer	Collectively, the set of functions and commands used by an interrogator to identify and modify tags (also known as the *operating procedure*)

- European Telecommunications Standards Institute (ETSI), EN 302 208: *Electromagnetic Compatibility and Radio Spectrum Matters (ERM)—Radio-Frequency Identification Equipment Operating in the Band 865 MHz to 868 MHz with Power Levels up to 2 W, Part 2—Harmonized EN under article 3.2 of the R&TTE Directive*
- ISO/IEC Directives, Part 2: *Rules for the Structure and Drafting of International Standards*
- ISO/IEC 3309: *Information Technology—Telecommunications and Information Exchange Between Systems—High Level Data Link Control (HDLC) Procedures—Frame Structure*
- ISO/IEC 15961: *Information Technology, Automatic Identification and Data Capture—Radio Frequency Identification (RFID) for Item Management—Data Protocol: Application Interface*
- ISO/IEC 15962: *Information Technology, Automatic Identification and Data Capture Techniques—Radio Frequency Identification (RFID) for Item*

Management—Data Protocol: Data Encoding Rules and Logical Memory Functions

- ISO/IEC 15963: *Information Technology—Radiofrequency Identification for Item Management—Unique Identification for RF Tags*
- ISO/IEC 18000-1: *Information Technology—Radio Frequency Identification for Item Management—Part 1: Reference Architecture and Definition of Parameters to be Standardized*
- ISO/IEC 18000-6: *Information Technology Automatic Identification and Data Capture Techniques—Radio Frequency Identification for Item Management Air Interface—Part 6: Parameters for Air Interface Communications at 860–960 MHz*
- ISO/IEC 19762: *Information Technology AIDC Techniques—Harmonized Vocabulary—Part 3: Radio-Frequency Identification (RFID)*
- U.S. Code of Federal Regulations (CFR), Title 47, Chapter I, Part 15: *Radio-Frequency Devices, U.S. Federal Communications Commission*

Figure 4.4 depicts the set of relevant standards in the EPCglobal environment. In particular, the EPCglobal organization has defined an EPCglobal Architecture Framework in the document *The EPCglobal Architecture Framework, EPCglobal Final Version 1.4, December 2010*. The EPCglobal Architecture Framework is a

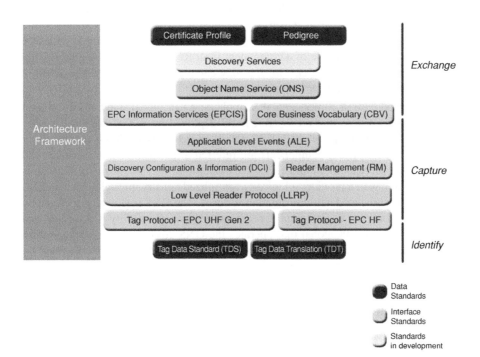

FIGURE 4.4   Standards that comprise the EPCglobal environment.

collection of interrelated standards ("EPCglobal Standards"), together with services operated by EPCglobal, its delegates, and others ("EPC Network Services"), all in service of a common goal of enhancing business flows and computer applications through the use of EPCs. It describes the collection of interrelated standards for hardware, software, and data interfaces, together with core services that are operated by EPCglobal and its delegates, all in service of a common goal of enhancing the supply chain through the use of EPCs. The architecture define core services that are operated by EPCglobal and its delegates, showing how the different components fit together to form a cohesive whole. It discusses (12):

- Individual hardware, software, and data interfaces are defined normatively by EPCglobal standards, or by standards produced by other standards bodies. EPCglobal standards are developed by the EPCglobal Community through the EPCglobal Standard Development Process (SDP). EPCglobal standards are normative, and implementations are subject to conformance and certification requirements. An example of an interface is the UHF Class-1 Gen-2 tag air interface, which specifies a radio-frequency communications protocol by which an RFID tag and an RFID reader device may interact. This interface is defined normatively by the UHF Class-1 Gen-2 tag air interface standard.
- The design of hardware and software components that implement EPCglobal standards are proprietary to the solution providers and end users that create such components. While EPCglobal standards provide normative guidance as to the behavior of interfaces between components, implementers are free to innovate in the design of components so long as they correctly implement the interface standards. An example of a component is an RFID tag that is the product of a specific tag manufacturer. This tag may comply with the UHF Class-1 Gen-2 tag air interface standard.
- A special case of components that implement EPCglobal standards are shared network services that are operated and deployed by EPCglobal itself (or by other organizations to which EPCglobal delegates responsibility), or by other third parties. These components are referred to as EPC network services and provide services to all end users. An example of an EPC Network Service is the ONS, which provides a logically centralized registry through which an EPC may be associated with information services. The ONS is logically operated by EPCglobal; from a deployment perspective this responsibility is delegated to a contractor of EPCglobal that operates the ONS "root" service, which in turn delegates responsibility for certain lookup operations to services operated by other organizations.

4.3.7 Satellite Technology

Due to its global reach and the ability to support mobility in all geographical environments (including Antarctica), satellite communications can play a critical role in many broadly distributed M2M applications. This topic deserves more attention and development because it offers interesting commercial possibilities.

REFERENCES

1. Lee GM, Park J, Kong N, Crespi N. The Internet of Things – Concept and Problem Statement. July 2011. Internet Research Task Force, July 11, 2011, draft-lee-iot-problem-statement-02.txt.
2. Manderson T, Halpern JM. Locator/ID Separation Protocol (lisp). IETF Working Group.
3. Huston G, Lindqvist K. Site Multihoming by IPv6 Intermediation (shim6). IETF Working Group, 2010.
4. Lee GM, Choi JK, et al. Naming Architecture for Object to Object Communications. HIP Working Group, Internet Draft, March 8, 2010, draft-lee-object-naming-02.txt.
5. EPCglobal® Organization Web Site, http://www.gs1.org/epcglobal.
6. Mulligan G. IPv6 Over Low power WPAN (6lowpan). Description of Working Group, IETF, 2012, http://datatracker.ietf.org/wg/6lowpan/charter/, http://www.ietf.org/mail-archive/web/6lowpan/.
7. Maeder A. How to Deal with a Thousand Nodes: M2M Communication Over Cellular Networks. IEEE WoWMoM 2012 Panel, San Francisco, California, USA June 25–28, 2012.
8. Tidblad AA. The Future of Battery Technologies – Part I, Intertek White Paper, November 2009, icenter@intertek.com.
9. Fleming N. Smartphone Batteries: When will They Last Longer?. bbc.com online article, February 27, 2012.
10. Urien P, Lee GM, Pujolle G. HIP Support for RFIDs. HIP Research Group, Internet Draft, draft-irtf-hiprg-rfid-03, July 2011.
11. EPCglobal®, EPC™ Radio-Frequency Identity Protocols, Class-1 Generation-2 UHF RFID, Protocol for Communications at 860 MHz–960 MHz, Version 1.0.9, January 2005.
12. EPCglobal®, *The EPCglobal Architecture Framework*, EPCglobal Final Version 1.4, December 2010, Ken Traub Editor.
13. Minoli D, Sohraby K, Zanti T. *Wireless Sensor Networks*, Wiley 2007, New York, NY.

CHAPTER 5

EVOLVING IoT STANDARDS

For many years, embedded systems have been deployed as specialized vertical applications with unique functions and attributes. As the need arises for broad-scale deployment, with the ensuing requirement of being able to easily connect these embedded machines to control systems and to users that require interaction with them, standards become fundamentally important. This chapter provides a short survey of some key evolving standards that can be used to support IoT applications. Mainstream layer 1/2 communication standards (specifically, Zigbee, Bluetooth, and long-term evolution [LTE]) and layer 3 communication standards (specifically, IPv6, Mobile IPv6, and IPv6 technologies directly applied to the IoT) are discussed in Chapters 6 through 9; this chapter, therefore, covers the multitude of other support standards that come into play in the deployment of IoT and machine-to-machine (M2M) services (also known as machine-type communication [MTC] in third-generation partnership project [3GPP] environments).

5.1 OVERVIEW AND APPROACHES

Despite technological advances in many supporting technologies that are advancing IoT concepts, difficulties associated with interworking and multisupplier approaches still hamper the cost-effective implementation and rollout of the technology. When there is insufficient standardization, capability mismatches between different devices

Building the Internet of Things with IPv6 and MIPv6: The Evolving World of M2M Communications,
First Edition. Daniel Minoli.
© 2013 John Wiley & Sons, Inc. Published 2013 by John Wiley & Sons, Inc.

easily arise. While IoT systems can utilize existing Internet protocols, as mentioned earlier, in a number of cases the power-, processing-, and capabilities-constrained IoT environment can benefit from additional protocols that help optimize the communications and lower the computational requirements. Developers have expressed the desire for having the IoT utilize existing Internet protocol stack, to a large extent and to the degree possible. However, one should expect some challenges and modifications because of the larger capability variations than in the current Internet, and because of the fact that there is no human in the loop for most applications (M2M), although humans may be in the loop in human-to-machine (H2M) situations. Also, as hinted in Chapter 4, power consideration drive the need for leaner protocol stacks.

Standards covering many of the underlying technologies are important because proprietary solutions fragment the industry. Standards are particularly critical when there is a requirement to physically or logically connect entities across an interface. Some areas requiring standardization include, but are not limited to, the following (1–3):

- Developing IP/routing/transport/web protocols subsets that scale down to IOT devices; specifically, lightweight routing protocols for the IoT;
- Describing architectures that employ gateways and middleware;
- Developing mobility management;
- Internetworking of IoT things;
- Lightweight implementations of cryptographic stacks; and building a suitable security infrastructure: end-to-end security capabilities for the IoT things;
- Developing standards for applications, specifically, data formats; and
- Discouraging on domain-specific solutions.

There is a practical desire, motivated by financial consideration, to build optimized solutions that can solve the problem in a particular setting, but these solutions may not be general enough for all situations. Such "point solutions" invariably leads to interoperability problems. Some observers make the case that Internet protocols were successful because they were good enough, scalable, and useful, not because they were particularly optimized for any hardware back in the early days (3).

Fortunately, several global organizations are currently working on global M2M standards. Several standardization efforts are underway addressing layer-specific protocols, optimized architectures, and policy, including but not limited to the following:

- The Internet Engineering Task Force (IETF) IPv6 routing protocol for low power and lossy networks (RPL)/routing over low power and lossy networks (ROLL);
- IETF constrained application protocol (CoAP);

- IETF constrained RESTful environments (CoRE);
- IETF IPv6 over low power WPAN (6LoWPAN);
- 3GPP MTC; and
- ETSI M2M. Recall that M2M involves communication without (or only limited) human intervention where the human is not the input agent but possibly (but not always) the output agent. For example, ETSI TS/TR 102 addresses M2M architecture and services (e.g., smart metering, e-health, auto, and city).

A number of specific considerations need to be taken when designing protocols and architectures for interconnecting smart objects to the Internet. Key concerns are scalability, power efficiency, interworking between different technologies and network domains, usability and manageability, and security and privacy (4). IoT standardization deals with physical interfaces, access connectivity (e.g., low power IEEE 802.15.4 based wireless standards such as IEC62591, 6LoWPAN, and ZigBee Smart Energy (SE) 2.0, DASH7/ISO/IEC 18000-7), networking (such as IPv6), and applications. IETF 6LoWPAN, ROLL, and CoRE aim at making IPv6 work well on constrained devices. 3GPP MTC seeks to include scalability in LTE. ETSI M2M aims at making devices communicate to service platforms and applications (5). Other activities include:

- IEEE 802: addresses LANs, WLANs, and PANs (personal area networks), particularly the IEEE802.15.4 wireless standards such as IEC62591, 6LoWPAN, and ZigBee, ZigBee IP (ZIP), ZigBee SE 2.0—IEEE 802 now includes over 100 standards. Specifically, the ZigBee Alliance's ZIP standard is a first definition of an open standards-based IPv6 stack for smart objects, the goal being to bring IPv6 network protocols over 802.15.4 wireless mesh networks to reality.
- IEEE P2030/SCC21: addresses smart grid (SG) interoperability.
- Emerging IEEE P1901.2 standard for Orthogonal Frequency Division Multiplexing (OFDM)-based communication over power lines and offers guaranteed interoperability. This standard is key to fostering SG deployments.
- ETSI TS/TR 102: addresses M2M architecture, services, smart metering, e-health, auto, and city.
- 3GPP SA1-SA3: addresses services, architecture, and security.
- JTC1 SC 6 and China NITSC: address sensor networks.
- TIA: TR-50: addresses smart device communications.
- CENELEC: addresses device addressability.

In summary, three major strands of press time standardization include the following: (i) ETSI: for end-to-end framework for M2M; (ii) 3GPP: to enable operators to support services; and (iii) IEEE: to optimize the radio access/physical layer.

5.2   IETF IPv6 ROUTING PROTOCOL FOR RPL ROLL

Low power and lossy networks (LLNs) are[1] a class of networks in which both the routers and their interconnect are constrained. LLN routers typically operate with constraints on processing power, memory, and energy (battery power); their interconnects are characterized by high loss rates, low data rates, and instability. LLNs comprise a few dozen routers up to thousands of routers. Supported traffic flows include point-to-point (between devices inside the LLN), point-to-multipoint (from a central control point to a subset of devices inside the LLN), and multipoint-to-point (from devices inside the LLN toward a central control point). The IPv6 Routing Protocol for LLNs (RPL) is a mechanism proposed by the IETF to support multipoint-to-point traffic from devices inside the LLN toward a central control point, as well as point-to-multipoint traffic from the central control point to the devices inside the LLN (6).

LLNs consist largely of constrained nodes (with limited processing power, memory, and sometimes energy when they are battery operated or energy scavenging). These routers are interconnected by lossy unstable links, resulting in relatively high packet loss rates and typically supporting only low data rates. Another characteristic of such networks is that the traffic patterns are not simply point-to-point, but in many cases point-to-multipoint or multipoint-to-point. Furthermore, such networks may potentially comprise up to thousands of nodes. These characteristics offer unique challenges to a routing solution. To address these issues, the IETF ROLL Working Group has defined application-specific routing requirements for an LLN routing protocol; it has also specified the RPL. A set of IETF companion documents to the basic specification provides further guidance in the form of applicability statements specifying a set of operating points appropriate to the building automation, home automation, industrial, and urban application scenarios.

Existing routing protocols include OSPF/IS-IS (open shortest path first/ intermediate system to intermediate system), OLSRv2 (optimized link state routing protocol version 2), TBRPF (topology-based reverse path forwarding), RIP (routing information protocol), AODV (ad hoc on-demand distance vector), DYMO (dynamic MANET on-demand), and DSR (dynamic source routing). Some of the metrics to be considered for IoT applications include the following:

- Routing state memory space—limited memory resources of low power nodes;
- Loss response—what happens in response to link failures;
- Control cost—constraints on control traffic;
- Link and node cost—link and node properties are considered when choosing routes.

The existing protocols all fail one or more of these goals for IoT applications. For example, for *protocol state memory size* OSPF/IS-IS fails; for *loss* OSPF/IS-IS fails;

---

[1] This discussion is based on and summarized from the IETF document draft-ietf-roll-rpl-19 [6]; it included to motivate the reader to consult the full document and/or related IETF documents for an inclusive view of the issue.

for *control* OSPF/IS-IS fails; for *link cost* OSPF/IS-IS would pass; and for *node cost* OSPF/IS-IS fails (see Reference 7 for additional information). Hence, the need for a new protocol.

In order to be useful in a wide range of LLN application domains, RPL separates packet processing and forwarding from the routing optimization objective. Examples of such objectives include minimizing energy, minimizing latency, or satisfying constraints. An RPL implementation, in support of a particular LLN application, will include the necessary objective function(s) as required by the application.

Consistent with the layered architecture of IP, RPL does not rely on any particular features of a specific link layer technology. RPL is designed to be able to operate over a variety of different link layers, including ones that are constrained, potentially lossy, or typically utilized in conjunction with highly constrained host or router devices, such as but not limited to low power wireless or PLC (power line communication) technologies.

RPL operations, however, require bidirectional links. In some LLN scenarios, communication links may exhibit asymmetric properties. Therefore, the reachability of a router needs to be verified before the router can be used as a parent. RPL expects an external mechanism to be triggered during the parent selection phase in order to verify link properties and neighbor reachability. Neighbor unreachability detection (NUD) is such a mechanism, but alternates are possible, including bidirectional forwarding detection described in RFC 5881 and hints from lower layers via layer 2 triggers. In general, a detection mechanism that is reactive to traffic is favored in order to minimize the cost of monitoring links that are not being used.

RPL also expects an external mechanism to access and transport some control information, referred to as the "RPL Packet Information," in data packets. The RPL packet information enables the association of a data packet with an RPL instance and the validation of RPL routing states. The IPv6 Hop-by-Hop RPL option is an example of such a mechanism. The mechanism is required for all packets except when strict source routing is used which, by nature, prevents endless loops and alleviates the need for the RPL packet information. Future companion specifications may propose alternate ways to carry the RPL packet information in the IPv6 packets and may extend the RPL packet information to support additional features.

RPL provides a mechanism to disseminate information over the dynamically formed network topology. The dissemination enables minimal configuration in the nodes, allowing nodes to operate mostly autonomously.

In some applications, RPL assembles topologies of routers that own independent prefixes. Those prefixes may or may not be aggregatable depending on the origin of the routers. A prefix that is owned by a router is advertised as "on-link."

RPL also introduces the capability to bind a subnet together with a common prefix and to route within that subnet. A source can inject information about the subnet to be disseminated by RPL, and that source is authoritative for that subnet. Because many LLN links have non-transitive properties, a common prefix that RPL disseminates over the subnet must not be advertised as on-link.

RPL may, in particular, disseminate IPv6 neighbor discovery (ND) information prefix information option (PIO) and the route information option (RIO). ND

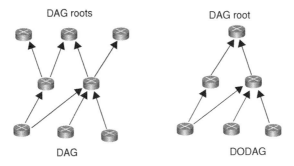

FIGURE 5.1 DAGs and DODAGs.

information that is disseminated by RPL conserves all its original semantics for router to host, with limited extensions for router to router, though it is not to be confused with routing advertisements and it is never to be directly redistributed in another routing protocol. An RPL node often combines host and router behaviors.

Some basic definitions in RPL are as follows (see Fig. 5.1):

- Directed acyclic graph (DAG) is a directed graph with no cycles.
- Destination-oriented DAG (DODAG) is a DAG rooted at a single destination.

RPL defines optimization objective when forming paths toward roots based on one or more metrics. Metrics may include both link properties (reliability, latency) and node properties (e.g., powered on not). RPL defines a new ICMPv6 message with three possible types:

- DAG information object (DIO)—carries information that allows a node to discover an RPL instance, learn its configuration parameters, and select DODAG parents;
- DAG information solicitation (DIS)—solicit a DODAG information object from an RPL node;
- Destination advertisement object (DAO)—used to propagate destination information upward along the DODAG.

A node rank defines a node's relative position within a DODAG with respect to the DODAG root.

The approach in RPL is to build a topology (instance) where routes to these nodes are optimized (namely, DODAG(s) rooted at these nodes). DODAG construction proceeds as follows (7):

- Nodes periodically send link-local multicast DIO messages;
- Stability or detection of routing inconsistencies influence the rate of DIO messages;

- Nodes listen for DIOs and use their information to join a new DODAG, or to maintain an existing DODAG;
- Nodes may use a DIS message to solicit a DIO;
- Based on information in the DIOs, the node chooses parents that minimize path cost to the DODAG root.

RPL is optimized for many-to-one and one-to-many traffic patterns. Routing state is minimized: stateless nodes have to store only instance(s) configuration parameters and a list of parent nodes. The protocol takes into account both link and node properties when choosing paths. Additionally, link failures do not trigger global network re-optimization. The reader is referred to the draft specification discussed in the key reference (6) for an extensive discussion of the capabilities, formats, and procedures of this protocol.

5.3 CONSTRAINED APPLICATION PROTOCOL (CoAP)

5.3.1 Background

The IETF constrained RESTful environments (CoRE) Working Group has recently undertaken standardization work the CoAP. CoAP is a simple application layer protocol targeted to simple electronic devices (e.g., IoT/M2M things) to allow them to communicate interactively over the Internet. CoAP is designed for low power sensors (especially wireless sensor network [WSN] nodes described in Chapters 3 and 4) and for actuators that need to be controlled or monitored remotely, using IP/Internet networks. CoAP can be seen as a specialized web transfer protocol for use with constrained networks and nodes for M2M applications, such as smart energy and building automation. CoAP operates with HTTP (hypertext transfer protocol) for basic support with the web, allowing proxies to be built providing access to CoAP resources via HTTP in a uniform way, while also supporting multicast and enjoying low overhead CoAP can run on most devices that support user datagram protocol (UDP) or a similar protocol. Some key aspects of the protocol are as follows: (i) minimal complexity for the mapping with HTTP; (ii) low header overhead and low parsing complexity; (iii) support for the discovery of resources; (iv) simple resource subscription process; and (v) simple caching based on max-age.

CoAP makes use of two message types, requests and responses, using a simple binary base header format. The base header may be followed by options in Internet control message protocol (ICMP)-style type-length-value format. CoAP is by default bound to UDP and, optionally, to transmission control protocol (TCP). Any bytes after the headers in the packet are considered the message body if any. The length of the message body is implied by the datagram length. When bound to UDP, the entire message must fit within a single datagram. When used with 6LoWPAN as defined in RFC 4944, messages fit into a single IEEE 802.15.4 frame.

The constrained nodes for which CoAP is targeted often have 8-bit microcontrollers with small amounts of ROM and RAM, while networks such as 6LoWPAN often have high packet error rates and a typical throughput of 10s of Kbps. CoAP provides a method/response interaction model between application end-points, supports built-in resource discovery, and includes key web concepts such as URIs (uniform resource identifiers) and content-types. CoAP easily translates to HTTP for integration with the web while meeting specialized requirements such as multicast support, very low overhead, and simplicity for constrained environments (8).

The use of Web Services (WS) on the Internet has become ubiquitous in most applications; it depends on the fundamental representational state transfer (REST) architecture of the web (see Section 5.4). The CoRE working group[2] aims at realizing the REST architecture in a suitable form for constrained IoT/M2M nodes (e.g., 8-bit microcontrollers with limited RAM and ROM) and IoT/M2M networks (e.g., 6LoW-PAN). Constrained networks such as 6LoWPAN support the expensive fragmentation of IPv6 packets into small link-layer frames. One design goal of CoAP has been to keep message overhead small, thus limiting the use of fragmentation.

One of the main goals of CoAP is to design a generic web protocol for the special requirements of this constrained environment, especially considering energy, building automation, and other M2M applications. The objective of CoAP is not to statically compress HTTP, but rather to realize a subset of REST common with HTTP, but optimized for M2M applications. Although CoAP can be used for compressing simple HTTP interfaces, it also offers features for M2M such as built-in discovery, multicast support, and asynchronous message exchanges. CoAP has the following main features:

- Constrained web protocol fulfilling M2M requirements;
- UDP binding with optional reliability supporting unicast and multicast requests;
- Asynchronous message exchanges;
- Low header overhead and parsing complexity;
- URI and content-type support;
- Simple proxy and caching capabilities;
- A stateless HTTP mapping, allowing proxies to be built providing access to CoAP resources via HTTP in a uniform way or for HTTP simple interfaces to be realized alternatively over CoAP; and
- Security binding to datagram transport layer security (DTLS).

The interaction model of CoAP is similar to the client/server model of HTTP. However, M2M interactions typically result in a CoAP implementation acting in both client and server roles (called an end-point). A CoAP request is equivalent to that of HTTP and is sent by a client to request an action (using a method code) on a resource (identified by a URI) on a server. The server then sends a response with a response code; this response may include a resource representation. Unlike

---

[2]This discussion is based on and summarized from the IETF document draft-ietf-core-coap-09 (8); it is included to motivate the reader to consult the full document and/or related IETF documents for an inclusive view of the issue.

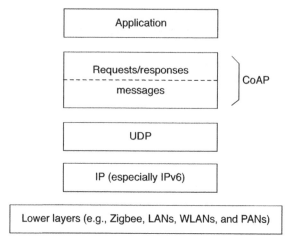

FIGURE 5.2 Abstract layering of CoAP.

HTTP, CoAP deals with these interchanges asynchronously over a datagram-oriented transport such as UDP. This is done logically using a layer of messages that supports optional reliability (with exponential back-off). CoAP defines four types of messages: confirmable (CON), non-confirmable (NON), acknowledgement, reset; method codes and response codes included in some of these messages make them carry requests or responses. The basic exchanges of the four types of messages are transparent to the request/response interactions.

One could think of CoAP logically as using a two-layer approach, a CoAP messaging layer used to deal with UDP and the asynchronous nature of the interactions, and the request/response interactions using method and response codes (see Fig. 5.2). CoAP is, however, a single protocol, with messaging and request/response just features of the CoAP header. Figure 5.3 depicts the overall protocol stack that is being considered in the CoAP context.

The reader is referred to the draft specification discussed in the key reference (8) for an extensive discussion of the capabilities, formats, and procedures of this protocol. A short summary follows.

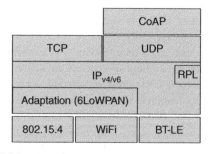

FIGURE 5.3 Overall protocol stack in CoAP's environment.

5.3.2 Messaging Model

The CoAP messaging model is based on the exchange of messages over UDP between end-points. It uses a short fixed-length binary header (4 bytes) that may be followed by compact binary options and a payload. This message format is shared by requests and responses. Each CoAP message contains a message ID used to detect duplicates and for optional reliability.

Reliability is provided by marking a message as CON. A CON message is retransmitted using a default timeout and exponential back-off between retransmissions, until the recipient sends an acknowledgement message (ACK) with the same message ID from the corresponding end-point. When a recipient is not able to process a CON message, it replies with a reset message (RST) instead of an ACK. A message that does not require reliable delivery, for example, each single measurement out of a stream of sensor data, can be sent as a NONmessage. These are not acknowledged, but still have a message ID for duplicate detection. When a recipient is not able to process a NON message, it may reply with an RST.

Since CoAP is based on UDP, it also supports the use of multicast IP destination addresses, enabling multicast CoAP requests.

5.3.3 Request/Response Model

CoAP request and response semantics are carried in CoAP messages, which include either a method code or response code, respectively. Optional (or default) request and response information, such as the URI and payload content-type, are carried as CoAP options. A token option is used to match responses to requests independent of the underlying messages.

A request is carried in a CON or NON message, and if immediately available, the response to a request carried in a CON message is carried in the resulting ACK message. This is called a piggy-backed response. If the server is not able to respond immediately to a request carried in a CON message, it simply responds with an empty ACK message so that the client can stop retransmitting the request. When the response is ready, the server sends it in a new CON message (which then in turn needs to be acknowledged by the client). This is called a separate response. Likewise, if a request is sent in a NON message, then the response is usually sent using a new NON message, although the server may send a CON message.

CoAP makes use of GET, PUT, POST, and DELETE methods in a similar manner to HTTP.

5.3.4 Intermediaries and Caching

The protocol supports the caching of responses in order to efficiently fulfill requests. Simple caching is enabled using freshness and validity information carried with CoAP responses. A cache could be located in an end-point or an intermediary.

Proxying is useful in constrained networks for several reasons, including (i) network traffic limiting, (ii) to improve performance, (iii) to access resources of sleeping devices, or (iv) for security reasons. The proxying of requests on behalf of another CoAP end-point is supported in the protocol. The URI of the resource to request is included in the request, while the destination IP address is set to the proxy.

The reader is referred to the draft specification discussed in the key reference (8) for an extensive discussion of the capabilities, formats, and procedures of this protocol.

5.4 REPRESENTATIONAL STATE TRANSFER (REST)

As noted, CoAP uses REST techniques. REST was first described in 2000 by Roy Fielding in his University of California dissertation which analyzed a set of web-focused software architecture principles for distributed computing. REST aims at supporting scalability of component interactions, generality of interfaces, and independent deployment of components. Hence, it defines a set of architectural principles by which one can design WS that focus on a system's resources, including how resource states are addressed and transferred over HTTP by a plethora of clients written in different languages (9). Stated differently, REST is an architectural style of large-scale networked software that takes advantage of the technologies and protocols of the World Wide Web; it describes how distributed data objects, or resources, can be defined and addressed, stressing the easy exchange of information and scalability (10). A REST-based WS follows four basic design principles:

- Use HTTP methods explicitly.
- Be stateless.
- Expose directory structure-like URIs.
- Transfer XML, JavaScript Object Notation (JSON), or both.

5.5 ETSI M2M

ETSI recently created a dedicated Technical Committee, with the mission to develop standard M2M communications. The group seeks to provide an end-to-end view of M2M standardization and is expected to co-operate closely with ETSI's ongoing activities on next-generation networks (NGNs), radio communications, fiber optics and powerline, as well as collaboration with 3GPP standards group on mobile communication technologies. The reference model used in this text is the M2M model developed by this group, as defined in various evolving standards, including the ETSI M2M Release 1 standards described in ETSI TS 102 689 (requirements), ETSI TS 102 690 (functional architecture), and ETSI TS 102 921 (interface descriptions). ETSI has also published a number of documents defining common use cases. These documents were cited in other chapters and are not re-listed here.

Key elements in the M2M environment include the following (11):

- M2M device: A device capable of replying to request for data contained within those device or capable of transmitting data contained within those devices autonomously;
- M2M area network (device domain): A network that provides connectivity between M2M devices and M2M gateways, for example, a PAN;
- M2M gateway: A gateway (say a router or higher layer network element) that uses M2M capabilities to ensure M2M devices interworking and interconnection to the communication network;
- M2M communication networks (network domain): A wider-range network that supports communications between the M2M gateway(s) and M2M application; examples include but are not limited to xDSL, LTE, WiMAX, and WLAN; and
- M2M applications: Systems that contain the middleware layer where data goes through various application services and is used by the specific business-processing engines.

The reader is referred to the architecture specification cited above for an extensive discussion of the M2M environment.

5.6 THIRD-GENERATION PARTNERSHIP PROJECT SERVICE REQUIREMENTS FOR MACHINE-TYPE COMMUNICATIONS

5.6.1 Approach

Current mobile networks are optimized for human-to-human (H2H) traffic and not for M2M/MTC interactions; hence, optimizations for MTC are advantageous. For example, one needs lower costs to reflect lower MTC ARPUs (average revenue per user); also, there is a need to support triggering. Hence, 3GPP has started work on M2M specification in 2010 for interoperable solutions, particularly in the 3G/4G/LTE context. Table 5.1 provides a superset of specifications that are applicable to MTC services. Figure 5.4 depicts the service model, while Figure 5.5 depicts the architecture. In that architecture, the interfaces are as follows:

- MTCu: provides MTC devices access to the 3GPP network for the transport of user traffic;
- MTCi: the reference point for MTC server to connect the 3GPP network via 3GPP bearer service; and
- MTCsms: the reference point for MTC server to connect the 3GPP network via 3GPP SMS.

The key document *3rd Generation Partnership Project Service Requirements for Machine Type Communications—Release 10* focused on overload and congestion control, extended access barring (EAB), low priority access, APN (access point

TABLE 5.1 3GPP Specifications Related to MTC

3GPP Specifications	Specifications Associated with or Affected by MTC Work
22.011	Service accessibility
22.368	Service requirements for MTC; stage 1
23.008	Organization of subscriber data
23.012	Location management procedures
23.060	General packet radio service (GPRS); service description; stage 2
23.122	Non-access-stratum (NAS) functions related to mobile station (MS) in idle mode
23.203	Policy and charging control architecture
23.401	GPRS enhancements for evolved universal terrestrial radio access network (E-UTRAN) access
23.402	Architecture enhancements for non-3GPP accesses
23.888	System improvements for MTC
24.008	Mobile radio interface layer 3 specification; core network protocols; stage 3
24.301	NAS protocol for evolved packet system (EPS); stage 3
24.368	NAS configuration management object (MO)
25.331	Radio resource control (RRC); protocol specification
29.002	Mobile application part (MAP) specification
29.018	GPRS; serving GPRS support node (SGSN)—visitors location register (VLR); Gs interface layer 3 specification
29.060	GPRS; GPRS tunneling protocol (GTP) across the Gn and Gp interface
29.118	Mobility management entity (MME)—VLR SGs interface specification
29.274	3GPP EPS; evolved GTP for control plane (GTPv2-C); stage 3
29.275	Proxy mobile IPv6 (PMIPv6)-based mobility and tunneling protocols; stage 3
29.282	Mobile IPv6 vendor-specific option format and usage within 3GPP
31.102	Characteristics of the universal subscriber identity module (USIM) application
33.868	Security aspects of MTC
36.331	Evolved universal terrestrial radio access (E-UTRA); RRC; protocol specification
37.868	RAN improvements for MTC
43.868	GERAN improvements for MTC
44.018	Mobile radio interface layer 3 specification; RRC protocol
44.060	GPRS; MS–base station system (BSS) interface; radio link control/medium access control (RLC/MAC) protocol
45.002	Multiplexing and multiple access on the radio path

name)-based congestion control, and downlink throttling (12). For MTC communication, the following communication scenarios are identified and described in the Release 10 document:

(i) MTC devices communicating with one or more MTC server;

(ii) MTC devices communicating with each other.

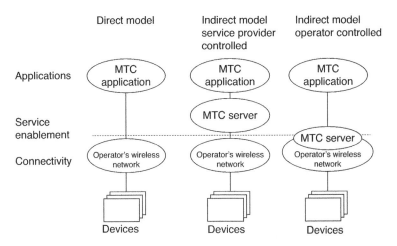

FIGURE 5.4   M2M in 3GPP—service models.

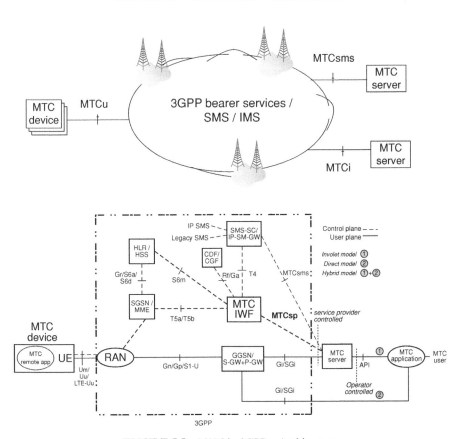

FIGURE 5.5   M2M in 3GPP—Architecture.

For MTC devices communicating with one or more MTC servers, the following use cases exist:

(a) MTC server controlled by the network operator; namely the MTC server is located in the operator domain. Here
  – The network operator offers API (e.g., Open Systems Architecture [OSA]) on its MTC server(s)
  – MTC user accesses MTC server(s) of the network operator via API
(b) MTC server not controlled by the network operator; namely MTC server is located outside the operator domain. Here
  – The network operator offers the network connectivity to the MTC server(s) located outside of the network operator domain

The communication scenario where the MTC devices communicate directly without intermediate MTC server is not considered in this release of the specification.

MTC applications do not all have the same characteristics. This implies that not every system optimization is suitable for every MTC application. Therefore, MTC features are defined in Release 10 to provide structure for the different system optimization possibilities that can be invoked. Such MTC features are offered on a per subscription basis. MTC features can be individually activated. The following MTC features have been defined:

– Low mobility
– Time controlled
– Time tolerant
– Packet switched (PS) only (here the MTC feature PS only is intended for use with MTC devices that only require packet switched services)
– Small data transmissions
– Mobile originated only
– Infrequent mobile terminated
– MTC monitoring
– Priority alarm
– Secure connection
– Location-specific trigger
– Network provided destination for uplink data
– Infrequent transmission

5.6.2 Architectural Reference Model for MTC

The latest Release 11 (an extensive document) focuses on numbers and addressing, on improvements of device triggering, and on interfaces between MTC server and mobile network (13, 14). Referring to Figure 5.5, MTCsp is a new control interface for interactions with MTC server; MTC-IWF is a new interworking function between (external) MTC server and operator core network handling security, authorization, authentication, and charging.

The end-to-end application, between the user equipment (UE) used for MTC and the MTC application, uses services provided by the 3GPP system, and optionally services provided by an MTC server. The 3GPP system provides transport and communication services (including 3GPP bearer services, IMS, and SMS) including various optimizations that can facilitate MTC. Figure 5.5 shows UE used for MTC connecting to the 3GPP network (UTRAN, E-UTRAN, GERAN, I-WLAN, and so on) via the Um/Uu/LTE-Uu interface. The architecture encompasses a number of models as follows:

- Direct model—direct communication provided by the 3GPP operator: The MTC application connects directly to the operator network without the use of any MTC server;
- Indirect model—MTC service provider controlled communication: The MTC server is an entity outside of the operator domain. The MTCsp and MTCsms are external interfaces (i.e., to a third-party M2M service provider);
- Indirect model—3GPP operator controlled communication: The MTC server is an entity inside the operator domain. The MTCsp and MTCsms are internal to the public land mobile network (PLMN);
- Hybrid model: The direct and indirect models are used simultaneously in the hybrid model, for example, connecting the user plane using the direct model and doing control plane signalling using the indirect model.

Some believe that there may be E.164 telephone number issues as related to M2M: in several countries, regulators have indicated that there are not enough (mobile) numbers available for M2M applications. 3GPP postulates that solutions will have to support $100\times$ more M2M devices than devices for H2H communications. Proposed solutions include: (i) mid-term solution: special M2M number ranges with longer telephone numbers (e.g., 14 digits); (ii) long-term solution: no longer provide E.164 telephone numbers for M2M applications.

Figure 5.6 provides a view to the various protocol stacks defined in Release 11.

The reader is referred to the Technical Report by 3GPP (13) for an extensive discussion of architectural aspects and system requirements for MTC/M2M communication. The second part of Chapter 6 discusses some 3GPP networks that may come into play in the MTC/M2M context.

5.7 CENELEC

Recently, the European Committee for Electrotechnical Standardization (CENELEC) has accepted the transport profile of Siemens' distribution line carrier communication protocol, CX1, as a standardization proposal. The standard aims at supporting open

User-plane

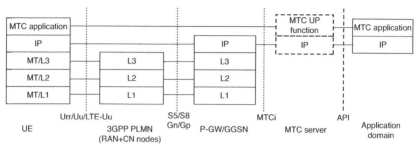

Control plane

MTC server-MTC-IWF MTCsp reference point

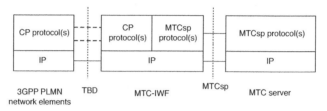

MTC Server-SMS SC MTCsms reference point

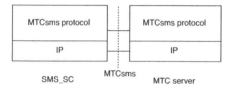

FIGURE 5.6 User and control plane stack for MTC architecture—as described in Release 11—Technical Report 3GPP TR 23.888 V1.7.0 (2012–08).

and fault tolerant communication via powerline in intelligent power supply grids. As the basis for the transmission protocol, which uses the low voltage network as a communication channel for data of grid sensors and smart meters, the transport profile has been designed to ensure interoperability in accordance with EU Mandate M/441. CENELEC TC 13 was planning to forward the CX1 transport profile to TC 57 of the International Electrotechnical Commission (IEC) as a proposal for inclusion in the IEC standardization process. CX1 is already used to connect meters and other intelligent terminal devices in Siemens' SG metering systems, such as in the load switching devices that will replace household ripple control receivers. The systems collect energy consumption data and network information, which are then relayed to a control center for further processing (15). CX1 utilizes spread spectrum modulation, in which multiple frequencies within the same frequency band are used simultaneously to transmit a single signal. This means that interference, which often occurs at certain frequencies, has only a negligible effect on signal transmission. In addition, the communication protocol can handle any change in the physical communication parameters of a low voltage power supply grid, such as signal attenuation, noise, network disruption and signal coupling, as well as operational changes in network configuration. The protocol can also be integrated into existing IEC protocol-based network automation and energy management infrastructures.

5.8 IETF IPv6 OVER LOWPOWER WPAN (6LoWPAN)

6LoWPAN is an IPv6 adaption layer for low power wireless PAN (LoWPAN).

IPv6-over-IEEE 802.15.4 described in RFC 4944 specifies how IPv6 is carried over an IEEE 802.15.4 network with the help of an adaptation layer which sits between the MAC layer and the IP network layer. As it should be clear at this juncture, a link in a LoWPAN is characterized as lossy, low power, low bit-rate, short range, with many nodes saving energy with long sleep periods.

It turns out that multicast as used in IPv6 ND described in RFC 4861 is not desirable in such a wireless low power and lossy network. Moreover, LoWPAN links are asymmetric and non-transitive in nature. A LoWPAN is potentially composed of a large number of overlapping radio ranges. Although a given radio range has broadcast capabilities, the aggregation of these is a complex non-broadcast multi-access (NBMA) structure with generally no LoWPAN-wide multicast capabilities. Link-local scope is in reality defined by reachability and radio strength. Thus, one can consider a LoWPAN to be made up of links with undetermined connectivity properties, along with the corresponding address model assumptions defined therein. Hence, there is work underway to develop optimizations to IPv6 ND (RFC 4861) specifically aimed at low power and lossy networks such as LoWPANs (16).

This topic is covered in Chapter 9, after the reader has acquired some background on IPv6.

5.9 ZigBee IP (ZIP)

ZigBee is a wireless PAN IEEE 802.15.4 standard, which we cover in Chapter 6. Here we simply make some passing reference to the ZigBee Alliance's ZIP standard, which is a first definition of an open standards-based IPv6 stack for smart objects. The goal is to extend the use of IP networking into resource-constrained devices over a wide range of low power link technologies. The effort related to ZIP development has made significant progress to bring IPv6 network protocols over 802.15.4 wireless mesh networks to reality. ZIP is a protocol stack based on IETF- and IEEE-defined standards such as 6LoWPAN and IEEE 802.15.4 to be used for the Smart Energy 2.0 (SE 2.0) profile.

ZIP enables low power 802.15.4 nodes to participate natively with other IPv6-enabled WiFi, Homeplug, and Ethernet nodes without the complexity and cost of application layer gateways. To accomplish this, the ZIP stack incorporates a number of standardized IETF protocols including 6LoWPAN for IP header compression and ND, and RPL for mesh routing. ZIP further employs other IETF standards to support network joining procedures, service discovery, and TLS/SSL-based security mechanisms (17). At press time, the ZIP specification was nearing release of its 0.9 draft and had already progressed through numerous certification events. In particular, there has been interest in validating that ZIP will comfortably support SEP2 unicast and multicast messaging over an 802.15.4-based HAN mesh. It was anticipated that production ready, certified stacks would be available mid-2013. Early implementers included Cisco, Exegin, and Grid2Home, among others. Proponents expect that ZIP-based product offerings would soon be interoperating within the SG.

5.10   IP IN SMART OBJECTS (IPSO)

The IPSO Alliance is an advocate for IP-networked devices for use in energy, consumer, healthcare, and industrial applications. The objective of the Alliance is not to define technologies or standards, but to document the use of IP-based technologies defined at the standard organizations such as IETF with focus on support by the Alliance of various use cases. The IPSO Alliance is a non-profit association of more than 60 members at press time from leading technology, communications, and energy companies around the world. The mission is to provide a foundation for industry growth through building stronger relationships, fostering awareness, providing education, promoting the industry, generating research, and creating a better understanding of IP and its role in connecting smart objects. Goals include (18):

- Promote IP as the premier solution for access and communication for smart objects.
- Promote the use of IP in smart objects by developing and publishing white papers and case studies and providing updates on standards progress from associations like IETF, among others, and through other supporting marketing activities.
- Understand the industries and markets where smart objects can have an effective role in growth when connected using the Internet protocol.
- Organize interoperability tests that will allow members and interested parties to show that products and services using IP for smart objects can work together and meet industry standards for communication.
- Support IETF and other standards development organizations in the development of standards for IP for smart objects.

APPENDIX 5.A: LEGACY SUPERVISORY CONTROL AND DATA ACQUISITION (SCADA) SYSTEMS

This appendix provides a short summary of SCADA, a legacy, but widely deployed system used to monitor and control a plant or equipment in industries such as but not limited to energy, oil and gas refining, water and waste control, transportation, and telecommunications. This section is summarized and synthesized from reference (19) from the National Communications System (NCS). M2M approaches seek to enhance, modernize, and extend the basic concepts found in SCADA (M2M is not intended to be directly interoperable with SCADA but can be supported with proxies/gateways.)

A SCADA system gathers remote operational information, transfers the information to a central site, then alerts a management station that an event has occurred, carrying out necessary analysis and control. These systems can be relatively simple, such as one that monitors environmental conditions of a small office building, or very complex, such as a system that monitors all the activity in a nuclear power plant or the activity of a municipal water system. Traditionally, SCADA systems have made use of public switched network (PSN) facilities for monitoring purposes; wireless technologies are now being widely deployed for purposes of monitoring.

A SCADA system encompasses the transfer of data between a SCADA central host computer and a number of remote terminal units (RTUs) and/or programmable logic controllers (PLCs); the central host typically supports operator terminals. Specifically, a SCADA system consists of:

- One or more field data interface devices, usually RTUs or PLCs, which interface to field sensing devices and local control switchboxes and actuators;
- A communications system used to transfer data between field data interface devices and control units and the computers in the SCADA central host; the communication may use telephone, cable, radio, cellular, satellite, etc. or any combination of these;
- A central host computer server or servers (sometimes called a SCADA center, master station, or master terminal unit [MTU]);
- A collection of standard and/or custom software systems [sometimes called human machine interface (HMI) software or man machine interface (MMI) software] used to provide the SCADA central host and operator terminal application, support the communications system, and monitor and control remotely located field data interface devices.

There have been three generations of SCADA systems:

- First generation—monolithic approach
- Second generation—distributed approach
- Third generation—networked approach

In a SCADA system, the RTU accepts commands to operate control points, sets analog output levels, and responds to requests. The RTU provides status, as well as discrete and accumulated data to the SCADA master station. The data representations sent are not identified in any fashion other than by unique addressing. The addressing is designed to correlate with the SCADA master station database. The RTU has no knowledge of which unique parameters it is monitoring in the real world; it simply monitors certain points and stores the information in a local addressing scheme. Each protocol consists of two message sets or pairs. One set forms the master protocol, containing the valid statements for master station initiation or response, and the other set is the RTU protocol, containing the valid statements an RTU can initiate and respond to. In most but not all cases, these pairs can be considered a poll or request for information or action and a confirming response. The SCADA protocol between master and RTU forms a viable model for RTU-to-intelligent electronic device (IED) communications. Currently, there are several different protocols in use; the most common are:

- IEC 60870-5 series, specifically IEC 60870-5-101 (commonly referred to as 101) and
- Distributed network protocol version 3 (DNP3).

IEC 60870-5 Series

IEC 60870-5 specifies a number of frame formats and services that may be provided at different layers. IEC 60870-5 is based on a three-layer enhanced performance architecture (EPA) reference model (see Fig. 5A.1) for efficient implementation within RTUs, meters, relays, and other IEDs. Additionally, IEC 60870-5 defines basic application functionality for a user layer; such user layer is situated between the open system interconnection (OSI) application layer and the application program. This user layer adds interoperability for such functions as clock synchronization and file transfers.

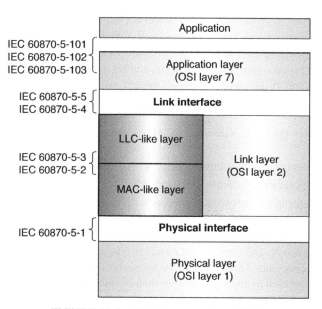

FIGURE 5A.1   SCADA protocols and EPA.

The following descriptions provide the basic scope of each of the five documents in the base IEC 60870-5 telecontrol transmission protocol specification set. Standard profiles are necessary for uniform application of the IEC 60870-5 standards. A profile is a set of parameters defining the way a device acts; such profiles have been created.

- IEC 60870-5-1 (1990–02) specifies the basic requirements for services to be provided by the data link and physical layers for telecontrol applications. In particular, it specifies standards on coding, formatting, and synchronizing data frames of variable and fixed lengths that meet specified data integrity requirements. At the physical layer, the Standard 101 Profile additionally allows the selection of International Telecommunication Union-Telecommunication Standardization Sector (ITU-T) standards that are compatible with Electronic Industries Association (EIA) standards RS-232 and RS-485 and also support fiber optics interfaces.
- IEC-60870-5-2 (1992–04) provides a selection of link transmission procedures using a control field and optional address field; the address field is optional because some point-to-point topologies do not require either source or destination addressing.
- IEC 60870-5-3 (1992–09) specifies rules for structuring application data units in transmission frames of telecontrol systems. These rules are presented as generic standards that may be used to support a variety of present and future telecontrol applications. This section of IEC 60870-5 describes the general structure of application data and basic rules to specify application data units without specifying details about information fields and their contents.
- IEC 60870-5-4 (1993–08) provides rules for defining information data elements and a common set of information elements, particularly digital and analog process variables that are frequently used in telecontrol applications.
- IEC 60870-5-5 (1995–06) defines basic application functions that perform standard procedures for telecontrol systems, which are procedures that reside beyond layer 7 (application layer) of the ISO reference model. These utilize standard services of the application layer. The specifications in IEC 60870-5-5 (1995–06) serve as basic standards for application profiles that are then created in detail for specific telecontrol tasks.

DNP3

DNP3 is a protocol for transmission of point-to-point data using serial communications. It has been used primarily by utilities, but can also be used in other areas. The DNP3 is specifically developed for interdevice communication involving SCADA RTUs and provides for both RTU-to-IED and master-to-RTU/IED. It is based on the three-layer EPA model contained in the IEC 60870-5 standards, with some alterations to meet additional requirements of a variety of users in the electric utility industry. DNP3 was developed with the following goals in mind:

- High data integrity. The DNP3 data link layer uses a variation of the IEC 60870-5-1 (1990–02) frame format FT3. Both data link layer frames and application layer messages may be transmitted using confirmed service.
- Flexible structure. The DNP3 application layer is object based, with a structure that allows a range of implementations while retaining interoperability.
- Multiple applications. DNP3 can be used in several modes, including: (i) polled only; (ii) polled report-by-exception; (iii) unsolicited report-by-exception (quiescent mode); and (iv) a mixture of modes. It can also be used with several physical layers, and as a layered protocol it is suitable for operation over local and some wide area networks.
- Minimized overhead. DNP3 was designed for existing wire-pair data links with operating bit rates as low as 1200 bps and attempts to use a minimum of overhead while retaining flexibility. Selection of a data reporting method, such as report-by-exception, further reduces overhead.
- Open standard. DNP3 is a non-proprietary, evolving standard controlled by a users group whose members include RTU, IED, and master station vendors, and representatives of the electric utility and system consulting community.

REFERENCES

1. Gluhak A, Krco S, et al. A survey on facilities for experimental internet of things research. Communications Magazine, IEEE, November 2011;49(11):58–67.
2. Ladid L. Keynote Speech, International Workshop on Extending Seamlessly to the Internet of Things (ESLOT 2012), in conjunction with IMIS-2012 International Conference, July 4–6, 2012, Palermo, Italy.
3. Arkko J. Interoperability Challenges in the Internet of Things. Interconnecting Smart Objects with the Internet Workshop 2011, 25th March 2011, Prague.
4. Internet Architecture Board, Interconnecting Smart Objects with the Internet Workshop 2011, 25th March 2011, Prague.
5. Kutscher D, Farrell S. Towards an Information-Centric Internet with more Things. Interconnecting Smart Objects with the Internet Workshop 2011, 25th March 2011, Prague.
6. Winter T, editor. ROLL/RPL: IPv6 Routing Protocol for Low Power and Lossy Networks, March 2011, draft-ietf-roll-rpl-19.
7. Kuryla S. RPL: IPv6 Routing Protocol for Low Power and Lossy Networks, Networks and Distributed Systems Seminar, March 1, 2010.
8. Shelby Z, Hartke K, Bormann C, Frank B. Constrained Application Protocol (CoAP). CoRE Working Group, March 12, 2012, Internet-Draft, draft-ietf-core-coap-09.
9. Richardson L, Ruby S. RESTful Web Service, O'Reilly Media, 2007, Sebastopol, CA.
10. Kay R. QuickStudy: Representational State Transfer (REST). ComputerWorld, August 6, 2007.

11. Lin T-M. M2M: Machine to Machine Communication (From ETSI/3GPP Aspect). White Paper, Industrial Technology Research Institute of Taiwan, R.O.C, 2010.

12. 3rd Generation Partnership Project, Technical Specification Group Services and System Aspects; Service Requirements for Machine Type Communications (MTC); Stage 1 (Release 10); Technical Specification 3GPP TS 22.368 V10.1.0 (2010–06).

13. 3rd Generation Partnership Project, Technical Specification Group Services and System Aspects; System Improvements for Machine-Type Communications; Stage 1 (Release 11); Technical Report 3GPP TR 23.888 V1.7.0 (2012–08).

14. Norp T. Mobile Network Improvements for M2M, a 3GPP Perspective. ETSI M2M Workshop, October 2011. TNO, P.O. Box 342, NL-7300 AH Apeldoorn.

15. Mrosik J. International PLC data communication standard for grid automation and smart metering proposed by Siemens. On line Magazine, Nov 15, 2012, http://www. metering .com.

16. Shelby Z, editor. Neighbor Discovery Optimization for Low Power and Lossy Networks (6LoWPAN), Updates: 4944 (if approved), August 24, 2012, IETF draft-ietf-6lowpan-nd-21.

17. Duffy P. Zigbee IP: Extending the Smart Grid to Consumers., Cisco Blog – The Platform, June 4, 2012, Cisco Systems, Inc., 170 West Tasman Dr., San Jose, CA 95134 USA.

18. IPSO Alliance, http://www.ipso-alliance.org/.

19. National Communications System, Supervisory Control and Data Acquisition (SCADA) Systems, Technical Information Bulletin 04-1, NCS TIB 04-1, October 2004, P.O. Box 4052, Arlington, VA 22204-4052. http://www.ncs.gov.

CHAPTER 6

LAYER 1/2 CONNECTIVITY: WIRELESS TECHNOLOGIES FOR THE IoT

This chapter surveys basic lower-layer wireless technologies to support IoT/machine-to-machine (M2M) applications, as it appears that many such implementations will entail wireless connectivity at the PHY/MAC layer. Available wireless networks[1] that can be utilized for IoT/M2M applications include the following:

- Personal area networks (PANs): Zigbee®, Bluetooth®, especially Bluetooth low energy (BLE), near field communications (NFC), and proprietary systems (e.g., ANT+,[2] NIKE+[3]); specifically, there is interest in low-power wireless personal area networks (LoWPANs); some of these PANs are also classified as low-rate wireless personal area networks (LR-WPANs);

---

[1] Some refer to the entire "wireless networks" field as wireless information and communication technology (WICT).

[2] ANT/ANT+ is a proprietary wireless sensor network technology targeted at manufacturers of bike computers, speed/cadence sensors, foot pods, power meters, heart rate monitors, calorimeters, body mass index-measuring devices, blood pressure monitors, blood glucose meters, and so on, promoted by the ANT+ Alliance. It is principally used for compatible Garmin device. For example, an ANT+ heart rate strap will send heart rate data to a watch, phone, bike computer, tablet, and/or any other device that reads ANT+ heart rate.

[3] Nike+® is a proprietary wireless technology developed by Nike and Apple to allow users to monitor their activity levels while exercising.

Building the Internet of Things with IPv6 and MIPv6: The Evolving World of M2M Communications, First Edition. Daniel Minoli.
© 2013 John Wiley & Sons, Inc. Published 2013 by John Wiley & Sons, Inc.

- Wireless local area networks (WLANs): Wi-Fi® IEEE Standard 802.11 (including vendor-specific implementations for low power[4]);
- Metropolitan area networks (MANs): WiMAX;
- Wireless sensor networks (WSN): application-specific technology, in general;
- Third generation (3G)/4G cellular: Universal mobile telecommunications system (UMTS), general packet radio service (GPRS), enhanced data rates (EDRs) for GSM evolution (EDGE), and long-term evolution (LTE); and,
- Global: Satellite networks.

While IoT/M2M connectivity might be achieved by wired means, for example power line communication (PLC)-based grid management, some operators have used wireless technology for meter reading. Furthermore, although energy suppliers routinely utilize supervisory control and data acquisition (SCADA)-based systems to enable remote telemetry functions in the power grid and, and although, traditionally, SCADA systems have used wireline networks to link remote power grid elements with a central operations center, at this time an increasing number of utilities are turning to public cellular networks to support these functions. Some of the wireline technologies, including PLC, are briefly discussed in the appendix to this chapter.

6.1 WPAN TECHNOLOGIES FOR IoT/M2M

A PAN (also called WPAN) is a network used for communication among intelligent devices physically close to a person (including smartphones, tablets, body monitors, and so on). PANs can be used to support wireless body area networks (WBANs) (also known as wireless medical body area networks [WMBANs] and/or medical body area network systems [MBANSs]), but they can also be used to support other applications. As discussed in Chapter 3, Medical applications include, among others, vital sign monitoring, respiration monitoring, electrocardiography (ECG), pH monitoring, glucose monitoring, disability assistance, muscle tension monitoring, and artificial limb support. Nonmedical applications of WBANs include, among others, video streaming, data transfer, and entertainment and gaming. The reach of a PAN is typically a few meters. The devices in question are sometimes known as short-range devices (SRDs) (1). PANs can be used for communication among the personal devices themselves (intrapersonal communication), or for connecting to a higher level network such as the Internet. Table 6.1 (partially based on Reference 2) summarizes a coarse comparison between three wireless technologies, highlighting the features of BANs/WBANs. The WBAN technologies can satisfy, in various degrees, major requirements that the healthcare industry considers important: (i) very low-power

---

[4]In recent years, several improvements have been made to the Wi-Fi LAN standard; some of these improvements (including IEEE Standard 802.11v) are aimed at reducing its power consumption. Wi-Fi is optimized for traditional office automation (OA) large data transfer, where high throughput is needed; it is not generally intended for coin cell operation.

TABLE 6.1 Comparison of Technologies

	WBAN	WSN	Cellular Wireless Networks
Traffic	Application specific, sporadic/cyclic, modest data rate		Multimedia, high data rate
Topology	Dynamic	Random, dynamic	Few infrastructure changes
Configuration/ maintenance	Some flexibility Specialists are needed	Self-configurable, unattended operation	Managed by large organizations/ carriers
Battery	Multimonth to multiyear battery life		Replaced as needed
Network size	Dense distribution limited by body size	Unlimited number (typically 10^2–10^6)	Tens of nodes
Node	Low/modest complexity		High complexity
Overall design goals	Limited electromagnetic exposure, energy efficiency	Energy efficiency, self-operability cost optimization	Bandwidth efficiency. QoS (throughput/ delay)
Standardization	Multiple (IEEE) standards especially at lower layers	Relatively little standardization	Multiple international standards, ITU-T, ETSI, etc.

sensor consumption, (ii) very low transmitted power, and (iii) high reliability and quality of service (QoS).

Focusing specifically on WBANs, the key wireless standards include ZigBee/IEEE 802.15.4 along with the Personal, Home and Hospital Care (PHHC) Profile—ZigBee Health Care, IEEE 802.15.1 (Bluetooth), and the newer IEEE 802.15.6 and IEEE 802.15.4j; other standards include ISO/IEEE 11073 and ETSI TR 101 557 V1.1.1 (2012–02). Note that both ZigBee and Bluetooth have been extended and modified in recent years to satisfy particular requirements of medical/fitness industries (3). Low-power consumption IEEE 802.11 Wi-Fi is considered generally less attractive at this time, although some proponents argue in favor.[5]

In this chapter, we focus predominantly on PANs and 3G/4G technologies. See Table 6.2 for a tabulation of some important technologies. It is not the goal of this

---

[5]Proponents make the case that no other wireless technology is as IP friendly as Wi-Fi. For example, ZigBee IP that requires the use of a bridge. ZigBee may have lower node costs, but it requires new infrastructure. Wi-Fi also provides the highest bandwidth of any wireless technologies—some low-power implementations provide up to 11 Mbps, with a fallback to 1 Mbps. ZigBee offers less than 250 Kbps, with no fallback. Wi-Fi also provides well-proven encryption, authentication, and end-to-end network security (WPA2, EAP, TLS/SSL); ZigBee still requires testing, since some security holes have been identified (4). On the other hand, Wi-Fi's power requirements are high. Work is being conducted in Wi-Fi groups to lower power consumption. Currently, however, proprietary drivers are needed, with the technology only applicable to the personal computer market where receiver power budgets are higher (5).

TABLE 6.2   Key Wireless Technology and Concepts Supporting IoT/M2M Applications

Technology/Concept	Description
3GPP	3GPP unites six telecommunications standard bodies, known as "organizational partners" and provides their members with a stable environment to produce the reports and specifications that define 3GPP technologies. These technologies are constantly evolving through—what have become known as—generations of commercial cellular/mobile systems. 3GPP was originally the standards partnership evolving Global System for Mobile communication (GSM) systems toward the 3G. However, since the completion of the first LTE and the Evolve Packet Core (EPC) specifications, 3GPP has become the focal point for mobile systems beyond 3G. From 3GPP Release 10 onward, 3GPP is compliant with the latest ITU-R requirements for IMT-Advanced "Systems beyond 3G." The standard now allows for operation at speeds up to100 Mbps for high-mobility and 1 Gbps for low-mobility communication. The original scope of 3GPP was to produce Technical Specifications and Technical Reports for a 3G Mobile System based on evolved GSM CNs and the radio access technologies that they support (i.e., Universal Terrestrial Radio Access (UTRA) both frequency division duplex [FDD] and time division duplex [TDD] modes). The scope was subsequently amended to include the maintenance and development of the GSM Technical Specifications and Technical Reports including evolved radio access technologies (e.g. GPRS and EDGE) (6). The term "3GPP specification" covers all GSM (including GPRS and EDGE), W-CDMA, and LTE (including LTE-Advanced) specifications. The following terms are also used to describe networks using the 3G specifications: UTRAN, UMTS (in Europe), and FOMA (in Japan)
3GPP2 (Third-Generation Partnership Project 2)	3GPP2 is a collaborative 3G telecommunications specification-setting project comprising North American and Asian interests developing global specifications for ANSI/TIA/EIA-41 Cellular Radiotelecommunication Intersystem Operations network evolution to 3G and global specifications for the radio transmission technologies (RTTs) supported by ANSI/TIA/EIA-41. 3GPP2 was born out of the International Telecommunication Union's (ITU) International Mobile Telecommunications "IMT-2000" initiative, covering HS, broadband, and Internet protocol (IP)-based mobile systems featuring network-to-network interconnection, feature/service transparency, global roaming, and seamless services independent of location (7)

(continued)

TABLE 6.2   *(Continued)*

Technology/Concept	Description
6LoWPAN: IPv6 over low-power area networks (IEEE 802.15.4)	6LoWPAN is now a widely accepted approach to run IP on 802.15.4 based on RFC 4944 (September 2007). It is supported in TinyOS, Contiki, and in standards such as ISA100, ZigBee SE 2.0. RFC 4944 makes 802.15.4 look like an IPv6 link. It provides basic encapsulation, efficient representation of packets $< \sim 100$ bytes. It addresses topics such as (8): • Fragmentation (how to map 1280-byte MTU to packets 128 bytes or less); • First approach to stateless header compression; • Datagram tag/datagram offset; • Mesh forwarding; • Identify originator/final destination; • Minimal use of complex MAC layer concepts
ANT/ANT+	ANT^{TM} is a low-power proprietary wireless technology introduced in 2004 by the sensor company Dynastream. The system operates in the 2.4 GHz band. ANT devices can operate for years on a coin cell. ANT's goal is to allow sports and fitness sensors to communicate with a display unit. ANT+^{TM} extends the ANT protocol and makes the devices interoperable in a managed network. ANT+ recently introduced a new certification process as a prerequisite for using ANT+ branding (5)
Bluetooth	Bluetooth is a PAN technology based on IEEE 802.15.1. It is a specification for short-range wireless connectivity for portable personal devices initially developed by Ericsson. The Bluetooth SIG made their specifications publicly available in the late 1990s, at which time the IEEE 802.15 Group has took the Bluetooth work and developed a vendor-independent standard. The sublayers of IEEE 802.15:include: (i) RF layer; (ii) baseband layer; (iii) the link manager; and (iv) the L2CAP. Bluetooth has evolved through four versions; all versions of the Bluetooth standards maintain downward compatibility. BLE is a subset to Bluetooth v4.0 with an entirely new protocol stack for rapid build-up of simple links. BLE is an alternative to the "power management" features that were introduced in Bluetooth v1.0 to v3.0 as part of the standard Bluetooth protocols (Bluetooth is a trademark of the Bluetooth Alliance, a commercial organization that certifies the interoperability of specific devices designed to the respective IEEE standard.)

TABLE 6.2 *(Continued)*

Technology/Concept	Description
EDGE (Enhanced Data Rates for Global Evolution)	An enhancement of the GSM™ radio access technology to provide faster bit rates for data applications, both circuit and packet switched. As an enhancement of the existing GSM PHY layer, EDGE is realized via modifications of the existing layer 1 specifications rather than by separate, standalone specifications. Other than providing improved data rates, EDGE is transparent to the service offering at the upper layers, but is an enabler for HS circuit switched data (HSCSD) and enhanced GPRS (EGPRS). By way of illustration, the GPRS can offer a data rate of 115 Kbps, whereas EDGE can increase this to 384 Kbps. This is comparable with the rate for early implementations of Wideband Code Division Multiple Access (W-CDMA), leading some parties to consider EDGE as a 3G technology rather than 2G (a capability of 384 Kbps allows EDGE systems to meet the ITU's IMT-2000 requirements). EDGE is generally viewed as a bridge between the two generations: a sort of 2.5G (9)
DASH7	A long range low-power wireless networking technology, with the following features: • Range: dynamically adjustable from 10 m to 10 km • Power: <1 milliwatt power draw • Data rate: dynamically adjustable from 28 Kbps to 200 Kbps • Frequency: 433.92 MHz (available worldwide) • Signal propagation: penetrates walls, concrete, water • Real-time locating precision: within 4 m • Latency: configurable, but worst case is less than 2 s • P2P cessaging • IPv6 support • Security: 128-bit AES, public key • Standard: ISO/IEC 18000-7; advanced by the DASH7 Alliance
GPRS (General Packet Radio Service)	Packet-switched functionality for GSM, which is essentially circuit switched. GPRS is the essential enabler for always-on data connection for applications such as web browsing and push-to-talk over cellular. GPRS was introduced into the GSM specifications in Release 97 and usability was further approved in Releases 98 and 99. It offers faster data rates than plain GSM by aggregating several GSM time slots into a single bearer, potentially up to eight, giving a theoretical data rate of 171 Kbps. Most operators do not offer such high rates, because obviously if a slot is being used for a GPRS bearer, it is not available for other traffic. Also, not all mobiles are able to aggregate all combinations of slots.

(continued)

TABLE 6.2 *(Continued)*

Technology/Concept	Description
	The "GPRS class number" indicates the maximum speed capability of a terminal, which might be typically 14 Kbps in the uplink direction and 40 Kbps in the downlink, comparable with the rates offered by current wireline dial-up modems. Mobile terminals are further classified according to whether or not they can handle simultaneous GSM and GPRS connections: class A = both simultaneously, class B = GPRS connection interrupted during a GSM call, automatically resumed at end of call, class C = manual GSM/GPRS mode switching. Further data rate increases have been achieved with the introduction of EDGE (9)
GSM EDGE Radio Access Network (GERAN)	GERAN is an Radio Access Network (RAN) architecture, based on GSM/EDGE radio access technologies. GERAN is the term given to the second generation digital cellular GSM radio access technology, including its evolutions in the form of EDGE and, for most purposes, the GPRS. The GERAN is harmonized with the UTRAN through a common connectivity to the UMTS CN, making it possible to build a combined network for GSM/GPRS and UMTS. GERAN is also the name of the 3GPP™ Technical Specification Group responsible for its development. The technical specifications which together comprise a 3GPP system with a GERAN are listed in 3GPP TS 41.101
IEEE 802.15.4	IEEE Standard for Local and MANs. Part 15.4: *Low-Rate Wireless Personal Area Networks (LR-WPANs)*. IEEE 802.15.4-conformant devices support a wide range of industrial and commercial applications. The amended MAC sublayer facilitates industrial applications such as process control and factory automation in addition to the MAC behaviors that support the Chinese wireless personal area network (CWPAN) standard
IEEE 802.15.4j (TG4j) MBANs	The purpose of Task Group 4j (TG4j) is to create an amendment to 802.15.4, which defines a PHY layer for IEEE 802.15.4 in the 2360 to 2400 MHz band and complies with FCC MBAN rules. The amendment may also define modifications to the MAC needed to support this new PHY layer. This amendment allows 802.15.4- and MAC-defined changes to be used in the MBAN band (10)
Infrared Data Association (IrDA®)	IrDA is an SIG consisting of about 40 members at press time. The SIG is pursuing a 1 Gbps connectivity link; however, this link only operates over a distance of less than 10 cm. One of the challenges with IR signaling is its requirement for LOS requirement. Additionally, IrDA is also not very power efficient (power per bit) when compared with radio technologies

TABLE 6.2 *(Continued)*

Technology/Concept	Description
ISA100.11a	ISA SP100 standard for wireless industrial networks developed by the International Society of Automation (ISA) to address all aspects of wireless technologies in a plant. The ISA100 Committee addresses wireless manufacturing and control systems in the areas of the: (i) environment in which the wireless technology is deployed; (ii) technology and life cycle for wireless equipment and systems; and (iii) application of wireless technology. The wireless environment includes the definition of wireless, radio frequencies (starting point), vibration, temperature, humidity, electromagnetic compatibility (EMC), interoperability, coexistence with existing systems, and physical equipment location. ISA100.11a Working Group Charter addresses (11): <ul><li>Low-energy consumption devices, with the ability to scale to address large installations</li><li>Wireless infrastructure, interfaces to legacy infrastructure and applications, security, and network management requirements in a functionally scalable manner</li><li>Robustness in the presence of interference found in harsh industrial environments and with legacy systems</li><li>Coexistence with other wireless devices anticipated in the industrial work space</li><li>Interoperability of ISA100 devices</li></ul>
LTE (Long Term Evolution)	LTE is the 3GPP initiative to evolve the UMTS technology toward a 4G. LTE can be viewed as an architecture framework and a set of ancillary mechanisms that aim at providing seamless IP connectivity between UE and the packet (IPv4, IPv6) data network without any disruption to the end-users' applications during mobility. In contrast to the circuit-switched model of previous-generation cellular systems, LTE has been designed to support *only* packet-switched services
NFC (Near Field Communication)	A group of standards for devices such as PDAs, smartphones, and tablets that support the establishment of wireless communication when such devices are in immediate proximity of a few inches. These standards encompass communications protocols and data exchange formats; they are based on existing RFID standards including ISO/IEC 14443 and FeliCa (a contactless RFID smart card system developed by Sony, e.g., utilized in electronic money cards in use in Japan). NFC standards include ISO/IEC 18092, as well as other standards defined by the NFC Forum. NFC standards allow two-way communication between endpoints (earlier generation systems were one-way systems only). Unpowered NFC-based tags can also be read by NFC devices; therefore, this technology can substitute for earlier one-way systems. Applications of NFC include contactless transactions

(continued)

TABLE 6.2   (*Continued*)

Technology/Concept	Description
NIKE+	Nike+® is a proprietary wireless technology developed by Nike and Apple to allow users to monitor their activity levels while exercising. Its power consumption is relatively high, returning only 40 days of battery life from a coin cell. It is a proprietary radio that only works between Nike and Apple devices. Nike+ devices are shipped as a single unit: processor, radio, and sensor (5)
RF4CE (Radio Frequency for Consumer Electronics)	RF4CE is based on ZigBee and was standardized in 2009 by four CE companies: Sony, Philips, Panasonic, and Samsung. Two silicon vendors support RF4CE: Texas Instruments and Freescale Semiconductor, Inc. RF4CE's intended use is as a device RC system, for example for television set-top boxes. The intention is that it overcomes the common problems associated with IR: interoperability, line of sight, and limited enhanced features (5)
Satellite systems	Satellite communication plays a key role in commercial, TV/media, government, and military communications because of its intrinsic multicast/broadcast capabilities, mobility aspects, global reach, reliability, and ability to quickly support connectivity in open-space and/or hostile environments. Satellite communications is a LOS one-way or two-way RF transmission system that is comprised of a transmitting station (uplink), a satellite system that acts as a signal regeneration node, and one or more receiving stations (downlink). Satellites can reside in a number of orbits. A geosynchronous (GEO) satellite circles the earth at the earth's rotational speed and with the same direction of rotation, therefore appearing at the same position in the sky at a particular time each day. When the satellite is in the equatorial plane, it appears to be permanently stationary when observed at the earth's surface, so that an antenna pointed to it will not require tracking or (major) positional adjustments at periodic intervals of time (this satellite arrangement is also known as "geostationary"). The geostationary orbit is at 35,786 km (22,236 mi) of altitude from the earth's surface. Other orbits include the following: low earth orbits (LEOs), medium earth orbits (MEOs) (aka intermediate circular orbits [ICOs]), polar orbits, and highly elliptical orbits (HEOs). LEOs are either elliptical or (more commonly) circular orbits that are at a height of 2000 km or less above the surface of the earth. The advantage of LEOs is that they significantly reduce the propagation delay of the signal. The orbit period at these altitudes varies between 90 min and 2 h and the maximum time during which a satellite in LEO orbit is above the local horizon for an observer on the earth is up to 20 min.

TABLE 6.2   (*Continued*)

Technology/Concept	Description
	With LEOs, there are long periods during which a given satellite is out of view of a particular ground station; this may be acceptable for some applications, for example, for earth monitoring. Coverage can be extended by deploying more than one satellite and using multiple orbital planes. A complete global coverage system using LEO orbits requires a large number of satellites ($>12+$), in multiple orbital planes, and in various orbits. See Reference 12 for extensive treatment of this topic
UTRAN (UMTS Terrestrial Access Network)	A collective term for the NodeBs (base stations) and radio network controllers (RNCs) that comprise the UMTS RAN. NodeB is the equivalent to the BTS concept used in GSM. The UTRAN allows connectivity between the UE and the CN
UMTS (Universal Mobile Telecommunications System)	UMTS is a 3G mobile cellular technology for networks supporting voice and data (IP) based on the GSM standard developed by the 3GPP
Very small aperture terminal (VSAT)	A complete end-user terminal (typically with a small 4–5 ft antenna) that is designed to interact with other terminals in a satellite delivered data IP-based network, commonly in a "star" configuration through a hub. Contention and/or traffic engineering are typical of these services. Hub or network operator to control the system and present billing based on a data throughput, or other form of usage basis. VSATs are utilized in a variety of remote applications and are designed as low-cost units (say \$1500–\$3000 depending on application and data rate)
Wi-Fi	WLANs based on the IEEE 802.11 family of standards, including 802.11a, 802.11b, 802.11g, and 802.11n (13). (Wi-Fi is a trademark of the Wi-Fi Alliance, a commercial organization that certifies the interoperability of specific devices designed to the respective IEEE standard.)
WiMAX	WiMAX is defined as Worldwide Interoperability for Microwave Access by the WiMAX Forum, formed in June 2001 to promote conformance and interoperability of the IEEE 802.16 standard. The WiMAX Forum describes WiMAX as "a standards-based technology enabling the delivery of last mile wireless broadband access as an alternative to cable and DSL." (53)
Wireless Meter-Bus (M-Bus)	The Wireless M-Bus standard (EN 13757–4:2005) specifies communications between water, gas, heat, and electric meters and is becoming widely accepted in Europe for smart metering or AMI applications. Wireless M-Bus is targeted to operate in the 868 MHz band (from 868 MHz to 870 MHz); this band enjoys good trade-offs between RF range and antenna size. Typically chip manufacturers, for example Texas Instruments, have both single-chip (SoC) and two-chip solutions for Wireless M-Bus

(*continued*)

TABLE 6.2   (*Continued*)

Technology/Concept	Description
WSN (Wireless Sensor Network)	A sensor network is an infrastructure comprised of sensing (measuring), computing, and communication elements that gives the administrator the ability to instrument, observe, and react to events and phenomena in a specified environment. Typically, the connectivity is by wireless means, hence the term WSN. See reference (14) for an extensive treatment of this topic
WirelessHART (aka IEC 62591)	WirelessHART is a wireless sensor networking technology based on the highway addressable remote transducer protocol (HART). In 2010, WirelessHart was approved by the International Electrotechnical Commission (IEC) as IEC 62591 as a wireless international standard. IEC 62591 entails operation in the 2.4 GHz ISM band using IEEE 802.15.4 standard radios and makes use of a time-synchronized, self-organizing, and self-healing mesh architecture. WirelessHART/IEC 62591 was defined for the requirements of process field device networks. It is a global IEC-approved standard that specifies an interoperable self-organizing mesh technology in which field devices form wireless networks that dynamically mitigate obstacles in the process environment. This architecture creates a cost-effective automation alternative that does not require wiring and other supporting infrastructure (15)
ZigBee RF4CE specification	The specialty-use driven specification was designed for simple, two-way device-to-device control applications that do not require the full-featured mesh networking capabilities offered by ZigBee 2007. ZigBee RF4CE offers lower memory size requirements, thereby enabling lower cost implementations. The simple device-to-device topology provides easy development and testing, resulting in faster time to market. ZigBee RF4CE provides a multivendor interoperable solution for consumer electronics featuring a simple, robust, and low-cost communication network for two-way wireless connectivity. Through the ZigBee Certified program, the Alliance independently tests platforms implementing this specification and has a list of ZigBee Compliant Platforms offering support for ZigBee RF4CE (16)
ZigBee specification	The core ZigBee specification defines ZigBee's smart, cost-effective, and energy-efficient mesh network based on IEEE 802.15.4. It is a self-configuring, self-healing system of redundant, low-cost, very low-power nodes that enable ZigBee's unique flexibility, mobility, and ease of use. ZigBee is available as two feature sets, ZigBee PRO and ZigBee. Both feature sets define how the ZigBee mesh networks operate. ZigBee PRO, the most widely used specification, is optimized for low-power consumption and to support large networks with thousands of devices (16). (ZigBee is a trademark of the ZigBee Alliance, a commercial organization that certifies the interoperability of specific devices designed to the respective IEEE standard.)

(*continued*)

TABLE 6.2   (*Continued*)

Technology/Concept	Description
Z-wave	Z-wave is a wireless ecosystem that aims at supporting connectivity of home electronics, and the user, via Remote Control (RC). It uses low-power radio waves that easily travel through walls, floors, and cabinets. Z-wave control can be added to almost any electronic device in the home, even devices that one would not ordinarily think of as "intelligent," such as appliances, window shades, thermostats, smoke alarms, security sensors, and home lighting. Z-wave operates around 900 MHz (the band used by some cordless telephones but avoids interference with Wi-Fi devices). Z-wave was developed by Zen-Sys, a Danish startup around 2005; the company was later acquired by Sigma Designs. The Z-wave Alliance was established in 2005; it is comprised of about 200 industry leaders dedicated to the development and extension of Z-wave as the key enabling technology for "smart" home and business applications

chapter to provide an in-depth technical review of all these technologies, since each would require a text of its own, but the goal is to expose the reader to a plethora of available choices (furthermore, we are not attempting to exhaustively list all possibly applicable wireless or wireline standards, but to focus on a handful of key ones).

The following network topologies are applicable to personal low-power radio networks (5) (also see Table 6.3):

- **Broadcast:** environment where a message is sent from a device in the hope that it is received by a receiver within range. The broadcaster does not receive signals;
- **Mesh:** environment where a message can be relayed from one point in a network to any other by hopping through multiple nodes;
- **Star:** environment where a central device can communicate with a number of connected devices;
- **Scanning:** environment where a scanning device is constantly in receive mode, waiting to pick up a signal from anything transmitting within range;
- **Point-to-point:** in this mode, a one-to-one connection exists, where only two devices are connected over the communication path.

6.1.1 Zigbee/IEEE 802.15.4

As we have seen, the commercialization of consumer-based IoT services requires the introduction of wireless, low-power, battery-powered sensors and actuators in people's premises. Until recently, this space has been comprised of several PHY/MAC-specific nonstandardized protocol stacks that do not interoperate. ZigBee's focus has been aimed at the "little devices" (things, objects) often overlooked in an IT-centric

TABLE 6.3 Topologies Supported by PAN Wireless Technologies

		ZigBee	RF4CE	BLE	Wi-Fi	NFC	ANT/ANT+	NIKE+	IrDA
Topology	Broadcast	No	No	Yes	No	No	Yes	No	No
	Mesh	Yes	Yes	Yes	No	No	Yes	No	No
	Point-to-point	Yes	Yes	Yes	Yes	Yes	Yes	Yes	Yes
	Scanning	Yes	Yes	Yes	No	No	Yes	Yes	No
	Star	Yes	Yes	Yes	Yes	No	Yes	No	No
Technology aspects	Range	100 m	100 m	280 m	150 m	5 cm	30 m	10 m	10 cm
	Processor costs	N/A	N/A	N/A	High cost	High cost	Low cost	Low cost	N/A
	Radio cost	Low cost	Low cost	Low cost	High cost (~$3)	High cost (~$1)	Very low cost	Very low cost	Very low cost
	Throughput	~100 Kbps	(same as ZigBee)	~305 Kbps	~6 Mbps (lowest power 802.11b mode)	~424 Kbps	~20 Kbps	~272 bps	~1 Gbps
	Latency	~20 ms	(same as ZigBee)	~2.5 ms	~1.5 ms	Manufacturer specific (typically polled every second)	~Zero	~1 s	~25 ms
	Peak current draw (manganese dioxide lithium coin batteries such as the CR2032)	~40 mA	(same as ZigBee)	~12.5 mA	>100 mA	~50 mA	~17 mA	~12.3 mA	~10.2 mA
	Power per bit	185.9 µW/bit	(same as ZigBee)	0.153 µW/bit	0.00525 µW/bit for high throughput	NA	0.71 µW/bit	2.48 µW/bit	11.7 µW/bit

Note 1: ANT/ANT+, NIKE+, and IrDA systems are only cited in passing in this chapter.
Note 2: Some parameters included here are based on data derived in Reference 5.

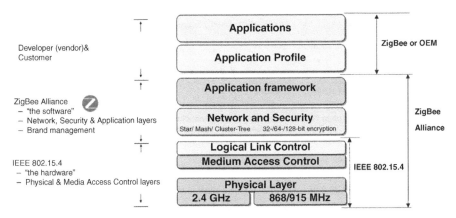

FIGURE 6.1   ZigBee protocol stack (overview).

world, such as light switches, thermostats, electricity meters, remote controls (RCs), as well as more complex sensor devices found in the healthcare, commercial building, and industrial automation sectors (17). To avoid multiple separate consumer networks, a PHY/MAC-agnostic solution is needed upon which IP standards and other well-known higher-layer protocols can run with little changes (18). ZigBee is one such open standard, as discussed below. ZigBee IP (ZIP) discussed in Chapter 5 is an example where Zigbee systems operate in an IP context. Here we focus more on the wireless lower-layer aspects of Zigbee and not the IP part *per se*.

ZigBee makes use of the physical radio specified by IEEE 802.15.4; it adds logical network capabilities, and security and application software. Figure 6.1 depicts the ZigBee protocol stack at a general level and Figure 6.2 depicts the stack at a more specific level. ZigBee utilizes the globally available, license-free 2.4 GHz industrial, scientific, and medical (ISM) frequency band to provide low data rate wireless applications (more generally, under IEEE 802.15.4, wireless links can operate in three unlicensed frequency bands, namely the 858 MHz band, the 902-to-928 MHz band, and the 2.4 GHz band[6]).

IEEE 802.15.4 defines a robust radio PHY (physical) layer and MAC (medium access control) layer, while ZigBee defines the network, security, and application framework for an IEEE 802.15.4-based system. (Table 6.4 provides an overview of the IEEE 802.15 family of PAN standards.) ZigBee networks support star, mesh, and cluster-tree topologies. These capabilities enable a network to have over 65,000 devices on a single wireless network. ZigBee offers low-latency communication between devices without the need for the initial network synchronization delays as required by Bluetooth. ZigBee can create robust self-forming, self-healing wireless mesh networks. The ZigBee mesh network connects sensors and controllers without being restricted by distance or range limitations; ZigBee mesh networks allow all

---

[6]858 MHz in Europe; 902-to-928 MHz in the United States and Australia; 2.5 GHz in India; and 2.4 GHz in most countries worldwide

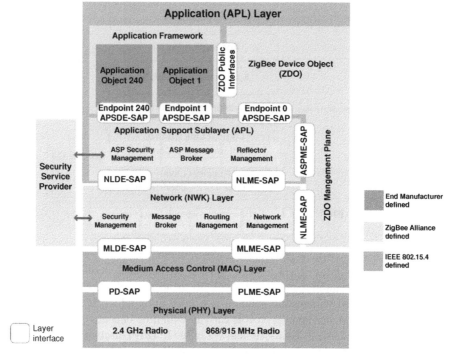

FIGURE 6.2   ZigBee protocol stack (details).

participating devices to communicate with one another and act as repeaters transferring data between devices.

ZigBee is available as two feature sets, ZigBee PRO™ and ZigBee. Both feature sets define how the ZigBee mesh networks operate. ZigBee PRO, the most widely used specification, is optimized for low-power consumption and to support large networks with thousands of devices (16). In October 2007, the ZigBee Alliance announced an expanded set of features for the ZigBee protocol. This new stack profile is universally referred to as ZigBee PRO and for the most part defines specific stack settings and makes mandatory many of the features that are optional in the ZigBee stack that was ratified in 2006. ZigBee PRO also adds some new application profiles such as automatic meter reading, commercial building automation, and home automation. In general, ZigBee PRO features implement support for larger networks, for example stochastic addressing to assign addresses using probability analysis to simplify network formation. The Alliance likes to position ZigBee PRO as a seamless extension of 2006 ZigBee (a ZigBee 2006 node can join a 2007 network, and vice-versa, but designers cannot mix 2006 routers with 2007 routers) (19). ZigBee PRO implements a technique known as frequency agility (not hopping): a network node is able to scan for clear spectrum (with a choice of 16 available channels) and communicate its findings back to the ZigBee coordinator so that a new channel can

TABLE 6.4   The IEEE 802.15™ Family of Wireless PANs

Standard and Date	Description
IEEE 802.15.1™-2005	IEEE Standard for Information technology—Telecommunications and Information Exchange between systems: Local and MAN-specific requirements. Part 15.1: *Wireless Medium Access Control (MAC) and Physical layer (PHY) specifications for Wireless Personal Area Networks (WPANs)*
IEEE 802.15.2™-2003	IEEE Recommended Practice for Telecommunications and Information Exchange between systems: Local and MAN-specific requirements. Part 15.2: *Coexistence of Wireless Personal Area Networks with Other Wireless Devices Operating in Unlicensed Frequency Band*
IEEE 802.15.3™-2003	IEEE Standard for Information Technology—Telecommunications and Information Exchange between systems: Local and MAN-specific requirements. Part 15.3: *Wireless Medium Access Control (MAC) and Physical layer (PHY) specifications for High Rate Wireless Personal Area Networks (WPAN)*
IEEE 802.15.3b™-2005	IEEE Standard for Information Technology—Telecommunications and Information Exchange between systems: Local and MAN-specific requirements. Part 15.3b: *Wireless Medium Access Control (MAC) and Physical layer (PHY) specifications for High Rate Wireless Personal Area Networks (WPANs) Amendment 1: MAC Sublayer*
IEEE 802.15.3c™-2009	IEEE Standard for Information Technology—Telecommunications and Information Exchange between systems: Local and MAN-specific requirements. Part 15.3: *Wireless Medium Access Control (MAC) and Physical layer (PHY) specifications for High Rate Wireless Personal Area Networks (WPANs) Amendment 2: Millimeter-wave-based Alternative PHY layer extension*
IEEE 802.15.4™-2011	IEEE Standard for Local and MANs. Part 15.4: *Low-Rate Wireless Personal Area Networks (LR-WPANs)*
IEEE 802.15.4e™-2011	IEEE Standard for Local and MANs. Part 15.4: *Low-Rate Wireless Personal Area Networks (LR-WPANs) Amendment 1: MAC sublayer*
IEEE 802.15.5™-2009	IEEE Standard for Recommended Practice for Information technology - Telecommunications and information exchange between systems: Local and MANs - Specific requirements Part 15.5: Mesh Topology Capability in WPANs.
IEEE 802.15.6™-2012	IEEE Standard for Local and MANs. Part 15.6: *Wireless Body Area Networks*
IEEE 802.15.7™-2011	IEEE Standard for Local and MANs. Part 15.7: *Short-Range Wireless Optical Communication Using Visible Light*

be used across the network (5). ZigBee PRO networks have the ability to aggregate routes through the use of "many-to-one" routing; this allows each device to share the same routing path reducing broadcast and network traffic and greatly improves the efficiency and stability of the network routing table. The ZigBee 802.15.4 spec defines a maximum packet size of 128 octets; this packet size is optimal for short control messages, but there may be instances where the network needs to send larger messages; therefore, ZigBee PRO now has the means to automatically fragment and reassemble a message at a receiving node relieving the host application of this overhead.

At press time, there were over 600 certified products from 400 companies. The interoperability process has been fostered by the ZigBee Alliance. The ZigBee Alliance is a global ecosystem of 400+ companies in the M2M/IoT space developing standards and producing products for use in commercial building automation, consumer electronics, health care and fitness, home automation, energy management, retail management, and wireless telecommunications. The Alliance was established in October 2002 to create global standards to connect a wide range of devices into secure, low-cost, low-power, and easy-to-use wireless sensor and control networks. Nine interoperable standards published by the Alliance enable manufacturers to bring to market a variety of energy management, commercial, and consumer application products.

LR-WPANs applications require a low-cost, small-size, highly reliable technology which offers long battery life, measured in months or even years, and automatic or semiautomatic installation. The IEEE 802.15.4 standard supports these requirements by trading off higher speed and performance for architectures that benefit from low-power consumption and low cost. ZigBee is a low-power wireless specification that introduces mesh networking to the low-power wireless space and is targeted toward applications such as smart meters, home automation, and RC units. ZigBee technology provides reasonably efficient low-power connectivity and ability to connect a large number of devices into a single network. Some studies have shown that for the home, two wireless PHY layer communications technologies that best meet the overall performance and cost requirements are Wi-Fi (802.11/n) and ZigBee (802.15.4) (20). 6LoWPAN, discussed in Chapter 9, makes use of the IEEE 802.15.4 PAN structure. Other researchers, however, argue that ZigBee's relative complexity (as seen in the protocol stack of Fig. 6.2) and the apparent fact that the power consumption of ZigBee devices is higher than the consumption of some alternatives (e.g., BLE) tend to make ZigBee not always the most ideal solution *for unmaintained devices that need to operate for extensive periods of time from a limited power source*; hence, while many home applications make ideal use of ZigBee, other IoT/M2M applications can also be supported by other approaches.

The PHY layer of the reference model specifies the network interface components, their parameters, and their operation. To support the operation of the MAC layer, the PHY layer includes a variety of features, such as receiver energy detection (RED), link quality indicator (LQI), and clear channel assessment (CCA). The PHY layer is also specified with a number of operational low-power features, including low-duty cycle operations, strict power management, and low transmission overhead. IEEE 802.15.4 defines several addressing modes: it allows the use of either IEEE 64-bit extended addresses or (after an association event) 16-bit addresses unique within the PAN. The MAC layer handles network association and disassociation. It also regulates access to the medium; this is achieved through two modes of operation, namely beaconing and nonbeaconing. The beaconing mode is specified for environments where control and data forwarding is achieved by an always active device. The nonbeaconing mode specifies the use of unslotted, nonpersistent CSMA-based MAC protocol. The network layer provides the functionality required to support network routing capabilities, configuration and device discovery, association and disassociation, topology management, MAC layer management, and routing and security management. Three network topologies, namely star, mesh, and cluster tree, are supported. The security layer leverages the basic security services specified by the IEEE 802.15.4 security model to provide support for infrastructure security and application data security. The application layer consists of the application support sublayer (APS), the ZigBee device object (ZDO), and the manufacturer-defined application objects. The responsibilities of the APS sublayer include maintaining tables for binding devices together, based on their services and their needs, and forwarding messages between bound devices. Refer to Table 6.3 for some technical parameters of this technology.

ZigBee channels are similar to those for BLE in that they are 2 MHz wide; however, they are separated by 5 MHz, thus wasting spectrum, to some degree. ZigBee is not a frequency-hopping technology; therefore, it requires careful planning during deployment in order to ensure that there are no interfering signals in the vicinity (5). The design of the PHY layer is driven by the need for low-cost, power-effective PHY layer for cost-sensitive, low data rate monitoring and control applications. Under IEEE 802.15.4, wireless links can operate in three unlicensed frequency bands, already identified above, namely in the 858 MHz band, in the 902-to-928 MHz band, and in the 2.4 GHz band. Based on these frequency bands, the IEEE 802.15.4 standard defines three physical media (14):

- Direct sequence spread spectrum (DSSS) using binary phase shift keying (BPSK), operating in the 868 MHz at a data rate of 20 Kbps;
- DSSS using BPSK, operating in the 915 MHz at a data rate of 40 Kbps; and
- DSSS using offset quadrature phase shift keying (O-QPSK), operating in the 2.4 GHz at a data rate of 140 Kbps.

These operating frequency bands are depicted in Figure 6.3. The spreading code of the 868 MHz and the 915 MHz PHY layers is a 15-chip m-sequence. Both specifications use BPSK with differential encoding data modulation scheme. The data rate of 868 MHz layer is 20 Kbps, while the data rat of the 915 MHz specification is 40 Kbps. The resulting chip rate is 300 Kchips/s for the 868 MHz PHY layer and 600 Kchips/s for the 915 MHz PHY layer. The data modulation of the 2.4 GHz PHY layer is a 16-ary orthogonal modulation. Consequently, 16 symbols are orthogonal set of 32-chip Pseudorandom Noise (PN) codes. The resulting data rate is 250 Kbps (4 bits/symbol, 62.5 Ksymbols/s). The specification uses O-QPSK with half-sine pulse shaping, which is equivalent to minimum shift keying; the resulting chip rate is 2.0 Mchips/s.

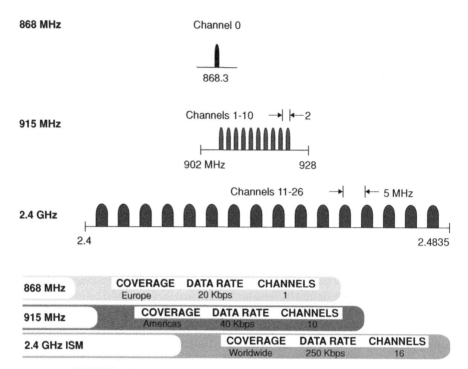

FIGURE 6.3 IEEE 802.15.4 PHY layer operating frequency bands.

IEEE 802.15.4 defines four types of frames: beacon frames, MAC command frames, acknowledgement frames, and data frames (see Fig. 6.4). As noted earlier, IEEE 802.15.4 networks can either be nonbeacon enabled or beacon enabled. The latter is an optional mode in which devices are synchronized by a so-called coordinator's beacons. This allows the use of superframes within which a contention-free guaranteed time service (GTS) is possible. In nonbeacon-enabled networks, data frames are sent via the contention-based channel access method of unslotted carrier sense multiple access/collision detect (CSMA/CD). In nonbeacon-enabled networks, beacons are not used for synchronization; however, they are still useful for link-layer device discovery to aid in association and disassociation events (21).

The packet structure of the IEEE 802.15.4 PHY layer is depicted in Figure 6.5. The first field of this structure contains a 32-bit preamble; this field is used for symbol synchronization. The next field represents the start of packet delimiter; this field of 8 bits is used for frame synchronization. The 8-bit PHY header field specifies the length of the PHY service data unit (PSDU). The PSDU field can carry up to 127 bytes of data.

In order to accommodate the MAC protocol, the IEEE 802.15.4 standard distinguishes devices based on their hardware complexity and capability. Accordingly, the standard defines two classes of physical devices, namely a full function device (FFD) and a reduced function device (RFD). These device types differ in their use and

Data Frame Format

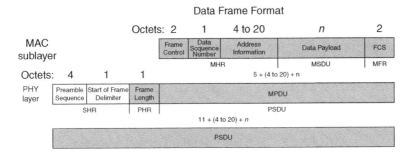

Acknowledgement Frame Format

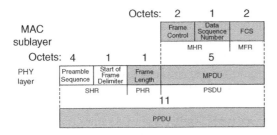

MAC Command Frame Format

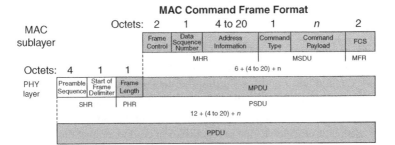

Beacon Frame format

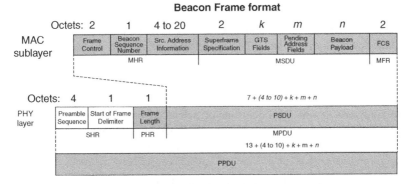

FIGURE 6.4 IEEE 802.15.4 frames.

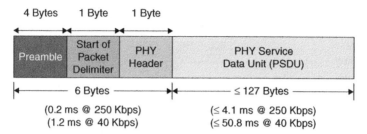

FIGURE 6.5   IEEE 802.15.4 PHY layer packet structure.

how much of the standard they implement. An FFD is equipped with the adequate resources and memory capacity to handle all the functionalities and features specified by the standard. It can, therefore, assume multiple network responsibilities; it can also communicate with any other network device. An RFD is a simple device that carries a reduced set of functionalities, for lower cost and complexity. It typically contains a physical interface to the wireless modem and executes the specified IEEE 802.15.4 MAC layer protocol. Furthermore, it can only associate and communicate with an FFD. Based on these physical device types, ZigBee defines a variety of logical device types. These logical devices are distinguished based on their physical capabilities and the role they play in the deployed network (14). There are three categories of logical devices:

- *Network coordinator*: An FFD device responsible for network establishment and control. The coordinator is responsible for choosing key parameters of the network configuration and for starting the network. It also stores information about the network and acts as the repository for security keys.
- *Router*: An FFD device that supports the data routing functionality, including acting as an intermediate device to link different components of the network and forwarding message between remote devices across multihop paths. A router can communicate with other routers and end devices.
- *End Devices*: An RFD device that contains (just) enough functionality to communicate with its parent node, namely the network coordinator or a router. An end device does not have the capability to relay data messages to other end devices.

A PAN coordinator is the designated principal controller of the WPAN. Every network has exactly one PAN coordinator, selected from within all the coordinators of the network. A coordinator is a network device configured to support network functionalities and additional responsibilities, including:

- Managing a list of all associated network devices;
- Exchanging data frames with network devices and peer coordinator;

- Allocating 16-bit short addresses to network devices. The short addresses, assigned on-demand, are used by the associated devices in lieu of the 64-bit addresses for subsequent communications with the coordinator;
- Generating, on a periodic basis, beacon frames. These frames are used to announce the PAN identifier, the list of outstanding frames, and other network and device parameters.

Based on these logical device types, a ZigBee WPAN can be organized into one of three possible topologies, namely a star, a mesh (peer-to-peer), or a cluster tree. (See Fig. 6.6.) The *star* network topology supports a single coordinator, with up to 65,536 devices. In this topology configuration, one of the FFD-type devices assumes the role of network coordinator. All other devices act as end devices. The selected coordinator is responsible for initiating and maintaining the end devices on the network. Upon initiation, the end devices can only communicate with the coordinator. The *mesh* configuration allows path formation from any source device to any destination device, using tree- and table-driven routing algorithms. *Cluster-tree* networks enable a peer–peer network to be formed with a minimum of routing overhead, using multihop routing. The topology is suitable for latency-tolerant applications. A cluster-tree network is self-organized and supports network redundancy to achieve a high degree of fault resistance and self-repair. The cluster can be rather large, comprising up to 255 clusters of up to 254 nodes each, for a total of 64,770 nodes. It may also span large physical areas. Any FFD can be a coordinator. Only one coordinator is selected for the PAN. The PAN coordinator forms the first cluster and assigns to it a cluster identity (CID) of value 0. Subsequent clusters are then formed with a designated cluster head for each cluster.

Public application profiles are agreements for messages, message formats, and processing actions. Profiles enable developers to create interoperable, distributed application entities residing on separate devices. These applications (written by the device manufacturer) send commands, request data, and process commands and

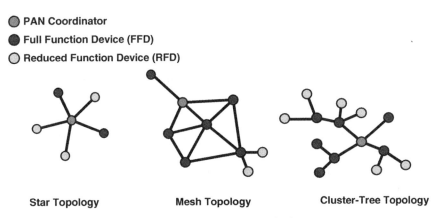

FIGURE 6.6   Network topologies.

requests over the ZigBee network. The ZDO represents a predefined base class of functionality upon which all applications are written. The ZDO creates an abstraction so that the developer can focus on writing application-specific code rather than dealing with the low-level details. The ZDO provides an interface between the application objects, the profile (e.g., the ZigBee Health Care), and the APS. The ZDO satisfies the common requirements of all applications operating in a ZigBee protocol stack. The ZDO is responsible for initializing the APS, the network layer, and the security service provider. Table 6.5 lists specific application standards defined and supported by ZigBee and the ZigBee Alliance.

Note: IEEE 802.15.4 mandates link-layer security based on Advanced Encryption Standard (AES), but it does not specify capabilities for bootstrapping, key management, and security at higher layers.

The ZigBee Alliance's focus on health care has resulted in the development of the ZigBee Health Care public application profile, also known as the PHHC Profile or simply the Medical Profile. ZigBee Health Care was designed for use by assistive devices operating in noninvasive health care. ZigBee Health Care provides an industry-wide standard for exchanging data between a variety of medical and non-medical devices. The PHHC Profile supports secure monitoring and management of noncritical, low-acuity healthcare services in support of chronic disease management. This profile also provides support for IEEE 11073-conformant devices (e.g., glucometers, pulse oximeters, ECGs, blood pressure monitors, respirometers, weight scales, and thermometers). The ZigBee Health Care definitions are comprised of device specializations defined by IEEE, including IEEE 11073 device specializations of standards point-of-care medical device communication. One of the standards that are part of this family, the 11073–20601 standard, is a transport-independent, optimized exchange protocol. This standard forms the basis of the data exchanges between the devices that will support the PHHC Profile. This protocol provides methods for (i) establishing logical connections between devices, (ii) presenting the capabilities of devices, and (iii) servicing communication needs. In summary, the ZigBee Health Care public application profile fully supports ISO/IEEE 11073 for point-of-care medical device communication and provides support for additional devices. The ZigBee Health Care also supports all device specializations; device specializations for a number of medical devices already exist including the pulse oximeter, blood pressure monitor, pulse monitor, weight scale, and glucose meter (16, 17).

Earlier, we mentioned ZIP as an example of an IP-based stack (IPv6 in particular) that supports Zigbee. A typical ZIP product implementation would have parameters similar to these:

- ZigBee: ZigBee Pro compliant and Full ZigBee Smart Energy (SE) Profile support
- Radio: IEEE 802.15.4 compliant ZigBee radio
- Operating frequency: 2405–2483.5 MHz, supports ZigBee channels 11 to 26, 5 MHz spacing
- Receiver sensitivity: −95 dBm

TABLE 6.5   Application Standards Defined and Supported by ZigBee and the ZigBee Alliance

Standard	Application Description
ZigBee Building Automation (used for efficient commercial spaces)	ZigBee Building Automation offers a global standard for interoperable products enabling the secure and reliable monitoring and control of commercial building systems. It is the only BACnet®-approved wireless mesh network standard for commercial buildings
ZigBee Health Care (used for health and fitness monitoring)	ZigBee Health Care offers a global standard for interoperable products enabling secure and reliable monitoring and management of noncritical, low-acuity healthcare services targeted at chronic disease, aging independence and general health, and wellness and fitness. ZigBee Alliance has joined forces with the Continua Health Alliance, a nonprofit, open industry coalition of the finest healthcare and technology companies collaborating to improve the quality of personal health care. Continua has endorsed ZigBee Health Care as its low-power LAN standard in the Continua 2010 Design Guidelines
ZigBee Home Automation (used for smart homes)	ZigBee Home Automation offers a global standard for interoperable products enabling smart homes that can control appliances, lighting, environment, energy management and security, as well as the expandability to connect with other ZigBee networks
ZigBee Input Device (easy-to-use touchpads, mice, keyboards, wands)	ZigBee Input Device is a global standard for greener, innovative, and easy-to-use mice, keyboards, touchpads, wands, and other input devices used with computers and CE devices. This standard allows consumers to use their devices from greater distances or even from another room because operation is not limited to LOS. The standard operates with existing ZigBee Remote Control-equipped HDTVs, set-top boxes, and other devices and existing computers. ZigBee Input Device is a standard designed specifically for the ZigBee RF4CE specification
ZigBee Light Link (LED lighting control)	ZigBee Light Link gives the lighting industry a global standard for interoperable and very easy-to-use consumer lighting and control products. It allows consumers to gain wireless control over all their LED fixtures, light bulbs, timers, remotes, and switches. Products using this standard will let consumers change lighting remotely to reflect ambiance, task, or season, all while managing energy use and making their homes greener. Since ZigBee Light Link is a ZigBee standard, lighting products will interoperate effortlessly with products using other ZigBee standards already in consumers' homes, including ZigBee Home Automation, ZigBee Input Device, ZigBee Remote Control, and ZigBee Health Care

(continued)

TABLE 6.5   *(Continued)*

Standard	Application Description
ZigBee network devices (assist and expand ZigBee networks)	ZigBee network device is the category for device specific standards designed to assist and expand ZigBee PRO-based networks. These universal devices can work on just about any ZigBee PRO network; they also work with most ZigBee standards. ZigBee Gateway is the first standard to join this category, and work is underway to develop standards for bridge and range extender devices. ZigBee Gateway makes it easy to connect Internet-based service provider systems with ZigBee users everywhere, allowing them both to take advantage of cost and energy efficiencies. This standard complements a number of ZigBee standards using the ZigBee PRO specification: (i) ZigBee Building Automation; (ii) ZigBee Health Care; (iii) ZigBee Home Automation; (iv) ZigBee Retail Services; (v) ZigBee SE; and (vi) ZigBee Telecom Services
ZigBee Remote Control (used for advanced RCs)	ZigBee Remote Control provides a global standard for advanced, greener, and easy-to-use RF remotes that remove LOS restrictions while also delivering two-way communication, longer range of use, and extended battery life. It was designed for a variety of CE devices including HDTV, home theater equipment, set-top boxes, and other audio equipment
ZigBee Retail Services (used for smarter shopping)	ZigBee Retail Services is a global standard of interoperable products to monitor, control, and automate the purchase and delivery of goods. It will also help retailers' manage their supply chain. ZigBee Retail Services will support a fully integrated ecosystem of technology suppliers, merchants, distribution centers, and both residential and commercial consumers in providing a standard way to purchase, fulfill, automate, and monitor the purchase and delivery of goods
ZigBee Smart Energy (SE) (used for home energy savings)	ZigBee SE is a leading standard for interoperable products that monitor, control, inform, and automate the delivery and use of energy and water. It helps create greener homes by giving consumers the information and automation needed to easily reduce their consumption and save money, too. ZigBee SE version 1.1, the newest version for product development, adds several important features including dynamic pricing enhancements, tunneling of other protocols, prepayment features, over-the-air updates, and guaranteed backward compatibility with certified ZigBee SE products version 1.0. All ZigBee SE products are ZigBee certified to perform regardless of manufacturer, allowing utilities and consumers to purchase with confidence. Every product needed to implement a robust ZigBee SE HAN is available. These products make it easy for utilities and governments to deploy smart grid solutions that are secure, easy to install, and consumer friendly

(continued)

TABLE 6.5   *(Continued)*

Standard	Application Description
	SE Profile version 2.0 was under development at press time, in cooperation with a number of other standard development groups. SE 2.0 offers IP-based control for AMI and HANs; the IP-based protocol is used to monitor, control, and automate the delivery and use of energy and water. This version will not replace ZigBee SE version 1, rather it will offer utilities and energy service providers another choice when creating their AMI and HANs. In addition to all the services and devices found in ZigBee SE version 1, version 2.0 will feature control of PEV charging, installation, configuration and firmware download for HAN devices, prepay services, user information and messaging, load control, demand response and common information, and application profile interfaces for wired and wireless HANs. Development partners include HomeGrid, HomePlug Powerline Alliance, International Society of Automative Engineers SAE International, IPSO Alliance, SunSpec Alliance, and the Wi-Fi Alliance
	On August 25, 2012, the Alliance closed the final public comment period on the latest draft 0.9 version of the Draft Standard (public application profile) and supporting documents. This was the final comment period because SE Profile 2 development is nearly complete. Public and member comments will be integrated to produce a final version 1 of the standard
ZigBee Telecom Services (used for value-added services)	ZigBee Telecom Services offers a global standard for interoperable products enabling a wide variety of value-added services, including information delivery, mobile gaming, location-based services, secure mobile payments, mobile advertising, zone billing, mobile office access control, payments, and peer-to-peer data-sharing services. This single standard offers an affordable and easy way to introduce innovative new services that touch almost everyone using mobile phones and other portable electronic devices. It offers a variety of value-added services for mobile phone network operators, retailers, businesses, and governments

Source: ZigBee Alliance.

- Transmitter power: +18 dBm output power (<100 mW)
- Ethernet and TCP/IP specifications:
  - Ethernet 10/100 base TX with auto negotiation
  - Supports standard socket-based communications
  - Protocols supported: IPv6, UDP, TCP, Telnet, ICMP, ARP, DHCP, BOOTP, Auto IP, HTTP, SMTP, TFTP, HTTPS, SSH, SSL, FTP, PPP, SNMP
  - Encryption: end-to-end AES 128-bit encryption, 3DES and RC4 encryption for SSH and SSL
  - Authentication: SHA-1, MD5

It should be noted that ZigBee and Bluetooth protocols are substantially different and are designed for different purposes: ZigBee is designed for low-to-very-low-duty cycle static and dynamic environments with many active nodes; Bluetooth, on the other hand, is designed for high QoS, variety of duty cycles, and moderate data rates in networks with limited active nodes.

6.1.2 Radio Frequency for Consumer Electronics (RF4CE)

The specialty-use-driven ZigBee RF4CE protocol has been designed for simple, two-way device-to-device control applications that do not require the full-featured mesh networking capabilities offered by ZigBee 2007. ZigBee RF4CE offers lower memory size requirements, thereby enabling lower cost implementations.

RF4CE is based on ZigBee and was standardized in 2009 by four consumer electronics (CE) companies: Sony, Philips, Panasonic, and Samsung.

The ZigBee RF4CE specification defines an RC network that defines a simple, robust, and low-cost communication network allowing wireless connectivity in applications for CE devices. The ZigBee RF4CE specification enhances the IEEE 802.15.4 standard by providing a simple networking layer and standard application layer that can be used to create a multivendor interoperable solution for use within the home. Some of the characteristics of ZigBee RF4CE include the following (16):

- Operation in the 2.4 GHz frequency band according to IEEE 802.15.4;
- Frequency agile solution operating over three channels;
- Incorporates power-saving mechanisms for all device classes;
- Discovery mechanism with full application confirmation;
- Pairing mechanism with full application confirmation;
- Multiple star topology with inter-PAN communication;
- Various transmission options including broadcast;
- Security key generation mechanism;
- Utilizes the industry standard AES-128 security scheme;
- Specifies a simple RC control profile for CE products;
- Support alliance-developed standards or manufacturer-specific profiles.

RF4CE's intended use is as a device RC system, for example for television set-top boxes. The intention is that it overcomes the common problems associated with infrared (IR): interoperability, line-of-sight (LOS), and limited enhanced features (5). At least wo-chip vendors supported RF4CE as of press time: Texas Instruments and Freescale Semiconductor, Inc.

6.1.3 Bluetooth and its Low-Energy Profile

6.1.3.1 Overview Bluetooth is a WPAN technology based on IEEE 802.15.1. It is a specification for short-range wireless connectivity for portable personal devices, including computer peripherals. It is now one of the most popular technologies in

consumer electronics. Bluetooth was initially developed by Ericsson; in the late 1990s, the Bluetooth Special Interest Group (SIG) made their specifications publicly available. Soon thereafter, the IEEE 802.15 Group took the Bluetooth work and developed a vendor-independent standard. The Bluetooth SIG, in conjunction with the IEEE, has managed enhancements of the basic standard over the years. Bluetooth has evolved through four versions (see Table 6.6); all versions of the Bluetooth standards maintain downward compatibility. The Bluetooth SIG has approximately 17,000 member companies in telecommunication, computing, and CE.

TABLE 6.6   Versions of Bluetooth

Version	Description
Bluetooth v1.0 and v1.0B	Original versions; had limited interoperability
Bluetooth v1.1	This is original IEEE Standard 802.15.1–2002
Bluetooth v1.2	Ratified as IEEE Standard 802.15.1–2005. Incorporates a number of enhancements compared with v1.1 including (i) faster connection and discovery; (ii) use of AFH spread spectrum; (iii) supports higher transmission speeds up to 721 Kbps; and (iv) adds flow control mechanisms
Bluetooth v2.0 + EDR	Published in 2004. Incorporates a number of enhancements compared with v1.1 including faster data transfer of about 3 Mbps and lower power consumption through a reduced duty cycle. Note: To be exact, Version 2.0 devices have a higher power consumption; however, the fact that the transmission rate is three times faster (thereby reducing the transmission burst times), effectively reduces consumption to half that of 1.x devices
Bluetooth v2.1 + EDR	Published in July 2007. This release adds secure simple pairing (SSP), which improves the pairing process for Bluetooth devices while improving security; it also incorporates a subrating mechanism that reduces the power consumption in low-power mode
Bluetooth v3.0 + HS	Published in April 2009. This release supports a theoretical data transfer speeds of up to 24 Mbps by using the Bluetooth link for negotiation and establishment of a session for high data rate traffic carried over a collocated 802.11 link. It adds alternate MAC/PHY (AMP) for the use of 802.11 as a HS transport. Note: The HS portion of the specification is not mandatory, and only devices with the "+HS" label actually support the Bluetooth over 802.11 HS data transfer. The enhanced power control feature updates the power control feature to remove the open loop power control and also to clarify ambiguities in power control as related to EDR
Bluetooth v4.0	Published in June 2010. This version includes *Classic Bluetooth*, *Bluetooth high speed*, and BLE protocols. Bluetooth high speed is based on Wi-Fi and Classic Bluetooth consists of legacy Bluetooth protocols

Bluetooth is a short-range data exchange communication protocol widely used in cellular phones, smartphones, tablets, and PDAs (has a range of about 10 m, or a maximum of 100 m with power boost). Bluetooth is designed for a small variety of tasks, such as synchronization, voice headsets, cell-modem calls, and mouse and keyboard input. The Bluetooth specification defines a low-power, low-cost technology that provides a standardized platform for eliminating cables between mobile devices and facilitating connections between products.

Bluetooth operates in the 2.4-GHz ISM band and has a bandwidth of approximately 1–3 Mbps (newer version support higher speeds). Bluetooth uses frequency-hopping spread spectrum. While the cost of Bluetooth equipment is significantly lower than the cost of WLAN, the transmission range of 10 m or less and the data transfer rate 12 Mbps or less (in Version 2.0 of the standard) are often considered a drawback. By comparison, EEE 802.11a/b/g/n is a collection of related technologies that operate in the 2.4-GHz ISM band, the 5-GHz ISM band, and the 5-GHz U-NII bands; it provides the highest power and longest range of the common unlicensed wireless technologies. Transmission data rates can reach 54 Mbps (twice as much with the latest 802.11n protocol). Typically, hardware implementation of some or all of 802.11 protocols comes preinstalled on most new laptop computers; the technology is often also available for PDAs and cellular phones. Also by comparison, the IEEE 802.15.4 (ZigBee) standard supports a maximum data rate of 250 Kbps, with rates as low as 20 Kbps; however, it has the lowest power requirement of the group: ZigBee devices are designed to run several years on a single set of batteries, making them ideal candidates for unattended or difficult-to-reach locations. See Table 6.7.

The sublayers of IEEE 802.15 are as follows: (i) RF layer; (ii) baseband layer; (iii) the link manager (an MAC-level protocol); and (iv) the logical link control and adaptation protocol (L2CAP) (also an MAC-level protocol). Bluetooth is designed for high QoS applications, a variety of duty cycles, and moderate data rates in networks with limited active nodes. Compared with WLANs, Bluetooth is limited as a transmission technology in terms of both bandwidth and distance. The functionality of the layers is as follows:

- **RF layer**: The air interface is based on antenna power range starting from 0 dBm up to 20 dBm, 2.4 GHz band, and the link range from 0.1 to 10 m.
- **Baseband layer**: The baseband layer establishes the Bluetooth *piconet*. The piconet is formed when two Bluetooth devices connect. In a piconet, one device acts as the master and the other devices act as slaves.
- **Link manager**: The link manager establishes the link between Bluetooth devices. Additional functions include security, negotiation of Baseband packet sizes, power mode and duty cycle control of the Bluetooth device, and the connection states of a Bluetooth device in a piconet.
- **L2CAP**: This sublayer provides the upper-layer protocols with connectionless and connection-oriented services. The services provided by this layer include protocol multiplexing capability, segmentation and reassembly of packets, and group abstractions.

TABLE 6.7   Wireless Protocol Comparison

IEEE Standard Property	802.11 WLANs	802.15.1/ Bluetooth	802.15.4/ ZigBee
Battery life measured in:	Minutes to hours	Hours to days	Days to years
Data throughput	• 802.11a: up to 54 Mbps • 802.11b: up to 11 Mbps • 802.11g: up to 54 Mbps • 802.11n: up to 150 Mbps (at 40 MHz operation at 5 GHz) • 802.11ac: up to 867 Mbps (160 MHz operation at 5 GHz)	~1 Mbps (Version 1) to 3 Mbps (Version 2)	~0.25 Mbps
Power consumption	Medium	Low	Very low
Range	~250 m (this figure is for 802.11n, otherwise ~100 m) Note: IEEE 802.11y-2008 extended operation of 802.11a to the licensed 3.7 GHz band (co-primary basis in the 3650 to 3700 MHz band in the U.S. band); this increased power limits allow a range up to 5000 m. This band has traditionally been used for satellite communications and is known as the C-band	~10 to 100 m	~10 m

BLE (originally known as WiBree and/or Bluetooth ultra low power [ULP][7]) is a low-power subset to Bluetooth v4.0, with an entirely new protocol stack for rapid build-up of simple links. BLE is an alternative to the "power management" features that were introduced in Bluetooth v1.0 to v3.0 as part of the standard Bluetooth protocols. BLE is aimed at very low-power applications running off a coin cell: it is capable of reporting data from a sensor for up to a year from a small button battery without recharging. Although the BLE data rate and radio range are lower than the same metrics in classic Bluetooth, the low-power and long battery life make it suitable for short-range monitoring applications in medicine. BLE sensor devices are typically required to operate for many years without needing a new battery; they commonly use a coin cell, for example, the popular CR2032 (22). The aim of the BLE technology is to enable power-sensitive devices to be permanently connected to the Internet. BLE per se is primarily aimed at mobile telephones, where it is envisaged

---

[7]BLE started as a project in the Nokia Research Centre with the name Wibree. In 2007, the technology was adopted by the Bluetooth SIG and renamed Bluetooth ultra low power; later, it was renamed Bluetooth low energy.

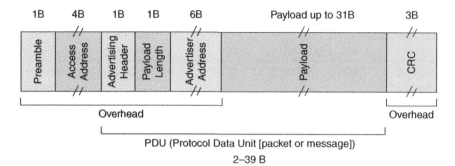

FIGURE 6.7 BLE packet.

that a star network topology, similar to Bluetooth, will often be created between the phone and an ecosystem of other devices.

Figure 6.7 depicts the BLE packet, while Figure 6.8 shows the frequency plan. Current chip designs allow for two types of implementation—dual mode and single mode. In a single-mode implementation, the BLE protocol stack is implemented solely. In a dual-mode implementation, BLE functionality is integrated into an existing Classic Bluetooth controller. Most new Bluetooth chipsets from leading Bluetooth silicon manufacturers are expected to support Bluetooth and the new BLE functionality; a number of companies had announced support of BLE by press time, including Broadcom and Texas Instruments.

As implied in Figure 6.8, there are some coexistence scenarios in a corporate setting, in a home, or in a small office home office (SOHO) where Wi-Fi is used. The IEEE 802.11b and 802.11g specifications postulate a partitioning of the spectrum into 14 overlapping, staggered channels whose center frequencies are 5 MHz apart; within this partitioning of the ISM spectrum, channels 1, 6, and 11 (and, if available in the regulatory domain, channel 14) do not overlap. These channels (or other sets with similar gaps) can be used so that multiple networks can operate in close proximity without interfering with each other. See Figure 6.9. The spectral mask for 802.11b requires that the signal be at least 30 dB down from its peak energy at ±11 MHz from the center frequency and at least 50 dB down from its peak energy at ±22 MHz from the center frequency. Note that if the transmitter is sufficiently powerful, the signal can be quite strong even beyond the ±22 MHz point (e.g., a powerful transmitter on channel 6 can easily overwhelm a weaker transmitter on channel 11); in most situations, however, the signal in a given channel is sufficiently attenuated to minimally interfere with a transmitter on any other channel. Each BLE channel is 2 MHz wide, but the spacing and placement of ZigBee channels implies that only four channels are likely to be free in the presence of average Wi-Fi network settings (typically, channels 1, 6, and 11 are defaults). With an on-air signaling data rate of only 250 Kbps and the inability to implement hopping, ZigBee is at risk of nondelivery of its packets; BLE, on the other hand, makes much more efficient use of the spectrum and employs adaptive frequency hopping (AFH) as proven by

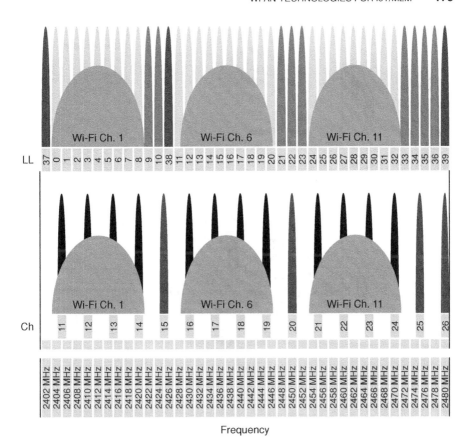

Frequency

FIGURE 6.8   Frequency spectrum. Top: BLE channel allocations (each channel is 2 MHz wide). Bottom: ZigBee channel allocations (each channel is 2 MHz wide but there is a 5 MHz spacing; in the presence of a multichannel Wi-Fi, only four channels may actually to be available).

Bluetooth. As noted earlier, a device that operates Bluetooth v4.0 may not necessarily implement other versions of Bluetooth; in such cases, it is known as a single-mode device (5).

In the recent past, Bluetooth was used in health care mostly just for interconnection of various medical apparatus. The situation is changing with the development of the Bluetooth Health Device Profile (HDP). Under Bluetooth, a profile defines the characteristics and features including function of a Bluetooth system. The HDP is used for connecting application data source devices such as blood pressure monitors, weight scales, glucose meters, thermometers, and pulse oximeters to application data sink devices such as mobile phones, laptops, desktop computers, and health appliances without the need for cables. This profile can be combined with BLE to make sure that medical devices can be in the operational conditions for many months and even years (3). The topic is revisited below.

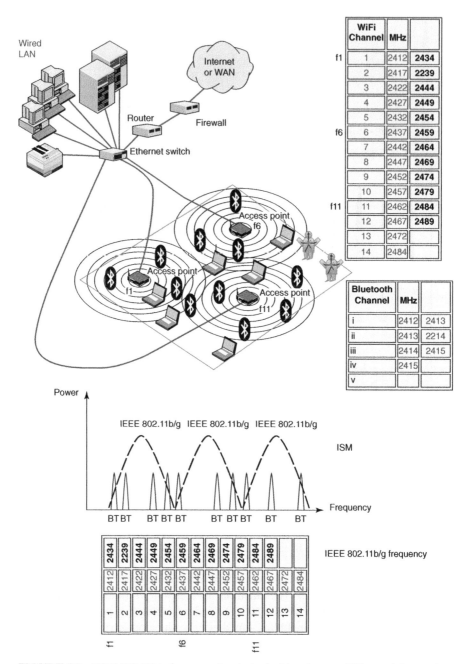

WiFi Channel	MHz	
1	2412	**2434**
2	2417	**2239**
3	2422	**2444**
4	2427	**2449**
5	2432	**2454**
6	2437	**2459**
7	2442	**2464**
8	2447	**2469**
9	2452	**2474**
10	2457	**2479**
11	2462	**2484**
12	2467	**2489**
13	2472	
14	2484	

Bluetooth Channel	MHz	
i	2412	2413
ii	2413	2214
iii	2414	2415
iv	2415	
v		

FIGURE 6.9   IEEE 802.11b/g frequency bands, typical topology, and Bluetooth interaction.

6.1.3.2 Details   As noted, Bluetooth is a specification for short-range RF-based connectivity for portable personal devices. The specification originally started out as a de facto industry standard; more recently, the IEEE Project 802.15.1 developed a wireless PAN standard based on the Bluetooth v1.1 Foundation Specifications. The IEEE 802.15.1 standard was published in 2002. Bluetooth is principally directed to the support of personal communication devices such as telephones, printers, headsets, PC keyboards/mice, etc. The technology has restricted performance characteristics by design; hence, its applicability to WSN is rather limited in most cases.

As part of its effort, the IEEE has reviewed and provided a standard adaptation of the Bluetooth Specification v1.1 Foundation MAC (L2CAP, LMP, and baseband) and PHY (radio). Also specified is a clause on service access points (SAPs) that includes an LLC/MAC interface for the ISO/IEC 8802-2 LLC. A Protocol Implementation Conformance Statement (PICS) proforma has been developed. Also specified is an informative high-level behavioral ITU-T Z.100 specification and description language (SDL) model for an integrated Bluetooth MAC sublayer (23).

The system uses omnidirectional radio waves that can transmit through walls and other nonmetal barriers. Unlike other wireless standards, the Bluetooth wireless specification includes both link-layer and application layer definitions for product developers. Radios that comply with the Bluetooth wireless specification operate in the unlicensed, 2.4-GHz ISM radio spectrum ensuring communication compatibility worldwide.

Bluetooth radios use a spread spectrum, frequency-hopping, full-duplex signal. While point-to-point connections are supported, the specification allows up to seven simultaneous connections to be established and maintained by a single radio (24). AFH available with newer versions allows for better graceful coexistence with IEEE 802.11 WLAN systems. The signal hops among 79 frequencies at 1 MHz intervals to give an acceptable degree of interference immunity between multiple Bluetooth devices and between a Bluetooth device and a WLAN device (at least in the case where not all the available frequencies are used by the WLAN—this is likely the case in a SOHO environment where only one or two access points are used at a location). Refer again to Figure 6.9. In order to minimize interference with other protocols that use the same band, the protocol can change channels up to 1600 times per second. If there is interference from other devices, the transmission does not stop, but its speed is downgraded.

Bluetooth version 1.2 allowed a maximum data rate of 1 Mbps; this results in an effective throughput of about 723 Kbps. In late 2004, a new version of Bluetooth, known as Bluetooth Version 2, was ratified; among other features, it included EDR. With EDR, the maximum data rate is able to reach 3 Mbps (throughput of 2.1 Mbps) within a range of 10 m (up to 100 m with a power boost). Older and newer Bluetooth devices can work together with no special effort (25). Because a device such as a telephone headset can transmit the same information faster with Bluetooth 2.0+EDR, it will use less energy since the radio is on for shorter periods of time. The data rate is improved by more efficient coding of the data sent across the air; this also means that for the same amount of data, the radio will be active less of the time, thus reducing the power consumption (24). Newer Bluetooth devices are efficient at using small amounts of power when not actively transmitting: for example, the headset is able to burst two to three times more data in a transmission; it is able to sleep longer between transmissions. Noteworthy features of Bluetooth Core Specification Version 2.0 + EDR include:

- Three times faster transmission speed compared with pre-existing technology
- Lower power consumption through reduced duty cycle
- Simplification of multilink applications due to increased available bandwidth
- Backward compatibility to earlier versions
- Improved BER (bit error rate) performance

In the recent past, hardware developers were shifting from Bluetooth 1.1 to Bluetooth 1.2 and then Bluetooth 2.0. To be exact, Version 2.0 devices have a higher power consumption; however, the fact that the transmission rate is three times faster (thereby reducing the transmission burst times) effectively reduces consumption to half that of 1.x devices.

Devices are able to establish a trusted relationship; a device that wants to communicate only with a trusted device can cryptographically authenticate the identity of the other device. Trusted devices may also encrypt the data that they exchange over the air.

A Bluetooth device playing the role of "master" can communicate with up to seven devices playing the role of "slave" (these groups of up to eight devices are called piconets). At any given instant in time, data can be transferred between the master and one slave; but the master switches rapidly from slave to slave in a round-robin fashion. (Simultaneous transmission from the master to multiple slaves is possible, but not used much in practice.) The Bluetooth specification also allows connecting two or more piconets together to form a scatternet, with some devices acting as a bridge by simultaneously playing the master role in one piconet and the slave role in another piconet.

6.1.3.3 *Bluetooth HDP*   Until recently, Bluetooth systems for medical application made use of proprietary implementations and data format; typically applications are placed on top of the serial port profile (SPP); however, they were not interoperable across vendors. To address the interoperability issue, the Bluetooth SIG started a program several years ago to define a new medical application, and in 2008 it released the HDP elluded to earlier.

The end result of this work was the HDP specification that included the multi-channel adaptation protocol (MCAP) and that made use of the device ID (DI) profile. Figure 6.10 describes the architecture of a Bluetooth system with the HDP and applications. Table 6.8 describes the key components (26). HDP provides several critical features; these include control channel connection/disconnection, data link creation (reliable or streaming), data link deletion, data link abort, data link reconnection, data transmission (over one or more data links), and clock synchronization.

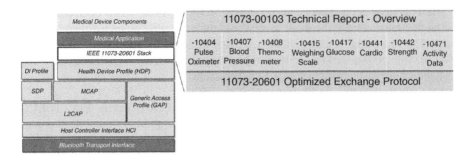

FIGURE 6.10 Bluetooth protocol and a HDP in a medical device application.

TABLE 6.8 **Description of the HDP Functional Blocks**

Functional Block	Description
Medical application	Describes the actual device application, including its user interface, application behavior, and integration layer to the IEEE 11073-20601 stack implementation
IEEE 11073-20601	Stack performs building, transmission, reception, and parsing of IEEE PDU packets for the associated agent/manager being developed. This component will directly link to the HDP
DI profile	Bluetooth profile designed to provide device-specific information through the use of the service discovery protocol (SDP). If vendor-specific information is required as part of a particular medical device, this profile provides specific behavior to acquire this information. A good HDP implementation offers APIs to register and query for such vendor-specific information. These APIs can then be integrated directly into the medical application
HDP	The core Bluetooth profile designed to facilitate transmission and reception of medical device data. The APIs of this layer interact with the lower-level MCAP layer, but also perform SDP behavior to connect to remote HDP devices
SDP	The discovery protocol used by all Bluetooth profiles to register and/or discover available services on remote devices so that connections over L2CAP can be established
MCAP	Used by HDP and facilitates the creation of a communications link (MCL) for exchanging generic commands, and also one or more data links (MDL) to transfer actual medical device data. MCAP is specific for the HDP and guarantees reliable transmission of data
Generic access profile (GAP)	Describes the required features of all core Bluetooth profiles including inquiry, connection, and authentication procedures
L2CAP	Supports protocol multiplexing, packet segmentation and reassembly, QoS, retransmission, and flow control for the Bluetooth packets transmitted through MCAP
Host controller interface (HCI)	Describes the commands and events that all Bluetooth hardware implementations (controllers) can understand
Bluetooth transport interface	Describes the UART, USB, SDIO, three-wire, ABCSP, etc. transport interface to the actual Bluetooth hardware components being used. Typically, UART and USB are the most widely used transports

HDP devices act as sinks and/or sources. A source is the small device that will act as the transmitter of the medical data (weight scale, glucose meter, thermometer, etc.). The sink is the feature-rich device that will act as the receiver of the medical data (mobile phone, desktop computer, health appliances, etc.). HDP devices acting as a source device are weight scales, blood pressure meters, thermometers, or glucose meters which transmit application data over a reliable data channel to a sink (PC, mobile phone, or PDA). Other source devices such as pulse oximeter, EEG, or ECG transmit application data over a streaming data channel to a sink (PC, mobile phone, or PDA). Multiple source devices transmit application data over reliable and streaming data channels to a sink. This data can then be routed on to a physician through an alternate transport (e.g., the Internet or a mobile phone network) to a medical server application at a hospital. A source device may be a combination device (pulse oximeter with thermometer capability) utilizing multiple data channels (26).

HDP does not define the data format and data content. The Bluetooth SIG requires for HDP the usage of the IEEE 11073-20601 Personal Health Device Communication Application Profile as the only allowed protocol for data exchange between HDP devices and the IEEE 11073-104xx Device Specification. IEEE 11073-20601 defines the data exchange protocol and IEEE 11073-104xx defines the data format including size and coding of all data exchanged between HDP devices. The data exchange protocol includes services for a reliable communication, mechanism for event reporting, object access via GET/SET, and the domain information (object-oriented description with attributes for the device configuration). Device description and attribute definitions are using ASN.1. Refer again to Figure 6.10 for the architecture of a Bluetooth device with IEEE 11073-20601 and device specifications with IEEE 11073 (-104xx). The length of transmitted data is in most cases 896 bytes for transmit and 224 bytes for receive. The exception is the oximeter (transmit: 9216 bytes; receive: 256 bytes).

6.1.4 IEEE 802.15.6 WBANs

At press time, the IEEE 802.15 Task Group (TG) 6 was in the process of developing a communication standard optimized for low-power devices and operation on, in, or around the human body (but nonetheless not limited to humans) to serve a variety of applications including medical, CE/personal entertainment, and others. The technology is intended to support low-power in-body/on-body nodes to serve a variety of medical and nonmedical applications. The IEEE TG postulated that for a successful implementation of WBAN, a standard model was required, which would be able to address both medical and CE applications.

The IEEE 802.15 TG6 was formed in November 2007 and begun operations as TG6 in January 2008. It had received 34 proposals, which were merged into a single candidate proposal. A draft of the standard was developed in March 2009. The draft has undergone significant editing and underwent five Letter Ballots; the last was Letter Ballot 79. On July 22, 2011, the draft was approved to start Sponsor Ballot. The standard defines an MAC layer supporting several PHY layers.

The selection of the PHYs (frequency bands) was an important issue.[8] Generally, the available frequencies for WBANs are regulated by communication authorities in different countries. Medical Implant Communication Service (MICS) band is a licensed band used for implant communication and has the same frequency range (402–405 MHz) in most of the countries. Wireless Medical Telemetry Services (WMTS) is a licensed band used for medical telemetry system. Both MICS and WMTS bandwidths do not support high data rate applications. The ISM band supports high data rate applications and is available worldwide. However, there are high chances of interference as many wireless devices including IEEE 802.1 and IEEE 802.15.4 operate at ISM band. The current IEEE 802.15.6 standard defines three PHY layers as follows: the narrowband (NB) layer, the ultra wideband (UWB) layer, and the human body communications (HBC) layer. The selection of each PHY depends on the application requirements. On the top of the PHY layer, the standard defines a sophisticated MAC protocol that controls access to the channel. For time-referenced resource allocations, the hub (or the coordinator) divides the time axis (or the channel) into a series of superframes. The superframes are bounded by beacon periods of equal length. To ensure high-level security, the standard defines three levels: (a) level 0—unsecured communication, (b) level 1—authentication only, (c) level 2—both authentication and encryption (27). Table 6.9, also from Reference 27, describes the PHY layers.

Regarding the MAC layer in IEEE 802.15.6, the entire channel is divided into superframe structures. Each superframe is bounded by a beacon period of equal length. The hub selects the boundaries of the beacon period and thereby selects the allocation slots. The hub may also shift the offsets of the beacon period. Generally, the beacons are transmitted in each beacon period except in inactive superframes or unless prohibited by regulations such as in MICS band. The IEEE 802.15.6 network operates in one of three modes listed in Table 6.10 and also from Reference 27. The access mechanisms used in each period of the superframe are divided into three categories: (1) random access mechanism, which uses either CSMA/CA or a slotted Aloha procedure for resource allocation, (2) improvized and unscheduled access (connectionless contention-free access), which uses unscheduled polling/posting for resource allocation, and (3) scheduled access and variants (connection-oriented contention-free access), which schedules the allocation of slots in one or multiple upcoming superframes. These mechanisms are described in detail in the standard.

6.1.5 IEEE 802.15 WPAN TG4j MBANs

The purpose of TG4j is to create an amendment to 802.15.4, which defines a PHY layer for IEEE 802.15.4 in the 2360 to 2400 MHz band and complies with Federal Communications Commission (FCC) MBAN rules. The amendment may also define modifications to the MAC needed to support this new PHY layer. This amendment allows 802.15.4- and MAC-defined changes to be used in the MBAN band. TG4j work

---

[8]This discussion is based on and summarized from reference (7) which the reader should consult for additional details.

TABLE 6.9 **PHY Layer Specification for the IEEE 802.15.6 Standard**

PHY	Description
NB PHY	The NB PHY is responsible for activation/deactivation of the radio transceiver, CCA within the current channel, and data transmission/reception. The Physical Protocol Data Unit (PPDU) frame of NB PHY contains a Physical Layer Convergence Procedure (PLCP) preamble, a PLCP header, and a PSDU. The PLCP preamble helps the receiver in the timing synchronization and carrier-offset recovery; it is the first component transmitted. The PLCP header conveys information necessary for a successful decoding of a packet to the receiver. The PLCP header is transmitted after PLCP preamble using the given header data rate in the operating frequency band. The last component of PPDU is PSDU which consists of an MAC header, MAC frame body, and frame check sequence (FCS) and is transmitted after PLCP header using any of the available data rates in the operating frequency band. A WBAN device should be able to support transmission and reception in one of the frequency bands available, including the following: 402–405 MHz; 420–450 MHz; 863–870 MHz; 902–928 MHz; 950–956 MHz; 2360–2400 MHz; and 2400–2483.5 MHz. The table further shows the data rate-dependent modulation parameters for PLCP header and PSDU. In NB PHY, the standard uses differential binary phase-shift keying (DBPSK), differential quadrature phase-shift keying (DQPSK), and differential 8-phase-shift keying (D8PSK) modulation techniques except 420–450 MHz which uses a Gaussian minimum shift keying (GMSK) technique
UWB PHY	UWB PHY operates in two frequency bands: low band and high band. Each band is divided into channels, all of them characterized by a bandwidth of 499.2 MHz. The low band consists of three channels (1–3) only. The channel 2 has a central frequency of 3993.6 MHz and is considered a mandatory channel. The high band consists of eight channels (4–11) where channel 7 with a central frequency 7987.2 MHz is considered a mandatory channel, while all other channels are optional. A typical UWB device should support at least one of the mandatory channels. The UWB PHY transceivers allow low implementation complexity and generate signal power levels in the order of those used in the MICS band. The UWB PPDU that contains a synchronization header (SHR), a PHY header (PHR), and PSDU. The SHR is composed of a preamble and a start frame delimiter (SFD). The PHR conveys information about the data rate of the PSDU, length of the payload, and scrambler seed. The information in the PHR is used by the receiver in order to decode the PSDU. The SHR is formed of repetitions of Kasami sequences of length 63. Typical data rates range from 0.5 Mbps up to 10 Mbps, with 0.4882 Mbps as the mandatory one

TABLE 6.9   (*Continued*)

PHY	Description
HBC PHY	HBC PHY operates in two frequency bands centered at 16 MHz and 27 MHz with the bandwidth of 4 MHz. Both operating bands are valid for the United States, Japan, and Korea, and the operating band at 27MHz is valid for Europe. HBC is the electrostatic field communication (EFC) specification of PHY, which covers the entire protocol for WBAN such as packet structure, modulation, preamble/SFD, etc. The PPDU structure of EFC that is composed of a preamble, SFD, PHY header, and PSDU. The preamble and SFD are fixed data patterns. They are pre-generated and sent ahead of the packet header and payload. The preamble sequence is transmitted four times in order to ensure packet synchronization while the SFD is transmitted only once. When the packet is received by the receiver, it finds the start of the packet by detecting the preamble sequence, and then it finds the start of the frame by detecting the SFD

TABLE 6.10   MAC Layer Modes for the IEEE 802.15.6 Standard

Beacon Mode	Description
Beacon mode with beacon period superframe boundaries	In this mode, the beacons are transmitted by the hub in each beacon period except in inactive superframes or unless prohibited by regulations. The superframe structure of IEEE 802.15.6 is divided into exclusive access phase 1 (EAP1), random access phase 1 (RAP1), type I/II phase, EAP2, random access phase 2 (RAP2), type I/II phase, and a contention access phase (CAP). In EAP, RAP, and CAP periods, nodes contend for the resource allocation using either CSMA/CA or a slotted Aloha access procedure. The EAP1 and EAP2 are used for highest priority traffic such as reporting emergency events. The RAP1, RAP2, and CAP are used for regular traffic only. The type I/II phases are used for uplink allocation intervals, downlink allocation intervals, bilink allocation intervals, and delay bilink allocation intervals. In type I/II phases, polling is used for resource allocation. Depending on the application requirements, the coordinator can disable any of these periods by setting the duration length to zero
Nonbeacon mode with superframe boundaries	In this mode, the entire superframe duration is covered by either a type I or a type II access phase but not by both phases
Nonbeacon mode without superframe boundaries	In this mode, the coordinator provides unscheduled type II polled allocation only

started in 2010 and a standard could emerge in 2013.[9] The title of the standard under development is: *IEEE Standard for Information Technology—Telecommunications and Information Exchange Between Systems: Local and Metropolitan Area Network-Specific Requirements. Part 15.4: Wireless Medium Access Control (MAC) and Physical Layer (PHY) Specifications for Low-Rate Wireless Personal Area Networks (WPANs) Amendment: Alternative Physical Layer Extension to support Medical Body Area Network (MBAN) services operating in the 2360–2400 MHz band.*

IEEE 802.15.4 has always supported operation in appropriate frequency bands, and an opportunity is now available to extend the operation of 15.4 into a band that is reserved for MBAN use by the FCC. As noted elsewhere in this text, the FCC has issued a Notice of Proposed Rule Making (NPRM) (FCC NPRM 09-57) to allocate the band 2360 to 2400 MHz for MBANSs using body sensor devices. Service and technical rules allow such devices to operate in this band either on a licensed-by-rule basis under the Medical Device Radiocommunication Service (MedRadio Service) in Part 95 or on a licensed and nonexclusive basis under Part 90 along with a frequency coordination model to minimize interference to incumbent users in the band. This project defines an alternate PHY and the necessary modifications to the MAC that are needed to support the PHY operation according to the FCC rules in the MBAN band (10). The proposed amendment to IEEE 802.15.4 provides a solution for the use of the MBAN spectrum that makes use of existing silicon solutions. The proposed amendment to IEEE 802.15.4 targets both on and off body applications.

By way of comparison, and as noted above, the IEEE P802.15.6 group is also working on BANs with potential medical applications. The two projects address a common application but provide a different set of capabilities. IEEE 802.15.6 is addressing communication in the vicinity of, or inside, a human body. The proposed amendment to IEEE 802.15.4 will address low data rate applications. IEEE P802.15.6 is targeting significant high data rates and lower power consumption applications.

6.1.6 ETSI TR 101 557

The 2012 ETSI TR 101 557 Technical Report (TR) has been produced by the ETSI Technical Committee, Electromagnetic Compatibility and Radiospectrum Matters (ERM) to address bandwidth allocations for WBANs/MBANSs. Previously (in 2011) ERM developed a system reference document (SRdoc) (TR 102 889-2) for technical characteristics for SRD equipment for *wireless industrial applications* using technologies different from UWB. ETSI has also identified two of the candidate frequency bands proposed for MBANSs (2360–2400 MHz and 2483.5–2500 MHz) as candidate bands for these wireless industrial applications. Both applications are

---

[9]Final agreement on the features of the amendment were agreed to during the March, 2012 meeting in Waikoloa, Letter Ballot #81 was approved by the Work Group, opened on March 28, 2012 and closed on April 27, 2012. The Letter Ballot passed with 90.83% Yes votes and generated 575 comments. There were 2 recirculations of the letter ballot, Letter Ballot #82 and Letter Ballot #84, both of which also passed. There were no new comments on the final recirculation ballot and no remaining NO votes. The Work Group has asked the Executive Committee to approve the amendment for Sponsor Ballot at the September 2012 meeting in Palm Springs, USA.

license-exempt SRD applications but can be both considered as critical within their environment and hence why the usual SRD bands are not intended to be used by these systems. MBANSs are used to provide wireless networking of multiple body sensors and actuators used for monitoring patient physiological parameters, patient diagnosis, and patient treatment, primarily in healthcare facilities as well as in other healthcare monitoring situations such as ambulances and the patient's home; the use of MBANSs holds the promise of improved quality and efficiency of patient care by reducing or eliminating a wide array of hardwired, patient-attached cables used by present monitoring technologies. MBANSs are intended to be used mainly in hospitals or, at a later stage of the treatment, at the patient's home. In any case, the environment for the application is far away from the application of wireless sensors used for machine automation in a factory environment. This is *why these two applications in such clearly defined but totally different environments will not harmfully interfere with each other* (1).

The ISM radio bands are radio bands allocated internationally for the said purpose. The ISM bands are defined by the ITU-R in 5.138, 5.150, and 5.280 of the radio regulations. Unfortunately, individual countries' use of the bands designated in these sections may differ due to variations in national radio regulations. In the United States, uses of the ISM bands are governed by Part 15 and Part 18 of the FCC rules. There are a number of ISM bands, but the most well known is the one covering the 2400–2500 MHz region (some other bands include allocations of 6.7 MHz, 13.5 MHz, 26.9 MHz, 40.6 MHz, 433 MHz, 902 MHz, and 5725 MHz).

In Europe, MBANS proponents (e.g., Philips, Zarlink, Texas Instruments, and Dutch Ministry of Economic Affairs Agriculture and Innovation) have an interest in addressing a growing market for MBANS services in the frequency range 1785–2500 MHz, but are concerned that no specific regulatory guidance from CEPT/ECC exists for administrations wishing to implement the MBANSs. A spectrum of 40 MHz between 1785 MHz and 2500 MHz is required for MBANS operation. A 40 MHz spectrum designation plays a key role in enabling MBANS devices achieve harmonized coexistence with other services. It enables MBANS equipment to use low-power and limited duty cycle while providing sufficient space for MBANSs to avoid interference to/from other services. It is also needed to support MBANS coexistence in high-density deployment scenarios. The proposed 40 MHz designation affords meaningful frequency diversity that would allow MBANS devices to use lower transmission power and therefore mitigate potential interference to other services. Initially, only the band 2360–2400 MHz has been proposed by the SRdoc to be considered for use by MBANS. However, during the SRdoc development process, the 1785–1805 MHz, 2400–2483.5 MHz, and 2483.5–2500 MHz bands were suggested as other candidate bands to be considered for designation for MBANS use. See Figure 6.11 for a view to the ITU-R radio regulations current allocation of the candidate bands (1710–2500 MHz). Also see Reference 1 for an extensive discussion of band availability and options, particularly for Europe.

In ETSI TR 101 557, it is proposed that the bigger portion (75%) of the required operational band should be used only inside the healthcare facilities such as hospitals, clinics, emergency rooms, etc. (indoor use), and the smaller portion (25%) should

Allocation to services		
Region 1	**Region 2**	**Region 3**
Europe, Africa, Middle East west of the Persian Gulf, former Soviet Union, and Mongolia.	Americas, Greenland, and some of the eastern Pacific Islands	Asia, and most of Oceania
1710 MHz to 1930 MHz	**FIXED** **MOBILE**	
2300 MHz to 2450 MHz FIXED MOBILE Amateur Radiolocation	**2300 MHz to 2450 MHz** FIXED MOBILE RADIOLOCATION Amateur	
2450 MHz to 2483.5 MHz FIXED MOBILE Radiolocation	**2450 MHz to 2483.5 MHz** FIXED MOBILE RADIOLOCATION	
2483.5 MHz to 2500 MHz FIXED MOBILE MOBILE-SATELLITE (space-to-Earth) Radiolocation	**2483.5 MHz to 2500 MHz** FIXED MOBILE MOBILE-SATELLITE (space-to-Earth) RADIOLOCATION RADIODETERMINATION-SATELLITE (space-to-Earth)	**2483.5 MHz to 2500 MHz** FIXED MOBILE MOBILE-SATELLITE (space-to-Earth) RADIOLOCATION Radiodetermination-satellite (space-to-Earth)

FIGURE 6.11 Current allocation of the candidate bands (1710–2500 MHz) in the ITU-R radio regulations. *Note:* the ISM (industrial, scientific and medical) radio band in the 2.5 GHz region covers the region 2400–2500 MHz. Bluetooth, 802.11/Wi-Fi, IEEE 802.15.4, and ZigBee may use this band, possibly among other bands.

be used both inside and outside the boundaries of healthcare facilities (indoor and outdoor). The required emission bandwidth is up to 5 MHz for proper operation of the MBANS. The emission bandwidth used would depend on the data-rate requirement of the particular MBANS application. For high data-rate applications (e.g., 250 Kbps and beyond), the bandwidth would be 3–5 MHz. For low data-rate applications, the bandwidth would be 1–3 MHz. For MBANS transmitters operating within the health-care facility sub-band (indoor), the maximum transmitted power over the emission bandwidth is 1 mW EIRP (effective isotropic radiated power). For MBANS transmitters operating within the location-independent sub-band, the maximum transmitted power over the emission bandwidth is 20 mW EIRP. The proposed MBANSs will operate at limited duty cycle to reduce power consumption and avoid interference to other services. It is expected that the duty cycle of a MBANS for in-hospital use will not be more than 25%. For location-independent MBANS applications, such as in patient homes, a much lower duty cycle of usually less than 2% is expected (1).

6.1.7 NFC

NFC can be used for IoT/M2M applications; it provides wireless connectivity, but it is not a WBAN technology. NFC[10] is a form of contactless communication between devices such as smartphones, tablets, and other devices. Contactless communication allows a user to wave the smartphone over an NFC-compatible device to send information without needing to touch the devices together or go through multiple steps setting up a connection. NFC is an offshoot of radio frequency identification (RFID), with the exception that NFC is designed for use by devices within close proximity to each other. NFC utilizes electromagnetic radio fields while technologies such as Bluetooth and Wi-Fi rely on radio transmissions. NFC technology is popular in parts of Europe and Asia and is spreading throughout the United States. As noted elsewhere in this text, Google has launched Google Wallet that supports MasterCard PayPass; PayPal offers money transfers between smartphones; and other companies are expected to offer comparable services. As the technology grows, more NFC-compatible smartphones will be available and more stores will offer NFC card readers for customer use.

The technology behind NFC allows a device, known as a reader, interrogator, or active device, to create an electromagnetic field that interacts with another NFC-compatible device or a small NFC tag holding the information the reader requires. Passive devices, such as the NFC tag in smart posters, store information, and communicate with the reader, but these devices do not actively read other devices. Peer-to-peer communication through two active devices is also possible with NFC, allowing both devices to send and receive information. Three forms of NFC technology exist—Type A, Type B, and FeliCa; all three types are similar, but communicate in slightly different ways.

Compatibility is the key to the growth of NFC as a popular payment and data communication method; hence, NFC-based device must be able to communicate with other wireless technologies and be able to interact with different types of NFC transmissions. NFC maintains interoperability between different wireless communication methods such as Bluetooth and other NFC standards (e.g., FeliCa, popular in Japan) through the NFC Forum. Founded in 2004 by Sony, Nokia, and Philips, the forum enforces standards that manufacturers must meet when designing NFC-compatible devices; this ensures that NFC is secure and remains easy to use with different versions of the technology.

Standards exist to ensure all forms of NFC technology can interact with other NFC-compatible devices and will work with newer devices in the future. Two major

---

[10]This discussion is based on materials from the NearFieldCommunication.org, an advocacy group for NFC applications. The organization aims at offering insightful information that keeps stakeholders informed on both the benefits and possible drawbacks of this evolving technology.

specifications exist for NFC technology: ISO/IEC 14443 and ISO/IEC 18000-3. The first defines the ID cards used to store information, such as that found in NFC tags. The latter specifies the RFID communication used by NFC devices. ISO/IEC 18000-3 is an international standard for all devices communicating wirelessly at the 13.56 MHz frequency using Type A or Type B cards, as is the case for NFC. The devices must be within 4 cm of each other before they can transfer information. The standards define how a device and the NFC tag it is reading should communicate with one another. The device is known as the interrogating device while the NFC tag is simply referred to as the tag.

To operate, the interrogator sends out a signal to the tag. If the devices are close enough to each other, the tag becomes powered by the interrogator's signal. Since the interrogator's signal powers the tag, the tag can be small in size and can function without any battery or power source of its own. The two devices create a high-frequency magnetic field between the loosely coupled coils in both the interrogating device and the NFC tag. Once this field is established, a connection is formed and the information can be passed between the interrogator and the tag. The interrogator sends the first message to the tag to find out what type of communication the tag uses, such as Type A or Type B. When the tag responds, the interrogator sends its first commands in the appropriate specification. The tag receives the instruction and checks if it is valid. If not, nothing occurs. If it is a valid request, the tag then responds with the requested information. For sensitive transactions such as credit card payments, a secure communication channel is first established, and all information sent is encrypted.

NFC tags function at half duplex; the interrogator functions at full duplex. Half duplex refers to a device that can only send or receive, but not both at once; full duplex can do both simultaneously. An NFC tag can only receive or send a signal, while the interrogating device can receive a signal at the same time it sends a command. Commands are transmitted from the interrogator using phase jitter modulation (PJM) to modify the surrounding field and send out a signal. The tag answers using inductive coupling by sending a charge through the coils in it.

Devices using NFC may be active or passive. A passive device, such as an NFC tag, contains information that other devices can read but does not read any information itself; an example could be a poster or a commercial sign on a wall where other devices can read the information, but the sign itself only transmits the stored information to authorized devices. Active devices can read information and send it. An active NFC device, such as a smartphone, is not only able to collect information from NFC tags, but it is also able to exchange information with other compatible phones or devices and could even alter the information on the NFC tag if authorized to make such changes.

To ensure security, NFC often establishes a secure channel and uses encryption when sending sensitive information such as credit card numbers. Users can further protect their private data by keeping antivirus software on their smartphones and adding a password to the phone.

As noted, NFC is limited to a distance of approximately 4 cm; Bluetooth does offer a longer signal range for connecting during data communication and transfers. NFC technology consumes little power when compared to standard Bluetooth technology (but not when compared with BLE which uses less power than NFC). Only when NFC has to power a passive, unpowered source such as an NFC tag does it require more power than a traditional Bluetooth transmission. Another benefit of NFC technology comes in its ease of use. Bluetooth requires users to manually set up connections between smartphones and takes several seconds. NFC connects automatically in a fraction of a second. Although the users must be close to one another to use NFC technology, it is faster and easier to set up than a Bluetooth connection. Also see the technical parameters depicted in Table 6.3 for this technology.

6.1.8 Dedicated Short-Range Communications (DSRC) and Related Protocols

DSRC is a two-way short-to-medium-range wireless communications capability that permits very high data transmission critical in communications-based active safety applications. DSRC-based communications is a major research priority of the Joint Program Office (ITS JPO) at the U.S. Department of Transportation (U.S. DOT) Research and Innovative Technology Administration (RITA). The cross-modal program is conducting research using DSRC and other wireless communications technologies to ensure safe, interoperable connectivity to help prevent vehicular crashes of all types and to enhance mobility and environmental benefits across all transportation system modes. In Report and Order FCC-03-324, the FCC allocated 75 MHz of spectrum in the 5.9 GHz band for use by Intelligent Transportation Systems (ITS) vehicle safety and mobility applications. Vehicle-to-vehicle (V2V) and vehicle-to-infrastructure (V2I) applications utilizing DSRC may have the potential to significantly reduce many of the most deadly types of crashes through real-time advisories alerting drivers to imminent hazards—such as veering close to the edge of the road; vehicles suddenly stopped ahead; collision paths during merging; the presence of nearby communications devices and vehicles; and sharp curves or slippery patches of roadway ahead. Convenience V2I services such as e-parking and toll payment are also able to communicate using DSRC. Anonymous information from electronic sensors in vehicles and devices can also be transmitted over DSRC to provide better traffic and travel condition information to travelers and transportation managers. DSRC was developed with a primary goal of enabling technologies that support safety applications and communication between vehicle-based devices and infrastructure to reduce collisions. DSRC is the only short-range wireless alternative today that provides (28):

- Designated licensed bandwidth: For secure, reliable communications to take place. It is primarily allocated for vehicle safety applications by FCC Report and Order FCC 03-324.
- Fast network acquisition: Active safety applications require the immediate establishment of communication and frequent updates.
- Low latency: Active safety applications must recognize each other and transmit messages to each other in milliseconds without delay.

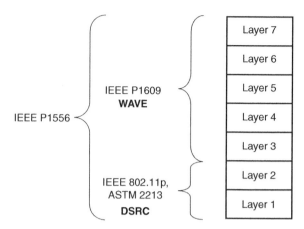

FIGURE 6.12   Relationship of WAVE, DSRC, and other protocols.

• High reliability when required: Active safety applications require a high level of link reliability. DSRC works in high vehicle speed mobility conditions and delivers performance immune to extreme weather conditions (e.g., rain, fog, snow, etc.).

• Priority for safety applications: Safety applications on DSRC are given priority over nonsafety applications.

• Interoperability: DSRC ensures interoperability, which is the key to successful deployment of active safety applications, using widely accepted standards. It supports both V2V and V2I communications.

• Security and privacy: DSRC provides safety message authentication and privacy.

The ASTM (American Society for Testing and Materials) Standard E2213-03,[11] based on IEEE 802.11a, is planned to be used for IoT applications in ITS environments. It uses a band around 5.9 GHz allocated to DSRC applications in the ITS environment—to be exact, the applicable band is now[12] 5.850–5.925 GHz range, which is divided into seven channels (each 10 MHz—these are licensed channels). Transmission has a range of 300–1000 m and a data rate of 6–27 Mbps. Half-duplex operation is used: a station can only send or transmit, but not both at the same time. DSRC devices are IEEE 802.11 systems using the WAVE (wireless access in vehicular environments) mode of operation in the DSRC band. The 5.9 GHz DSRC was originally developed for the U.S. market, and currently it is at the beginning of commercialization. Figure 6.12 depicts the relationship of WAVE, DSRC, and other support protocols.

---

[11] ASTM E2213-03 Standard Specification for Telecommunications and Information Exchange Between Roadside and Vehicle Systems—5 GHz Band Dedicated Short-Range Communications (DSRC) Medium Access Control (MAC) and Physical Layer (PHY) Specifications.

[12] Originally, the band was in the 915 MHz region, with a single unlicensed channel.

IEEE 802.11p (*802.11p-2010—IEEE Standard for Information technology: Local and Metropolitan Area Network-Specific Requirements. Part 11: Wireless LAN Medium Access Control (MAC) and Physical Layer (PHY) Specifications Amendment 6: Wireless Access in Vehicular Environments*) is an amendment that specifies the extensions to IEEE Standard 802.11 for WLANs providing reliable wireless communications while in a vehicular environment. IEEE 802.11p is based on ASTM Standard E2213-03 and defines the MAC layer for wireless communication in vehicular environments. It supports two different stacks:

- IPv6, but only on service channels (not control channel)
- WAVE short message protocol (WSMP): can be sent on any channel and allows applications to directly control physical characteristics (channel number and transmitter power)

The IEEE 802.11p standard is positioned as an underlying protocol for car-to-car and car-to-infrastructure applications worldwide. At the PHY layer, it has essentially the same structure as 802.11a and 802.11g: the modulation format, based on orthogonal frequency-division multiplexing (OFDM), the forward-error-correction (FEC), the structure of the preamble sequences, and the pilot-symbol schemes are identical. Furthermore, 802.11p uses the same medium access scheme common to all IEEE 802.11 standards, namely CSMA/CA (29).

WAVE is a mode of operation used by IEEE 802.11 devices to operate in the DSRC band. WAVE is part of the IEEE 1609 specification, which defines the architecture, the communications model, the management structure, the security, and physical access. The key architecture components are: (i) the on-board unit (OBU), (ii) the road side unit (RSU), and (iii) the WAVE interface. Figure 6.13, loosely based on Reference 30, depicts the WAVE protocol stack. Supportive standards are as follows (31):

- P1609.1 *Resource Manager* describes key components of WAVE system architecture and defines data flows and resources; it also defines command message formats and data storage formats. Finally it also specifies the types of devices that may by supported by OBU;
- P1609.2 *Security Services for Applications and Management Messages* defines secure message formats and processing and describes circumstances for using secure message exchanges;
- P1609.3 *Networking Services* defines network and transport layer services, including addressing and routing, in support of secure WAVE data exchange; it defines WAVE short messages (WSMs), providing an efficient WAVE-specific alternative to IP that can be directly supported by applications. Also it defines the MIB for WAVE protocol stack;
- P1609.4 *Multichannel Operations* defines enhancements to 802.11 MAC to support WAVE.

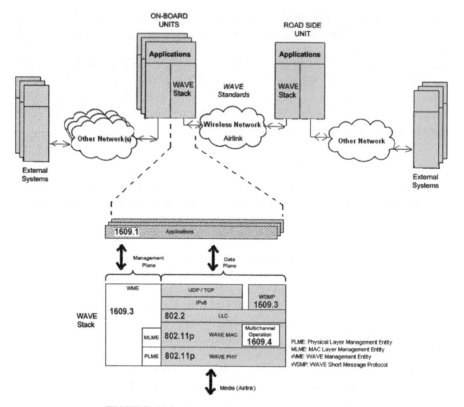

FIGURE 6.13 WAVE elements and protocol stack.

6.1.9 Comparison of WPAN Technologies

This section makes some general comparisons between some of the key PAN technologies discussed in this chapter, following observations and conclusion made in Reference 5. A basic comparison was already provided in Table 6.3, while Table 6.11 (also synthesized from Reference 5) describes some additional factors to take into account when comparing PAN technologies.

ANT/ANT+ is a mass production technology, establishing itself as the "sports and fitness" space. It is a proprietary technology, and it is unlikely that it will become pervasive. It had only been integrated into three mobile handsets at press time. ANT endeavors at operating from limited power sources and has built a niche ecosystem. ANT/ANT+ is not perceived to be a major IoT/M2M technology, but it is part of the ecosystem. The same can be said about NIKE+.

BLE is the closest competitor to ANT/ANT+ from an overall raw performance perspective. BLE is targeting the same markets as the competitive alternatives, but it offers the mobile handset manufacturers access to a larger product opportunity environment. BLE provides the best power per bit requirements of the PAN

TABLE 6.11   Some Additional Factors to Take into Account when Comparing PAN Technologies

Issue	Description
Implementation complexity	Implementation complexity is established by assessing the amount of software that would be required to implement a simple program along with hardware requirements It was noted in the text that BLE chipsets come in two categories: single mode and Bluetooth + BLE. Single-mode configurations are shipped as an SoC that contains the host processor and radio. The protocol stack is integrated in the silicon and exposes some simple application programming interfaces (API) for a developer to use. As a result, there is little effort required by the developer when creating a new product. Single-mode BLE devices are often shipped from silicon vendors as precertified units. This means that original end manufacturers (OEMs) do not need to spend resources qualifying their new products. If the developer decides to deviate significantly from a given reference design, then it is possible that some features may need retesting. The hardware for a single-mode LE device is simple. The main costs associated with a low-power sensor are the processor, radio, antenna, battery, battery connector, sensor, regulator, and the printed circuit board (PCB). A BLE device is expected to cost about $3 in components (about $2 for the Bluetooth IC and the EEPROM) and $1 for the rest (particularly the battery and the RF crystal); these component costs will be lower when mass production is activated. Dual-mode Bluetooth chipsets, as used in a mobile handset, have a host processor present. Silicon vendors normally ship a protocol stack that executes on the host processor and provides a simple API to access Bluetooth and LE. Dual-mode Bluetooth chips may also contain their own application processor. Such devices have the sensitive protocol stack burnt into read-only memory (ROM) and expose an API as a virtual machine. These types of chips are often found in consumer electronics, like headsets, where more than just sensing applications are necessary
Protocol efficiency	A wireless transmission protocol consists of the payload and overhead. The efficiency of the protocol can be defined as the ratio of payload to total packet length. If a protocol is inefficient, it will effectively imply that the transmission channel and the radio emanations are used to transferring nonpayload information; this will rapidly discharge the battery while transferring a limited amount of useful data. Alternatively, a protocol that is very efficient will transfer a larger amount of useful data on a single charge. There is a trade-off between reliability and efficiency; for example an ultra-efficient protocol that does not incorporate a checksum or error corrections; given the intrinsic possibility of interference in the 2.4 GHz band, this may require retransmissions (assuming that there are upper-layer protocols to address this predicament). For example, BLE protocol efficiency is around 66%

(*continued*)

TABLE 6.11 *(Continued)*

Issue	Description
Power efficiency	Power efficiency is one of the most critical factors in selecting the PAN technology for a given application. This efficiency is typically measured as the power per bit An ANT device is configured to transmit 32 bytes/s and consumes 61 μA. The power per bit = 0.183 mW/256 bits = 0.71 μW/bit In BLE, connectable advertising packets (adverts) are broadcast every 500 ms. Each packet has 20 bytes of useful payload and consumes 49 μA at 3 V. For this particular setup, the power per bit is 0.153 μW/bit For IrDA, the power per bit is 11.7 μW/bit A NIKE+ foot pod lasts 1000 h and transmits its payload every second. The power per bit is 2.48 μW/bit Wi-Fi consumes approximately 116 mA at 1.8 V when transmitting a 40 Mbps user datagram protocol (UDP) payload. Power per bit is 0.00525 μW/bit. Unfortunately, current consumption does not reduce when throughput is reduced in a Wi-Fi chipset. Hence, this measure is not completely comparable to the other data cited here. Also Wi-FI's peak current consumption exceeds the capabilities of a coin battery A Zigbee device consumes 0.035706 W when transferring 24 bytes of data. Hence, the power per bit is 0.035706/192 = 185.9 μW/bit
Peak power consumption	Peak power consumption is an important parameter when designing long-life devices. The common CR2032 coin cell can only provide about 15 mA peaks without damage (drawing 30 mA at peaks will reduce realized capacity by about 10% of manufacturers' stated figures). Acceptable continuous standard loads are typically 2 mA or less, in order to achieve published capacity figures. The PAN technologies discussed in this chapter have peak current requirements in the 10–50 mA, with the exception of Wi-Fi, which has a higher requirement
Robustness and coexistence	Packet transfer reliability impacts on battery life and the user experience: if a data packet is undeliverable due to suboptimal transmission environments, or interference from nearby radios, a transmitter may keep retransmitting until the packet is successfully delivered, expanding battery energy. A method to address these issues is to use channel hopping (which also helps with interference). If a wireless system is restricted to a single channel, its reliability may deteriorate in congested environments. Bluetooth and BLE use channel hopping: Bluetooth devices use AFH, which allows each node to map out frequently congested areas of the spectrum to be avoided in future transactions Coexistence is typically thought of as the ability of technologies to operate in the presence of other radios in the same room or building. ZigBee can interplay with a Wi-Fi access point; as can BLEs (refer to earlier figures on this issue). Colocation of PAN technologies with WLANs must be carefully designed, especially as Wi-Fi output power increases with advances in technology

(continued)

TABLE 6.11   *(Continued)*

Issue	Description
	BLE implements passive interference avoidance schemes. For example, AFH can be used to keep clear of channels where interference is detected. BLE advertising channels are also specifically chosen to be in the least congested regions of the 2.4 GHz ISM band. Wi-Fi has active coexistence technology implemented, when integrated with a device containing Bluetooth, and a mechanism to reduce its data rates, when interferers are detected from neighboring wireless technology. ZigBee does not implement a coexistence scheme, but it does have the ability to continuously listen for clear time on its channel. If the channel is heavily used, ZigBee throughput and latency are adversely affected, eventually halting. ZigBee PRO has a feature known as frequency agility (not the same as hopping) where it may be possible to search for a clear channel (of the 16 channels defined) and then re-establish the network

Note: Synthesized from Reference 5; consult reference for additional details.

technologies, exceeded only by Wi-Fi. BLE is likely to turn out to be an important IoT/M2M technology in the healthcare and/or home environment, for example for peripheral and/or smartphone connectivity.

Wi-Fi is normally intended for bulk traffic transfer at high speed (HS). It should come as no surprise that Wi-Fi is the most complicated technology to integrate into a system. Wi-Fi requires various drivers and a full protocol stack. In addition, such systems typically consume significant power at the PC end of the link to minimize latency.

ZigBee and RF4CE are practically the same technology and appear prima facia to require more power compared with the other PAN radio technologies. These systems are likely to turn out to be important IoT/M2M technologies in the healthcare and/or home environment.

NFC is not seen as a competitor to most low-power wireless technologies; the interest in this technology is that it brings new use cases to the mobile space. IR transmit-only devices are inexpensive and may still remain a viable option in low-end televisions for the near future, but the technology is also relatively power hungry. IR is being replaced in many areas by non-LOS radio technology.

6.2 CELLULAR AND MOBILE NETWORK TECHNOLOGIES FOR IoT/M2M

6.2.1 Overview and Motivations

Developers of IoT/M2M applications that are geographically dispersed over a city, region, or nation may find cellular networks to be the practical connectivity technology of choice. This section looks at some key capabilities of these networks. In the near future, M2M applications are expected to become important sources of traffic (and revenues) for cellular data networks. For example, energy suppliers routinely utilize SCADA-based systems to enable remote telemetry functions in the power grid. Traditionally, SCADA systems have used wireline networks to link remote power grid elements with a central operations center; however, at this time an increasing number of utilities are turning to public cellular networks to support these functions. Naturally, reliability and security are key considerations; endpoints typically will support virtual private network (VPN) built on IPsec mechanisms in addition to other embedded firewall capabilities.

In starting the discussion about mobile networks, one should keep in mind that IoT/M2M traffic has specific characteristics, discussed briefly in Chapter 4, which relate to the priority of the data being communicated, the size of the data, the real-time streaming needs on one end of the requirements spectrum to the extremely high delay tolerance of the data on the other end of the requirements spectrum, and varying degrees of mobility; cellular/mobile networks are characterized by varying capacity, bandwidth, link conditions, link utilization, and overall network load, which affect their ability to reliably transfer such M2M data (32). These details have to be reconciled in order to be able to cost-effectively utilize cellular technologies for a broad set of applications (while some applications may be less sensitive to cost consideration, many more applications will indeed require optimized connectivity cost metrics). Initial 3GPP efforts have focused on the ability to differentiate MTC-type devices, allowing operators to selectively handle such devices in congestion/overload situations. Specifically, low priority indicator has been added to the relevant UE (user equipment)-to-network procedures; with this, overload and congestion control is done on both core network (CN) and radio access network (RAN) based on this indicator (33).

There are different opinions as to which cellular technologies are practical and/or ideal for M2M. Some proponents claim that many developers are concentrating on 4G products. However, the cost of 4G modules is two times more expensive than 3G modules and three times more expensive than 2G modules; hence some proponents only recommend a 4G device if it is going to be deployed in an urban setting and the cost of connectivity was unimportant. Others argue that if a service provider or organization wanted to deploy an inexpensive system with a short lifespan of 1 or 2 years, they could go with 2G; but if a service provider or organization wanted to build a device to have longevity of around 10 years, then they should consider using 3G (34).

6.2.2 Universal Mobile Telecommunications System

UMTS is a 3G mobile cellular technology for networks supporting voice and data (IP) based on the GSM standard developed by the 3GPP (Third-Generation Partnership Project). UMTS is a component of the ITU IMT-2000 standard set and is functionally comparable with the CDMA2000 standard set for networks based on the competing cdmaOne technology. UMTS can carry many traffic types from real-time circuit switched to IP-based packet switched.

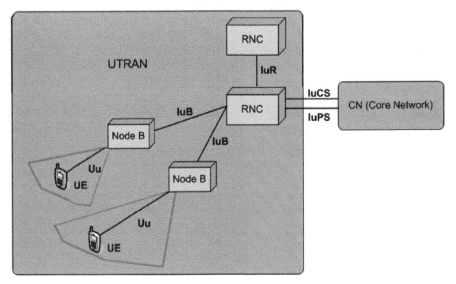

FIGURE 6.14   UTRAN.

Universal terrestrial radio access network (UTRAN) is a collective term for the NodeBs (base stations) and radio network controllers (RNC) that comprise the UMTS RAN. NodeB is the equivalent to the base transceiver station (BTS) concept used in GSM. The UTRAN allows connectivity between the UE and the CN. As seen in Figure 6.14, UTRAN contains the base stations, which are called NodeBs, and the RNC; the RNC provides control functionalities for one or more NodeBs.

As noted earlier, video can be supported over the data (IP) capability of a 3G system; mobility is generally supported at the PHY level, but could also be supported with the MIPv6 mechanisms. The challenge of 3G system is related to bandwidth availability.

6.2.3 LTE

6.2.3.1 Overview   LTE is the 3GPP initiative to evolve the UMTS technology toward a 4G. LTE can be viewed as an architecture framework and a set of ancillary mechanisms that aims at providing seamless IP connectivity between UE and the packet (IPv4, IPv6) data network without any disruption to the end-users' applications during mobility. In contrast to the circuit-switched model of previous-generation cellular systems, LTE has been designed to support *only* packet-switched services.

System architecture evolution (SAE) is the corresponding evolution of the GPRS/3G packet CN evolution. LTE/SAE standards are defined in 3GPP Rel.8 specifications. Colloquially, the term LTE is typically used to represent both LTE and SAE.

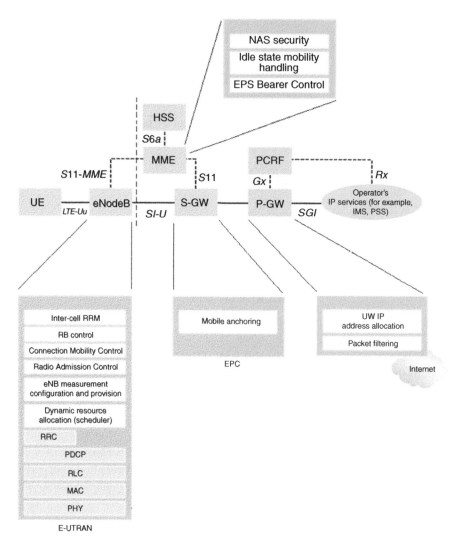

FIGURE 6.15 The EPS network elements.

The key element provided by LTE/SAE is the EPS (evolved packet system), that is, together LTE and SAE comprise the EPS. EPS provides the user with IP connectivity to a packet data network for accessing the Internet, as well as for supporting services such as streaming video. Figure 6.15 shows the overall network architecture, including the network elements and the standardized interfaces. The EPS consists of the:

- New air interface E-UTRAN (evolved UTRAN) and
- The evolved packet core (EPC) network

TABLE 6.12   Basic Comparison Between Two Generations of Cellular Technologies

3G Systems	4G/LTE/SAE Systems

Competing standards
Limited set of devices
Lack of applications
Multiple bands and frequency
Slow rollout
Interoperability and
   interworking
	– Complex technology
	  • 130+ 3GPP specifications
	  • 35 specs for devices, 56 specs for eNodeB, 41 specs
	    for EPC
	  • New network and functional elements (e.g., MME,
	    SGW, PGW, PCRF, . . .)
	  • New interfaces (**S6a**, **S8**, S9, S13, S13', . . .)
	  • **S6a**/S6d in LTE is the equivalent of MAP-based Gr
	    and D in Pre-Rel.8
	  • S13/S13' in LTE is the equivalent of MAP-based Gf
	    in Pre-Rel.8
	  • New protocols (PMIP, GTPv2, diameter, SIP, . . .)
	– Limited availability of network/user devices
	– Voice, video, data, and messaging
	  • Lack of voice support in early LTE networks
	– Multiple frequency/spectrum fragmentation
	– Expanded ecosystem
	– Interoperability and interworking
	  • 15 network types with which to interoperate
	    • Access networks
	    • Converged core
	    • CS core and PS core
	– Billing and settlement capabilities

Hence, while the term "LTE" encompasses the evolution of the UMTS *radio access* through the E-UTRAN, it is accompanied by an evolution of the *nonradio aspects* under the term SAE, which includes, as just noted, the EPC network.

Table 6.12 (based on observations made in Reference 35) provides a short comparison between two generations of cellular technologies.

In principle, LTE promises the following benefits:

• Simplified network architecture (Flat IP based);
• Efficient interworking;
• Robust QoS framework;
• Common evolution for multiple technologies;
• Real-time, interactive, low-latency true broadband;
• Multisession data;
• End-to-end enhanced QoS management (see below);
• Policy control and management;
• High level of security.

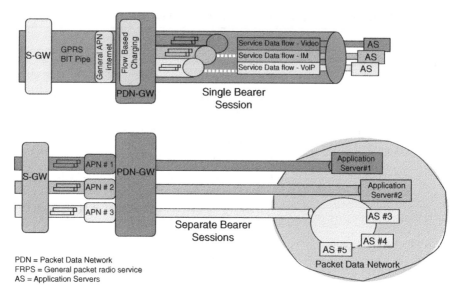

FIGURE 6.16   Bearers in EPS.

The EPS uses the concept of *bearers* to route IP traffic from a gateway in the packet data network to the UE. A bearer is an IP packet flow with a defined QoS between the gateway and the UE. The E-UTRAN and EPC together set up and release bearers as required by applications. An EPS bearer is often associated with a QoS. Multiple bearers can be established for an end-user in order to provide different QoS streams or connectivity to different packet data networks or applications reachable via that network. For example, a user might be engaged in watching a video clip while at the same time performing web browsing or FTP download; a video bearer would provide the necessary QoS for the video stream, while a best-effort bearer would be suitable for the web browsing or file transfer session (see Fig. 6.16). This is achieved by means of several EPS network elements that have different roles.

6.2.3.2   Core Network   At a high level, the network is comprised of the CN (i.e., the EPC) and the access network E-UTRAN. While the CN consists of many logical nodes, the access network is comprised of essentially just one node, the evolved NodeB (eNodeB), which connects to the UEs. Each of these network elements is interconnected over interfaces that are standardized in order to allow multivendor interoperability.

The logical CN nodes are shown in Figure 6.15 and briefly discussed in Table 6.13 (36, 37). The CN is responsible for the overall control of the UE and establishment of the bearers. The main logical nodes of the CN are: (i) PDN gateway (P-GW); (ii) serving gateway (S-GW); and (iii) mobility management entity (MME). In addition to these nodes, the CN also includes other logical nodes and functions such as the Home Subscriber Server (HSS) and the Policy Control and Charging Rules Function

TABLE 6.13   CN Nodes

Function	Description
Policy Control and Charging Rules Function (PCRF)	The PCRF is responsible for policy control decision-making, as well as for controlling the flow-based charging functionalities in the Policy Control Enforcement Function (PCEF), which resides in the P-GW. The PCRF provides the QoS authorization (QCI and bit rates) that decides how a certain data flow will be treated in the PCEF and ensures that this is in accordance with the user's subscription profile
Home Subscriber Server (HSS)	The HSS contains users' Systems Architecture Evolution (SAE) subscription data such as the EPS-subscribed QoS profile and any access restrictions for roaming. It also holds information about the packet data networks to which the user can connect. This could be in the form of an access point name (APN) (which is a label according to DNS naming conventions describing the access point to the PDN) or a PDN address (indicating subscribed IP address(es)). In addition, the HSS holds dynamic information such as the identity of the MME to which the user is currently attached or registered. The HSS may also integrate the authentication center (AUC), which generates the vectors for authentication and security keys
Packet data network Gateway (P-GW)	The P-GW is responsible for IP address allocation for the UE, as well as QoS enforcement and flow-based charging according to rules from the PCRF. It is responsible for the filtering of downlink user IP packets into the different QoS-based bearers. This is performed based on traffic flow templates (TFTs). The P-GW performs QoS enforcement for GBR bearers. It also serves as the mobility anchor for interworking with non-3GPP technologies such as CDMA2000 and WiMAX® networks
Serving Gateway (S-GW)	All user IP packets are transferred through the S-GW, which serves as the local mobility anchor for the data bearers when the UE moves between eNodeBs. It also retains the information about the bearers when the UE is in the idle state (known as "EPS Connection Management — IDLE" [ECM-IDLE]) and temporarily buffers downlink data while the MME initiates paging of the UE to re-establish the bearers. In addition, the S-GW performs some administrative functions in the visited network such as collecting information for charging (e.g., the volume of data sent to or received from the user) and lawful interception. It also serves as the mobility anchor for interworking with other 3GPP technologies such as GPRS and UMTS
Mobility Management Entity (MME)	The MME is the control node that processes the signaling between the UE and the CN. The protocols running between the UE and the CN are known as the nonaccess stratum (NAS) protocols. The main functions supported by the MME can be classified as: (i) *Functions related to bearer management*—This includes the establishment, maintenance, and release of the bearers and is handled by the session management layer in the NAS protocol and (ii) *Functions related to connection management*—This includes the establishment of the connection and security between the network and UE and is handled by the connection or mobility management layer in the NAS protocol layer

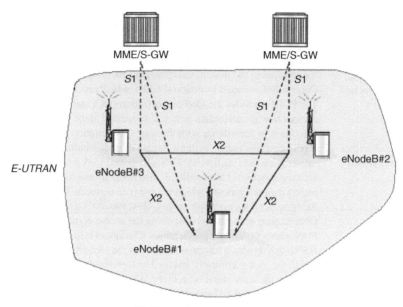

FIGURE 6.17   E-UTRAN.

(PCRF). Since the EPS only provides a bearer path of a certain QoS, control of multimedia applications such as packet video is provided by the IP multimedia subsystem (IMS), which is considered to be outside the EPS itself.

6.2.3.3 Access Network   The access network of LTE, E-UTRAN, consists of a network of eNodeBs, as illustrated in Figure 6.17. For normal user traffic (as opposed to broadcast), there is no centralized controller in E-UTRAN; hence the E-UTRAN architecture is said to be flat. The eNodeBs are normally interconnected with each other by means of an interface known as "X2" and to the EPC by means of the S1 interface—more specifically, to the MME by means of the S1–MME interface and to the S-GW by means of the S1–U interface. The protocols that run between the eNodeBs and the UE are known as the "AS protocols." The E-UTRAN is responsible for all radio-related functions, as depicted in Table 6.14 (36, 37). On the network side, all of these functions reside in the eNodeBs, each of which can be responsible for managing multiple cells. Unlike some of the previous second-generation and 3G technologies, LTE integrates the radio controller function into the eNodeB; this allows tight interaction between the different protocol layers of the RAN, thus reducing latency and improving efficiency. Such distributed control eliminates the need for a high-availability, processing-intensive controller, which in turn has the potential to reduce costs and avoid "single points of failure." Furthermore, as LTE does not support soft handover, there is no need for a centralized data-combining function in the network. One consequence of the lack of a centralized controller node is that, as the UE moves, the network must transfer all information related to a UE, that

TABLE 6.14   E-UTRAN Functions

Function	Description
Radio resource management (RRM)	This function covers all activities related to the radio bearers, such as radio bearer control, radio admission control, radio mobility control, scheduling, and dynamic allocation of resources to UEs in both uplink and downlink
Header compression	This function is used to ensure efficient use of the radio interface by compressing the IP packet headers that could otherwise represent a significant overhead, especially for small packets such as Voice Over IP (VoIP) or video
Security	All data sent over the radio interface is encrypted
Connectivity to the EPC	This function consists of the signaling toward MME and the bearer path toward the S-GW

is, the UE context, together with any buffered data, from one eNodeB to another; mechanisms are, therefore, needed to avoid data loss during handover.

6.2.3.4 Roaming A network run by one operator in a jurisdiction (or service area) is known as a "public land mobile network (PLMN)." Roaming is the capability where users are allowed to connect to PLMNs other than those to which they are directly subscribed, as shown in Figure 6.18. A roaming user is connected to the E-UTRAN, MME, and S-GW of the visited LTE network; however, LTE/SAE allows the P-GW of either the visited or the home network to be used (36, 37). Using the home network's P-GW allows the user to access the home operator's services even while in a visited network.

6.2.3.5 Interworking Interworking with other networks is also critically important. The EPS also supports interworking and mobility (handover) with networks such as GSM, UMTS, CDMA2000, and WiMAX (worldwide interoperability for microwave access). The architecture for interworking with 2G and 3G GPRS/UMTS networks is depicted in Figure 6.19; in Figure 6.19 the S-GW acts as the mobility anchor for interworking with other 3GPP technologies such as GSM and UMTS, while the P-GW serves as an anchor allowing seamless mobility to non-3GPP networks such as CDMA2000 or WiMAX. The P-GW may also support a Proxy Mobile Internet Protocol (PMIPv6)-based interface.

6.2.3.6 Protocol Architecture The protocol architecture spans the user plane and the control plane. The user plane protocols operate as follows: an IP packet for a UE is encapsulated in an EPC-specific protocol and tunneled between the P-GW and the eNodeB for transmission to the UE. Different tunneling protocols are used across different interfaces; A 3GPP-specific tunneling protocol called the GPRS tunneling protocol (GTP) is used over the CN interfaces, S1, and S5/S8. The E-UTRAN user plane protocol stack is shown in Figure 6.20 top, consisting of the packet data

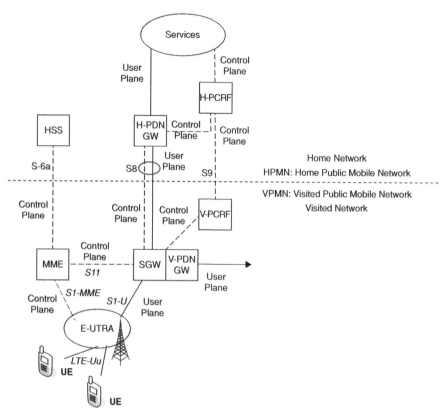

FIGURE 6.18   Roaming architecture for 3GPP accesses with P-GW in home network.

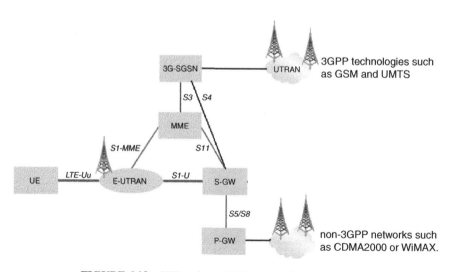

FIGURE 6.19   LTE and pre-LTE interworking mechanisms.

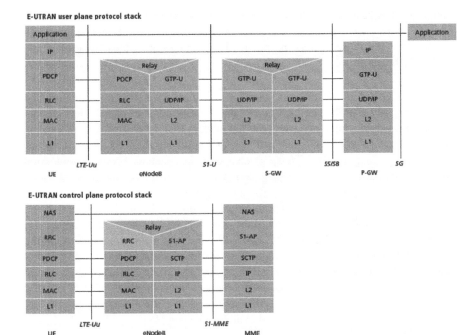

FIGURE 6.20 LTE protocol stack at the E-UTRAN.

convergence protocol (PDCP), radio link control (RLC) and MAC sublayers that are terminated in the eNodeB on the network side. The protocol stack for the control plane between the UE and MME is shown in Figure 6.12 bottom. The lower layers perform the same functions as for the user plane; the radio resource control (RRC) protocol is known as "layer 3" in the AS protocol stack and it is the key controlling function in the AS, being responsible for establishing the radio bearers and configuring all the lower layers using RRC signaling between the eNodeB and the UE (36, 37).

6.2.3.7 Multiple QoS Management
In order to support multiple QoS requirements, different bearers are set up within the EPS, each being associated with a QoS, being that in a typical environment, multiple applications may be running in a UE at any time, each one having different QoS requirements. In the access network, it is the responsibility of the eNodeB to ensure the necessary QoS for a bearer over the radio interface. Bearers can be classified into two categories:

- Minimum guaranteed bit rate (GBR) bearers that can be used for applications such as mobile video. These bearers have an associated GBR value for which dedicated transmission resources are permanently allocated at bearer establishment or modification (bit rates higher than the GBR may be allowed for a GBR bearer if resources are available).

- Non-GBR bearers that do not guarantee any particular bit rate. These bearers can be used for applications such as, but not limited to, web browsing or FTP transfer. For these bearers, no bandwidth resources are allocated permanently to the bearer.

Each bearer has an associated QoS class identifier (QCI), and an allocation and retention priority (ARP). The QCI is a scalar identifying a set of transport characteristics and used to infer node-specific parameters that control packet-forwarding treatment. Each packet flow is mapped to a QCI value based on the level of service required by the application. Transport characteristics include bearer with/without GBR, priority, packet loss rate, packet latency budget, and so on. Packet-forwarding treatment includes scheduling weights, admission thresholds, queue management thresholds, and link-layer protocol configuration. Nine QCI values were defined and standardized in the Release 8 version of the specifications, as depicted in Table 6.15; standardization ensures that an LTE operator can expect uniform traffic-handling behavior throughout the network regardless of the manufacturers of the eNodeB equipment. The usage of the QCI avoids the transmission of a full set of QoS-related parameters over the network interfaces and reduces the complexity of QoS negotiation. The QCI, along with ARP and, if where needed, GBR and maximum bit rate (MBR), determines the QoS associated to an EPS bearer. Hence, each QCI is characterized by priority, packet delay budget, and acceptable packet loss rate; the QCI label for a bearer determines how it is handled in the eNodeB. A mapping between EPS and pre-Release 8 QoS parameters has been defined to allow proper interworking with legacy networks.

TABLE 6.15   Standardized QCIs in LTE (Current List)

Resource Type	QCI	APP	Packet Delay Budget (ms)	Packet Loss Rate	Examples
GBR	1	2	100	10^{-2}	Voice
GBR	2	4	150	10^{-3}	Video streaming (live)
GBR	3	5	300	10^{-6}	Video streaming (buffered)
GBR	4	3	50	10^{-3}	Interactive gaming
Non-GBR	5	1	100	10^{-6}	IMS signaling
Non-GBR	6	7	100	10^{-3}	Voice, video (live streaming), interactive gaming
Non-GBR	7	6	300	10^{-6}	Video streaming (buffered)
Non-GBR	8	8	300	10^{-6}	WWW, e-mail, FTP, progressive video, p2p file sharing, TCP-based apps
Non-GBR	9	9	300	10^{-6}	

The priority and packet delay budget (and to some extent the acceptable packet loss rate) from the QCI label determine the RLC mode configuration and how the scheduler in the MAC handles packets sent over the bearer (e.g., in terms of scheduling policy, queue management policy, and rate-shaping policy). For example, a packet with higher priority can be expected to be scheduled before a packet with lower priority. For bearers with a low acceptable loss rate, an acknowledged mode can be used within the RLC protocol layer to ensure that packets are delivered successfully across the radio interface. The ARP of a bearer is used for call admission control— that is, to decide whether or not the requested bearer should be established in case of radio congestion. It also governs the prioritization of the bearer for pre-emption with respect to a new bearer establishment request. Once successfully established, a bearer's ARP does not have any impact on the bearer-level packet-forwarding treatment (e.g., for scheduling and rate control). Such packet-forwarding treatment should be solely determined by the other bearer-level QoS parameters such as QCI, GBR, and MBR (36, 37).

6.2.3.8 *Signaling*   2G/3G networks use SS7-MAP protocol for the following functions:

- location
- subscriber access
- handover
- authentication
- security/identity management
- handover services

In LTE/SAE (3GPP Rel.8), Diameter Base Protocol (RFC 3588) has been chosen by 3GPP for many of these procedures and is increasingly used for interoperator signaling network and roaming infrastructure. For example, registration messages received will be based on diameter (rather than SS7-MAP). The LTE interfaces based on diameter include the following (35):

- Packet core-related interfaces toward HSS and EIR
  - S6a (MME to HSS) and S6d (SGSN to HSS)
  - S6b, S6c (external AAA functions for non-3GPP accesses)
  - S13 (MME to EIR) and S13' (SGSN to EIR)
- Network signaling for policy control and charging
  1. S9 (H-PCRF to V-PCRF)
  2. S7 (PCRF to P-GW)
  3. Gx (PCRF to PCEF)
  4. Gxc (PCRF to S-GW)
  5. Rx (AF to PCRF)
  6. Gy (PCEF to OCS)

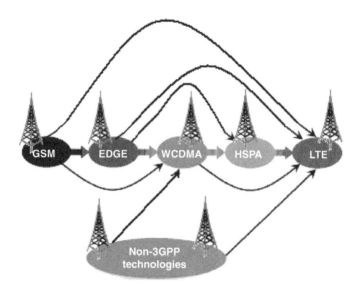

FIGURE 6.21   Evolution to LTE.

6.2.3.9 Evolution Paths to 4G/LTE   Mobile operators are evolving toward LTE/SAE using different evolution paths, as follows (see Fig. 6.21):

- 3GPP environments: GSM, GPRS, EDGE, WCDMA, HSPA
- Non-3GPP environments: 1xRTT, EV-DO, 3xRTT, WLAN, WiMAX

Some of the challenges in LTE deployment were hinted in Table 6.12, the key factors being the complexity of the technology and the plethora of interfaces that have to be supported. The evolution from a 2G/3G baseline will also be nontrivial. Network element evolution from 2G/3G to LTE includes the following upgrades in the provider network:

- GERAN and UTRAN -> **E-UTRAN**
- SGSN/PDSN-FA ->**S-GW**
- GGSN/PDSN-HA ->**PDN-GW**
- HLR/AAA ->**HSS**
- VLR ->**MME**

In addition, the following signaling evolution from 2G/3G to LTE is needed:

- SS7-MAP/ANSI-41/RADIUS ->**Diameter**
- GTPc-v0 and v1 ->**GTPc-v2**
- MIP ->**PMIP**

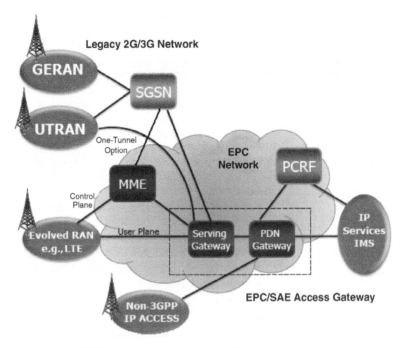

FIGURE 6.22 EPS and support of legacy environments.

After the LTE environment is established in a portion of the provider's environment, legacy components of the provider's network can be supported by the LTE infrastructure as depicted pictorially in Figure 6.22 (35).

APPENDIX 6.A: NON-WIRELESS TECHNOLOGIES FOR IoT: POWERLINE COMMUNICATIONS

This appendix provides a brief description of some non-wireless networking technologies that have been considered for IoT/M2M. See Table 6A.1 for a listing of some of the key technologies. SCADA was discussed in the context of standards in the Appendix to Chapter 5. Here we focus on PLC.

PLC refers to any technology that enables data transfer through powerlines by using advanced modulation technology. Data communication can take place at NB or broadband speeds. The technology has been around since the 1950s, but initially only supported NB applications for relay management, for example for public lighting. Broadband over PLC only began at the end of the 1990s. PLC is thus a term used to identify technologies, equipments, applications and services aiming at providing users with communication means over existing "powerlines" (cables transmitting electricity). The term broadband over powerline (BPL) is used to underline the technology capability to address broadband services. As for the term access PLC, it

TABLE 6A.1   Listing of Some of the Key Non-Wireless Technologies used for IoT-Like Services Over the Years

Technology/Concept	Description
KNX and KNX-RF	KNX (administered by the KNX Association) is an OSI-based network communications protocol for intelligent buildings defined in standards CEN EN 50090 and ISO/IEC 14543. KNX is the follow-on standard built on the European Home Systems Protocol (EHS), BatiBUS, and the European Installation Bus (EIB or Instabus). Effectively, KNX uses the communication stack of EIB but augmented with the PHY layers and configuration modes BatiBUS and EHS; thus, KNX includes the following PHYs: • Twisted pair wiring (inherited from the BatiBUS and EIB Instabus standards). This approach uses differential signaling with a signaling speed of 9.6 Kbps. MAC is controlled with the CSMA/CA method; • Powerline networking (inherited from EIB and EHS); • Radio (KNX-RF); • IR; and, • Ethernet (also known as EIBnet/IP or KNXnet/IP).
M-Bus	The M-Bus is a European standard for remote reading of gas and electric meters; it is also usable for all other types of consumption meters. It is specified as follows: • EN 13757-2 (PHY and link layer) • EN 13757-3 (application layer) • Note: the frame layer uses IEC 870 and the network (packet layer) is optional A radio variant of M-Bus (wireless M-Bus) is also specified in EN 13757-4
PLC	PLC (also called powerline communication as a singular term; also called powerline telecommunications [or PLT]) refers to any technology that enables data transfer through powerlines. Data communication can take place at NB or broadband speeds. The technology has been around since the 1950s, but initially only supported NB applications for relay management, for example for public lighting. Broadband over PLC only began at the end of the 1990s. PLC is thus a term used to identify technologies, equipments, applications, and services aiming at providing users with communication means over existing "powerlines" (cables transmitting electricity). The term BPL is used to underline the technology capability to address broadband services. As for the term access PLC, it is used to identify those PLC solutions aiming at providing consumers with broadband services through the external electricity grid, while in-home PLC is used to identify PLC solutions aiming at applications within the home (38)

TABLE 6A.1   (*Continued*)

Technology/Concept	Description
SCADA	A long-existing industrial control system (ICS). It is a centralized system used to monitor and control systems deployed over large geographic areas, such as a power grid. There are three main elements in a SCADA system, multiple RTUs (remote telemetry units), a communications apparatus, and a HMI (human machine interface) mechanism
xDSL	A 1990s technology that exploits unused frequencies on copper telephone lines to transmit traffic typically at multimegabit speeds. DSL can allow voice and HS data to be sent simultaneously over the same line. Because the service is "always available," end-users do not need to dial in or wait for call set-up. Asymmetrical variations include ADSL, G.lite ADSL (or simply G.lite), VDSL (ITU-T G.993.1), and VDSL2 (ITU-T G.993.2). The standard forms of ADSL (ITU G.992.3, G.992.5, and ANSI T1.413—Issue 2) are all built upon the same technical foundation, discrete multitone (DMT). The suite of ADSL standards facilitates interoperability between all standard forms of ADSL (39)

is used to identify those PLC solutions aiming at providing consumers with broadband services through the external electricity grid, while in-home PLC is used to identify PLC solutions aiming at applications within the home (38). A brief history is as follows (40):

- **1950**: at a frequency of 10 Hz, 10 kW of power, one-way: town lighting, relay RC;
- **Mid-1980s**: beginning of research into the use of the electrical grid to support data transmission; on bands between 5 and 500 KHz, always in a one-way direction;
- **1997**: first tests for bidirectional data signal transmission over the electrical supply network and the beginning of research by Ascom (Switzerland) and Norweb (United Kingdom);
- **2000**: first tests carried out in France by EDF R&D and Ascom;
- **2011-12**: Publication of IEEE 1901 standards.

PLC transmission works by superimposing a high-frequency signal at low-energy levels over the 50 Hz electrical signal. The powerline is transformed into a communication network through the superposition of a low-energy information signal to the power wave. In order to ensure a suited coexistence and separation between the two systems, the frequency range used for communication is very far from the one used for the power wave (50 Hz in Europe): 3–148.5 kHz for PLC NB applications and from 1–30 MHz for PLC broadband applications. The modulated signal is transmitted via the power infrastructure and can be received and decoded remotely. Thus, the PLC signal is received by any PLC receiver located on the same electrical network. An integrated coupler at the PLC receiver entry points eliminates low frequency components before the signal is treated.

There now is standardization work underway in the PLC Forum and in ETSI. CENELEC has issued regulations for transmission in defined bands. The CENELEC A-band is reserved by law in CENELEC regulated countries for the exclusive use of utilities and their licensees. The CENELEC C-band is available for consumer and commercial use without restriction, but a common access protocol and coexistence protocol is mandated (41).

A plethora of NB (some Kbps) and broadband (tens or even hundreds of Mbps) applications can be provided through access and in-home PLC solutions, for the benefit of end consumers and of utilities (to increase their performances and improve their service quality). NB applications include home control, home automation, automatic meter reading, remote surveillance, and control of home appliances. Broadband applications include (for access PLC) Internet access, telephony, TV and (for in-home PLC) Internet access sharing, computer resource sharing, and AV whole-house distribution. PLC can be used in places where radio frequency (RF) cannot be used or is unreliable; for example, smart meters in the basement of a building are unlikely to be able to use RF to communicate with the neighborhood data concentrator—PLC communication can utilize the power wires to reach the data concentrator. It is estimated today that more than 80 PLC initiatives in more than 40 countries have been launched, worldwide, by electric utilities. Pilot sites, technological or commercial trials, and deployments are numerous in Europe. Among the most important initiatives are the ones developed by EDF (France), EDP (Portugal), EEF (Switzerland), ENDESA and IBERDROLA (Spain), PPC (Germany), and SSE (Scotland) (38).

IEEE 1901 is a group of PLC standards that enables transmission of data over AC electrical powerlines. Its goal was to replace a set of different powerline specs now in existence but maintaining a mandatory coexistence with legacy PLC approaches. There are two basic standards: (i) a BPL standard and (ii) a low-frequency narrowband (LF NB) standard.

- The IEEE 1901™ BPL standard was finalized and published in December 2010. The standard was sponsored by the IEEE Communications Society. The BPL standard is designed for use in a wide range of applications including SE, transportation, and LANs in both the home and the enterprise. Networking products that fully comply with IEEE 1901 will deliver data rates in excess of 500 Mbps in LAN applications. In first-mile/last-mile applications, IEEE 1901-compliant devices will achieve ranges of up to 1500 m. The technology specified by IEEE 1901 uses sophisticated modulation techniques to transmit data over standard AC powerlines of any voltage at transmission frequencies of less than 100 MHz. In the transportation sector, for example, the standard's data rates and range make it possible to deliver A/V entertainment to the seats of airplanes, trains, and other mass transit vehicles. Electric vehicles (EVs) can download a new entertainment playlist to the A/V system while the car is charging overnight. In the home, PLC will complement wireless LANs by providing a link through walls and other RF impediments as well as over distances beyond the normal range of wireless networks. It will complement wireless networks in hotels and other multistory buildings by carrying multimedia data over the longer distances and allowing wireless to complete the communication link over the last few meters. IEEE 1901 may also benefit utilities, service providers, and consumer electronics companies—anyone with a stake in smart grid technologies—as well as smart-meter providers and home appliance manufacturers (42).

- The IEEE has been working on IEEE P1901.2™, a standard for LF NB (less than 500 kHz) PLC for smart grid applications. The specification entered its final approval process in early 2012 and was expected to be ratified soon thereafter. LF NB PLC is needed, according to proponents, to accelerate wider-scale rollout of smart grids. IEEE P1901.2 is designed to support smart grid applications such as grid to utility meter, EV to charging station, home area networking, and solar-panel communications. More than 30 semiconductor manufacturers, meter and systems manufacturers, software developers, service providers, and utilities have contributed to the work of the IEEE P1901.2 Working Group since its inception in fall 2009. The work was sponsored by the Powerline Communications Standards Committee of the IEEE Communications Society (ComSoc). IEEE P1901.2 is designed to specify secure PLC at data rates up to 500 Kbps and at transmission frequencies of less than 500 kHz for applications such as grid to utility meter, EV to charging station, home area networking and lighting, and solar-panel communications. The standard addresses LF NB PLC over low-voltage lines of less than 1000 V between transformer and meter, through transformer low-voltage to medium-voltage (1000 V up to 72 kV) and through transformer medium-voltage to low-voltage powerlines in both urban and long-distance (multikilometer) rural communications. IEEE P1901.2 supports the balanced and efficient use of the PLC channel by all classes of LF NB devices by defining detailed mechanisms for coexistence among standard technologies operating in the same field, data rate, and frequency band. This standard assures coexistence with broadband powerline (BPL) devices by minimizing out-of-band emissions in frequencies greater than 500 kHz. The standard addresses the necessary security requirements that assure communication privacy and allow use for security sensitive services. This standard defines the PHY layer and the medium access sublayer of the data link layer, as defined by the International Organization for Standardization (ISO) Open Systems Interconnection (OSI) Basic Reference Model (43).

    The PLCforum is a leading international association that represents the interests of manufacturers, energy utilities, and other organizations (universities, other PLC associations, consultants, etc.) active in the field of access and in-home PLC technologies.

Beyond the PLCforum, a number of industry groups and electric utilities, all around the world, are supporting the development of the PLC technology. Among industry groups are UPLC and PLCA (in the United States), PLC-J (in Japan), APTEL (in South America), PUA (PLC Utilities Alliance) in Europe, Utilitel in Australia, the Universal Powerline Alliance, and the HomePlug® Powerline Alliance, among others.

The HomePlug Alliance's mission[13] is to enable and promote rapid availability, adoption, and implementation of cost-effective, interoperable, and standards-based home powerline networks and products. By working with utility companies and the Wi-Fi Alliance and ZigBee Alliance, the HomePlug Alliance aims at helping to build the home area network (HAN) ecosystem that enables intelligent energy management and efficiency in the home and small businesses. With the goal of providing a complimentary wireless (ZigBee) and wired (HomePlug) infrastructure, the coverage for large homes and multidwelling units can be assured.

Basic applications include the use of in-home wires to distribute signals to support Smart Grid & Smart Energy, HDTV Networking, Whole Home Audio, and Gaming. Technology standards defined by the Alliance include the following:

- HomePlug Green PHY™ ("GP")
- IEEE 1901 Powerline Networking Standard
- HomePlug Broadband-Speed Technologies
- SE Profile 2

HomePlug Green PHY Specification. This is a new powerline networking specification that targets smart grid/SE applications. HomePlug GP is based on customer requirements for cost, coverage, and performance and driven by input from utility companies, as well as from companies that manufacture meters, automobiles, and appliances. In addition to low cost and power consumption, IPv6 networking and interoperability with the installed base of powerline products are critical to the success of products. As such, HomePlug GP will be interoperable with both HomePlug AV and IEEE 1901, just cited; this means that HomePlug Green PHY is a certification profile of IEEE 1901. HomePlug Green PHY has ample bandwidth to support critical functionality such as IP networking, but with power consumption estimated to be 75% lower than HomePlug AV, with similar cost savings projected. The specification is designed to the specific requirements of Smart Grid applications while interoperating with HomePlug AV and AV2 products and the IEEE 1901 standard. GP chips are already available; certified products are expected to ship in early 2013.

- Principal applications: Monitor and control devices via low speed, low-cost PLC, including smart energy applications such as demand response, load control, energy efficiency Home/Building Automation. It targets smart grid

---

[13]This section is based on material from The HomePlug® Powerline Alliance (44).

applications such as HVAC/thermostats, smart meters, home appliances, and plug-in electric vehicles (PEVs).
- Features: (i) interoperable with HomePlug AV; (ii) HomePlug GP is a profile of IEEE P1901; and (iii) low-power consumption, low cost
  - Estimated, up to 75% lower cost, 75% less power consumption than Home-Plug AV
  - Internet (IP) networking: 802.2, IPv6 support
  - Minimum 1 Mbps effective data rate (3.8 Mbps peak PHY rate)
  - Support for firmware updates

IEEE 1901 Powerline Networking Standard. Regarding IEEE 1901.2010—For HS communication devices (HomePlug AV), the HomePlug Alliance and its members first collaborated with IEEE in 2005 with the inception of the P1901 workgroup, tasked to develop a standard for HS communication devices. In December 2008, the IEEE P1901 working group voted to include HomePlug technology in the baseline standard for PLC. The IEEE 1901.2010 standard was ratified in September 2010, and multiple semiconductor vendors are now shipping integrated circuits (ICs) based on the standard. In addition, the installed base of tens of millions of HomePlug AV products are fully interoperable with the 1901 standard, ensuring a seamless roadmap for existing users of HomePlug technology. The HomePlug Alliance conducts a comprehensive compliance and interoperabilty (C&I) program for products based on the HomePlug AV IEEE P1901 standard, ensuring that reliable, interoperable products are available from multiple suppliers. Additionally, the HomePlug Alliance plans to launch a new certification program—Netricity PLC—to provide C&I testing of products built on the IEEE P1901.2 LF NB PLC standard.

HomePlug Broadband-Speed Technologies. In June 2011, the HomePlug Alliance put its support behind the IEEE P1905 working group's efforts to define the first standard for hybrid home networks. A P1905 network would include combinations of stationary home networking devices such as set-top boxes, home gateways, Blu-Ray players and televisions, and mobile devices such as laptops, tablets, and smartphones. The IEEE P1905 standard provides an abstraction layer to established powerline, wireless, coaxial cable, and Ethernet home networking technologies. The standard enables consumers and service providers to combine the capabilities of otherwise disparate networks to maximize a home network's overall performance and reliability. IEEE P1905's abstraction layer common interface allows applications and upper-layer protocols to be agnostic to the underlying home networking technologies. Packets can arrive and be transmitted over any technology according to QoS priorities. IEEE P1905 also simplified the network set-up by providing common set-up procedures for adding devices, establishing secure links, implementing QoS, and managing the network.

SE Initiative. In 2008, a number of utility companies (American Electric Power, Consumers Energy, Pacific Gas and Electric Company, Reliant Energy, Sempra, and Southern California Edison) announced that they are working with the ZigBee and

HomePlug alliances to develop a common application layer integrated solution for advanced metering infrastructure (AMI) and HANs. The three groups are expanding the application layer, enabling it to run on HomePlug technology, and providing utilities with industry standards for both wireless and wired HAN options when implementing new AMI programs. Shortly after the formation of the group, the Electric Power Research Institute (EPRI) began to collaborate to develop a common language for HAN devices to utilize the AMI. This arrangement further expands the Smart Grid by creating a standard communication approach between AMI systems and HANs, as well as a common set of certification procedures. As noted elsewhere, the term "smart energy" refers generally to actions and technologies that are used to improve the efficiency of energy consumption. Energy demand and costs are increasing rapidly, so utility companies are focusing on adopting communications and networking technologies to help consumers monitor and reduce their energy consumption.

REFERENCES

1. ETSI TR 101 557 V1.1.1 (2012-02), Electromagnetic Compatibility and Radio spectrum Matters (ERM); System Reference document (SRdoc); Medical Body Area Network Systems (MBANSs) in the 1785 MHz to 2500 MHz range.
2. Coronel P, Schott W, Schwieger K, Zimmermann E, Zasowski T, Chevillat P, editors. Briefing on Wireless Body Area and Sensor Networks, 8th Wireless World Research Forum (WWRF8bis) Meeting, Beijing, China, February 2004; (ii) 11th Wireless World Research Forum Meeting, Oslo, Norway, June 2004.
3. Practel, Inc., Role of Wireless ICT in Health Care and Wellness—Standards, Technologies and Markets, May 2012, Published by Global Information, Inc. (GII), 195 Farmington Avenue, Suite 208 Farmington, CT 06032 USA.
4. Gainspan, Gainspan Low-Power Embedded WI-FI VS ZigBee. GainSpan Corporation, 3590 N. First Street, Suite 300, San Jose, CA 95134, Available at http://www.gainspan.com.
5. Smith P. Comparing Low-Power Wireless Technologies. Tech Zone, Digikey Online Magazine, Digi-Key Corporation, 701 Brooks Avenue, South Thief River Falls, MN 56701 USA.
6. 3rd Generation Partnership Project (3GPP) Organization, Available at www.3gpp.org.
7. Third Generation Partnership Project 2 Organization, Available at http://www.3gpp2.org.
8. Bormann C. Getting Started with IPv6 in Low-Power Wireless. "Personal Area" Networks (6LoWPAN), Universität Bremen TZI, IETF 6lowpan WG and CoRE WG Co-Chair, IAB Tutorial on Interconnecting Smart Objects with the Internet, Prague, Saturday, 2011-03-26, Available at http://www.iab.org/about/workshops/smartobjects/tutorial.html.
9. ETSI Documentation, ETSI, 650 Route des Lucioles F-06921 Sophia Antipolis Cedex—FRANCE.
10. Krasinski R, Nikolich P, Heile RF. IEEE 802.15.4j Medical Body Area Networks Task Group PAR, IEEE P802.15 Working Group for Wireless Personal Area Networks (WPANs), January18, 2011.

11. ISA, 67 Alexander Drive, P.O. Box 12277, Research Triangle Park, NC 27709, info@isa.org.

12. Minoli D. Satellite Systems Engineering in an IPv6 Environment. Boca Raton, FL: Francis and Taylor; 2009.

13. Minoli D. Hotspot Networks: Wi-Fi for Public Access Locations. New York, NY: McGraw-Hill; 2002.

14. Minoli D, *Wireless Sensor Networks* (co-authored with K. Sohraby and T. Znati). Hoboken, NJ: Wiley; 2007.

15. Emerson Process Management, IEC 62591 WirelessHART, System Engineering Guide, Revision 2.3, Emerson Process Management, 2011.

16. ZigBee Alliance, Available at http://www.zigbee.org/.

17. ZigBee Wireless Sensor Applications for Health, Wellness and Fitness, March 2009, ZigBee Alliance, Available at www.zigbee.org.

18. Duffy P. Zigbee IP: Extending the Smart Grid to Consumers. Cisco Blog – The Platform, June 4, 2012, Cisco Systems, Inc., 170 West Tasman Dr., San Jose, CA 95134 USA.

19. Shandle J. What does ZigBee Pro mean for your application?. EETimes Online Magazine, 11/27/2007, Available at http://www.eetimes.com.

20. Drake J, Najewicz D, Watts W. Energy efficiency comparisons of wireless communication technology options for smart grid enabled devices. White Paper, General Electric Company, GE Appliances & Lighting, December 9, 2010.

21. Montenegro G, Kushalnagar N, Hui J, Culler D. Transmission of IPv6 Packets over IEEE 802.15.4 Networks, RFC 4944, Updated by RFC 6282, RFC 6775 (was draft-ietf-6lowpan-format), September 2007.

22. Kingsley S. Personal Body Networks go Wireless at 2.4GHz. ElectronicsWeekly Online Magazine, 16 May 2012, Available at http://www.electronicsweekly.com.

23. IEEE 802.15 WPAN Task Group 1 (TG1), WPAN Home Page, Monday, June 20, 2005.

24. Bluetooth SIG Home page, Available at www.bluetooth.com (more info at www.bluetooth .org).

25. Fleishman G. Inside Bluetooth 2.0., Macworld, February 9, 2005.

26. Latuske R. Bluetooth Health Device Profile (HDP). White Paper, September 2009, ARS Software GmbH, Stanberger Strasse 22, D-82131, Gauting/Munchen, Germany, Available at http://www.ars2000.com/.

27. Kwak KS, Ullah S, Ullah N An Overview of IEEE 802.15.6 Standard (Invited Paper), ISABEL 2010 in Rome, Italy. UWB-ITRC Center, Inha University, 253 Yonghyun-dong, Nam-gu, Incheon (402–751), South Korea.

28. U.S. Department of Transportation, Research and Innovative Technology Administration. Intelligent Transportation Systems. December 2012, Available at http://www.its.dot.gov.

29. Fuxjäger P, Costantini A, et al. IEEE 802.11p Transmission Using GNURadio. Forschungszentrum Telekommunikation Wien, Donau-City-Strasse 1, A-1220 Vienna, Austria. And, University of Salento, 73100 Lecce, Italy. 2007.

30. TechnoCom. The WAVE Communications Stack: IEEE 802.11p, 1609.4 and, 1609.3. Presentation, September, 2007, TechnoCom, 2030 Corte del Nogal, Suite 200, Carlsbad, CA 92011 Available at http://www.ieeevtc.org/plenaries/vtc2007fall/34.pdf.

31. Weigle M. Standards: WAVE / DSRC /802.11p in Vehicular Networks, CS 795/895, Spring 2008, Old Dominion University.

32. IEEE WoWMoM 2012 Panel, San Francisco, California, USA June 25–28, 2012.

33. Rao YS, Pica F, Krishnaswamy D. 3GPP Enhancements for Machine Type Communications Overview. IEEE WoWMoM 2012 Panel, San Francisco, California, USA June 25–28, 2012.

34. Principi B. CTIA: Should M2M skip 3G and go right to 4G?. May 9, 2012, Online Article, Available at http://www.telecomengine.com.

35. Clark M, Neal BJ, Gullstrand C. Preparing for LTE Roaming. Syniverse Technologies, 120 Moorgate London, EC2M 6UR United Kingdom, March 2011, Available at www.syniverse.com.

36. Alcatel-Lucent. LTE—The UMTS Long Term Evolution: From Theory to Practice. Strategic Whitepaper, Available at www.alcatel-lucent.com, Wiley; 2009.

37. Sesia S, Toufik I, Baker M, editors, *LTE – The UMTS Long Term Evolution: From Theory to Practice.* Wiley; 2009.

38. PLCforum. Available at http://www.plcforum.org/frame_plc.html.

39. DSL Forum, DSL Forum, 48377 Fremont Blvd, Suite 117, Fremont, CA 94538, Available at http://www.dslforum.org.

40. Cacciaguerra F. Introduction to Power Line Communications (PLC). November 2003, Kioskea.net Online Magazine, Available at http://en.kioskea.net/contents/cpl/cpl-intro.php3.

41. Power Line Communications (PLC), Echelon Corporation, 550 Meridian Ave., San Jose, CA 95126 USA. Available at http://www.echelon.com.

42. Yu S. Final IEEE 1901 Broadband Over Power Line Standard Now Published. IEEE Press Release, February 1, 2011.

43. Yu S. IEEE P1901.2™ Standard FOR Low-Frequency, Narrowband Power Line Communications Enters Letter Balloting, IEEE Press Release, January 2012.

44. The HomePlug® Powerline Alliance, Available at http://www.homeplug.org.

45. 3GPP2 X.S0011-002-D. cdma2000 Wireless IP Network Standard: Simple IP and Mobile IP Access Services. Available at http://www.3gpp2.org/Public_html/specs/X.S0011-002-D_v1.0_060301.pdf, February 2006.

46. Alcatel-Lucent. Alcatel-Lucent Researches Opportunities for Delivering Enhanced Video Sharing Services with DOCOMO Euro-Labs. Press Release, Paris and Barcelona, February 15, 2011. Available at www.alcatel-lucent.com.

47. California Software Labs. Basic Streaming Technology and RTSP Protocol—A Technical Report, 2002. California Software Labs, 6800 Koll Center Parkway, Suite 100 Pleasanton CA 94566, USA.

48. Machine-to-Machine Communications (M2M); M2M Service Requirements. ETSI TS 102 689 V1.1.1 (2010-08). ETSI, 650 Route des Lucioles F-06921 Sophia Antipolis Cedex—FRANCE.

49. Machine-to-Machine Communications (M2M); Functional Architecture Technical Specification, ETSI TS 102 690 V1.1.1 (2011-10), ETSI, 650 Route des Lucioles F-06921 Sophia Antipolis Cedex—FRANCE.

50. H.720. Overview of IPTV Terminal Devices and End-Systems. (also known as ex H.IPTV-TDES.0), October 2008. ITU-T Study Group 16. International Telecommunication Union, Telecommunication Standardization Bureau, Place des Nations, CH-1211 Geneva 20.

51. Near Field Communication.org, Advocacy Group, Available at http://www.nearfield communication.or.

52. Patil B, Dommety G. Why the Authentication Data Suboption is Needed for Mobile IPv6 (MIPv6). RFC 5419, January 2009.

53. WiMAX Network Architecture—WiMAX End-to-End Network Systems Architecture. May 2008, Available at http://www.wimaxforum.org/documents/documents/WiMAX_ Forum_Network_Architecture_Stage_23_Rel_1v1.2.zip.

CHAPTER 7

LAYER 3 CONNECTIVITY: IPv6 TECHNOLOGIES FOR THE IoT

7.1 OVERVIEW AND MOTIVATIONS

Internet Protocol Version 6 (IPv6) is a newer version of the network layer protocol that is designed to coexist (but not directly interwork) with IPv4. In the long term, IPv6 is expected to replace IPv4, but that will not happen overnight. IPv6 provides improved internetworking capabilities compared to what is presently available with IPv4. The current IPv4 has been in use for over 30 years, but it exhibits some challenges in supporting emerging demands for address space cardinality, high-density mobility, multimedia, and strong security. IPv6 offers the potential of achieving scalability, reacheability, end-to-end interworking, quality of service (QoS), and commercial-grade robustness that is needed for contemporary and emerging web services, data services, mobile video, and Internet of things (IoT) applications.

We retain the position stated in Chapter 1 that *IoT may well become the "killer-app" for IPv6*. Using IPv6 with its abundant address spaces, globally unique object (thing) identification and connectivity can be provided in a standardized manner without additional status or address (re)processing; hence, its intrinsic advantage over IPv4 or other schemes. We are not implying in this text that IPv6 is strictly and uniquely required to support IoT, just that it provides an ideal, future-proof, scalable mechanism for such services, whether in a terrestrial mode or in a satellite-based mode (1, 2).

Building the Internet of Things with IPv6 and MIPv6: The Evolving World of M2M Communications,
First Edition. Daniel Minoli.
© 2013 John Wiley & Sons, Inc. Published 2013 by John Wiley & Sons, Inc.

IP was designed as a packet-based technology (protocol) in the late 1970s–early 1980s for the purpose of connecting computers that were in separate geographic locations. Starting in the early 1990s, developers realized that the communication needs of the twenty-first century needed a protocol with some new features and capabilities, while at the same time retaining the useful features of the existing protocol. IPv6 was initially developed in the early 1990s because of the anticipated need for more end-system addresses based on anticipated Internet growth, encompassing mobile phone deployment, smart home appliances, and billions of new users in developing countries (e.g., BRIC: Brazil, Russia, India, China). Technologies and applications such as voice over IP (VoIP), "always-on access" (e.g., cable modems), broadband and/or ethernet-to-the-home, converged networks, evolving ubiquitous computing applications, and IoT will be driving this need even more in the next few years (3).

IPv6 is now being slowly deployed worldwide: there is documented institutional and commercial interest and activity in Europe and Asia, and there also is evolving interest in the United States. The expectation is that in the next few years deployment of this new protocol will occur worldwide. For example, the U.S. Department of Defense (DoD) announced that from October 1, 2003, all new developments and procurements needed to be IPv6 capable; the DoD's goal was to complete the transition to IPv6 for all intra- and internetworking across the agency by 2008, which was accomplished. The U.S. Government Accountability Office (GAO) has recommended that all agencies become proactive in planning a coherent transition to IPv6. The current expectation is that IPv4 will continue to exist for the foreseeable future, while IPv6 will be used for new broad-scale applications. The two protocols are not directly interworkable, but tunneling and dual-stack techniques allow coexistence and co-working.

While the basic function of the network layer internetworking protocol is to move information across networks, IPv6 has more capabilities built into its foundation than IPv4. Link-level communication does not generally require a node identifier (address) since the device is intrinsically identified with the link-level address; however, communication over a group of links (a network) does require unique node identifiers (addresses). The IP address is an identifier that is applied to each device connected to an IP network. In this setup, different entities taking part in the network (servers, routers, user computers, and so on) communicate among each other using their IP address, as an entity identifier. The current IPv4 naming scheme was developed in the 1970s and had capacity for about 4.3 billion addresses, which were grouped into 255 blocks of 16 million addresses each. In IPv4, addresses consist of four octets. With IPv4, the 32-bit address can be represented as **AdrClass|netID|hostID**. The network portion can contain either a network ID or a network ID and a subnet. Every network and every host or device has a unique address, by definition. For ease of human conversation, IP addresses are represented as separated by periods, for example: 166.74.110.83, where the decimal numbers are a shorthand and corresponds to the binary code described by the byte in question (an 8-bit number takes a value in the 0–255 range). Since the IPv4 address has 32 bits, there are nominally 2^{32} different IP addresses (as noted, approximately 4.3 billion nodes, if all combinations are used).

TABLE 7.1   Projected RIR Unallocated Address Pool Exhaustion (as of April 2011)

RIR	Assigned Addresses (/8s)	Remaining Addresses (/8s)
AFRINIC	8.3793	4.6168
APNIC	53.7907	1.2093
ARIN	77.9127	6.0130
LACNIC	15.6426	4.3574
RIPE NCC	45.0651	3.9349

RIR, regional Internet registry; AFRINIC, African Network Information Centre; ARIN, American Registry for Internet Numbers; APNIC, Asia-Pacific Network Information Centre; LACNIC, Latin America and Caribbean Network Information Centre; RIPE NCC, Réseaux IP Européens Network Coordination Centre (the RIR for Europe, the Middle East, and parts of Central Asia).

IPv4 has proven, by means of its long life, to be a flexible and powerful networking mechanism. However, IPv4 is starting to exhibit limitations, not only with respect to the need for an increase of the IP address space, driven, for example, by new populations of users in countries such as China and India; by new technologies with "always connected devices" (e.g., cable modems, networked PDAs, 3G/4G mobile smartphones, and so on); and by new services such as global rollout of VoIP, IP Television (IPTV), and social networking. A full deployment of IoT applications will certainly stress the IPv4 environment. A regional Internet registry (RIR) manages the allocation and registration of Internet resources such as IPv4 addresses, IPv6 addresses, and autonomous system (AS) numbers, in a specific region of the world. As of February 1, 2011, only 1% of all possible IPv4 addresses were left unassigned. This has led to a predicament known as *IPv4 Run-Out*. The entire address space was expected to be more or less exhausted by September 2011, according to the IPv4 Address Report (see Table 7.1) (4, 5). The IPv4 address allocation is based on the following hierarchy:

> Internet assigned numbers authority (IANA) → RIRs → internet service providers (ISPs) → the public (including businesses).

Thus, a key desirable capability is the increase in address space such that it is able to cover all elements of the universe set under consideration. For example, all computing devices could have a public IP address, so that they can be uniquely tracked[1]; today inventory management of dispersed IT assets cannot be achieved with IP mechanisms alone. With IPv6, one can use the network to verify that such equipment is deployed in place and active; even non-IT equipment in the field can be tracked by having an IP address permanently assigned to it. IPv6 creates a new IP address format, such that the number of IP addresses will not exhaust for several decades or longer, even though an entire new crop of devices are expected to connect to Internet over the coming years.

---

[1]Note that this has some potential negative security issues as attackers could be able to own a machine and then exactly know how to go back to that same machine again. Therefore, reliable security mechanisms need to be understood and put in place in IPv6 environments.

IPv6 also adds improvements in areas such as routing and network configuration. IPv6 has extensive automatic configuration (autoconfiguration) mechanisms and reduces the IT burden, making configuration essentially plug-and-play. Specifically, new devices that connect to intranet or Internet will be "plug-and-play" devices. With IPv6, one is not required to configure dynamic non-published local IP addresses, the gateway address, the subnetwork mask, or any other parameters. The equipment automatically obtains all requisite configuration data when it connects to the network. Autoconfiguration implies that a dynamic host configuration protocol (DHCP) server is not needed and/or does not have to be configured (2, 6, 7).

IPv6 was originally defined in RFC 1883 that was then obsolete by RFC 2460, "Internet Protocol, Version 6 (IPv6) Specification," S. Deering, R. Hinden (December 1998).[2] A large body of additional RFCs has emerged in recent years to add capabilities and refine the concept.

The advantages of IPv6, some of which we already noted in Chapter 1, can be summarized as follows:

- Scalability and expanded addressing capabilities: IPv6 has 128-bit addresses versus 32-bit IPv4 addresses. With IPv4, the theoretical number of available IP addresses is $2^{32} \sim 10^{10}$. IPv6 offers a 2^{128} space. Hence, the number of available unique node addressees is $2^{128} \sim 10^{39}$. IPv6 has more than 340 undecillion (340,282,366,920,938,463,463,374,607,431,768,211,456) addresses, grouped into blocks of 18 quintillion addresses.

- "Plug-and-play": IPv6 includes a "plug-and-play" mechanism that facilitates the connection of equipment to the network. The requisite configuration is automatic; it is a serverless mechanism.

- IPv6 makes it easy for nodes to have multiple IPv6 addresses on the same network interface. This can create the opportunity for users to establish overlay or communities of interest (COI) networks on top of other physical IPv6 networks. Department, groups, or other users and resources can belong to one or more COIs, where each can have its own specific security policy (8).

- Security: IPv6 includes security in its specifications such as payload encryption and authentication of the source of the communication. It calls for end-to-end security, with built-in, strong IP-layer encryption and authentication (embedded security support with mandatory IP Security [IPsec] implementation). It follows that IPv6 network architectures can easily adapt to an end-to-end security model where the end hosts have the responsibility of providing the security services necessary to protect any data traffic between them; this results in greater flexibility for creating policy-based trust domains that are based on varying parameters including node address and application (9).

- In IPv6, creating a Virtual Private Network (VPN) is easier and more standard than in IPv4, because of the (authentication header [AH] and encapsulating

---

[2]The "version 5" reference was employed for another use—an experimental real-time streaming protocol—and to avoid any confusion, it was decided not to use this nomenclature.

security protocol [ESP]) extension headers. The performance penalty is lower for the VPN implemented in IPv6 compared to those built in IPv4 (10).

- Optimized protocol: IPv6 embodies IPv4 best practices but removes unused or obsolete IPv4 characteristics. This results in a better-optimized IP. Also, merging two IPv4 networks with overlapping addresses (say, if two organizations merge) is complex; it will be much easier to merge networks with IPv6.
- Real-time applications: To provide better support for real-time traffic (e.g., VoIP, IPTV), IPv6 includes "labeled flows" in its specifications. By means of this mechanism, routers can recognize the end-to-end flow to which transmitted packets belong. This is similar to the service offered by multiprotocol label switching (MPLS), but it is intrinsic with the IP mechanism rather than an add-on. Also, it preceded this MPLS feature by a number of years.
- Mobility: IPv6 includes more efficient and robust mobility mechanisms (enhanced support for mobile IP, mobile computing devices, and mobile video). Specifically, mobile IPv6 (MIPv6) as defined in RFC 3775 is now starting to be deployed (11).
- Streamlined header format and flow identification.
- Extensibility: IPv6 has been designed to be extensible and offers support for new options and extensions.

ISPs and carriers have been preparing for IP-address exhaustion for a number of years, and there are transition plans in place. The expectation is that IPv6 can make IP devices less expensive, more powerful, and even consume less power; the power issue is not only important for environmental reasons, but also improves operability (e.g., longer battery life in portable devices, such as mobile phones).

7.2 ADDRESS CAPABILITIES

7.2.1 IPv4 Addressing and Issues

IPv4 addresses can be from an officially assigned public range or from an internal intranet private (but not globally unique) block. As noted, IPv4 theoretically allows up to 2^{32} addresses, based on a four-octet address space. Hence, there are 4,294,967,296 unique values, which can be considered as a sequence of 256 "/8s," where each "/8" corresponds to 16,777,216 unique address values. Public, globally unique addresses are assigned by IANA. IP addresses are addresses of network nodes at layer 3; each device on a network (whether the Internet or an intranet) must have a unique address. In IPv4, it is a 32-bit (4-byte) binary address used to identify a host's network ID. It is represented by the nomenclature a.b.c.d (each of a, b, c, and d being from 1 to 255) (0 has a special meaning). Examples are 167.168.169.170, 232.233.229.209, and 200.100.200.100.

The problem is that during the 1980s, many public, registered addresses were allocated to firms and organizations without any consistent control. As a result, some organizations have more addresses that they actually might need, giving rise to the present dearth of available "registerable" layer 3 addresses. Furthermore, not all IP addresses can be used due to the fragmentation described above.

One approach to the issue would be a renumbering and a reallocation of the IPv4 addressing space. However, this is not as simple as it appears since it requires worldwide coordination efforts. Moreover, it would still be limited for the human population and the quantity of devices that will be connected to Internet in the medium-term future. At this juncture, and as a temporary and pragmatic approach to alleviate the dearth of addresses, network address translation (NAT) mechanisms are employed by organizations and even home users. This mechanism consists of using only a small set of public IPv4 addresses for an entire network to access the Internet. The myriad of internal devices are assigned IP addresses from a specifically designated range of Class A or Class C address that are locally unique but are duplicatively used and reused within various organizations. In some cases (e.g., residential Internet access use via Digital Subscriber Line [DSL] or cable), the legal IP address is only provided to a user on a time-lease basis, rather than permanently.

Internal intranet addresses may be in the ranges 10.0.0.0/8, 172.16.0.0/12, and 192.168.0.0/16. In the internal intranet private address case, a NAT function is employed to map the internal addresses to an external public address when the private-to-public network boundary is crossed. This, however, imposes a number of limitations, particularly since the number of registered public addresses available to a company is almost invariably much smaller (as small as 1) than the number of internal devices requiring an address. A number of protocols cannot travel through a NAT device, and hence the use of NAT implies that many applications (e.g., VoIP) cannot be used effectively in all instances. As a consequence, these applications can only be used in intranets. Examples include:

- Multimedia applications such as videoconferencing, VoIP, or video-on-demand/IPTV do not work smoothly through NAT devices. Multimedia applications make use of real-time transport protocol (RTP) and real-time control protocol (RTCP). These in turn use User Datagram Protocol (UDP) with dynamic allocation of ports and NAT does not directly support this environment.
- IPsec is used extensively for data authentication, integrity, and confidentiality. However, when NAT is used, IPsec operation is impacted, since NAT changes the address in the IP header.
- Multicast, although possible in theory, requires complex configuration in a NAT environment and hence, in practice, is not utilized as often as could be the case.

The need for obligatory use of NAT disappears with IPv6.

7.2.2 IPv6 Address Space

The IPv6 addressing architecture is described in RFC 4291 February 2006 (12). One of the major modifications in the addressing scheme in IPv6 is a change to the

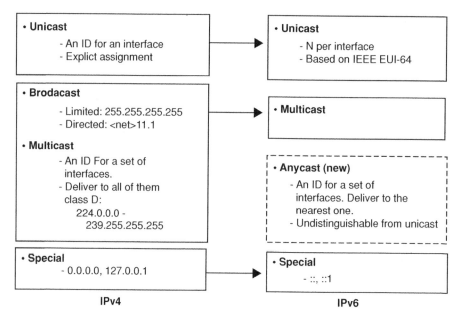

FIGURE 7.1 Address comparison between IPv4 and IPv6.

basic types of addresses and how they are utilized. *Unicast* addresses are utilized for a majority of traditional (enterprise) communications, as was the case in IPv4. However, *Broadcast* as a specific addressing type has been eliminated; in its place support for *multicast* addressing has been expanded and made a required part of the protocol. A new type of addressing called *anycast* has also been implemented. In addition, there are a number of special IPv6 addresses. Figure 7.1 compares the two address formats. Figure 7.2 provides a pictorial comparison of these three transmission (and address) modes. Logically, one can interpret the types of transmissions as follows[3]:

- Unicast transmission: "send to this one specific address"
- Multicast transmission: "send to every member of this specific group"
- Anycast transmission: "send to any one member of this specific group." Typically (motivated by efficiency goals), the transmission occurs to the closest (in routing terms) member of the group. Generally one interprets anycast to mean "send to the closest member of this specific group."

ETSI standards on the M2M system require support for anycast, unicast, multicast and broadcast communication modes; whenever possible, a global broadcast is

---

[3]Broadcast, by contrast, means "send this information/content to the entire universe of users in the address space."

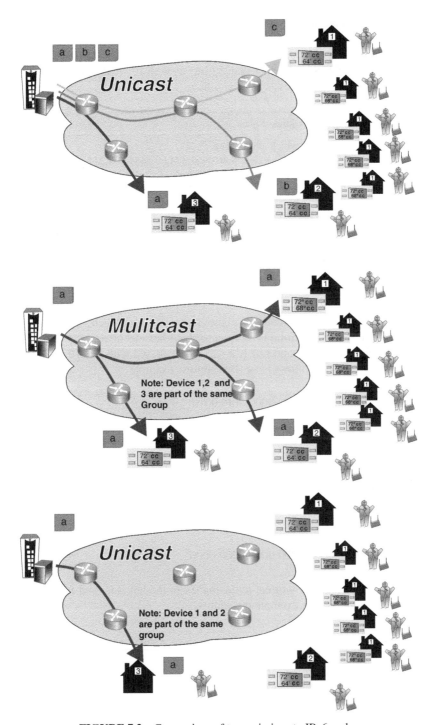

FIGURE 7.2   Comparison of transmissions to IPv6 nodes.

expected to be replaced by a multicast or anycast in order to minimize the load on the communication network (13).

The format of IPv6 addressing is described in RFC 2373. As noted, an IPv6 address consists of 128 bits, rather than 32 bits as with IPv4 addresses; the number of bits correlates to the address space, as follows:

IP Version	Size of Address Space
IPv6	128 bits, which allows for 2^{128} or 340,282,366,920,938,463,463,374,607,431,768,211,456 (3.4×10^{38}) possible addresses
IPv4	32 bits, which allows for 2^{32} or 4,294,967,296 possible addresses

The relatively large size of the IPv6 address is designed to be subdivided into hierarchical routing domains that reflect the topology of the modern-day Internet. The use of 128 bits provides multiple levels of hierarchy and flexibility in designing hierarchical addressing and routing. The IPv4-based Internet currently lacks this flexibility (14).

The IPv6 address is represented as eight groups of 16 bits each, separated by the ":" character. Each 16-bit group is represented by 4 hexadecimal digits, that is, each digit has a value between 0 and f (0,1, 2, ... a, b, c, d, e, f with a = 10, b = 11, and so on, to f = 15). What follows is an IPv6 address example

3223:0ba0:01e0:d001:0000:0000:d0f0:0010

An abbreviated format exists to designate IPv6 addresses when all endings are 0. For example

3223:0ba0::

is the abbreviated form of the following address:

3223:0ba0:0000:0000:0000:0000:0000:0000

Similarly, only one 0 is written, removing 0's in the left side, and four 0's in the middle of the address. For example the address

3223:ba0:0:0:0:0::1234

is the abbreviated form of the following address

3223:0ba0:0000:0000:0000:0000:0000:1234

There is also a method to designate groups of IP addresses or subnetworks that is based on specifying the number of bits that designate the subnetwork, beginning from left to right, using remaining bits to designate single devices inside the network. For example, the notation

3223:0ba0:01a0::/48

indicates that the part of the IP address used to represent the subnetwork has 48 bits. Since each hexadecimal digit has 4 bits, this points out that the part used to represent the subnetwork is formed by 12 digits, that is: "3223:0ba0:01a0." The remaining digits of the IP address would be used to represent nodes inside the network.

As noted, anycast addresses are a new type of address defined in IPv6 (as originally defined in RFC 1546). The purpose of the anycast address functionality is to enable capabilities that were difficult to implement in IPv4 environments. Datagrams sent to the anycast address are automatically delivered to the device in the network that is the easiest to reach. Anycast addresses can be used to define a group of devices, any one of which can support a service request from the user sent to a single specific IP address. One example is situations where one needs a service that can be provided by a set of different (dispersed) servers, but where one does not specifically care which one provides it; a specific example here may be an Internet or video (streaming) cache. Another example of anycast addressing is a router arrangement that allows datagrams to be transmitted to whichever router in a group of equivalent routers is closest to the point of transmission; a specific example here may be to allow load sharing between routers. It should be noted that there is no special anycast addressing format: anycast addresses are the same as unicast addresses from an address format perspective. In practicality, an anycast address is defined and created in a self-declarative manner when a unicast address is assigned to more than one device interface.

Special IPv6 addresses, as follows (see Table 7.2 for additional details) (15):

- Auto-return or loopback virtual address. This address is specified in IPv4 as the 127.0.0.1 address. In IPv6, this address is represented as ::1.
- Not specified address (::). This address is not allocated to any node since it is used to indicate absence of address.
- IPv6 over IPv4 dynamic/automatic tunnel addresses. These addresses are designated as IPv4-compatible IPv6 addresses and allow the sending of IPv6 traffic over IPv4 networks in a transparent manner. They are represented as, for example, ::156.55.23.5.
- IPv4 over IPv6 addresses automatic representation. These addresses allow for IPv4-only nodes to still work in IPv6 networks. They are designated as "mapped from IPv4 to IPv6 addresses" and are represented as ::FFFF:, for example ::FFFF.156.55.43.3.

TABLE 7.2   A Set of IPv6 Addresses of Particular Note

Node-scoped unicast	::1/128 is the loopback address (per RFC 4291)
	::/128 is the unspecified address (per RFC 4291)
	Addresses within this block should not appear on the public Internet
IPv4-mapped addresses	::FFFF:0:0/96 are the IPv4-mapped addresses (per RFC 4291).
	Addresses within this block should not appear on the public Internet
IPv4-compatible addresses	::ipv4-address/96 are the IPv4-compatible addresses (per RFC4291).
	These addresses are deprecated and should not appear on the public Internet
Link-scoped unicast	FE80::/10 are the link-local unicast (per RFC 4291) addresses.
	Addresses within this block should not appear on the public Internet
Unique local	FC00::/7 are the unique-local addresses (per RFC 4193). Addresses within this block should not appear by default on the public Internet
Documentation prefix	The 2001:db8::/32 are the documentation addresses (per RFC 3849). They are used for documentation purposes such as user manuals, RFCs, and so on. Addresses within this block should not appear on the public Internet
6to4	2002::/16 are the 6to4 addresses (per RFC 3056). The 6to4 addresses may be advertised when the site is running a 6to4 relay or offering a 6to4 transit service. However, the provider of this service should be aware of the implications of running such service (per RFC 3964), which include some specific filtering rules for 6to4. IPv4 addresses disallowed in 6to4 prefixes are listed in (per RFC 3964)
Teredo	2001::/32 are the Teredo addresses (per RFC 4380). The Teredo addresses may be advertised when the site is running a Teredo relay or offering a Teredo transit service
6bone	5F00::/8 were the addresses of the first instance of the 6bone experimental network (per RFC 1897)3FFE::/16 were the addresses of the second instance of the 6bone experimental network (per RFC 2471)Both 5F00::/8 and 3FFE::/16 were returned to IANA (per RFC 3701). These addresses are subject to future allocation, similar to current unallocated address space. Addresses within this block should not appear on the public Internet until they are reallocated
ORCHID	2001:10::/28 are ORCHID addresses (per RFC 4843). These addresses are used as identifiers and are not routable at the IP layer. Addresses within this block should not appear on the public Internet
Default route	::/0 is the default unicast route address
IANA special-purpose IPv6 address block	An IANA registry (iana-ipv6-special-registry) is set (per RFC 4773) for special-purpose IPv6 address block assignments used for experiments and other purposes. Addresses within this registry should be reviewed for Internet routing considerations
Multicast	FF00::/8 are multicast addresses (per RFC 4291). They have a 4-bit scope in the address field where only some values are of global scope (per RFC 4291). Only addresses with global scope in this block may appear on the public Internet
	Multicast routes must not appear in unicast routing tables

7.3 IPv6 PROTOCOL OVERVIEW

Table 7.3 summarizes the core protocols that comprise IPv6. IPv6 basic protocol capabilities include the following:

- Addressing
- Anycast
- Flow Labels
- ICMPv6
- Neighbor discovery (ND)

Like IPv4, IPv6 is a connectionless datagram protocol used primarily for addressing and routing packets between hosts. Connectionless means that a session is not established before exchanging data. "Unreliable" means that delivery is not guaranteed. IPv6 always makes a best-effort attempt to deliver a packet. An IPv6 packet might be lost, delivered out of sequence, duplicated, or delayed. IPv6 *per se* does not attempt to recover from these types of errors. The acknowledgment of packets delivered and the recovery of lost packets is done by a higher-layer protocol, such as TCP (14). From a packet-forwarding perspective, IPv6 operates in a similar, nearly identical manner to IPv4.

TABLE 7.3   Key IPv6 Protocols

Protocol (Current Version)	Description
IPv6: RFC 2460 Updated by RFC 5095, RFC 5722, RFC 5871	IPv6 is a connectionless datagram protocol used for routing packets between hosts
Internet control message protocol for IPv6 (ICMPv6): RFC 4443 Updated by RFC 4884	A mechanism that enables hosts and routers that use IPv6 communication to report errors and send status messages
Multicast listener discovery (MLD): RFC 2710 Updated by RFC 3590, RFC 3810	A mechanism that enables one to manage subnet multicast membership for IPv6. MLD uses a series of three ICMPv6 messages. MLD replaces the Internet group management protocol (IGMP) v3 that is employed for IPv4
ND: RFC 4861 Updated by RFC 5942	A mechanism that is used to manage node-to-node communication on a link. ND uses a series of five ICMPv6 messages. ND replaces address resolution protocol (ARP), ICMPv4 router discovery, and the ICMPv4 redirect message ND is implemented using the neighbor discovery protocol (NDP)

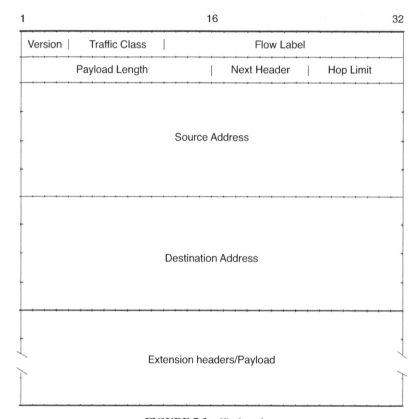

FIGURE 7.3 IPv6 packet.

An IPv6 packet, also known as an IPv6 datagram, consists of an IPv6 header and an IPv6 payload, as shown Figure 7.3. The IPv6 header consists of two parts, the IPv6 base header and optional extension headers. See Figure 7.4. Functionally, the optional extension headers and upper-layer protocols, for example TCP, are considered part of the IPv6 payload. Table 7.4 shows the fields in the IPv6 base header. IPv4 headers and IPv6 headers are not directly interoperable: hosts and/or routers must use an implementation of both IPv4 and IPv6 in order to recognize and process both header formats (see Fig. 7.5). This gives rise to a number of complexities in the migration process between the IPv4 and the IPv6 environments. The IP header in IPv6 has been streamlined and defined to be of a fixed length (40 bytes). In IPv6, header fields from the IPv4 header have been removed, renamed, or moved to the new optional IPv6 extension headers. The header length field is no longer needed since the IPv6 header is now a fixed-length entity. The IPv4 "type of service" is equivalent to the IPv6 "traffic class" field. The "total length" field has been replaced with the "payload length" field. Since IPv6 only allows for fragmentation to be performed by the IPv6 source and destination nodes, and not individual routers, the IPv4 segment control

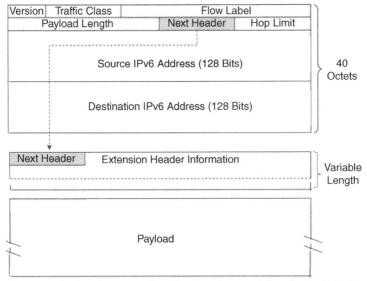

IPv6 extension headers are optional headers that may follow the basic IPv6 header. An IPv6 PDU may include zero, one, or multiple extension headers. When multiple extension headers are used, they form a chained list of headers identified by the Next Header field of the previous header.

FIGURE 7.4   IPv6 extension headers.

fields (identification, flags, and fragment offset fields) have been moved to similar fields within the fragment extension header. The functionality provided by the "time to live (TTL[4])" field has been replaced with the "hop limit" field. The "protocol" field has been replaced with the "next header type" field. The "header checksum" field was removed, which has the main advantage of not having each relay spend time processing the checksum. The "options" field is no longer part of the header as it was in IPv4. Options are specified in the optional IPv6 extension headers. The removal of the options field from the header enables more efficient routing; only the information that is needed by a router needs to be processed (16).

One area requiring consideration, however, is the length of the IPv6 PDU: the 40-octet header can be a problem for real-time IP applications such as VoIP and IPTV. Header compression (HC) becomes critical for many applications, as noted in Section 7.4. Also, there will be some bandwidth inefficiency in general, which could be an issue in limited-bandwidth environments or applications (e.g., wireless networks, sensor networks, IoT networks).

Stateless address autoconfiguration (described in RFC 4862) defines how an IPv6 node generates addresses without the use of a DHCP for IPv6 (DHCPv6) server (17). "Autoconfiguration" is a new characteristic of the IPv6 protocol that facilitates network management and system set-up tasks by users. This characteristic is

---

[4]TTL has been used in many attacks and intrusion detection system (IDS) tricks in IPv4.

TABLE 7.4 IPv6 Base Header

IPv6 Header Field	Length (bits)	Function
Version	4	Identifies the version of the protocol. For IPv6, the version is 6
Traffic class	8	Intended for originating nodes and forwarding routers to identify and distinguish between different classes or priorities of IPv6 packets
Flow label	20	(sometimes referred to as flow ID) Defines how traffic is handled and identified. A flow is a sequence of packets sent either to a unicast or to a multicast destination. This field identifies packets that require special handling by the IPv6 node. The following list shows the ways the field is handled if a host or router does not support flow label field functions: • If the packet is being sent, the field is set to zero • If the packet is being received, the field is ignored
Payload length	16	Identifies the length, in octets, of the payload. This field is a 16-bit unsigned integer. The payload includes the optional extension headers, as well as the upper-layer protocols, for example, TCP
Next header	8	Identifies the header immediately following the IPv6 header. The following shows examples of the next header: • 00 = Hop-by-hop options • 01 = ICMPv4 • 04 = IP in IP (encapsulation) • 06 = TCP • 17 = UDP • 43 = Routing • 44 = Fragment • 50 = Encapsulating security payload • 51 = Authentication • 58 = ICMPv6
Hop limit	8	Identifies the number of network segments, also known as links or subnets, on which the packet is allowed to travel before being discarded by a router. The hop limit is set by the sending host and is used to prevent packets from endlessly circulating on an IPv6 internetwork When forwarding an IPv6 packet, IPv6 routers must decrease the hop limit by 1 and must discard the IPv6 packet when the hop limit is 0
Source address	128	Identifies the IPv6 address of the original source of the IPv6 packet
Destination address	128	Identifies the IPv6 address of intermediate or final destination of the IPv6 packet

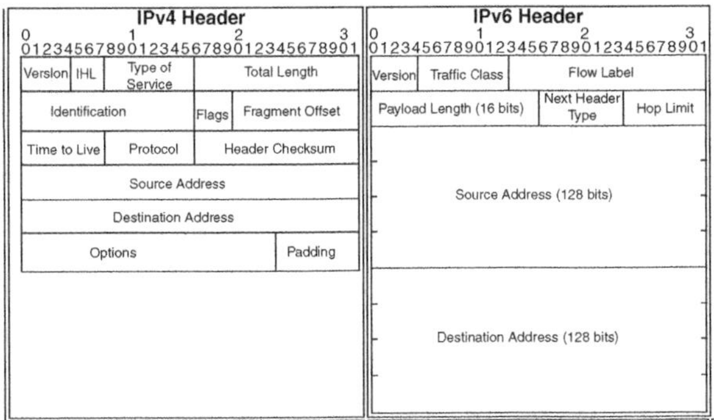

IPv4 Header	IPv6 Header	
Version (4-bit)	Version (4-bit)	IPv6 header contains a new value
Header length (4-bit)	—	Removed in IPv6, the basic IPv6 header has fixed length of 40 octets
Type of service (8-bit)	Traffic class (8-bit)	Same function for both headers
—	Flow label (20-bit)	New field added to tag a flow for IPv6 packets
Total PDU length (16-bit)	Payload length (16-bit)	Same function for both headers
Identification (16-bit)	—	Removed in IPv6 because fragmentation is no longer done by intermediate routers in the networks, but by the source node that originates the packet
Flags (3-bit)	—	Removed in IPv6 because fragmentation is no longer done by intermediate routers in the networks, but by the source node that originates the packet
Fragment offset (13-bit)	—	Removed in IPv6 because fragmentation is no longer done by intermediate routers in the networks, but by the source node that originates the packet
Time to live (8-bit)	Hop limit (8-bit)	Same function for both headers
Protocol number (8-bit)	Next header (8-bit)	Same function for both headers
Header checksum (16-bit)	—	Removed in IPv6; upper-layer protocols handle checksums
Source address (32-bit)	Source address (128-bit)	Same function, but source address is expanded in IPv6
Destination address (32-bit)	Destination address (128-bit)	Same function, but destination address is expanded in IPv6
Options (variable)	—	Removed in IPv6. Options handled differently
Padding (variable)	—	Removed in IPv6. Options handled differently
—	Extension headers	New way in IPv6 to handle Options fields, security

FIGURE 7.5   Comparison of IPv4 and IPv6 headers.

often called "plug-and-play" or "connect-and-work." Autoconfiguration facilitates initialization of user devices: after connecting a device to an IPv6 network, one or several IPv6 globally unique addresses are automatically allocated. Note, however, that an IPv6 address must be configured on a router's interface for the interface to forward IPv6 traffic. Configuring a site-local or global IPv6 address on a router's interface automatically configures a link-local address (LLA) and activates IPv6 for that interface.

DHCP allows systems to obtain an IPv4 address and other required information (e.g., default router or domain name system [DNS] server); a similar protocol, DHCPv6, has been published for IPv6. DHCP and DHCPv6 are known as stateful protocols because they maintain tables on (specialized) servers. However, IPv6 also has a new stateless autoconfiguration protocol that has no equivalent in IPv4. The stateless autoconfiguration protocol does not require a server component because there is no state to maintain (a DHCP server may typically run in a router or firewall). Every IPv6 system (other than routers) is able to build its own unicast global address

(18). "Stateless" autoconfiguration is also described as "serverless." The acronym SLAAC is also used; it expands to *stateless address autoconfiguration*. SLAAC was originally defined in RFC 2462. With SLAAC, the presence of configuration servers to supply profile information is not required.

The host generates its own address using a combination of the information that it possesses (in its interface or network card) and the information that is supplied by the router. As noted in RFC 4941, nodes use IPv6 SLAAC to generate addresses using a combination of locally available information and information advertised by routers. Addresses are formed by combining network prefixes with an interface identifier. On an interface that contains an embedded IEEE identifier, the interface identifier is typically derived from it. On other interface types, the interface identifier is generated through other means, for example, via random number generation (19). Some types of network interfaces come with an embedded IEEE identifier (i.e., a link-layer media access control [MAC] address), and in those cases, SLAAC uses the IEEE identifier to generate a 64-bit interface identifier (12). By design, the interface identifier is likely to be globally unique when generated in this fashion. The interface identifier is in turn appended to a prefix to form a 128-bit IPv6 address. Not all nodes and interfaces contain IEEE identifiers. In such cases, an interface identifier is generated through some other means (e.g., at random), and the resultant interface identifier may not be globally unique and may also change over time. Routers determine the prefix that identifies networks associated to the link under discussion. The "interface identifier" identifies an interface within a subnetwork and is often, and by default, generated from the MAC address of the network card. The IPv6 address is built combining the 64 bits of the interface identifier with the prefixes that routers determine as belonging to the subnetwork. If there is no router, the interface identifier is self-sufficient to allow the PC to generate a "link-local" address. The "link-local" address is sufficient to allow the communication between several nodes connected to the same link (the same local network).

In summary, all nodes combine interface identifiers (whether derived from an IEEE identifier or generated through some other technique) with the reserved link-local prefix to generate LLAs for their attached interfaces. Additional addresses can then be created by combining prefixes advertised in router advertisements via ND (defined in RFC 4861) (20) with the interface identifier.

Note: As seen addresses generated using SLAAC contain an embedded interface identifier that remains constant over time. Whenever a fixed identifier is used in multiple contexts, a security exposure could theoretically result. A correlation can be performed by an attacker who is in the path between the node in question and the peer(s) to which it is communicating, and who can view the IPv6 addresses present in the datagrams. Because the identifier is embedded within the IPv6 address, which is a fundamental requirement of communication, it cannot be easily hidden. Solutions to this issue have been proposed by generating interface identifiers that vary over time (19).

IPv6 addresses are "leased" to an interface for a fixed established time (including an infinite time). When this "lifetime" expires, the link between the interface and the address is invalidated and the address can be reallocated to other interfaces. For the suitable management of addresses expiration time, an address goes through two states (stages) while is affiliated to an interface (21):

(a) At first, an address is in a "preferred" state, so its use in any communication is not restricted.
(b) After that, an address becomes "deprecated," indicating that its affiliation with the current interface will (soon) be invalidated.

When it is in a "deprecated" state, the use of the address is discouraged, although it is not forbidden. However, when possible, any new communication (e.g., the opening of a new TCP connection) must use a "preferred" address. A "deprecated" address should only be used by applications that have already used it before and in cases where it is difficult to change this address to another address without causing a service interruption.

To ensure that allocated addresses (granted either by manual mechanisms or by autoconfiguration) are unique in a specific link, the *link duplicated address detection algorithm* is used. The address to which the duplicated address detection algorithm is being applied to is designated (until the end of this algorithmic session) as an "attempt address." In this case, it does not matter that such address has been allocated to an interface and received packets are discarded.

Next we describe how an IPv6 address is formed. The lowest 64 bits of the address identify a specific interface, and these bits are designated as "interface identifier." The highest 64 bits of the address identify the "path" or the "prefix" of the network or router in one of the links to which such interface is connected. The IPv6 address is formed by combining the prefix with the interface identifier.

It is possible for a host or device to have IPv6 and IPv4 addresses simultaneously. Most of the systems that currently support IPv6 allow the simultaneous use of both protocols. In this way, it is possible to support communication with IPv4-only networks as well as with IPv6-only networks and the use of the applications developed for both protocols (21).

Is it possible to transmit IPv6 traffic over IPv4 networks via tunneling methods. This approach consists of "wrapping" the IPv6 traffic as IPv4 payload data: IPv6 traffic is sent "encapsulated" into IPv4 traffic, and at the receiving end this traffic is parsed as IPv6 traffic. Transition mechanisms are methods used for the coexistence of IPv4 and/or IPv6 devices and networks. For example, an "IPv6-in-IPv4 tunnel" is a transition mechanism that allows IPv6 devices to communicate through an IPv4 network. The mechanism consists of creating the IPv6 packets in a normal way and encapsulating them in an IPv4 packet. The reverse process is undertaken in the destination machine that de-encapsulates the IPv6 packet.

There is a significant difference between the procedures to allocate IPv4 addresses, which focus on the parsimonious use of addresses (since addresses are a scare resource and should be managed with caution), and the procedures to allocate IPv6 addresses, which focus on flexibility. ISPs deploying IPv6 systems follow the RIRs' policies relating to how to assign IPv6 addressing space among their clients. RIRs are recommending ISPs and operators allocate to each IPv6 client a /48 subnetwork; this allows clients to manage their own subnetworks without using NAT. (The implication is that the *obligatory* need for NAT for intranet-based devices disappears in IPv6.)

In order to allow its maximum scalability, the IPv6 protocol uses an approach based on a basic header, with minimum information. This differentiates it from IPv4 where different options are included in addition to the basic header. IPv6 uses a header "concatenation" mechanism to support supplementary capabilities. The advantages of this approach include the following:

- The size of the basic header is always the same and is well known. The basic header has been simplified compared with IPv4, since only eight fields are used instead of 12. The basic IPv6 header has a fixed size; hence, its processing by nodes and routers is more straightforward. Also, the header's structure aligns to 64 bits, so that new and future processors (64 bits minimum) can process it in a more efficient way.

- Routers placed between a source point and a destination point (i.e., the route that a specific packet has to pass through) do not need to process or understand any "following headers." In other words, in general, interior (core) points of the network (routers) only have to process the basic header, while in IPv4 all headers must be processed. This flow mechanism is similar to the operation in MPLS, yet precedes it by several years.

- There is no limit to the number of options that the headers can support (the IPv6 basic header is 40 octets in length, while IPv4 one varies from 20 to 60 octets, depending on the options used).

In IPv6, interior/core routers do not perform packet fragmentation, but the fragmentation is performed end-to-end. That is, source and destination nodes perform, by means of the IPv6 stack, the fragmentation of a packet and the reassembly, respectively. The fragmentation process consists of dividing the source packet into smaller packets or fragments (21).

The IPv6 specification defines a number of extension headers (16) (also see Table 7.5) (22):

- Routing header—Similar to the source routing options in IPv4. The header is used to mandate a specific routing.
- AH—A security header that provides authentication and integrity.
- Encapsulating security payload (ESP) header—A security header that provides authentication and encryption.
- Fragmentation header—The Fragmentation Header is similar to the fragmentation options in IPv4.

TABLE 7.5   IPv6 Extension Headers

Header (Protocol ID)	Description
Hop-by-hop options header (protocol 0)	The hop-by-hop options header is used for Jumbogram packets and the router alert. An example of applying the hop-by-hop options header is resource reservation protocol (RSVP). This field is read and processed by every node and router along the delivery path
Destination options header (protocol 60)	This header carries optional information that is specifically targeted to a packet's destination address. The MIPv6 protocol specification makes use of the destination options header to exchange registration messages between MNs and the HA. Mobile IP is a protocol allowing MNs to keep permanent IP addresses even if they change point of attachment
Routing header (protocol 43)	This header can be used by an IPv6 source node to force a packet to pass through specific routers on the way to its destination. A list of intermediary routers may be specified within the routing header when the routing type field is set to 0
Fragment header (protocol 44)	In IPv6, the path MTU discovery (PMTUD) mechanism is recommended to all IPv6 nodes. When an IPv6 node does not support PMTUD and it must send a packet larger than the greatest MTU along the delivery path, the fragment header is used. When this happens, the node fragments the packets and sends each fragment using fragment headers; then the destination node reassembles the original packet by concatenating all the fragments
AH (protocol 51)	This header is used in IPsec to provide authentication, data integrity, and replay protection. It also ensures protection of some fields of the basic IPv6 header. This header is identical in both IPv4 and IPv6
Encapsulating security payload (ESP) header (protocol 50)	This header is also used in IPsec to provide authentication, data integrity, replay protection, and confidentiality of the IPv6 packet. Similar to the AH, this header is identical in both IPv4 and IPv6

- Destination options header—Header that contains a set of options to be processed only by the final destination node. MIPv6 is an example of an environment that uses such a header.
- Hop-by-hop options header—A set of options needed by routers to perform certain management or debugging functions.

7.4 IPv6 TUNNELING

IPv6 tunneling is used in a variety of settings, including in MIPv6. MIPv6 tunnels payload packets between the mobile node (MN) and the home agent (HA) in both directions. This tunneling uses IPv6 encapsulation discussed below.

IPv6 tunneling as defined in RFC 2473 (23) is a technique for establishing a "virtual link" between two IPv6 nodes for transmitting data packets as payloads of IPv6 packets. From the perspective of the two nodes, this "virtual link," called an *IPv6 tunnel*, appears as a point-to-point link on which IPv6 acts like a link-layer protocol. The two IPv6 nodes support specific roles. One node encapsulates original packets received from other nodes or from itself and forwards the resulting tunnel packets through the tunnel. The other node decapsulates the received tunnel packets and forwards the resulting original packets toward their destinations, possibly itself. The encapsulator node is called the tunnel entry-point node, and it is the source of the tunnel packets. The decapsulator node is called the tunnel exit point, and it is the destination of the tunnel packets. An IPv6 tunnel is a unidirectional mechanism— tunnel packet flow takes place in one direction between the IPv6 tunnel entry-point and exit-point nodes (see Fig. 7.6, top). Bidirectional tunneling is achieved by merging two unidirectional mechanisms, that is, configuring two tunnels, each in opposite direction to the other—the entry-point node of one tunnel is the exit-point node of the other tunnel (see Fig. 7.6, bottom).

Note: while tunnels between two nodes identified by unicast addresses are typical (such tunnels look like "virtual point to point links"), one can also define tunnels where the exit-point nodes are identified by anycast or multicast addresses.

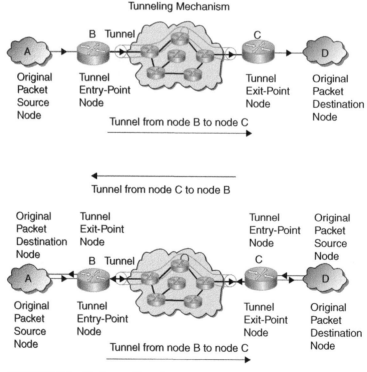

FIGURE 7.6   IPv6 tunneling. Top: Unidirectional. Bottom: Bidirectional.

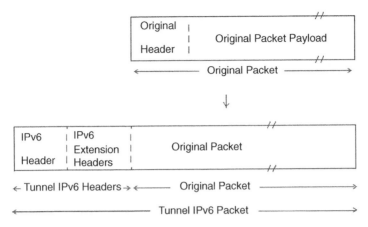

FIGURE 7.7   Encapsulating a packet.

IPv6 encapsulation entails prepending an IPv6 header to the original packet, and, optionally, a set of IPv6 extension headers, as depicted in Figure 7.7 that are collectively called tunnel IPv6 headers. The encapsulation takes place in an IPv6 tunnel entry-point node, as a result of an original packet being forwarded onto the virtual link represented by the tunnel. The original packet is processed during forwarding according to the forwarding rules of the protocol of that packet. At encapsulation, the source field of the tunnel IPv6 header is filled with an IPv6 address of the tunnel entry-point node and the destination field with an IPv6 address of the tunnel exit point. Subsequently, the tunnel packet resulting from encapsulation is sent toward the tunnel exit-point node.

IPv6 intermediate processing by intermediate nodes in the tunnel processes the IPv6 tunnel packets according to the IPv6 protocol. For example, a tunnel hop-by-hop options extension header is processed by each receiving node in the tunnel; a tunnel routing extension header identifies the intermediate processing nodes and controls at a finer granularity the forwarding path of the tunnel packet through the tunnel; a tunnel destination options extension header is processed at the tunnel exit-point node.

IPv6 decapsulation is the opposite process of encapsulation. Upon receiving an IPv6 packet destined to an IPv6 address of a tunnel exit-point node, its IPv6 protocol layer processes the tunnel headers. The strict left-to-right processing rules for extension headers are applied. When processing is complete, control is handed to the next protocol engine, which is identified by the next header field value in the last header processed. If this is set to a tunnel protocol value, the tunnel protocol engine discards the tunnel headers and passes the resulting original packet to the Internet or lower-layer protocol identified by that value for further processing. For example, in the case the next header field has the IPv6 tunnel protocol value, the resulting original packet is passed to the IPv6 protocol layer. (The tunnel exit-point node, which decapsulates the tunnel packets, and the destination node, which receives the resulting original packets, can be the same node.)

7.5 IPsec IN IPv6

As noted, IPsec provides network-level security where the application data is encapsulated within the IPv6 packet. IPsec itself is a set of two protocols: ESP, which provides integrity and confidentiality and AH, which provides integrity. IPsec utilizes the AH and/or ESP header to provide security (the AH and ESP header may be used separately or in combination). IPsec, with ESP, offers integrity and data origin authentication, confidentiality, and optional (at the discretion of the receiver) anti-replay features (using confidentiality without integrity is discouraged by the RFCs); in addition, ESP provides limited traffic flow confidentiality. Both the AH and ESP header may be employed as follows (16):

– "Tunnel mode"—The protocol is applied to the entire IP packet. This method is needed to ensure security over the entire packet, where a new IPv6 header and an AH or ESP header are wrapped around the original IP packet.
– "Transport mode"—The protocol is just applied to the transport layer (i.e., TCP, UDP, ICMP) in the form of an IPv6 header and AH or ESP header, followed by the transport protocol data (header, data). (see Fig. 7.8).

It should be noted that although the basic IPv6 standards have long been stable, considerable work continues in the IETF, particularly to resolve the issue of highly scalable multihoming support for IPv6 sites, and to resolve the problem of IP-layer interworking between IPv6-only and IPv4-only hosts. IPv6/IPv4 interworking at the application layers is handled within the original dual-stack model of IPv6 deployment: either one end of an application session will have dual-stack connectivity or a dual-stack intermediary such as a hypertext transfer protocol (HTTP) proxy or simple mail transfer protocol (SMTP) server will interface to both IPv4-only and IPv6-only hosts or applications (24).

7.6 HEADER COMPRESSION SCHEMES

Implementation of IPv6 gives rise to concerns related to expanded packet headers, especially for video and wireless (low bandwidth channel) applications. As noted in earlier sections, the packet header size doubled from 20 bytes in IPv4 to at least 40 bytes in IPv6. The use of network-layer encryption mechanism nearly doubles IP operational overhead. HC is, therefore, of interest. Currently, the use of HC in commercial networks is generally rare, but wireless and video applications (especially in an IPv6 environment) may well drive future deployment of the technology.

HC algorithms can reduce the performance and throughput impact of expanded IPv6 packet headers and protocol-imposed overhead. Consider the illustrative case where packets with constant 20 byte payloads are transmitted using a 40-byte IPv6 header. Consider a 1 Mbps link. Then during a 1-s period, about 666 kb transmitted over the link is IPv6 overhead, and only about 333 kb transmitted over the link is

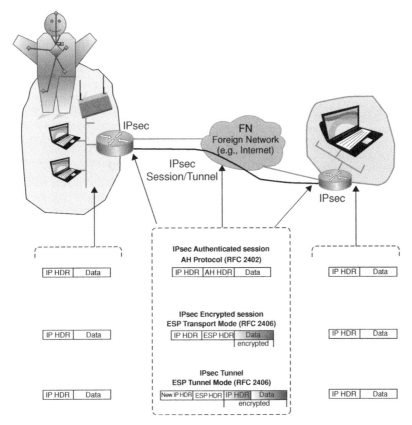

FIGURE 7.8   IPsec network environment.

actual user data. This implies that 66% of data transmitted is overhead. Now consider the case where the same packet of payload is sent with a 2-byte compressed header. Now over a 1-s period, about 90 kb transmitted is IPv6 overhead, and about 910 kb transmitted is actual user data. This implies that only 9% of data transmitted is overhead. This example shows that HC can theoretically decrease header overhead by 95%. Overhead is defined as "IP header bytes" divided by "total bytes transmitted." Naturally, the overhead for larger packets will be less as a total percentage. Studies show that although the average packet length of packets traveling over the Internet is around 350–400 bytes, a considerable portion of the Internet traffic is short (say, 40 bytes or less) (25). Depending on the encapsulation protocol, video packets can also be small. For example, under the DVB standard (e.g., DVB-T, DVB-C, DVB-S, DVB-S2), basic packets have a length of 204 bytes. This implies a significant percentage of overhead is incurred without HC. (For illustration, a 40-byte IPv6 header on a DVB packet would result in an overhead of $40/244 = 16.39\%$; if one assumes that header size is reduced to 2 bytes per packet, the overhead is $2/206 = 0.97\%$.)

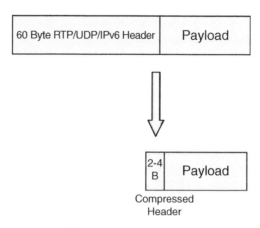

FIGURE 7.9   HC for IPv6.

There is additional protocol overhead. Applications carrying data carried within RTP will, in addition to link-layer framing, have an IPv4 header (20 octets), a UDP header (8 octets), and an RTP header (12 octets), for a total of 40 octets. With IPv6, the IPv6 header is 40 octets for a total of 60 octets. Applications transferring data using TCP have 20 octets for the transport header, for a total size of 40 octets for IPv4 and 60 octets for IPv6 (26).

Usually HC techniques are applied to a link, on a per-hop basis. Application of hop-by-hop HC techniques to network backbones is relatively rare because to achieve compression over the network, multiple compression–decompression cycles are required. This represents a scalability and resource issues on core network nodes. Developments in the IETF in the past few years provide a framework for applying HC over multiple-hop to backbone networks. For example, work has been done HC techniques to MPLS backbones and mobile ad hoc networks (MANETs) (where trade needs to be made between computational processing, power requirements, and bandwidth savings).

Traditionally, compression is applied to layer 3 (IP) and several layer 4 proto-col headers; for example, RTP/UDP/IPv6 headers can be compressed from 60 bytes to 2–4 bytes. See Figure 7.9. HC algorithms can also reduce the additional over-head introduced by network-layer encryption mechanisms (e.g., IPsec). Compression algorithms that address encryption/decryption have the ability to: (i) compress inner headers before encryption and (ii) compress outer ESP/IP headers after encryption. Two compression protocols emerged from the IETF in recent years:

(i) Internet protocol header compression (IPHC), a scheme designed for low bit error rate (BER) links (compression profiles were originally defined in RFC 2507 and RFC 2508, and further discussed in RFC 4995, 4996, and 4497); it provides compression of TCP/IP, UDP/IP, RTP/UDP/IP, and ESP/IP header; "enhanced" compression of RTP/UDP/IP (ECRTP) headers is defined in RFC 3545.

(ii) Robust header compression (ROHC) is a scheme designed for wireless links that provides greater compression compared to IPHC at the cost of greater implementation complexity (compression profiles were originally defined in RFC 3095 and RFC 3096 with further developments in other RFCs) (26–28); this is more suitable for high BER, long RTT links and supports compression of ESP/IP, UDP/IP, and RTP/UDP/IP headers.

Compression is applied over a link between a source node (i.e., compressor) and a destination node (i.e., decompressor). HC algorithms make use of protocol inter-packet header field redundancies to improve overall efficiency. Both compressor and decompressor store header fields of each packet stream and associate each stream with a context identifier (CID). Upon reception of a packet with an associated context, the compressor removes the IPv6 header fields from packet header and appends a CID. Upon reception of a packet with a CID, the decompressor inserts IPv6 header fields back into packet header and transmits packet (25). IPHC and ROHC are both specified in Release 4 and Release 5 of the Third-Generation Partnership Project (3GPP). Cisco Systems router Internetwork Operating System (IOS) provides IPHC implementation.

Point-to-point protocol (PPP) (defined in RFC 1661) provides (i) a method for encapsulating datagrams over serial links; (ii) a link control protocol (LCP) for establishing, configuring, and testing the data-link connection; and (iii) a family of network control protocols (NCPs) for establishing and configuring different network-layer protocols. In order to establish communications over a point-to-point link, each end of the PPP link must first send LCP packets to configure and test the data link. After the link has been established and optional facilities have been negotiated as needed by the LCP, PPP must send NCP packets to choose and configure one or more network-layer protocols. Once each of the chosen network-layer protocols has been configured, datagrams from each network-layer protocol can be sent over the link. The link will remain configured for communications until explicit LCP or NCP packets close the link down, or until some external event occurs (power failure at the other end, carrier drop, and so on) (29).

In RFC 5072, the NCP for establishing and configuring IPv6 over PPP, called IPV6CP, is defined. In RFC 5172, the compression parameter for use in IPv6 datagram compression is defined. The configuration option described in this just-cited RFC provides a way to negotiate the use of a specific IPv6 packet compression protocol. The IPv6-compression protocol configuration option is used to indicate the ability to receive compressed packets. IPv6-compression protocol field values have been assigned in for IPHC (0061) and for ROHC (0003).

7.7   QUALITY OF SERVICE IN IPv6

ETSI standards on the M2M system require that the M2M system should be able to make use of the QoS supported by underlying networks; M2M applications or service capabilities may use QoS capabilities of the underlying networks when implemented by the system (13). QoS is supported in IPv6. The IPv6 header has two QoS-related fields:

- 20-bit flow label, usable in IntServ-based environments. In IntServ environments, performance guarantees to traffic and resource reservations are provided on per-flow basis. A guaranteed and controlled load service capability is supported. IntServ approaches have scalability issues;
- 8-bit traffic class indicator usable in DiffServ-based environments. DiffServ environments are more common. The traffic class field may be used to set specific precedence or differentiated services code point (DSCP) values. These values are used in the exact same way as in IPv4. Performance guarantees are provided to traffic aggregates rather than to flows. DiffServ classifies all the network traffic into classes. Two distinct types (per hop behaviors) are supported:
- Expedited forwarding (EF): aims at providing QoS for the class by minimizing jitter and is generally focused on providing stricter guarantees;
- Assured forwarding (AF): inserts at most four classes with at most three levels of packets dropping categories.

There are no signaling protocol for resource allocation (admission control) and QoS mechanisms control. The following priority levels are typical, but variances are possible:

- Level 0—No specify priority
- Level 1—Background traffic (news)
- Level 2—Unattended data transfer (email)
- Level 3—Reserved
- Level 4—Attended bulk transfer (FTP)
- Level 5—Reserved
- Level 6—Interactive traffic (Telnet, Windowing)
- Level 7—Control traffic (routing, network management)

7.8 MIGRATION STRATEGIES TO IPv6

7.8.1 Technical Approaches

While the infrastructure is in place for IPv4 systems and IPv6 systems to run in parallel, widespread adoption of IPv6 has been slow because the two systems are not directly compatible (IPv6 and IPv4 protocols can coexist, but they cannot intercommunicate directly), and there been so far rather limited economic incentive for providers and end-user firms to introduce the technology (4). Therefore, migration to IPv6 environments is expected to be fairly complex. However, with the growth in the number of users and the IPv4 address exhaustion, large-scale deployment will invariably happen in the near future. IoT/M2M applications are expected to provide an impetus to the deployment of IPv6. Initially, internetworking between the two environments will be critical (6). Existing IPv4-endpoints and/or nodes will need to run dual-stack nodes or convert to IPv6 systems. Fortunately, the new protocol supports an IPv4-compatible IPv6 address that is an IPv6 address employing embedded IPv4 addresses. Tunneling, which we already described in passing, will play a major role in the beginning. There are a number of requirements that are typically applicable to an organization wishing to introduce an IPv6 service (30):

- The existing IPv4 service should not be adversely disrupted (e.g., as it might be by router loading of encapsulating IPv6 in IPv4 for tunnels);
- The IPv6 service should perform as well as the IPv4 service (e.g., at the IPv4 line rate, and with similar network characteristics);
- The service must be manageable and be able to be monitored (thus tools should be available for IPv6 as they are for IPv4);
- The security of the network should not be compromised, due to the additional protocol itself or a weakness of any transition mechanism used; and
- An IPv6 address allocation plan must be drawn up.

Well-known interworking mechanisms include the following, as described in RFC 2893:

- Dual IP layer (also known as dual stack): A technique for providing complete support for both IPs—IPv4 and IPv6—in hosts and routers;
- Configured tunneling of IPv6 over IPv4: Point-to-point tunnels made by encapsulating IPv6 packets within IPv4 headers to carry them over IPv4 routing infrastructures; and
- Automatic tunneling of IPv6 over IPv4: A mechanism for using IPv4-compatible addresses to automatically tunnel IPv6 packets over IPv4 networks.

Tunneling techniques include the following approaches, as described in RFC 2893:

- IPv6-over-IPv4 tunneling: The technique of encapsulating IPv6 packets within IPv4 so that they can be carried across IPv4 routing infrastructures.
- Configured tunneling: IPv6-over-IPv4 tunneling where the IPv4 tunnel endpoint address is determined by configuration information on the encapsulating node. The tunnels can be either unidirectional or bidirectional. Bidirectional configured tunnels behave as virtual point-to-point links.
- Automatic tunneling: IPv6-over-IPv4 tunneling where the IPv4 tunnel endpoint address is determined from the IPv4 address embedded in the IPv4-compatible destination address of the IPv6 packet being tunneled.
- IPv4 multicast tunneling: IPv6-over-IPv4 tunneling where the IPv4 tunnel endpoint address is determined using ND. Unlike configured tunneling, this does

not require any address configuration, and unlike automatic tunneling it does not require the use of IPv4-compatible addresses. However, the mechanism assumes that the IPv4 infrastructure supports IPv4 multicast.

Applications (and the lower-layer protocol stack) need to be properly equipped. Some examples of interoperability techniques include dual stacks and tunneling—IPv6-in-IPv4 (e.g., 6-to-4, 6rd, protocol 41), IPv4-in-IPv6, and IPv6-in-UDP (Teredo, TSP). There are four cases, as described in RFC 4038:

Case 1: IPv4-only applications in a dual-stack node. IPv6 protocol is introduced in a node, but applications are not yet ported to support IPv6. The protocol stack is as follows:

```
+----------------------+
|        appv4         | (appv4 - IPv4-only applications)
+----------------------+
|  TCP / UDP / others  | (transport protocols - TCP,
+----------------------+  UDP, and so on)
|     IPv4 | IPv6      | (IP protocols supported/enabled
+----------------------+  in the OS)
```

Case 2: IPv4-only applications and IPv6-only applications in a dual-stack node. Applications are ported for IPv6 only. Therefore, there are two similar applications, one for each protocol version (e.g., ping and ping6). The protocol stack is as follows:

```
+----------------------+ (appv4 - IPv4-only applications)
|   appv4 | appv6     | (appv6 - IPv6-only applications)
+----------------------+
|  TCP / UDP / others  | (transport protocols - TCP,
+----------------------+  UDP, and so on)
|     IPv4 | IPv6      | (IP protocols supported/
+----------------------+  enabled in the OS)
```

Case 3: Applications supporting both IPv4 and IPv6 in a dual-stack node. Applications are ported for both IPv4 and IPv6 support. Therefore, the existing IPv4 applications can be removed. The protocol stack is as follows:

```
+----------------------+
|       appv4/v6       | (appv4/v6 - applications
+----------------------+  supporting both IPv4 and IPv6)
|  TCP / UDP / others  | (transport protocols - TCP,
+----------------------+  UDP, and so on)
|     IPv4 | IPv6      | (IP protocols supported/
+----------------------+  enabled in the OS)
```

Case 4: Applications supporting both IPv4 and IPv6 in an IPv4-only node. Applications are ported for both IPv4 and IPv6 support, but the same applications may also have to work when IPv6 is not being used (e.g., disabled from the OS). The protocol stack is as follows:

```
+----------------------+
|       appv4/v6       |  (appv4/v6 - applications
+----------------------+   supporting both IPv4 and IPv6)
|  TCP / UDP / others  |  (transport protocols - TCP,
+----------------------+   UDP, and so on)
|         IPv4         |  (IP protocols supported/
+----------------------+   enabled in the OS)
```

The first two cases are not interesting in the longer term; only a few applications are inherently IPv4 or IPv6 specific and should work with both protocols without having to care about which one is being used.

It should be noted that the transition from a pure IPv4 network to a network where IPv4 and IPv6 coexist brings a number of extra security considerations that need to be taken into account when deploying IPv6 and operating the dual-protocol network and the associated transition mechanisms (7, 31).

Figure 7.10 depicts some basic scenarios of carrier-based IPv6 support. Case (a) and (b) represent traditional environments where the carrier link supports either a clear channel that is used to connect, say, two IPv4 routers, or is IP aware. (In each case, the "cloud" on the left could also be the IPv4 Internet or the IPv6 Internet.)

In Case (c), the carrier link is used to connect as a transparent link two IPv6 routers; the carrier link is not (does not need to be) aware that it is transferring IPv6 PDUs. In Case (d), the carrier system is IPv4 aware, so the use of that environment to support IPv6 requires IPv6 to operate in a tunneled mode over the non-IPv6 cloud, which is a capability of IPv6.

In Case (e), the carrier infrastructure needs to provide a gateway function between the IPv4 and the IPv6 world (this could entail re-packing the IP PDUs from the v4 format to the v6 format). Case (f) is the ideal long-term scenario where the "world has converted to IPv6" and "so did the carrier network."

In Case (g), the carrier IP-aware network provides a conversion function to support both IPv4 (as a baseline) and IPv6 (as a "new technology") handoffs. Possibly a dual-stack mechanism is utilized. In Case (h), the carrier IPv6-aware network provides a support function for IPv6 (as a baseline) and also a conversion function to support legacy IPv4 islands.

Some user organizations have expressed concerns about security in an IPv6 environment, fundamentally because of tunneling and firewall issues. The interested reader should consult Reference 7 for an extensive discussion of this topic and for tools and techniques to address the issues. Even network/security administrators that operate in a pure IPv4 environment need to be aware of IPv6-related security issues. In a standard IPv4 environment where IPv6 is not explicitly supported, any form of IPv6-based tunneling traffic must be considered abnormal, malicious traffic. For

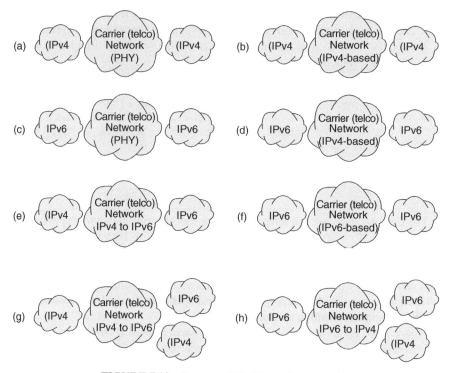

FIGURE 7.10   Support of IPv6 in carrier networks.

example, unconstrained 6to4-based traffic should be blocked (as noted elsewhere 6to4 is a transitional mechanism intended for individual independent nodes to connect IPv6 over the greater Internet). Most commercial-grade IPv4 firewalls block the IP protocol 41, the 6to4, and the tunnel protocol, unless it has been explicitly enabled (32).

7.8.2 Residential Broadband Services in an IPv6 Environment

One of the challenges related to the deployment of IPv6 is how to continue to support IPv4 services in residential broadband environments at the same time as the users migrate to a mixed IPv4 and IPv6 operational model. This is especially critical as IPv6 is technically incompatible with IPv4; this forces the introduction of some new concepts that change the present operation of broadband networks and has ramifications on how IPv6 can be offered to residential subscribers. Three approaches can be used, as covered in Reference 33 on which this discussion is based:

1. IPv6 support in telco environments using PPP over Ethernet (PPPoX) and/or asynchronous transfer mode (ATM) as defined in TR-187 of the Broadband Forum.

2. IPv6 support using PPPoX in conjunction with the bridged residential gateway (RG).
3. IPv6 support using IP over ethernet (IPoE) as defined in the Broadband Forum specification TR-177.

Approach 1. The introduction of IPv6 using PPPoX/layer 2 tunneling protocol (L2TP) has no implications on the access and aggregation network elements. PPP session authentication for IPv6 is identical to IPv4, using password authentication protocol/challenge handshake authentication protocol (PAP/CHAP) or option 82. IPv4 and IPv6 authentication can be done in a single authentication phase to RADIUS (remote authentication dial-in user service). Since PPPoX IPv6 control protocol (CP) is only defining the LLA, global IPv6 addresses are typically assigned using DHCP or SLAAC. To support an IPv6 routed RG using the PPP termination and aggregation/L2TP network server (PTA/LNS) model, the following mechanisms are required between the RG and the broadband network gateway/broadband remote access server (BNG/BRAS) to ensure IPv6 connectivity:

- PPPoX IPv6 CP is used for LLA assignment
- DHCPv6 prefix delegation (IA-PD—identity association for prefix delegation) is used to obtain a prefix for LAN address assignment
- Stateless DHCPv6 is used to obtain additional configuration parameters
- When the numbered RG model is deployed, stateful DHCPv6 (identity association for non-temporary addresses [IA-NA]) is used to obtain an RG management IPv6 address; in case of an unnumbered RG model, this is not required
- Route advertisements are required to assign the default gateway assignment

Approach 2. The utilization of the Bridged RG requires the following:

- PPPoX IPv6CP is used for LLA assignment
- SLAAC is used for the host to obtain a global-Unicast IPv6 address
- Stateless DHCP is used to obtain additional configuration parameters
- Route advertisements are used to assign the default gateway assignment

Therefore, to support IPv6 in a telco environment, PPPoX for IPv6 imposes no different requirements on N:1 virtual local area network (VLAN) or 1:1 VLAN architectures or on a bridged gateway model, compared to IPv4. However, PPPoX for IPv6 will always impact the BNG/BRAS, CPE, and home gateway using a routed gateway model.

Approach 3. The implications for introducing IPv6 IPoE mainly depend on the VLAN model used (1:1 or N:1) and the operational model of the home gateway (bridged or routed). The impact of IPv6 support for IPoE in a bridged RG model depends on whether DHCP or SLAAC is used to the end device. When deploying DHCP, the key difference from the routed RG IPoE model arises from the fact that there is no DHCP PD address required and only an IA address is assigned to the host. Care must be taken to ensure communication between IPv6 devices in the home remains local and is not sent through the BNG.

7.8.3 Deployment Opportunities

There was a lack of ubiquitous IPv6 utilization as of early 2013; this is partly due to the fact that the number of IPv6 nodes is rather low. However, IPv6 rollout has started to get traction. The approaching exhaustion of IPv4 address space will bring about a situation where ISPs are faced with a choice between one or more of three major alternatives (24):

1. Squeeze the use of IPv4 addresses even harder than today, using smaller and smaller address blocks per enterprise customer, and possibly trading address blocks with other ISPs.
2. Install multiple layers of NAT or share IPv4 addresses by other methods, such as address-plus-port mapping.
3. Deploy IPv6 and operate IPv4–IPv6 coexistence and interworking mechanisms.

RFC 5514 (April 2009) proposed to vastly increase the number of IPv6 hosts by transforming all social networking platforms into IPv6 networks. This would immediately add millions of IPv6 hosts to the existing IPv6 Internet.

Hosts (PCs, servers) and network infrastructure (routers, switches) are generally IPv6 ready at this time, but organizations may need to upgrade their overall end-to-end environment. Service providers such as Google have already rolled out an IPv6 site for customers already on that system. In fact, Google, Facebook, Yahoo!, Akamai, and Limelight Networks are among some of the larger companies that planed a one-day test run of IPv6 addresses as part of World IPv6 Day, on June 8, 2011, to encourage the transition to the new namespace. These organizations were planning to offer their content over IPv6 for a 24-hour "test flight," with the goal of the Test Flight Day being to motivate organizations across the industry—ISPs, hardware makers, operating system (OS) vendors, and web companies—to prepare their services for IPv6 to ensure a successful transition as IPv4 addresses run out. Internet users did not need to do anything different on World IPv6 Day. Web services, ISPs, and OS manufacturers were planning to be updating their systems to ensure Internet users receive uninterrupted service. In rare cases, users may still experience connectivity issues when visiting participating websites. Users were able to visit an IPv6 test site to check if their connectivity was impacted. Organizations that wanted to bring their company's website online using IPv6 during the World IPv6 Day needed to make it IPv6 accessible using dual-stack technology and provide an AAAA record for the site. Of course, IPv4 websites continued to be accessible over IPv4 during the event.

According to the Internet Society (ISOC), the World IPv6 Day saw more than 1000 major website operators switch over to IPv6-compatible main pages in the most extensive live run of the next-generation addressing protocol so far. The day turned out to be a technological success. Approximately two-thirds of the participants were reportedly so pleased with the results they left IPv6 enabled on their equipment going forward. Nonetheless, just 0.16% of Facebook users were IPv6 natives and 0.04% were using 6to4 tunneling capabilities, delivering around 1 million IPv6 visitors over the course of the day.

In DNS, host names are mapped to IPv6 addresses by AAAA (also known as Quad A) resource records (RRs). The IETF specifies the use AAAA RR for forward mapping and pointer RRs (PTRs) for reverse mapping. The IPv6 AAAA RR approach is described in RFC 3596. The forward DNS entry for an IPv6 entry in entered using AAAA. It can be entered using the full IPv6 address or by using the shorthand :: notation. PTRs are the opposite of AAAA RRs and are used in reverse map zone files to map an IPv6 address to a host name.

Tier 1 telecommunication firms have been upgrading their infrastructure over the past few years in anticipation of the eventual transition. The same has occurred for content providers. For example, Comcast has begun assigning IPv6 addresses to its cable modem customers in a "native dual-stack" configuration as of early 2011; under this configuration, customers have both IPv4 and IPv6 addresses and can access content and services over both systems. Comcast's first 25 IPv6-enabled customers went live January 11, 2011, in the Littleton, Colo. TimeWarner Cable has already signed up commercial customers on IPv6 and was planning to begin residential IPv6 trials in early 2011. TimeWarner Cable is also expected to adopt a dual-stack approach similar to that of Comcast. Domain infrastructure company VeriSign will also provide business services to assist companies with the transition in 2011 (4).

Having ISPs deploy IPv6 to customers' sites, in addition to IPv4 and without extra charge, is a way to break the existing impasse that has delayed IPv6 deployment: ISPs wait for customer demand before deploying IPv6; customers do not demand IPv6 as long as application vendors announce that their products work on existing infrastructures (that are based on IPv4 with NATs); application vendors focus their investments on NAT traversal compatibility as long as ISPs do not deploy IPv6. However, most ISPs are not willing to add IPv6 to their current offerings at no charge unless incurred investment and operational costs are small. For this, ISPs that provide router customer premise equipment (CPE) to their customers have the most favorable conditions: they can upgrade their router CPEs and can operate gateways between their IPv4 infrastructures and the global IPv6 Internet to support IPv6 encapsulation in IPv4. They then need no additional routing plans than those that already exist on these IPv4 infrastructures. Encapsulation using 6to4 methods, as specified in RFC 3056, is nearly sufficient for this: (i) it is simple; (ii) it is supported on many platforms including PC-compatible appliances; (iii) open-source portable code is available; and (iv) its stateless nature ensures good scalability. There is, however, a limitation of 6to4 that prevents ISPs from using it to offer full IPv6 unicast connectivity to their customers. While an ISP that deploys 6to4 can guarantee that IPv6 packets outgoing from its customer sites will reach the IPv6 Internet, and also can guarantee that packets coming from other 6to4 sites will reach its customer sites, it cannot guarantee that packets from native IPv6 sites will reach them. The problem is that a packet coming from a native IPv6 address needs to traverse (somewhere on its way) a 6to4 relay router to do the required IPv6/IPv4 encapsulation. There is no guarantee that routes toward such a relay exist from everywhere, nor is there a guarantee that all such relays do forward packets toward the IPv4 Internet. Also, if an ISP operates one or several 6to4 relay routers and opens IPv6 routes toward them in the IPv6 Internet, for the 6to4 prefix 2002::/16, it may receive in these relays packets destined to an unknown number of other 6to4 ISPs. If it does not forward these packets, it creates a "black hole" in which packets may be systematically lost, breaking some of the IPv6 connectivity. If it does forward them, it can no longer dimension its 6to4 relay routers in proportion to the traffic of its own customers; QoS, at least for customers of other 6to4 ISPs, will then not be guaranteed (34). To address these issues RFC 5569, *6rd—IPv6 Rapid Deployment*, also known simply as *6rd*, proposes to slightly modify 6to4 so that:

1. Packets coming from the global Internet, entering *6rd* gateways of an ISP are only packets destined to customer sites of this ISP.
2. All IPv6 packets destined to *6rd* customer sites of an ISP, and coming from anywhere else on the IPv6 Internet, traverse a *6rd* gateway of this ISP.

The principle of the RFC 5569 proposal is that to build on 6to4 and suppress its limitation, it is sufficient that:

1. 6to4 functions are modified to replace the standard 6to4 prefix 2002::/16 by an IPv6 prefix that belongs to the ISP-assigned address space, and to replace the 6to4 anycast address by another anycast address chosen by the ISP.
2. The ISP operates one or several 6rd gateways (upgraded 6to4 routers) at its border between its IPv4 infrastructure and the IPv6 Internet.
3. CPEs support IPv6 on their customer-site side and support 6rd (upgraded 6to4 function) on their provider side.

There is no guarantee that this proposal will be broadly accepted, but it represents one press-time approach for IPv6 deployment.

REFERENCES

1. Minoli D. *IP Multicast with Applications to IPTV and Mobile DVB-H*. New York: Wiley; 2008.
2. Minoli D. *Satellite Systems Engineering in an IPv6 Environment*. Francis and Taylor; 2009.
3. Minoli D. *Voice Over IPv6 – Architecting the Next-Generation VoIP*. New York: Elsevier; 2006.
4. Rashid FY. IPv4 Address Exhaustion Not Instant Cause for Concern with IPv6 in Wings, Eweek, 2011-02-01.
5. The IPv4 Address Report, Online resource, http://www.potaroo.net.

6. Minoli D, Amoss J. *Handbook of IPv4 to IPv6 Transition Methodologies For Institutional & Corporate Networks*. New York: Auerbach/CRC; 2008.

7. Minoli D, Kouns J. *Security in an IPv6 Environment*. Taylor and Francis; 2009.

8. An IPv6 Security Guide for U.S. Government Agencies—Executive Summary, The IPv6 World Report Series, Volume 4 February 2008, Juniper Networks, 1194 North Mathilda Avenue, Sunnyvale, CA 94089 USA.

9. Kaeo M, Green D, Bound J, Pouffary, Y. IPv6 Security Technology Paper. North American IPv6 Task Force (NAv6TF) Technology Report, July 22, 2006.

10. Lioy A. Security Features of IPv6Security Features of IPv6, Chapter 8 of *Internetworking IPv6 with Cisco Routers* by Silvano Gai McGraw-Hill, 1998; also available at www.ip6.com/us/book/Chap8.pdf.

11. Johnson D, Perkins C, Arkko J. Mobility Support in IPv6. RFC 3775, June 2004.

12. Hinden R, Deering S. IP Version 6 Addressing Architecture. RFC 4291, February 2006.

13. Machine-to-Machine Communications (M2M); M2M Service Requirements. ETSI TS 102 689 V1.1.1 (2010-08). 650 Route des Lucioles F-06921 Sophia Antipolis Cedex—FRANCE.

14. Microsoft Corporation, MSDN Library, Internet Protocol, 2004, http://msdn.microsoft.com.

15. Blanchet M. Special-Use IPv6 Addresses. draft-ietf-v6ops-rfc3330-for-ipv6-04.txt, January 15, 2008.

16. Hermann-Seton, P. Security Features in IPv6, SANS Institute 2002, As part of the Information Security Reading Room.

17. Thomson S, Narten T, Jinmei T. IPv6 Stateless Address Autoconfiguration. RFC 4862, September 2007.

18. Donzé F. IPv6 Autoconfiguration. The Internet Protocol Journal, June 2004;7 (2). Published Online, http://www.cisco.com.

19. Narten T, Draves R, Krishnan S. Privacy Extensions for Stateless Address Autoconfiguration in IPv6. RFC 4941, September 2007.

20. Narten T, Nordmark E, Simpson W, Soliman H. Neighbor Discovery for IP version 6 (IPv6). RFC 4861, September 2007.

21. IPv6 Portal, http://www.ipv6tf.org.

22. Desmeules R. *Cisco Self-Study: Implementing Cisco IPv6 Networks (IPv6)*. Cisco Press; June 6, 2003.

23. Conta A, Deering S. Generic Packet Tunneling in IPv6 Specification. RFC 2473, December 1998.

24. Carpenter B, Jiang S. Emerging Service Provider Scenarios for IPv6 Deployment. RFC 6036, October 2010.

25. Ertekin E, Christou C. IPv6 Header Compression. North American IPv6 Summit, June 2004.

26. Jonsson L-E, Pelletier G, Sandlund K. The RObust Header Compression (ROHC) Framework. RFC 4995, July 2007.

27. Pelletier G, Sandlund K, Jonsson L-E, West M. RObust Header Compression (ROHC): A Profile for TCP/IP (ROHC-TCP). RFC 4996, July 2007.

28. Finking R, Pelletier G. Formal Notation for RObust Header Compression (ROHC-FN). RFC 4997, July 2007.

29. Varada S, editor. IPv6 Datagram Compression. RFC 5172, March 2008.

30. 6NET. D2.2.4: Final IPv4 to IPv6 Transition Cookbook for Organizational/ISP (NREN) and Backbone Networks. Version: 1.0 (4th February 2005), Project Number: IST-2001-32603, CEC Deliverable Number: 32603/UOS/DS/2.2.4/A1.

31. Davies E, Krishnan S, Savola P. IPv6 Transition/Co-existence Security Considerations. RFC 4942, September 2007.

32. Warfield MH. Security Implications of IPv6", 16th Annual FIRST Conference on Computer Security Incident Handling, June 13–18, 2004—Budapest, Hungary.

33. Henderickx W. Making the Move to IPv6, alcatel-lucent White Paper, September 20, 2011.

34. Despres R. 6rd - IPv6 Rapid Deployment. RFC 5569, January 2010.

CHAPTER 8

LAYER 3 CONNECTIVITY: MOBILE IPv6 TECHNOLOGIES FOR THE IoT

This chapter provides an in-depth view of mobile IPv6 (MIPv6). It starts with an overview of the key concepts (Section 8.1) and then provides a more detailed protocol-level description (Section 8.2). MIPv6 is specified in RFC 3775; this RFC is known as the "MIPv6 base specification." For a more complete description of MIPv6 and several extensions to the base specification, the reader may wish to refer to Reference 1. MIPv6 is one of several approaches that can be utilized to manage mobility in an IoT/machine-to-machine (M2M) environment.

8.1 OVERVIEW

MIPv6 specifies a protocol that allows nodes to remain reachable while moving around in the IPv6 Internet. An entity that implements the MIPv6 protocol is a MIPv6 entity. There are three types of entities defined in the MIPv6 protocol:

- Mobile node (MN): A node that can change its point of attachment from one link to another while still being reachable via its home address.
- Correspondent node (CN): A peer node with which an MN is communicating. The CN may be either mobile or stationary. A CN does not necessarily require MIPv6 support, but it does require IPv6 support.

Building the Internet of Things with IPv6 and MIPv6: The Evolving World of M2M Communications,
First Edition. Daniel Minoli.
© 2013 John Wiley & Sons, Inc. Published 2013 by John Wiley & Sons, Inc.

- Home agent (HA): A router on an MN's home link with which the MN has registered its current care-of address (CoA) described below. While the MN is away from home, the HA intercepts packets on the home link destined to the MN's home address, encapsulates them, and routes them to the MN's CoA.

If an MN is not currently attached to its home network (also called the home link[1]), the MN is said to be "away from home." Each MN is *identified* by its home address (which we also call stationary home address), regardless of its current point of attachment to the remote network (e.g., the Internet); this is a globally unique, explicit IPv6 address. While situated away from its home, on a foreign link (also known as foreign network [FN][2]), an MN is also associated with an "in-care-of-address" known, in fact, as care-of address, or CoA, which provides information about the MN's current location. Clearly, the CoA changes depending on the current location of the MN. The CoA is used for *routing* (i.e., delivering) IPv6 packets addressed to an MN's home address; packets sent to the MN's home address are transparently routed to the MN via its current CoA. The CoA must be a unicast routable address, typically specified by the source address field in the IPv6 header; the IPv6 source address must be a topologically correct source address. The MN is assumed to be seeking to communicate with a CN, also an IPv6-ready node. The MIPv6 protocol enables IPv6 nodes to cache the binding of an MN's home address with its CoA; these underlying mechanisms ascertain that communications (e.g., TCP sessions) are maintained while the MN is physically moving, and, thus, connecting via an FNs. MIPv6 operations involve movement detection, IP address configuration, and location update. Table 8.1 provides some basic MIPv6 nomenclature used in this chapter as defined in Reference 2. Figure 8.1 depicts the basic MIPv6 environment.

The binding (association) between the two IP addresses utilized in MIPv6 (the home address and the CoA) is kept at a well-known location, the HA, which is used to support connectivity; the HA is a router in the MN's home network. The CN performs packet routing toward the MN using the routing header. The CN learns the position of an MN by processing binding updates (BUs). Whenever the MN connects to an FN, it sends a BU to the HA and CNs; an MN keeps a list of the CNs to which it sent a BU. The recipients of the BUs reply with a binding acknowledgement (BA). Security is a consideration; therefore, BU information requires protection and authentication; broadly speaking, IP Security (IPsec) can be used for this.[3] Figure 8.2 depicts the basic routing/forwarding operation of the HA (this is the tunnel mode).

Note: The MN may have multiple CoAs. The CoA sent to the HA in the BU is called the primary CoA. For example, in the case of a wireless networks, an MN might be reachable through multiple links at the same time (e.g., with overlapping

---

[1]The home link is defined as the link on which a mobile node's home subnet prefix is defined.

[2]The FN can be the Internet or a network that is connected to the Internet.

[3]BUs can be protected using IPSec extensions headers (as covered in Chapter 2), or by the use of the binding authorization data option (this option employs a binding management key [known as Kbm] which can be established through the return-routability procedure).

TABLE 8.1   Basic MIPv6 Terminology

Term	Description
Binding	The association of the home address of an MN with an in-CoA for that MN, along with the remaining lifetime of that association
Binding authorization	Mechanism where correspondent's registration is authorized, enabling the recipient to conclude that the sender has the right to specify a new binding
Binding cache	A cache of bindings for other nodes. This cache is maintained by HAs) and CNs. The cache contains both "correspondent registration" entries and "home registration" entries
Binding management key	(also known as Kbm) A key used for authorizing a binding cache management message (e.g., BU or BA). Return-routability provides a way to create a binding management key
BU list	A list that is maintained by each MN. The list has an item for every binding that the MN has or is trying to establish with a specific other node. Both correspondent and home registrations are included in this list. Entries from the list are deleted as the lifetime of the binding expires
Care-of address (CoA)	A unicast routable IPv6 address associated with an MN while visiting a foreign link; the subnet prefix of this IP address is a foreign subnet prefix. Among the multiple CoAs that an MN may have at any given time (e.g., with different subnet prefixes), the one registered with the MN's HA for a given home address is called its "primary" CoA
Care-of init cookie	A cookie sent to the CN in the care-of test init message, to be returned in the care-of test message
Care-of keygen token	A keygen token sent by the CN in the Care-of test message
Cookie	A cookie is a random number used by an MN to prevent spoofing by a bogus CN in the return-routability procedure
Correspondent node (CN)	A peer node with which an MN is communicating. The CN may be either mobile or stationary
Correspondent registration	A return-routability procedure followed by a registration, run between the MN and a CN
Destination option	Options that are carried by the IPv6 DESTINATION OPTIONS extension header. Destination options include optional information that is examined only by the IPv6 node given as the destination address in the IPv6 header, not by routers in between. MIPv6 defines one new destination option, the home address destination option
Foreign link	Any link other than the MN's home link. Also known as FN
Foreign subnet prefix	Any IP subnet prefix other than the MN's home subnet prefix
Home address	A unicast routable address assigned to an MN, used as the permanent address of the MN; this address is within the MN's home link. Standard IP routing mechanisms will deliver packets destined for an MN's home address to its home link. MNs can in principle have multiple home addresses, for instance when there are multiple home prefixes on the home link

(continued)

TABLE 8.1 *(Continued)*

Term	Description
Home agent (HA)	A router on an MN's home link with which the MN has registered its current CoA. While the MN is away from home, the HA intercepts packets on the home link destined to the MN's home address, encapsulates them, and tunnels them to the MN's registered CoA
HA list	HAs need to know which other HAs are on the same link. This information is stored in the HA list; the list is used for informing MNs during dynamic HAAD
Home init cookie	A cookie sent to the CN in the home test init (HoTi) message, to be returned in the home test (HoT) message
Home keygen token	A keygen token sent by the CN in the HoT message
Home registration	A registration between the MN and its HA, authorized by the use of IPsec
Home subnet prefix	The IP subnet prefix corresponding to an MN's home address
Interface identifier	A number used to identify a node's interface on a link. The interface identifier is the remaining low-order bits in the node's IP address after the subnet prefix
IP Security (IPsec) security association	A cooperative relationship formed by the sharing of cryptographic keying material and associated context. SAs are simplex; that is, two SAs are needed to protect bidirectional traffic between two nodes, one for each direction
Keygen token	A number supplied by a CN in the return-routability procedure to enable the MN to compute the necessary binding management key for authorizing a BU
Layer 2 (L2) handover	A process by which the MN changes from one link-layer connection to another
Layer 3 (L3) handover	Subsequent to an L2 handover, an MN detects a change in an on-link subnet prefix that would require a change in the primary CoA. For example, a change of access router subsequent to a change of wireless access point typically results in an L3 handover
Link-layer address	A link-layer identifier for an interface, such as IEEE 802 addresses on Ethernet links
Mobility message	A message containing a mobility header
Nonce	Random numbers used internally by the CN in the creation of keygen tokens related to the return-routability procedure. The nonces are not specific to an MN and are kept secret within the CN
Registration	The process during which an MN sends a BU to its HA or a CN, causing a binding for the MN to be registered
Return-routability procedure	A procedure that authorizes registrations by the use of a cryptographic token exchange
Routing header	A routing header may be present as an IPv6 header extension and indicates that the payload has to be delivered to a destination IPv6 address in some way that is different from what would be carried out by standard Internet routing
Unicast routable address	An identifier for a single interface such that a packet sent to it from another IPv6 subnet is delivered to the interface identified by that address

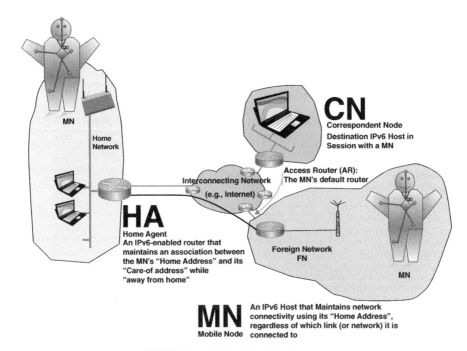

FIGURE 8.1 Basic MIPv6 environment.

wireless cells). The MN must ensure that its primary CoA always has a prefix that is advertised by its current default router.

Note: An MN may use various and multiple types of network interfaces to obtain durable and wide-area network connectivity, for example using protocols such as IEEE 802.2, 802.11, 802.16, cellular radios, etc. Note, however, that while an MN may have several CoA but only one, called the primary CoA, can be registered with its HA and the CNs. There are cases where it is desirable for the MN to get Internet access through multiple accesses simultaneously, in which case the MN would be configured with multiple active IPv6 CoAs. In RFC 5648, MIPv6 and Network Mobility (NEMO) basic support are extended to allow the binding of more than one CoA to a home address.

At least one IPv6-capable router on the home network must be able to act as HA. The HA supports the following functions:

- Maintains the MN's binding information;
- Intercepts packets that arrive at the MN's home network and whose destination address is its HA;
- Tunnels (i.e., provides IPv6 encapsulation) these packets to the MN; and
- Provides reverse tunneling from the MN to the CN (i.e., provides IPv6 de-encapsulation).
- MIPv6 makes use of IPv6 packet formats and procedures, and, furthermore,

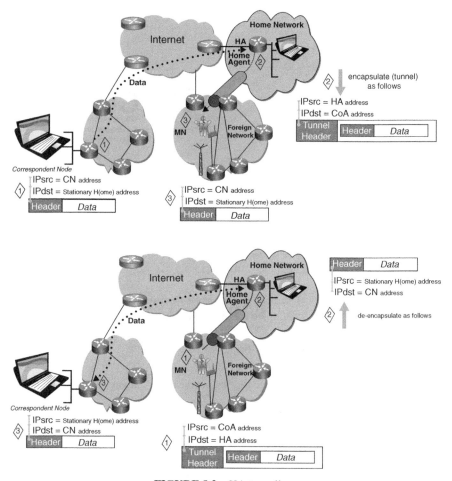

FIGURE 8.2 HA tunneling.

1. Establishes new extension header, specifically the mobility header (described further in Section 8.2).
2. Adds a new routing header type (routing header type 2); MIPv6 defines a routing header that allows packets to be routed directly from a CN to MN via the MN's CoA. This is achieved by inserting the MN's CoA into the IPv6 destination address field. Once the packet arrives at the location specified by the CoA, the MN retrieves its home address from the routing header; this is then used as the final destination of the packet. The newly defined routing header uses a different type than the type used for "regular" IPv6 routing; this, for example, allows firewalls to utilize different security rules for MIPv6 packets that would be used for source-routed IPv6 packets (see Fig. 8.3). And,

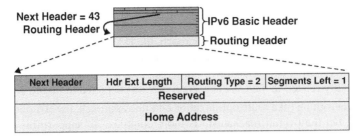

FIGURE 8.3   New routing header type for MIPv6.

3. Adds a new destination option; The destination option extension header is used to support home address option. This option is utilized in a packet sent by an MN while it is on an FN to inform the recipient of the MN's home address (see Fig. 8.4).

HA address discovery (HAAD) is an important mechanism. MIPv6 introduces four new Internet control message protocol version 6 (ICMPv6) messages to support its processes. Two of the new ICMPv6 messages are employed in the dynamic home agent address discovery (DHAAD) process; these messages support the (i) HAAD request (using the HA's anycast address of its own home subnet prefix) and (ii) HAAD reply. The other two ICMPv6 are used for renumbering and mobile configuration mechanisms; these messages support (i) mobile prefix solicitation and (ii) mobile prefix advertisement. The utilization of these four ICMPv6 messages plus the neighbor discovery protocol (NDP) makes MIPv6 independent of the underlying (layer 2) networking technology.

The NDP is modified with MIPv6 to support requisite mobility functions, as follows. The modified router advertisement message format has a single flag indicating HA service. The modified prefix information option format allows a router to advertise its global address. Other modifications include: (i) a new advertisement interval option format; (ii) a new HA information option format; and (iii) changes to sending router advertisements.

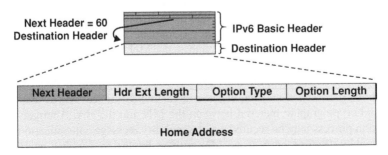

FIGURE 8.4   Destination option extension header.

Communications with MNs takes place in two ways:

1. Bidirectional tunneling. In this approach, the HA plays a crucial role, although this implies that the network traffic to this node can be high; however, the CN has no requirements related to mobility support—also, the MNs have no direct visibility related to the CN. This approach was depicted in Figure 8.2.
2. Direct routing (aka route optimization). In this approach, the HA plays a lesser role, but the overall mechanism is more complex. To support this operation, the MNs have three basic functions to manage communication (in addition to gaining access to the FN): (i) perform IPv6 packet encapsulation and de-encapsulation; (ii) send BUs and receive BAs (this entails processing the mobility header); and (iii) keep track of BUs that are sent. To support this operation, the CNs have three basic functions to manage communication: (i) process the mobility header (BUs, BAs); (ii) process/use routing headers type 2; and, (iii) maintain a binding cache. This approach is depicted in Figure 8.5.

If a binding exists, the MN will send the packets directly to the CN; otherwise, if a binding does not exist, the MN must use tunneling. MIPv6 route optimization as described in RFC 3775 enables MNs and CNs to communicate via a direct routing path despite changes in IP connectivity on the MN side. Both end nodes use a stable "home address" in identifying the MN at stack layers above IP, while payload packets are sent or received via a CoA that routes to the MN's current network attachment. MIPv6 swaps the home address and COA when a payload packet traverses the IP layer. The association between an MN's home address and CoA is the "binding" for the MN. It is the responsibility of the MN to update its binding at the CN through a "correspondent registration" when it changes IP connectivity. A correspondent registration further involves the MN's HA, which proxies the MN at the home address and mainly serves as a relay for payload packets exchanged with CNs that do not support route optimization. The MN keeps the HA up to date about its current CoA by means of "home registrations" (3). See Figure 8.6.

Higher-layer protocols, for example user datagram protocol (UDP), transmission control protocol (TCP), real-time streaming protocol (RTSP), real-time transport protocol (RTP), generally treat the MN's home address as its IP address for most packets. For packets sent that are part of transport-level connections established while the MN was at home, the MN must use its home address; for packets sent that are part of transport-level connections that the MN may still be using after moving to a new location, the MN also uses its home address.

In summary, the MIPv6 protocol requires the MN to own a home address and to have an assigned HA to the MN. The MN needs to register with the HA in order to enable its reachability and mobility, when away from its home link. The registration process itself may require an establishment of IPsec security associations (SAs) and cryptographic material between the MN and the HA. Alternatively, the registration process may be secured using a mobility message authentication option, which enables IPv6 mobility in an MN without having to establish an IPsec SA with its HA. According to the latest RFCs, the only SA that is preconfigured is

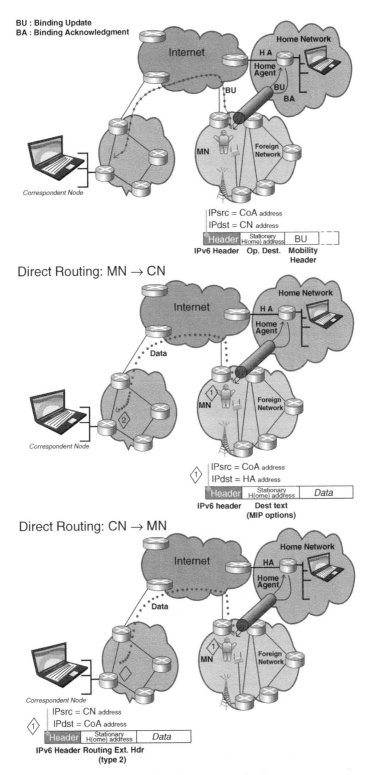

FIGURE 8.5 Direct communication.

Top: single CoA included in Binding Cache per RFC 3775)

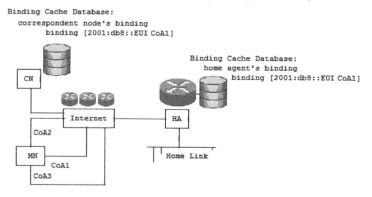

Bottom: Multiple CoAs included in Binding Cache per RFC 5648

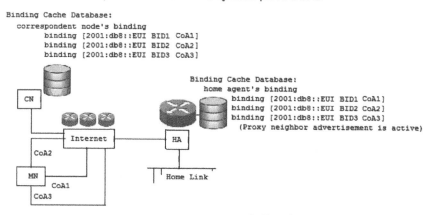

BID: Binding identification number

FIGURE 8.6 CoA registration.

a shared secret between the MN and the home authentication, authorization, and accounting (AAA) server; this is in contrast with an earlier version of the MIPv6 model. Automatically providing the collection of home address, HA address, and keying material is generally referred to as the MIPv6 bootstrapping problem (4).

Table 8.2 provides a listing (from reference 5) of MIPv6 implementations as available in the recent past.

The sections that follow provide more in-depth information about MIPv6 processes and procedures.

8.2 PROTOCOL DETAILS

The sections that follow are summarized from relevant RFCs, including RFC 3775. Only a subset of concepts is described; the interested reader should always consult the

TABLE 8.2   Recent Implementations on MIPv6 Technology (Partial List)

- 6 Wind
- Cisco—HA
- Elmic systems now Treck Inc.
- Ericsson
- HP—HP-UX (HA, CN) and Tru64 (HA, CN)
- Keio University (wide) —HA, MN, CN, and IPsec
- Microsoft Window XP, Vista
- NEC-MN, HA, CN, and IPsec
- Nokia-MN, HA, CN
- Samsung—MN, CN
- Siemens
- University of Helsinski (Linux) —MN, CN
- 6NET MIPv6 implementation survey

primary RFC for complete and detailed information. The key concepts were already discussed in Section 8.1, but this section provides additional details.

8.2.1 Generic Mechanisms

8.2.1.1 *MIPv6 Basic Operation*   As noted, an MN is always addressable at its home address, whether it is currently attached to its home link or is away from home. The "home address" is an IP address assigned to the MN within its home subnet prefix on its home link. While an MN is at home, packets addressed to its home address are routed to the MN's home link using traditional routing mechanisms. While an MN is attached to some foreign link away from home, it is also addressable at one or more CoAs. A CoA is an IP address associated with an MN that has the subnet prefix of a particular foreign link. The MN acquires its CoA using traditional IPv6 mechanisms, such as stateless or stateful autoconfiguration. As long as the MN stays in this location, packets addressed to this CoA will be routed to the MN. The MN may also accept packets from several CoAs, this being the case, for example, when it is moving to a new location but still reachable at the previous link. The MIPv6 specification requires that home and CoAs must be unicast routable addresses. The association between an MN's home address and CoA is known as a "binding" for the MN. While away from home, an MN registers its primary CoA with a router on its home link, requesting this router to function as the "HA" for the MN. The MN performs this binding registration by sending a BU message to the HA. The HA replies to the MN by returning a BA message. The exchange of BUs, BAs, and other control messages is referred to as "signaling."

Note: In addition to the binding cache, each HA also maintains an HA list. This list has information about routers on the same link that is acting as an HA and is used by the HAAD mechanism—a router is known to be acting as an HA, if it sends

TABLE 8.3 Binding Cache Content

Content	Description
Home address	The home address of the MN for which this is the binding cache entry. This field is used as the key for searching the binding cache for the destination address of a packet being sent
CoA	The CoA for the MN indicated by the home address field in this binding cache entry
Lifetime value	The lifetime value indicates the remaining lifetime for this binding cache entry. The lifetime value is initialized from the lifetime field in the BU that created or last modified this binding cache entry
Flag	This flag indicates whether or not this binding cache entry is a home registration entry (applicable only on nodes that support HA functionality)
Maximum value	The maximum value of the sequence number field received in previous BUs for this home address. The sequence number field is 16 bits long (it uses modulo 2^{16} math)
Usage information	Usage information for this binding cache entry. This is needed to implement the cache replacement policy in use in the binding cache. Recent use of a cache entry also serves as an indication that a BRR should be sent when the lifetime of this entry nears expiration

a router advertisement in which the HA (H) bit is set. The HA maintains a separate HA list for each link on which it is serving as an HA.

Any node communicating with an MN is referred to as a "correspondent node" of the MN and may itself be either a stationary device or a mobile device. MNs are also able to provide information about their current location to CNs. This happens through the correspondent registration. As a part of this procedure, a return-routability test is performed in order to authorize the establishment of the binding.

There are two possible modes for communications between the MN and a CN, as previously noted, as follows:

- The first mode, "bidirectional tunneling," *does not require MIPv6 support from the CN* and is available even if the MN has not registered its current binding with the CN. Packets from the CN are routed to the HA and then tunneled to the MN. Packets to the CN are tunneled from the MN to the HA ("reverse tunneled") and then routed normally from the home network to the CN. In this mode, the HA uses proxy neighbor discovery to intercept any IPv6 packets addressed to the MN's home address on the home link. Each intercepted packet is tunneled to the MN's primary CoA.

- The second mode, "route optimization[4]" (also called above, "direct routing"), requires the MN to register its current binding at the CN. Packets from the CN can be routed directly to the CoA of the MN. When sending a packet to any IPv6 destination, the CN checks its cached bindings (see Table 8.3) for an entry for

---

[4]The acronym RO is also used by some practitioners.

the packet's destination address. If a cached binding for this destination address is found, the node uses a new type of IPv6 routing header to route the packet to the MN by way of the CoA indicated in this binding. Routing packets directly to the MN's CoA allows the shortest communications path to be used. It also eliminates congestion at the MN's HA and home link. In addition, the impact of any possible failure of the HA or networks on the path to or from it is reduced.

When routing packets directly to the MN, the CN sets the destination address in the IPv6 header to the CoA of the MN. A new type of IPv6 routing header is also added to the packet to carry the desired home address. Similarly, the MN sets the source address in the packet's IPv6 header to its current CoAs. The MN adds a new IPv6 "home address" destination option to carry its home address. The inclusion of home addresses in these packets makes the use of the CoA transparent above the network layer (e.g., at the transport layer).

Note: MIPv6 requires the MN to know its HA address, its own home address, and the cryptographic materials (e.g., shared keys or certificates) needed to set up IPsec SAs with the HA in order to protect MIPv6 signaling. The MIPv6 base protocol does not specify any method to automatically acquire this information, which means that network administrators are normally required to manually set configuration data on MNs and HAs. However, in real deployments, manual configuration does not scale as the MNs increase in number (6). A bootstrapping process can be beneficial. Also, according to the latest RFCs, the only SA that is preconfigured is a shared secret between the MN and the home AAA server; this is in contrast with an earlier version of the MIPv6 model.

8.2.1.2 IPv6 Protocol Extensions   MIPv6 defines a new IPv6 protocol, using the mobility header. This header is used to carry the messages summarized in Table 8.4.

8.2.1.3 New IPv6 Destination Option   MIPv6 defines a new IPv6 destination option, the home address destination option. This option is described in more detail in Section 8.2.2.

8.2.1.4 New IPv6 ICMP Messages   As alluded to earlier, MIPv6 also introduces four new ICMPv6 message types, two for use in the dynamic HAAD mechanism and two for renumbering and mobile configuration mechanisms.

- *HAAD request.* The ICMP HAAD request message is used by an MN to initiate the dynamic HAAD mechanism. The MN sends the HAAD request message to the MIPv6 HA anycast address for its own home subnet prefix.
- *HAAD reply.* The ICMP HAAD reply message is used by an HA to respond to an MN that uses the dynamic HAAD mechanism.
- *Mobile prefix solicitation.* The ICMP mobile prefix solicitation message is sent by an MN to its HA while it is away from home. The purpose of the message is to solicit a mobile prefix advertisement from the HA, which will allow the MN

TABLE 8.4 Mobility Header Messages

Message	Description
HoTi HoT Care-of test init Care-of test	These messages are used to perform the return-routability procedure from the MN to a CN
BU	Message is used by an MN to notify a CN or the MN's HA of its current binding. The BU sent to the MN's HA to register its primary CoA is marked as a "home registration"
BA	Message is used to acknowledge receipt of a BU, if an acknowledgement was requested in the BU, the BU was sent to an HA, or an error occurred
BRR	Message is used by a CN to request an MN to re-establish its binding with the CN. This message is typically used when the cached binding is in active use, but the binding's lifetime is close to expiration. The CN may use, for instance, recent traffic and open transport layer connections as an indication of active use
Binding error	Message is used by the CN to signal an error related to mobility, such as an inappropriate attempt to use the home address destination option without an existing binding

to gather prefix information about its home network. This information can be used to configure and update home address(es) according to changes in prefix information supplied by the HA.

- *Mobile prefix advertisement.* An HA will send a mobile prefix advertisement to an MN to distribute prefix information about the home link while the MN is traveling away from the home network. This occurs in response to a mobile prefix solicitation with an advertisement, or by an unsolicited advertisement.

8.2.1.5 Mobile IPv6 Security
MIPv6 incorporates a number of security features. These include the protection of BUs both to HAs and to CNs, the protection of mobile prefix discovery, and the protection of the mechanisms that MIPv6 uses for transporting data packets:

- BUs are protected by the use of IPsec extension headers, or by the use of the binding authorization data option (this option employs a binding management key, Kbm, which can be established through the return-routability procedure).
- Mobile prefix discovery is protected through the use of IPsec extension headers.
- Mechanisms related to transporting payload packets—such as the home address destination option and type 2 routing header—have been specified in a manner that restricts their use in attacks.

Although these basic security mechanisms are adequate for some environments and applications, there are limitations with these for other environments.

8.2.2 New IPv6 Protocol, Message Types, and Destination Option

8.2.2.1 *Mobility Header* The mobility header is an extension header used by MNs, CNs, and HAs in all messaging related to the creation and management of bindings. The subsections within this section describe the message types that may be sent using the mobility header. The mobility header is identified by a next header value of 135 in the immediately preceding header and has the format depicted in Figure 8.7.

```
 Payload Proto |  Header Len   |   MH Type    |   Reserved
-+-+-+-+-+-+-+-+-+-+-+-+-+-+-+-+-+-+-+-+-+-+-+-+-+-+-+-+-+-+-+-
          Checksum           |
-+-+-+-+-+-+-+-+-+-+-+-+-+-+-+


                        Message Data


```

Payload Proto	8-bit selector. Identifies the type of header immediately following the mobility header. Uses the same values as the IPv6 next header field. This field is intended to be used by a future extension.
Header Len	8-bit unsigned integer, representing the length of the mobility header in units of 8 octets, excluding the first 8 octets.
MH Type	8-bit selector. Identifies the particular mobility message in question.
Reserved	8-bit field reserved for future use. The value must be initialized to zero by the sender and must be ignored by the receiver.
Checksum	16-bit unsigned integer. This field contains the checksum of the mobility header.
Message Data	A variable length field containing the data specific to the indicated mobility header type.

The message types are as follows:

Binding refresh request (BRR) Message	The BRR message requests a mobile node to update its mobility binding. This message is sent by correspondent nodes. The BRR message uses the MH Type value 0.
Home test init (HoTI) message	A mobile node uses the HoTI message to initiate the return-routability procedure and request a home keygen token from a correspondent node. The Home test init message uses the MH type value 1. This message is tunneled through the home agent when the mobile node is away from home. Such tunneling should employ IPsec ESP in tunnel mode between the HA and the mobile node. This protection is indicated by the IPsec security policy database.
Care-of test init (CoTI) message	A mobile node uses the CoTI message to initiate the return-routability procedure and request a care-of keygen token from a correspondent node. The Care-of test init message uses the MH type value 2.
Home test (HoT) message	The HoT message is a response to the Home test init message and is sent from the correspondent node to the mobile node. The HoT message uses the MH type value 3.
Care-of test (CoT) message	The CoT message is a response to the CoT Init message and is sent from the correspondent node to the mobile node. The CoT message uses the MH type value 4.
Binding update (BU) message	The BU message is used by a mobile node to notify other nodes of a new CoA for itself. The BU uses the MH type value 5.
Binding acknowledgement (BA) message	The BA is used to acknowledge receipt of a BU. The BA has the MH type value 6.
Binding error (BE) message	The BE message is used by the correspondent node to signal an error related to mobility, such as an inappropriate attempt to use the home address destination option without an existing binding. The BE message uses the MH type value 7.

FIGURE 8.7 Mobility header (details).

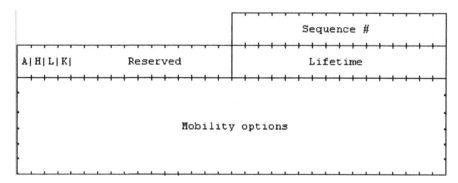

FIGURE 8.8   Message data field for BU (BU) message.

Two important messages are the BU message and the BA message.

The BU message is used by an MN to notify other nodes of a new CoA it has acquired. The format of the message data field in the mobility header for the BU message is shown in Figure 8.8. The fields/flags are described next.

- Acknowledge (A). The acknowledge (A) bit is set by the sending MN to request a BA be returned upon receipt of the BU.
- Home registration (H). The home registration (H) bit is set by the sending MN to request that the receiving node should act as this node's HA. The destination of the packet carrying this message must be that of a router sharing the same subnet prefix as the home address of the MN in the binding.
- Link-local address compatibility (L). The link-local address compatibility (L) bit is set when the home address reported by the MN has the same interface identifier as the MN's link-local address.
- Key management mobility capability (K). If this bit is cleared, the protocol used for establishing the IPsec SAs between the MN and the HA does not survive movements; it may then have to be rerun.
- Reserved. These fields are unused. They must be initialized to zero by the sender and must be ignored by the receiver.
- Sequence number. A 16-bit unsigned integer used by the receiving node to sequence BUs and by the sending node to match a returned BA with this BU.
- Lifetime. 16-bit unsigned integer. The number of time units remaining before the binding must be considered expired. A value of zero indicates that the binding cache entry for the MN must be deleted.
- Mobility options. Variable-length field of such length that the complete mobility header is an integer multiple of 8 octets long. This field contains zero or more Type/Length/Value (TLV)-encoded[5] mobility options. The following options are valid in a BU:

---

[5]Type, Length, Value.

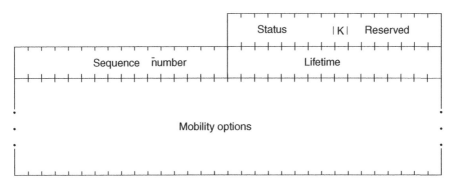

FIGURE 8.9   Message data field for BA message.

- Binding authorization data option (this option is mandatory in BUs sent to a CN);
- Nonce indices option;
- Alternate CoA option

The CoA is specified either by the source address field in the IPv6 header or by the alternate CoA option, if present. IPv6 source address must be a topologically correct source address. BUs for a CoA that is not a unicast routable address must be silently discarded. Similarly, the BU must be silently discarded if the CoA appears as a home address in an existing binding cache entry, with its current location creating a circular reference back to the home address specified in the BU (possibly through additional entries).

The BA message is used to acknowledge the receipt of a BU. The format of the message data field in the mobility header for the BA message is shown in Figure 8.9. The fields/flags are described next.

- Key management mobility capability (K). If this bit is cleared, the protocol used by the HA for establishing the IPsec SAs between the MN and the HA does not survive movements (it may then have to be rerun).
- Reserved. These fields are unused. They must be initialized to zero by the sender and must be ignored by the receiver.
- Status. 8-bit unsigned integer indicating the disposition of the BU. Values of the status field less than 128 indicate that the BU was accepted by the receiving node. Values greater than or equal to 128 indicate that the BU was rejected by the receiving node. The following status values were originally defined:

0	BU accepted
1	Accepted but prefix discovery necessary
128	Reason unspecified
129	Administratively prohibited
130	Insufficient resources

131	Home registration not supported
132	Not home subnet
133	Not HA for this MN
134	Duplicate address detection failed
135	Sequence number out of window
136	Expired home nonce index
137	Expired care-of nonce index
138	Expired nonces
139	Registration type change disallowed

- Sequence number. The sequence number in the BA is copied from the sequence number field in the BU. It is used by the MN in matching this BA with an outstanding BU.
- Lifetime. The granted lifetime, in time units of 4 s, for which this node should retain the entry for this MN in its binding cache.
- Mobility options. Variable-length field of such length that the complete mobility header is an integer multiple of 8 octets long. This field contains zero or more TLV-encoded mobility options. The receiver must ignore and skip any options which it does not understand.

BUs and BAs follow the rules discussed in RFC 3776[6] (7) and summarized in Table 8.5.

A CN registration involves six message transmissions at the MN, totaling about 376 bytes. This signaling overhead may be acceptable if movements are infrequent. For example, an MN that moves once every 30 min generates an average of 1.7 bps of signaling traffic. Higher mobility causes more substantial overhead, however. A cell size of 100 m and a speed of 120 km/h yields a change in IP connectivity every 3 s and about 1000 bps of signaling traffic. This is significant compared to a highly compressed voice stream with a typical data rate of 10,000 to 30,000 bps. Furthermore, base MIPv6 requires MNs to renew a correspondent registration at least every 7 min. The signaling overhead amounts to 7.16 bps if the MN communicates with a stationary node. It doubles if both peers are mobile. This overhead may be negligible when the nodes communicate, but it can be an issue for MNs that are inactive and stay at the same location for a while because these MNs are typically designed to go to standby mode to conserve battery power. Also, the periodic refreshments consume a fraction of the wireless bandwidth that one could use more efficiently (3).

8.2.2.2 Mobility Options Mobility messages can include zero or more mobility options. This allows optional fields that may not be needed in every use of a particular mobility header, as well as future extensions to the format of the messages. Such options are included in the message data field of the message itself, after the fixed portion of the message data. The presence of such options is be indicated by the header Len of the mobility header. See Figure 8.10.

---

[6]RFC 3776 has been updated in RFC 4877.

TABLE 8.5   BUs and BAs

MN Status	Message	Description
MN is away from its home	BUs	When the MN is away from its home, the BUs sent by it to the HA must support at least the following headers in the following order: IPv6 header (source = CoA, destination = HA) Destination options header 　Home address option (home address) ESP header in transport mode Mobility header 　BU 　Alternate CoA option (CoA)
	BAs	The BA sent back to the MN when it is away from home must support at least the following headers in the following order: IPv6 header (source = HA, destination = CoA) Routing header (type 2) 　Home address ESP header in transport mode Mobility header 　BA
MN is at home	BUs	When the MN is at home, the above rules are different since the MN can use its home address as a source address; this typically happens for the de-registration BU when the mobile is returning home. Here the BUs must support at least the following headers in the following order: IPv6 header (source = home address, destination = HA) ESP header in transport mode Mobility header 　BU
	BAs	The BA messages sent to the home address must support at least the following headers in the following order: IPv6 header (source = HA, destination = home address) ESP header in transport mode Mobility header 　BA

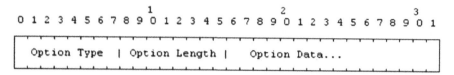

FIGURE 8.10 Format of mobility options.

8.2.2.3 Home Address Option

The home address option is carried by the destination option extension header (next header value = 60). It is used in a packet sent by an MN while away from home, to inform the recipient of the MN's home address. See Figure 8.11.

8.2.2.4 Type 2 Routing Header

MIPv6 defines a new routing header variant, the type 2 routing header, to allow the packet to be routed directly from a correspondent to the MN's CoA. The MN's CoA is inserted into the IPv6 destination address field. Once the packet arrives at the CoA, the MN retrieves its home address from the routing header; this address is used as the final destination address for the packet. The type 2 routing header is shown in Figure 8.12.

The new routing header uses a different type than defined for "regular" IPv6 source routing, enabling firewalls to apply different rules to source routed packets than to MIPv6. This routing header type (type 2) is restricted to carry only one IPv6 address. All IPv6 nodes that process this routing header must verify that the address contained within is the node's own home address in order to prevent packets from being forwarded outside the node. The IP address contained in the routing header must be a unicast routable address, being that it is the MN's home address. Furthermore, if the scope of the home address is smaller than the scope of the CoA, the MN must discard the packet.

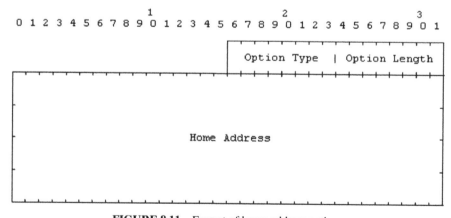

FIGURE 8.11 Format of home address option.

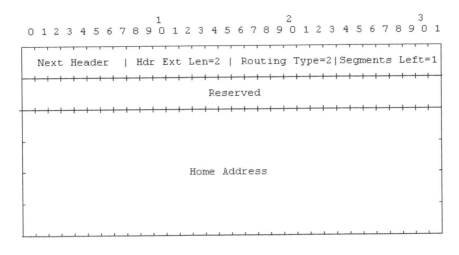

Next header	8-bit selector. Identifies the type of header immediately following the routing header. Uses the same values as the IPv6 next header field.
Hdr ext Len	2 (8-bit unsigned integer); length of the routing header in 8-octet units, not including the first 8 octets.
Routing type	2 (8-bit unsigned integer).
Segments left	1 (8-bit unsigned integer).
Reserved	32-bit reserved field. The value must be initialized to zero by the sender and must be ignored by the receiver.
Home address	The home address of the destination mobile node.

FIGURE 8.12   Type 2 routing header.

8.2.3   Modifications to IPv6 Neighbor Discovery

Modifications to existing protocols are described herewith as described in RFC 3775.

8.2.3.1   *Modified Router Advertisement Message*   MIPv6 modifies the format of the router advertisement message by the addition of a single flag bit to indicate that the router sending the advertisement message is serving as an HA on this link.

8.2.3.2   *Modified Prefix Information Option*   MIPv6 requires knowledge of a router's global address in building an HA list as part of the dynamic HAAD mechanism. MIPv6 extends neighbor discovery defined in RFC 2461 (8) to allow a router to advertise its global address by the addition of a single flag bit in the format of a prefix information option for use in router advertisement messages.

8.2.3.3   *New Advertisement Interval Option*   MIPv6 defines a new advertisement interval option, used in router advertisement messages to advertise the interval at which the sending router sends unsolicited multicast router advertisements.

8.2.3.4 New HA Information Option MIPv6 defines a new HA information option, used in router advertisements sent by an HA to advertise information specific to this router's functionality as an HA.

8.2.3.5 Changes to Sending Router Advertisements The basic NDP specification limits routers to a minimum interval of 3s between sending unsolicited multicast router advertisement messages from any given network interface (limited by MinRtrAdvInterval and MaxRtrAdvInterval). This limitation, however, is not suitable to providing timely movement detection for MNs. MNs detect their own movement by learning the presence of new routers as the MN moves into wireless transmission range of them (or physically connects to a new wired network), and by learning that previous routers are no longer reachable. MNs must be able to quickly detect when they move to a link served by a new router, so that they can acquire a new CoA and send BUs to register this CoA with their HA and to notify CNs as needed. One method that can provide for faster movement detection is to increase the rate at which unsolicited router advertisements are sent. MIPv6 relaxes this limit such that routers may send unsolicited multicast router advertisements more frequently. This method can be applied where the router is expecting to provide service to visiting MNs (e.g., wireless network interfaces), or on which it is serving as an HA to one or more MNs (who may return home and need to hear its advertisements).

8.2.4 Requirements for Various IPv6 Nodes

MIPv6 imposes specific requirements on the functions provided by different types of IPv6 nodes (except for a generic IPv6 node acting as CN). These are summarized in Table 8.6.

8.2.5 Correspondent Node Operation

IPv6 nodes with route optimization support must maintain a binding cache of bindings for other nodes (as shown in Table 8.3); a separate Binding Cache is typically maintained by each IPv6 node for each of its unicast routable addresses. Specifically, CNs are required to support the following functionality:

- Processing mobility headers
- Packet processing
- Return-routability procedure
- Processing bindings
- Cache replacement policy

8.2.5.1 Processing Mobility Headers Mobility header processing follows the process of Figure 8.13. Subsequent checks depend on the particular mobility header.

TABLE 8.6   Requirements for Various IPv6 Nodes

Nodes	Requirement
IPv6 nodes	Any IPv6 node may at any time be a CN of an MN, either sending a packet to an MN or receiving a packet from an MN. There are no MIPv6-specific requirements for such nodes and basic IPv6 capabilities are sufficient. If an MN attempts to set up route optimization with a node with only basic IPv6 support, an ICMP error will signal that the node does not support such optimizations and communications will flow through the HA
IPv6 nodes with support for route optimization. Nodes that implement route optimization are a subset of all IPv6 nodes on the Internet. The ability of a CN to participate in route optimization is essential for the efficient operation of the IPv6 environment	The node must be able to validate a home address option using an existing binding cache entry The node must be able to insert a type 2 routing header into packets being sent to an MN Unless the CN is also acting as an MN, it must ignore type 2 routing headers and silently discard all packets that it has received with such headers The node should be able to interpret ICMP messages. The node must be able to send Binding Error messages. The node must be able to process Mobility Headers. The node must be able to participate in a return-routability procedure. The node must be able to process BU messages. The node must be able to return a BA. The node must be able to maintain a Binding Cache of the bindings received in accepted BUs. The node should allow route optimization to be administratively enabled or disabled. The default should be enabled.
IPv6 routers. All IPv6 routers, even those not serving as an HA for MIPv6, have an effect on how well MNs can communicate	Every IPv6 router should be able to send an advertisement interval option in each of its router advertisements, to aid movement detection by MNs. The use of this option in router advertisements should be configurable Every IPv6 router should be able to support sending unsolicited multicast router advertisements at a fast rate (the used rate should then be configurable) Each router should include at least one prefix with the router address (R) bit set and with its full IP address in its router advertisements Routers supporting filtering packets with routing headers should support different rules for type 0 and type 2 routing headers so that filtering of source routed packets (type 0) will not necessarily limit MIPv6 traffic which is delivered via type 2 routing headers

(continued)

TABLE 8.6 *(Continued)*

Nodes	Requirement
IPv6 routers that serve as an HA. In order for an MN to operate correctly while away from home, at least one IPv6 router on the MN's home link must function as an HA for the MN	Every HA must be able to maintain an entry in its binding cache for each MN for which it is serving as the HA
	Every HA must be able to intercept packets (using proxy neighbor discovery) addressed to an MN for which it is currently serving as the HA, on that MN's home link, while the MN is away from home
	Every HA must be able to encapsulate such intercepted packets in order to tunnel them to the primary CoA for the MN indicated in its binding in the HA's binding cache
	Every HA must support decapsulating reverse tunneled packets sent to it from an MN's home address. Every HA must also check that the source address in the tunneled packets corresponds to the currently registered location of the MN
	The node must be able to process mobility headers.
	Every HA must be able to return a BA in response to a BU
	Every HA must maintain a separate HA list for each link on which it is serving as an HA
	Every HA must be able to accept packets addressed to the MIPv6 HA anycast address for the subnet on which it is serving as an HA and must be able to participate in dynamic HAAD
	Every HA should support a configuration mechanism to allow a system administrator to manually set the value to be sent by this HA in the HA preference field of the HA information option in router advertisements that it sends
	Every HA should support sending ICMP mobile prefix advertisements and should respond to mobile prefix solicitations. If supported, this behavior must be configurable, so that HAs can be configured to avoid sending such prefix advertisements according to the needs of the network administration in the home domain
	Every HA must support IPsec encapsulating security payload (ESP) for protection of packets belonging to the return-routability procedure
	Every HA should support the multicast group membership control protocols. If this support is provided, the HA must be capable of using it to determine which multicast data packets to forward via the tunnel to the MN
	HAs may support stateful address autoconfiguration for MNs

TABLE 8.6   (*Continued*)

Nodes	Requirement
IPv6 MNs	The node must maintain a BU list
	The node must support sending packets containing a home address option and follow the required IPsec interaction
	The node must be able to perform IPv6 encapsulation and decapsulation
	The node must be able to process type 2 routing header
	The node must support receiving a binding error message
	The node must support receiving ICMP errors
	The node must support movement detection, CoA formation, and returning home
	The node must be able to process mobility headers
	The node must support the return-routability procedure
	The node must be able to send BUs
	The node must be able to receive and process BAs
	The node must support receiving a BRR by responding with a BU
	The node must support receiving mobile prefix advertisements and reconfiguring its home address based on the prefix information contained therein
	The node should support use of the dynamic HAAD mechanism
	The node must allow route optimization to be administratively enabled or disabled. The default should be enabled
	The node may support the multicast address listener part of a multicast group membership protocol. If this support is provided, the MN must be able to receive tunneled multicast packets from the HA
	The node may support stateful address autoconfiguration mechanisms such as dynamic host configuration protocol version 6 (DHCPv6) on the interface represented by the tunnel to the HA

8.2.5.2 *Packet Processing*   Packet processing covers the following subactivities:

- Receiving packets with home address option
- Sending packets to an MN
- Sending binding error messages
- Receiving ICMP error messages

These subactivities are described next.

Receiving packets with home address option. The CN must process the option in a manner consistent with exchanging the home address field from the home address option into the IPv6 header and replacing the original value of the source address field there. After all IPv6 options have been processed, the upper layers can process the packet without the knowledge that it came originally from a CoA or that a home address option was used.

Packets containing a home address option must be dropped if the given home address is not a unicast routable address. MNs can include a home address destination

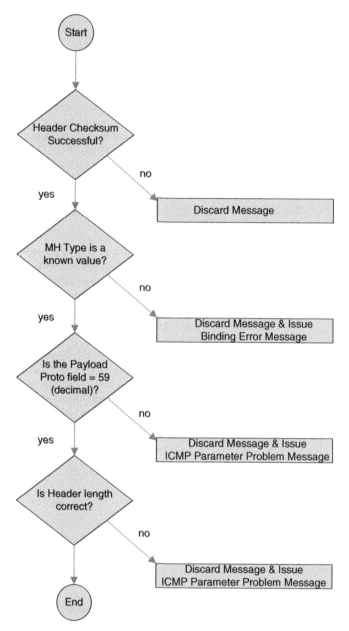

FIGURE 8.13 Mobility header processing.

option in a packet if they believe the CN has a binding cache entry for the home address of an MN. Packets containing a home address option must be dropped if there is no corresponding binding cache entry. A corresponding binding cache entry must have the same home address as appears in the home address destination option, and the currently registered CoA must be equal to the source address of the packet. These actions are not done for packets that contain a home address option and a BU. If the packet is dropped due to these conditions, the CN must send the binding error message.

Sending packets to an MN. Before sending any packet (except when sending an IPv6 neighbor discovery packet), the sending node should examine its binding cache for an entry for the destination address to which the packet is being sent. If the sending node has a binding cache entry for this address, the sending node should use a type 2 routing header to route the packet to this MN (the destination node) by way of its CoA. For example, if there are no additional routing headers in this packet beyond those needed by MIPv6, the CN could set the fields in the packet's IPv6 header and routing header as follows:

- The destination address in the packet's IPv6 header is set to the MN's home address (the original destination address to which the packet was being sent).
- The routing header is initialized to contain a single route segment, containing the MN's CoA copied from the binding cache entry. The segments left field is, however, temporarily set to zero.

If, on the other hand, the sending node has no binding cache entry for the destination address to which the packet is being sent, the sending node simply sends the packet normally, with no routing header. If the destination node is not an MN (or is an MN that is currently at home), the packet will be delivered directly to this node and processed normally by it. If, however, the destination node is an MN that is currently away from home, the packet will be intercepted by the MN's HA and tunneled to the MN's current primary CoA.

Sending binding error messages. A binding error message is sent directly to the address that appeared in the IPv6 source address field of the offending packet (if the source address field does not contain a unicast address, the binding error message must not be sent). The home address field in the binding error message is copied from the home address field in the home address destination option of the offending packet, or set to the unspecified address if no such option appeared in the packet.

Receiving ICMP error messages. When the CN has a binding cache entry for an MN, all traffic destined to the MN goes directly to the current CoA of the MN using a routing header. Any ICMP error message caused by packets on their way to the CoA will be returned in the normal manner to the CN. On the other hand, if the CN has no binding cache entry for the MN, the packet will be routed through the MN's home link. In all cases, any meaningful ICMP error messages caused by packets from a CN to an MN will be returned to the CN.

TABLE 8.7 Return-Routability Actions of the CN

Action	Description
Receiving HoTi messages	Upon receiving a HoTi message, the CN verifies that the packet does not include a home address destination option. Any packet carrying a HoTi message that fails to satisfy all of these tests must be silently ignored. Otherwise, in preparation for sending the corresponding HoT message, the CN checks that it has the necessary material to engage in a return-routability procedure. The CN must have a secret Kcn and a nonce; it does not have this material yet, it must produce it before continuing with the return-routability procedure
Receiving care-of test init messages	Upon receiving a HoTi message, the CN verifies that the packet does not include a home address destination option. Any packet carrying a care-of test init message that fails to satisfy all of these tests must be silently ignored. Otherwise, in preparation for sending the corresponding care-of test message, the CN checks that it has the necessary material to engage in a return-routability procedure
Sending HoT messages	The CN creates a home keygen token and uses the current nonce index as the home nonce index; it then creates a HoT message and sends it to the MN at the latter's home address
Sending care-of test messages	The CN creates a care-of keygen token and uses the current nonce index as the care-of nonce index; it then creates a care-of test message and sends it to the MN at the latter's CoA

8.2.5.3 Return-Routability Procedure Actions taken by a CN during the return-routability procedure are listed in Table 8.7.

8.2.5.4 Processing Bindings Messages related to bindings are as follows:

- **Receiving BUs**. Before accepting a BU, the receiving node must validate the BU. This validation entails the following: the packet must contain a unicast routable home address, either in the home address option or in the source address if the home address option is not present; also, the sequence number field in the BU is greater than the sequence number received in the previous valid BU for this home address, if any (if the receiving node has no BINDING CACHE entry for the indicated home address, it must accept any sequence number value in a received BU from this MN); also, other tests must pass.

- **Requests to cache a binding**. There is a need to process a valid BU that requests a node to cache a binding, for which the home registration (H) bit is not set in the BU. In this case, the receiving node should create a new entry in its binding cache for this home address, or update its existing binding cache entry for this home address, if such an entry already exists. The lifetime for the binding cache entry is initialized from the lifetime field specified in the BU, although this lifetime may be reduced by the node caching the binding; the lifetime for the binding cache entry cannot be greater than the lifetime value specified in the

BU. Any binding cache entry must be deleted after the expiration of its lifetime. The CN may refuse to accept a new binding cache entry if it does not have sufficient resources.

- **Requests to delete a binding**. There is a need to process a valid BU that requests a node to delete a binding when the home registration (H) bit is not set in the BU. Any existing binding for the given home address must be deleted. A binding cache entry for the home address must not be created in response to receiving the BU. If the binding cache entry was created by use of return-routability nonces, the CN must ensure that the same nonces are not used again with the particular home and CoA. If both nonces are still valid, the CN has to remember the particular combination of nonce indexes, addresses, and sequence number as illegal until at least one of the nonces has become too old.

- **Sending BAs**. A BA may be sent to indicate receipt of a BU. If the node accepts the BU and creates or updates an entry for this binding, the status field in the BA must be set to a value less than 128. Otherwise, the status field must be set to a value greater than or equal to 128.

- **Sending binding refresh requests (BRRs).** If a binding cache entry being deleted is still in active use when sending packets to an MN, then the next packet sent to the MN will be routed normally to the MN's home link. Communication with the MN continues, but the tunneling from the home network creates additional overhead and latency in delivering packets to the MN. If the sender is aware that the binding cache entry is still in active use, it may send a BRR message to the MN in an attempt to avoid this overhead and latency due to deleting and recreating the binding cache entry. This message is always sent to the home address of the MN. The CN may retransmit BRR messages as long as the rate limitation is applied. The CN must stop retransmitting when it receives a BU.

8.2.5.5 Cache Replacement Policy
A node may maintain a separate timer for each entry in its binding cache. When creating or updating a binding cache entry in response to a received and accepted BU, the node sets the timer for this entry to the specified lifetime period; entries in a node's binding cache are deleted after the expiration of the lifetime specified in the BU from which the entry was created or last updated. A node may also opt to drop any entry already in its binding cache in order to make space for a new entry. If the node sends a packet to a destination for which it has dropped the entry from its binding cache, the packet will be routed through the MN's home link; the MN can detect this and establish a new binding if necessary.

8.2.6 HA Node Operation

HA operations entail the following functions:

- Maintaining the binding cache and the HA list
- Processing mobility headers

- Processing bindings
  - Primary CoA registration
  - Primary CoA de-registration
- Packet processing
  - Intercepting packets for an MN
  - Processing intercepted packets
  - Multicast membership control
  - Stateful Address autoconfiguration
  - Handling reverse tunneled packets
  - Protecting return-routability packets
- Dynamic HAAD
- Sending prefix information to the MN

We have generally described this (or comparable) functionality earlier in this chapter; hence we will not discuss it further herewith.

8.2.7 Mobile Node Operation

MN operations entail the following functions:

- Maintaining the BU list
- Processing bindings
  - Sending BUs to the HA
  - Correspondent registration
  - Receiving BAs
  - Receiving BRRs
- Processing mobility headers
- Packet processing
  - Sending packets while away from home
  - Interaction with outbound IPsec processing
  - Receiving packets while away from home
  - Routing multicast packets
  - Receiving ICMP error messages
  - Receiving binding error messages
- HA and prefix management
  - Dynamic HAAD
  - Sending mobile prefix solicitations
  - Receiving mobile prefix advertisements
- Movement support
  - Movement detection

- ○ Forming new CoA
- ○ Using multiple CoA
- ○ Returning home
- • Return-routability procedure
  - ○ Sending test init messages
  - ○ Receiving test messages
  - ○ Protecting return-routability packets
- • Retransmissions and rate limiting

The BU list records information for each BU sent by this MN, in which the lifetime of the binding has not yet expired. The BU list includes all bindings sent by the MN either to its HA or to remote CNs; it also contains BUs which are waiting for the completion of the return-routability procedure before they can be sent. However, for multiple BUs sent to the same destination address, the BU list contains only the most recent BU (i.e., with the greatest sequence number value) sent to that destination.

Other aspects of the MN operations are covered next; however, only some key highlights are covered here; for additional details, consult RFC 3775 (2).

8.2.7.1 *Packet Processing*   For packets sent by an MN while it is at home, no special MIPv6 processing is required.

While an MN is away from home, it can continue to use its home address or it can use one or more CoAs as the source of the packet (thus eliminating the use of a home address option in the packet.) Using the MN's CoA as the source generally has a lower overhead than using the MN's home address, given that no extra options need be used. Such packets can be routed normally, that is, directly between their source and destination without relying on MIPv6 mechanisms. Summarizing this, if the MN uses an address other than one of its home addresses as the source of a packet sent while away from home, no special MIPv6 processing is required: packets are simply addressed and transmitted in the same way as any normal IPv6 packet.

For packets sent by the MN while away from home using the MN's home address as the source, MIPv6 processing of the packet is required. As we noted, this can be done in one of two ways:

- • *Route optimization*: This approach to the delivery of packets does not require going through the home network, and such, typically enables faster and more reliable transmission. The MN needs to ensure that a binding cache entry exists for its home address so that the CN can process the packet. An MN should arrange to supply the home address in a home address option and must set the IPv6 header's source address field to the CoA which the MN has registered to be used with this CN. The CN will then use the address supplied in the home address option to serve the function traditionally done by the source IP address in the IPv6 header. The MN's home address is then supplied to higher protocol layers and applications.

- *Reverse tunneling.* This is the mechanism that tunnels the packets via the HA, being needed if there is no binding yet with the CN; as such, it is not as efficient as the route optimization mechanism. This mechanism is used for packets that have the MN's home address as the source address in the IPv6 header, or with multicast control protocol. The process is as follows: (i) the packet is sent to the HA using IPv6 encapsulation; (ii) the source address in the tunnel packet is the primary CoA as registered with the HA; (iii) the destination address in the tunnel packet is the HA's address. Then, the HA will pass the encapsulated packet to the CN.

During packet processing, there will be an interaction between outbound MIPv6 processing and outbound IPsec processing for packets sent by an MN while away from home. This interaction is shown in Figure 8.14; in Figure 8.14, it is assumed that IPsec is being used in transport mode and that the MN is using its home address as the source for the packet. Note that the treatment of destination options (in RFC 2402) is extended as follows: the authentication header (AH) authentication data must be calculated as if the following were true: (i) the IPv6 source address in the IPv6 header contains the MN's home address; (ii) the home address field of the home address destination option contains the new CoA.

While away from home, an MN will receive packets addressed to its home address, by one of two methods:

- Packets sent by a CN, which does not have a binding cache entry for the MN, will be sent to the home address, captured by the HA, and tunneled to the MN. Here the MN must check that the IPv6 source address of the tunneled packet is the IP address of its HA. In this method, the MN may also send a BU to the original sender of the packet and subject to rate-limiting processes. The MN must also process the received packet in the manner defined for IPv6 encapsulation, which will result in the encapsulated (inner) packet being processed normally by upper-layer protocols within the MN as if it had been addressed (only) to the MN's home address.

- Packets sent by a CN that has a binding cache entry for the MN that contains the MN's current CoA will be sent by the CN using a type 2 routing header. The packet will be addressed to the MN's CoA, with the final hop in the routing header directing the packet to the MN's home address; the processing of this last hop of the routing header is entirely internal to the MN, since the CoA and home address are both addresses within the MN.

8.2.7.2 *Home Agent Address Discovery*   Sometimes when the MN needs to send a BU to its HA to register its new primary CoA, the MN may not know the address of any router on its home link that can serve as an HA for it. In this case, the MN may attempt to discover the address of a suitable HA on its home link. To do so,

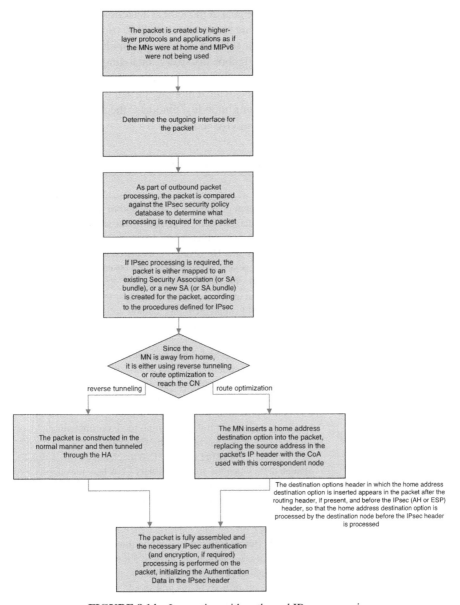

FIGURE 8.14   Interaction with outbound IPsec processing.

the MN sends an ICMP HAAD request message to the MIPv6 HA anycast address
for its home subnet prefix. The HA on its home link that receives this request message
will return an ICMP HAAD reply message. This message gives the addresses for the
HAs operating on the home link. The MN, upon receiving this HAAD reply message,
may then send its home registration BU to any of the unicast IP addresses listed in
the HA addresses field in the reply.

8.2.7.3 *Movement Support* The goal of movement detection is to detect Layer 3 handovers. While full-function roaming mechanisms might be useful in this context, as a minimum, one needs some generic method of detecting handoffs. Methods that make use of the facilities of IPv6 neighbor discovery, including router discovery and neighbor unreachability detection, may be of interest. Table 8.8 depicts some mechanisms for movement support. Due to the temporary packet flow disruption and signaling overhead involved in updating mobility bindings, the MN should avoid performing an L3 handover until it is strictly necessary.

TABLE 8.8   Basic Mechanisms for Movement Support

Activity	Description
Movement detection	Generic movement detection can use neighbor unreachability detection to detect when the default router is no longer bidirectionally reachable, in which case the MN must discover a new default router. However, this detection only occurs when the MN has packets to send, and in the absence of frequent router advertisements or indications from the link layer, the MN might become unaware of an L3 handover that occurred. Hence, the MN should supplement this method with other information whenever it is available to the MN (e.g., from lower protocol layers)
	When the MN detects an L3 handover, it selects a new default router as a consequence of router discovery and then performs prefix discovery with that new router to form new CoA(es). It then registers its new primary CoA with its HA. After updating its home registration, the MN then updates associated mobility bindings in CNs that it is performing route optimization
Forming new CoA	After detecting that it has moved an MN is expected to generate a new primary CoA using normal IPv6 mechanisms. This should also be done when the current primary CoA becomes deprecated
	After selecting a new primary CoA, the MN must send a BU containing that CoA to its HA. The BU must have the home registration (H) and acknowledge (A) bits set its HA. In order to form a new CoA, an MN may use either stateless or stateful (e.g., DHCPv6) address autoconfiguration
Using multiple CoAs	An MN may use more than one CoA at a time. To assist with smooth handovers, an MN should retain its previous primary CoA as a (non-primary) CoA and should still accept packets at this address, even after registering its new primary CoA with its HA
	Whenever an MN determines that it is no longer reachable through a given link, it should invalidate all CoAs associated with address prefixes that it discovered from routers on the unreachable link which are not in the current set of address prefixes advertised by the (possibly new) current default router

8.2.8 Relationship to IPV4 Mobile IPv4 (MIP)

A question might be "what is the relationship of MIPv6 to IPV4 MIPv4 defined in RFC 3344 (9)?" RFC 3775 (2) notes that the design of MIPv6 benefits both from the experiences gained from the development of MIP and also from the opportunities provided by IPv6. Therefore, MIPv6 shares many features with MIP, but is integrated into IPv6 and offers other improvements. The notable differences between MIP and MIPv6 are as follows:

- There is no need to deploy special routers as "foreign agents," as in MIP. MIPv6 operates in any location without any special support required from the local router.
- Support for route optimization is a fundamental part of the protocol, rather than a nonstandard set of extensions.
- MIPv6 route optimization can operate securely even without prearranged SAs. It is expected that route optimization can be deployed on a global scale between all MNs and CNs.
- Support is also integrated into MIPv6 for allowing route optimization to coexist efficiently with routers that perform "ingress filtering."
- The IPv6 neighbor unreachability detection assures symmetric reachability between the MN and its default router in the current location.
- Most packets sent to an MN while away from home in MIPv6 are sent using an IPv6 routing header rather than IP encapsulation, reducing the amount of resulting overhead compared to MIP.
- MIPv6 is decoupled from any particular link layer, as it uses IPv6 neighbor discovery instead of Address Resolution Protocol (ARP); this also improves the robustness of the protocol.
- The use of IPv6 encapsulation (and the routing header) removes the need in MIPv6 to manage "tunnel soft state."
- The dynamic HAAD mechanism in MIPv6 returns a single reply to the MN. The directed broadcast approach used in IPv4 returns separate replies from each HA.

MIPv6 offers a number of improvements over MIPv4 principally due to capabilities inherited from IPv6. For example, route optimization and dynamic HA discovery can only be achieved with MIPv6. One of the advantages of the large address space provided by IPv6 is that it allows MNs to obtain a globally unique CoA wherever they are; therefore, there is no need for network address translator (NAT) traversal techniques designed for MIPv4. This allows MIPv6 to be a significantly simpler and more bandwidth-efficient mobility management protocol. At the same time, during the transition toward IPv6, NAT traversal for existing private IPv4 networks needs to be considered (10).

REFERENCES

1. Minoli D. *Mobile Video with Mobile IPv6*. New York: Wiley; 2012.

2. Johnson D, Perkins C, Arkko J. Mobility Support in IPv6. RFC 3775, June 2004.

3. Arkko J, Vogt C, Haddad W. Enhanced Route Optimization for Mobile IPv6. RFC 4866, May 2007.

4. Korhonen J, editor. Bournelle J, Giaretta G, NakhjiriM. Diameter Mobile IPv6: Support for Home Agent to Diameter Server Interaction. February 2010, RFC 5778.

5. 6deploy.org. IPv6 Workshop – IPv6 Mobility Module. October 2008.

6. Giaretta G, Devarapalli V. Mobile IPv6 Bootstrapping in Split Scenario, RFC 5026, October 2007.

7. Arkko J, Devarapalli V, Dupont F. Using IPsec to Protect Mobile IPv6 Signaling Between Mobile Nodes and Home Agents. RFC 3776, June 2004.

8. Narten T, Nordmark E, Simpson W. Neighbor Discovery for IP Version 6 (IPv6). RFC 2461, December 1998.

9. Perkins C. editor. IP Mobility Support for IPv4. RFC 3344, August 2002.

10. Soliman H, editor. Mobile IPv6 Support for Dual Stack Hosts and Routers. RFC 5555, June 2009.

CHAPTER 9

IPv6 OVER LOW-POWER WPAN (6LoWPAN)

As we have seen at various points in this text, most (but certainly not all) IoT/M2M nodes have noteworthy design constraints. Developers make the case that the IEEE 802.15.4-2003 standard is very promising for the lower (physical and link) layers. As for higher layer functions, the goal is to utilize IP technology, specifically IPv6, considering the v6 capabilities and benefits described in Chapter 7. To that end, an IETF Working Group (WG) was chartered in 2005 to define IPv6 over IEEE 802.15.4, that is to say, IPv6 over low-power WPANs; the outcome is known as 6LoWPAN. Two initial deliverables were generated in 2007: (i) problem statement ("Goals and Assumptions") and (ii) format specification ("IPv6 over 802.15.4"). 6LoWPAN is now a widely accepted approach to run IP on 802.15.4 based on the just cited format specification. It is already supported in TinyOS, Contiki, and in standards such as ISA SP 100, ZigBee Smart Energy (SE) 2.0, and the IEEE 1451.5 standard for wireless transducers. The basic RFC makes 802.15.4 look like an IPv6 link; it provides basic encapsulation and efficient representation of packets smaller than 100 octets. Some highlights of this work are provided in this chapter. The material is abstracted and synthesized from the basic RFCs. The reader is referred to the original material for a more detailed description of the specifications.

Building the Internet of Things with IPv6 and MIPv6: The Evolving World of M2M Communications,
First Edition. Daniel Minoli.
© 2013 John Wiley & Sons, Inc. Published 2013 by John Wiley & Sons, Inc.

9.1   BACKGROUND/INTRODUCTION

The requirement for IPv6 connectivity in a LoWPAN is driven by the following (1):

- The many devices in a LoWPAN make network autoconfiguration and state-lessness highly desirable; as we have seen, IPv6 offers ready solutions;
- The large number of devices poses the need for a large address space, well met by IPv6;
- Given the limited packet size of LoWPANs, the IPv6 address format allows subsuming of IEEE 802.15.4 addresses, if so desired;
- Given the limited packet size, headers for IPv6 and layers above must be compressed whenever possible; and
- Simple interconnectivity of the LoWPANs to other IP networks including the Internet.

The WG has completed two RFCs: (i) "*IPv6 over Low-Power Wireless Personal Area Networks (6LoWPANs): Overview, Assumptions, Problem Statement, and Goals*" (RFC 4919) that documents and discusses the problem space, and (ii) "*Transmission of IPv6 Packets over IEEE 802.15.4 Networks*" (RFC 4944) that defines the format for the adaptation between IPv6 and 802.15.4. 6LoWPAN has also worked closely with the routing over low-power and lossy networks (LLNs) (roll) WG, which is developing IPv6 routing solutions for LLNs. See Table 9.1 for a detailed listing of the 6LoWPAN family of documents and specifications.

Recent additional work items of the WG include the following (2):

1. Produce "6LoWPAN Bootstrapping and 6LoWPAN IPv6 ND Optimizations" to define limited extensions to IPv6 neighbor discovery (RFC 4861) for use specifically in low-power networks. This document defines how to bootstrap a 6LoWPAN network and explore ND optimizations such as reusing the structure of the 802.15.4 network (e.g., by using the coordinators) and reduce the need for multicast by having devices talk to coordinators (without creating a single point of failure or changing the semantics of the IPv6 ND multicasts).

2. Produce "6LoWPAN Improved Header Compression" to describe mechanisms to allow enhancements to the 6LoWPAN headers. Specifically, this document describes the compression of addresses that are not link local. Additionally, the document may include other enhancements or optimizations of the HC1 or HC2 6LoWPAN headers.

3. Produce "6LoWPAN Architecture" to describe the design and implementation of 6LoWPAN networks. This document covers the concepts of "Mesh Under" and "Route Over," 802.15.4 design issues such as operation with sleeping nodes, network components (both battery and line powered), addressing, and IPv4/IPv6 network connections.

TABLE 9.1   6LoWPAN Family of Documents and Specifications

	Title	Date	Status
Active Internet Drafts			
draft-ietf-6LoWPAN-btle-11	Transmission of IPv6 packets over Bluetooth low energy	2012-10-12	IESG evaluation: AD follow-up (for 106 days)
			Submitted to IESG for publication
RFCs			
RFC 4919 (draft-ietf-6LoWPAN-problem)	IPv6 over Low-Power Wireless Personal Area Networks (6LoWPANs): Overview, Assumptions, Problem Statement, and Goals	2007-08	RFC 4919 (informational) errata
RFC 4944 (draft-ietf-6LoWPAN-format)	Transmission of IPv6 packets over IEEE 802.15.4 networks	2007-09	RFC 4944 (proposed standard) updated by RFC 6282, RFC 6775
RFC 6282 (draft-ietf-6LoWPAN-hc)	Compression format for IPv6 datagrams over IEEE 802.15.4-based networks	2011-09	RFC 6282 (proposed standard)
RFC 6568 (draft-ietf-6LoWPAN-usecases)	Design and Application Spaces for IPv6 over Low-Power Wireless Personal Area Networks (6LoWPANs)	2012-04	RFC 6568 (informational)
RFC 6606 (draft-ietf-6LoWPAN-routing-requirements)	Problem Statement and Requirements for IPv6 over Low-Power Wireless Personal Area Network (6LoWPAN) Routing	2012-05	RFC 6606 (informational)
RFC 6775 (draft-ietf-6LoWPAN-nd)	Neighbor Discovery Optimization for IPv6 over Low-Power Wireless Personal Area Networks (6LoWPANs)	2012-11 (new)	RFC 6775 (proposed standard)
Related Documents/Active Internet Drafts			
draft-bormann-6LoWPAN-ghc-05	6LoWPAN Generic Compression of Headers and Header-like Payloads	2012-09-06	I-D exists
draft-bormann-6LoWPAN-roadmap-03	6LoWPAN Roadmap and Implementation Guide	2012-10-22	I-D exists
draft-schoenw-6LoWPAN-mib-01	Definition of Managed Objects for IPv6 over Low-Power Wireless Personal Area Networks (6LoWPANs)		

4. As a separate Internet Draft, "6LoWPAN Routing Requirements" is aimed at describing 6LoWPAN-specific requirements on routing protocols used in 6LoWPANs, addressing both the "route-over" and "mesh-under" approach.

5. Produce "Use Cases for 6LoWPAN" to define, for a small set of applications with sufficiently unique requirements, how 6LoWPANs can solve those requirements, and which protocols and configuration variants can be used for these scenarios. The use cases will cover protocols for transport, application layer, discovery, configuration, and commissioning.

6. Produce "6LoWPAN Security Analysis" to define the threat model of 6LoW-PANs, to document the suitability of existing key management schemes, and to discuss bootstrapping/installation/commissioning/setup issues.

9.2 6LoWPANS GOALS

LoWPANs[1] in general and IEEE 802.15.4-2003-based systems in particular have design constraints that need to be taken into consideration when developing a protocol stack. These constraints fall into two categories:

- Communication constraints defined by the underlying personal area network (PAN):
  - Small packet size. Given that the maximum physical layer packet is 127 bytes, the resulting maximum frame size at the media access control layer is 102 octets. Link-layer security imposes further overhead, leaving 81 octets for data packets. Adding all layers for IP connectivity should still allow transmission in one frame, without incurring excessive fragmentation and reassembly. Furthermore "control/protocol packets" fit within a single 802.15.4 frame;
  - Support for both 16-bit short or IEEE 64-bit extended media access control addresses;
  - Low bandwidth. Data rates of 250 Kbps, 40 Kbps, and 20 Kbps for each of the currently defined physical layers (2.4 GHz, 915 MHz, and 868 MHz, respectively);
  - Topologies include star and mesh operation;
  - Other issues to address include limited configuration and management capabilities, need for service discovery, and need for security (confidentiality and integrity protection).
- System constraints driven by the intended application parameters:
  - Characteristic examples include low/battery power, low cost, low processing capabilities, small memory size, large population of devices, ad-hoc locations/logical topology, mobility, and unreliable nodal behaviors (e.g., due to uncertain radio connectivity, interference, sleep state, battery drain, device, etc.)

---

[1]This discussion is summarized and synthesized from Reference 1.

While many LoWPAN devices in a network are expected to have limited functionality (the "reduced function devices" or RFDs discussed in Chapter 6), other, more capable "full function devices" (FFDs) will also be present in the network. FFDs are expected to "aid" RFDs by providing functions such as network coordination, packet forwarding, interfacing with other types of networks, and so on. LoWPANs must support various topologies including mesh and star. Mesh topologies imply multihop routing to a desired destination. In this case, intermediate devices act as packet forwarders at the link layer (akin to routers at the network layer). Typically, these are "FFDs" that have more capabilities in terms of power, computation, etc. The requirements on the routing protocol are:

- Given the minimal packet size of LoWPANs, the routing protocol must impose low (or no) overhead on data packets.
- The routing protocols should have low routing overhead (low chattiness) balanced with topology changes and power conservation.
- The computation and memory requirements in the routing protocol should be minimal to satisfy the low-cost and low-power objectives. Thus, storage and maintenance of large routing tables is detrimental.
- Support for network topologies in which either FFDs or RFDs may be battery or mains powered. This implies the appropriate considerations for routing in the presence of sleeping nodes.

Table 9.2 summarizes IP Protocol considerations for LoWPANs as defined in RFC 4919.

9.3 TRANSMISSION OF IPv6 PACKETS OVER IEEE 802.15.4

RFC 4944[2] describes the frame format for transmission of IPv6 packets and the method of forming IPv6 link-local addresses and statelessly autoconfigured addresses on IEEE 802.15.4 networks. Additional specifications include a simple header compression scheme using shared context and provisions for packet delivery in IEEE 802.15.4 meshes.

IEEE 802.15.4 defines four types of frames: beacon frames, MAC command frames, acknowledgement frames, and data frames, as noted in Chapter 6. IPv6 packets must be carried on data frames. Data frames may optionally request that they be acknowledged. IPv6 packets will be carried in frames for which acknowledgements are requested so as to aid link-layer recovery. IEEE 802.15.4 networks can either be nonbeacon enabled or beacon enabled. 6LoWPAN (RFC 4944) does not require that IEEE networks run in beacon-enabled mode. In nonbeacon-enabled networks, data frames (including those carrying IPv6 packets) are sent via the contention-based channel access method of unslotted Carrier Sense Multiple Access/Collision Avoidance (CSMA/CA). In nonbeacon-enabled networks, beacons are not used for

---

[2]This discussion is summarized and synthesized from Reference 3.

TABLE 9.2 IP Protocol Considerations for LoWPANs as Defined in RFC 4919 (Partial List)

Item	Issues and Approaches
Fragmentation and reassembly layer	The PDUs in IEEE 802.15.4-2003 may be as small as 81 bytes. This is far below the minimum IPv6 packet size of 1280 octets and consistent with Section 5 of the IPv6 specification in RFC 2460; a fragmentation and reassembly adaptation layer must be provided at the layer below IP
Header compression	In the worst case the maximum size available for transmitting IP packets over an IEEE 802.15.4 frame is 81 octets, and that the IPv6 header is 40 octets long (without optional headers); this leaves only 41 octets for upper-layer protocols, such as UDP and TCP. UDP uses 8 octets in the header and TCP uses 20 octets. This leaves 33 octets for data over UDP and 21 octets for data over TCP. Additionally, as pointed above, there is also a need for a fragmentation and reassembly layer, which will use even more octets leaving very few octets for data. Thus, if one were to use the protocols as is, it would lead to excessive fragmentation and reassembly, even when data packets are just 10s of octets long. This mandated the need for header compression. 6LoWPAN expects using existing header compression techniques, but, if necessary, specifies new ones
Address autoconfiguration	6LoWPAN needs to define methods for creating IPv6 stateless address autoconfiguration. Stateless autoconfiguration (as compared to stateful) is attractive for 6LoWPANs, because it reduces the configuration overhead on the hosts. There is a need for a method to generate an "interface identifier" from the EUI-64 assigned to the IEEE 802.15.4 device
Mesh routing protocol	A routing protocol to support a multihop mesh network is necessary. There is much published work on ad-hoc multihop routing for devices, but these protocols are designed to use IP-based addresses that have large overheads. For example, the ad-hoc on-demand distance vector (AODV) routing protocol described in RFC 3561 uses 48 octets for a route request based on IPv6 addressing. Given the packet-size constraints, transmitting this packet without fragmentation and reassembly may be difficult. Thus, care should be taken when using existing routing protocols (or designing new ones) so that the routing packets fit within a single IEEE 802.15.4 frame

synchronization; however, they are still useful for link-layer device discovery to aid in association and disassociation events. RFC 4944 recommends that beacons be configured so as to aid these functions.

As we noted in Chapter 6, IEEE 802.15.4 allows the use of either IEEE 64-bit extended addresses or (after an association event) 16-bit addresses unique within the PAN. 6LoWPAN/RFC 4944 supports both 64-bit extended addresses and 16-bit short addresses; however, the RFC imposes additional constraints (beyond those imposed by IEEE 802.15.4) on the format of the 16-bit short addresses. Short addresses are transient in nature and are assigned by the PAN coordinator function during an association event; hence their validity and uniqueness is limited by the lifetime of that association. It should also be noted that because of the scalability issues posed by such a centralized allocation and single point of failure at the PAN coordinator, deployers should carefully weigh the trade-offs (and implement the necessary mechanisms) of growing such networks based on short addresses.

RFC 4944 assumes that a PAN maps to a specific IPv6 link. Note that multicast is not supported natively in IEEE 802.15.4; hence, IPv6 level multicast packets must be carried as link-layer broadcast frames in IEEE 802.15.4 networks.

The maximum transmission unit (MTU) size for IPv6 packets over IEEE 802.15.4 is 1280 octets. However, a full IPv6 packet does not fit in an IEEE 802.15.4 frame. 802.15.4 protocol data units (PDUs) have different sizes depending on how much overhead is present. Starting from a maximum physical layer packet size of 127 octets (aMaxPHYPacketSize) and a maximum frame overhead of 25 (aMaxFrameOverhead), the resultant maximum frame size at the media access control layer is 102 octets. Link-layer security imposes further overhead, which in the maximum case (21 octets of overhead in the AES-CCM-128 case, versus 9 and 13 for AES-CCM-32 and AES-CCM-64, respectively) leaves only 81 octets available. This implies that fragmentation and reassembly adaptation layer must be provided at the layer below IP.

Furthermore, the IPv6 header is 40 octets long and this leaves only 41 octets for upper-layer protocols, such as UDP. The latter uses 8 octets in the header, which leaves only 33 octets for application data. Additionally, as just noted, there is a need for a fragmentation and reassembly layer, which will use even more octets.

The encapsulation formats defined in the RFC (also called the "LoWPAN encapsulation") are the payload in the IEEE 802.15.4 MAC PDU. The LoWPAN payload (e.g., an IPv6 packet) follows this encapsulation header.

All LoWPAN-encapsulated datagrams transported over IEEE 802.15.4 are prefixed by an encapsulation header stack. Each header in the header stack contains a header type followed by zero or more header fields. While in an IPv6 header, the stack would contain, in the following order, addressing, hop-by-hop options, routing, fragmentation, destination options, and finally payload; in a LoWPAN header, the analogous header sequence is mesh (layer 2) addressing, hop-by-hop options (including layer 2 broadcast/multicast), fragmentation, and finally payload. Figure 9.1 shows typical header stacks that may be used in a LoWPAN network.

When more than one LoWPAN header is used in the same packet, they must appear in the following order:

1. Mesh addressing header
2. Broadcast header
3. Fragmentation header

All protocol datagrams (e.g., IPv6, compressed IPv6 headers, etc.) are preceded by one of the valid LoWPAN-encapsulation headers, examples of which are given

```
A LoWPAN-encapsulated IPv6 datagram

+---------------+--------------+---------+
| IPv6 Dispatch | IPv6 Header  | Payload |
+---------------+--------------+---------+


A LoWPAN-encapsulated LOWPAN_HC1 compressed IPv6 datagram

+--------------+-------------+---------+
| HC1 Dispatch | HC1 Header  | Payload |
+--------------+-------------+---------+
```

```
A LoWPAN-encapsulated LOWPAN_HC1 compressed IPv6 datagram that requires mesh
                                 addressing

+-----------+--------------+---------------+-------------+---------+
| Mesh Type | Mesh Header  | HC1 Dispatch  | HC1 Header  | Payload |
+-----------+--------------+---------------+-------------+---------+
```

```
A LoWPAN-encapsulated LOWPAN_HC1 compressed IPv6 datagram that requires
                              fragmentation

+-----------+--------------+---------------+-------------+---------+
| Frag Type | Frag Header  | HC1 Dispatch  | HC1 Header  | Payload |
+-----------+--------------+---------------+-------------+---------+
```

```
A LoWPAN-encapsulated LOWPAN_HC1 compressed IPv6 datagram that requires both
                     mesh addressing and fragmentation

+-------+-------+-------+-------+---------+---------+---------+
| M Typ | M Hdr | F Typ | F Hdr | HC1 Dsp | HC1 Hdr | Payload |
+-------+-------+-------+-------+---------+---------+---------+
```

```
A LoWPAN-encapsulated LOWPAN_HC1 compressed IPv6 datagram that requires both
mesh addressing and a broadcast header to support mesh broadcast/multicast:

+-------+-------+-------+-------+---------+---------+---------+
| M Typ | M Hdr | B Dsp | B Hdr | HC1 Dsp | HC1 Hdr | Payload |
+-------+-------+-------+-------+---------+---------+---------+
```

FIGURE 9.1   Typical header stacks that may be used in a LoWPAN network.

above. This allows uniform software treatment of datagrams without regard to the mode of their transmission.

The definition of LoWPAN headers, other than mesh addressing and fragmentation, consists of the dispatch value, the definition of the header fields that follow, and their ordering constraints relative to all other headers. Although the header stack structure provides a mechanism to address future demands on the LoWPAN adaptation layer, it is not intended to provide general-purpose extensibility.

Refer to the RFC 4944 as well as to the other RFCs and drafts identified in Table 9.1 for an extensive discussion of the 6LoWPAN technology.

REFERENCES

1. Kushalnagar N, Montenegro G, Schumacher C. RFC 4919: IPv6 over Low-Power Wireless Personal Area Networks (6LoWPANs): Overview, Assumptions, Problem Statement, and Goals. IETF, August 2007.

2. Mulligan G. IPv6 over Low power WPAN (6LoWPAN). Description of Working Group, IETF, 2012, http://datatracker.ietf.org/wg/6lowpan/charter/, http://www.ietf.org/mail-archive/web/6lowpan/.

3. Montenegro G, Kushalnagar N, Hui J, Culler, D. Transmission of IPv6 Packets over IEEE 802.15.4 Networks, RFC 4944, Updated by RFC 6282, RFC 6775 (was draft-ietf-6LoWPAN-format), September 2007.

GLOSSARY

3GPP (Third-Generation Partnership Project) The Third-Generation Partnership Project unites (six) telecommunications standards bodies, known as "organizational partners," and provides their members with a stable environment to produce the Reports and Specifications that define 3GPP technologies. Wireless technologies are constantly evolving through—what have become known as—generations of commercial cellular/mobile systems. 3GPP was originally the standards partnership evolving global system for mobile (GSM) systems toward the third generation. However, since the completion of the first LTE and the evolved packet core specifications, 3GPP has become the focal point for mobile systems beyond 3G. From 3GPP Release 10 onward, 3GPP is compliant with the latest ITU-R requirements for IMT-advanced "Systems beyond 3G." The standard now allows for operation at peak speeds of 100 Mbps for high-mobility and 1 Gbps for low-mobility communication.

    The original scope of 3GPP was to produce Technical Specifications and Technical Reports for a 3G Mobile System based on evolved GSM core networks and the radio access technologies that they support (i.e., Universal Terrestrial Radio Access [UTRA] both frequency division duplex [FDD] and time division duplex [TDD] modes). The scope was subsequently amended to include the maintenance and development of the GSM communication Technical Specifications and

Building the Internet of Things with IPv6 and MIPv6: The Evolving World of M2M Communications,
First Edition. Daniel Minoli.
© 2013 John Wiley & Sons, Inc. Published 2013 by John Wiley & Sons, Inc.

Technical Reports including evolved radio access technologies (e.g., general packet radio service [GPRS] and enhanced data rates for GSM evolution [EDGE]) (1). The term "3GPP specification" covers all GSM (including GPRS and EDGE), W-CDMA, and LTE (including LTE-advanced) specifications. The following terms are also used to describe networks using the 3G specifications: UTRAN, universal mobile telecommunications system (UMTS) (in Europe), and FOMA (in Japan).

3GPP2 (Third-Generation Partnership Project 2) The Third-Generation Partnership Project 2 is a collaborative third-generation (3G) telecommunications specifications-setting project comprising North American and Asian interests developing global specifications for ANSI/TIA/EIA-41 cellular radiotelecommunication intersystem operations network evolution to 3G and global specifications for the radio transmission technologies (RTTs) supported by ANSI/TIA/EIA-41. 3GPP2 was born out of the International Telecommunication Union's (ITU) International Mobile Telecommunications "IMT-2000" initiative, covering high-speed, broadband, and internet protocol (IP)-based mobile systems featuring network-to-network interconnection, feature/service transparency, global roaming, and seamless services independent of location. IMT-2000 is intended to bring high-quality mobile multimedia telecommunications to a worldwide mass market by achieving the goals of increasing the speed and ease of wireless communications, responding to the problems faced by the increased demand to pass data via telecommunications, and providing "anytime, anywhere" services (2). 3GPP2 provides globally applicable Technical Specifications for a 3G mobile system based on the evolving ANSI-41 core network and the relevant radio access technologies to be transposed by standardization bodies (organizational partners) into appropriate deliverables (e.g., standards).

6LoWPAN: IPv6 Over Low-Power Area Networks (IEEE 802.15.4) 6LoWPAN is now a widely accepted approach to run IP on 802.15.4 based on RFC 4944 (September 2007.) It is supported in TinyOS, Contiki, and in standards such as ISA100, ZigBee Smart Energy (SE) 2.0. RFC 4944 makes 802.15.4 look like an IPv6 link. It provides basic encapsulation and efficient representation of packets $< \sim100$ bytes. It addresses topics such as (3):

- Fragmentation (how to map 1280 byte MTU to packets 128 bytes or less);
- First approach to stateless header compression;
- Datagram tag/datagram offset;
- Mesh forwarding;
- Identify originator/final destination;
- Minimal use of complex MAC (media access control) layer concepts.

6over4 An IPv6 transition technology that provides IPv6 unicast and multicast connectivity through an IPv4 infrastructure with multicast support, using the IPv4 network as a logical multicast link.

6over4 Link-Local Address An IPv6 address of the form FE80::WWXX:YYZZ, where WWXX:YYZZ is the hexadecimal representation of w.x.y.z, a public or private IPv4 address assigned to the 6over4 device interface.

6over4 Unicast Address An IPv6 address of the form 64-bit prefix:0:0:WWXX: YYZZ, where WWXX:YYZZ is the hexadecimal representation of w.x.y.z, a public or private IPv4 address assigned to the 6over4 device interface.

6to4 An IPv6 transition technology that provides unicast connectivity between IPv6 networks and devices through an IPv4 infrastructure. 6to4 uses a public IPv4 address to build a global IPv6 prefix.

6to4 Address A global IPv6 address of the form 2002:WWXX:YYZZ: SLA_ID:interface ID, where WWXX:YYZZ is the hexadecimal representation of w.x.y.z, a public IPv4 address assigned to a 6to4 router's IPv4 interface and SLA_ID is the site-level aggregation identifier (SLA ID). The address space 2002::/16 is assigned to 6to4 addresses.

6to4 Host An IPv6 device that is configured with at least one 6to4 address (a global address with a 2002::/16 prefix). 6to4 devices do not require manual configuration and they create 6to4 addresses by means of standard autoconfiguration mechanisms.

6to4 Relay Router An IPv6/IPv4 router that forwards traffic between 6to4 routers and IPv6 Internet devices.

6to4 Router A router that participates in the 6to4 transition technology, providing unicast connectivity between IPv6 networks and devices through an IPv4 infrastructure.

Actuator An actuator is a mechanized device of various sizes (from ultra-small to very large) that accomplishes a specified physical action, for example controlling a mechanism or system, opening or closing a valve, starting some kind or rotary or linear motion, and initiating physical locomotion. It is the mechanism by which an entity acts upon an environment. The actuator embodies a source of energy, such as an electric current (battery, solar, motion), a hydraulic fluid pressure, or a pneumatic pressure; the device converts that energy into some kind of action or motion upon external command.

Address In this context a network-layer identifier assigned to an interface or set of interfaces that can be used as source or destination field in IP datagrams. An IP layer identifier for an interface or a set of interfaces.

The IPv6 128-bit address is divided along 16-bit boundaries. Each 16-bit block is then converted to a 4-digit hexadecimal number, separated by colons. The resulting representation is called colon-hexadecimal. This is in contrast to the 32-bit IPv4 address represented in dotted-decimal format, divided along 8-bit boundaries, and then converted to its decimal equivalent, separated by periods (4).

The following example shows a 128-bit IPv6 address in binary form:

0010000111011010000000001101001100000000000000000010111100111011
000000101 010101000000000111111111111111000101000100111000101 1010

The following example shows this same address divided along 16-bit boundaries:

0010000111011010   0000000011010011   0000000000000000
0010111100111011   0000001010101010   0000000011111111
1111111000101000   1001110001011010

The following example shows each 16-bit block in the address converted to hexadecimal and delimited with colons.

21DA:00D3:0000:2F3B:02AA:00FF:FE28:9C5A

IPv6 representation can be further simplified by removing the leading zeros within each 16-bit block. However, each block must have at least a single digit. The following example shows the address without the leading zeros:

21DA:D3:0:2F3B:2AA:FF:FE28:9C5A

Address Autoconfiguration The automatic configuration process for IPv6 addresses on an interface; specifically, the process for configuring IP addresses for interfaces in the absence of a stateful address configuration server, such as dynamic host configuration protocol version 6 (DHCPv6).

Address Maximum Valid Time Time period during which a unicast address, obtained by means of stateless autoconfiguration mechanism, is valid.

Address Resolution Procedure used by a node for determining the link-layer address of other nodes on a link. In an IPv6 context, the process by which a node resolves a neighboring node's IPv6 address to its link-layer address. In IPv4, the procedure is accomplished via the ARP protocol. In IPv6, the procedure is accomplished via neighbor advertisement and neighbor solicitation ICMPv6 messages.

Advanced Encryption Standard (AES) Cryptographic algorithm; National Institute of Standards and Technology (NIST)-approved standard. It was chosen by NIST because it is considered to be both faster and smaller than its competitors (5).

Advanced Meter Infrastructure (AMI) system An infrastructure that contains meters capable of two-way communications with a centralized grid control system. These are meters that can receive signals, including the cost of electricity and status of the grid, track electricity usage on a short-term basis, and automatically report the meter readings back to the utility (6).

Aggregatable Global Unicast Address Also known as global addresses, these addresses are identified by means of the 3-bit format prefix 001 (2000::/3). IPv6 global addresses are equivalent to IPv4 public addresses and they are routable in the IPv6 Internet.

Air Interface In radio-frequency identification (RFID) environments, the complete communication link between an interrogator and a tag including the physical layer, collision arbitration algorithm, command and response structure, and data-coding methodolog (7).

Ambient Intelligence Ambient intelligence is a vision where environment becomes smart, friendly, context aware, and responsive to any type of human needs. In such a world, computing and networking technology coexist with people in a ubiquitous, friendly, and pervasive way. Numerous miniature and interconnected smart devices create a new intelligence and interact with each other seamlessly. For health care, this translates into proliferation of remote monitoring and telemedicine (8).

AMI (Advanced Metering Infrastructure) The electric information service infrastructure between the end-user or end device and the electric company. A system for implementing smart grid (SG) and a principal means of realizing demand response. AMI has several methods to connect from end device to applications of utility, and there are many standards communication protocols. To communicate between physical service layers, some combinations and transformations of the protocols are required. AMI environment is very complex because it should be considered the area of home area network (HAN) and demand respond application (9).

AMR Automated meter reader

ANT™/ANT+™ ANT is a low-power proprietary wireless technology introduced in 2004 by the sensor company Dynastream. The system operates in the 2.4 GHz band. ANT devices can operate for years on a coin cell. ANT's goal is to allow sports and fitness sensors to communicate with a display unit. ANT+ extends the ANT protocol and makes the devices interoperable in a managed network. ANT+ recently introduced a new certification process as a prerequisite for using ANT+ branding (10).

Anycast Address A unicast address that is assigned to several interfaces and is used for the delivery of IP datagrams to one of the several interfaces. With an appropriate route, datagrams addressed to an anycast address will be delivered to a single interface—the nearest one.

Asymmetric Encryption Type of encryption in which encryption keys are different from decryption keys, and one key is computationally difficult to determine from the other. Uses an asymmetric algorithm (5).

Attempt Address Unicast address where uniqueness is no longer checked.

Authentication The process of proving the genuineness of an entity (such as a smart card) by means of a cryptographic procedure. Authentication entails using a fixed procedure to determine whether someone is actually the person he or she claims to be (5).

Authentication, Authorization, and Accounting (AAA) Authentication refers to the confirmation that a user who is requesting services is a valid user of the network services requested. Authorization refers to the granting of specific types of service (including "no service") to a user, based on their authentication, what services they are requesting, and the current system state. Accounting refers to the tracking of the consumption of network resources by users. This information may be used for management, planning, billing, or other purposes (11).

Authorization An authorization provides access (or legal power) to some protected service. In a CA system, the authorization gives access to encrypted services (channels, movies, and so on) (5).

Automatic IPv6 Tunnel Automatic creation of tunnels, generally through the use of various IPv6 address formats that contain the IPv4 tunnel endpoints.

Autonomous System (AS) A network domain that belongs to the same administrative authority.

Bandwidth The amount of information that can be sent through a connection. In digital settings, it is measured in bits-per-second. Full-motion full-screen video requires 2.5–12 Mbps depending on compression (e.g., MPEG-2, MPEG-4) and format (SD or HD).

Bluetooth Bluetooth is a personal area network (PAN) technology based on IEEE 802.15.1. It is a specification for short-range wireless connectivity for portable personal devices, initially developed by Ericsson. The Bluetooth special interest group (SIG) made their specifications publicly available in the late 1990s; soon thereafter the IEEE 802.15 group has took the Bluetooth work developed a vendor-independent standard. The sublayers of IEEE 802.15 are: (i) RF layer, (ii) baseband layer, (iii) the link manager, and (iv) the logical link control and adaptation protocol (L2CAP). Bluetooth has evolved through four versions; all versions of the Bluetooth standards maintain downward compatibility. Bluetooth low energy (BLE) is a subset to Bluetooth v4.0, with an entirely new protocol stack for rapid build-up of simple links. BLE is an alternative to the "power management" features that were introduced in Bluetooth v1.0 to v3.0 as part of the standard Bluetooth protocols.

The functionality is as follows:

- RF layer: The air interface is based on antenna power range starting from 0 dBm up to 20 dBm, 2.4 GHz band, and the link range from 0.1 to 10 m.
- Baseband layer: The baseband layer establishes the Bluetooth *piconet*. The piconet is formed when two Bluetooth devices connect. In a piconet, one device acts as the master and the other devices act as slaves.
- Link manager: The link manager establishes the link between Bluetooth devices. Additional functions include security, negotiation of baseband packet sizes, power mode and duty cycle control of the Bluetooth device, and the connection states of a Bluetooth device in a piconet.
- Logical link control and adaptation protocol (L2CAP): This sublayer provides the upper-layer protocols with connectionless and connection-oriented services. The services provided by this layer include protocol multiplexing capability, segmentation and reassembly of packets, and group abstractions.

(Bluetooth is a trademark of the Bluetooth Alliance, a commercial organization that certifies the interoperability of specific devices designed to the respective IEEE standard.)

Broadcasting Satellite Service (BSS) A satellite service that (for ITU Region 2 segments covering the majority of the Americas) operates at 17.3–17.8 GHz for the uplink and 12.2 to 12.7 GHz for the downlink. High-power geostationary satellites are utilized.

Buffering The temporary storing data before playing it back. A buffer is a temporary holding area in memory for data; buffers can be on the input or output side of a data-carrying link.

Certificate A digital certificate consists of three things, as follows: (1) The public-key portion of the certificate holder's public and private key pair. (2) Information that identifies the holder of the certificate (the owner of the corresponding private key). (3) The digital signature of a trusted entity attesting to the validity of the certificate (i.e., that the key and the certificate information truly go together) (5).

Circular Orbit (Satellite) A satellite orbit where the distance between the center of mass of the satellite and of the earth is constant.

Clarke Belt (Satellite) The circular orbit (geostationary orbit [GEO]) at approximately 35,786 km above the equator, where the satellites travel at the same speed as the earth's rotation and thus appear to be stationary to an observer on earth (named after Arthur C. Clarke who was the first to describe the concept of geostationary communication satellites).

Client The originating endpoint of a request; the destination endpoint of a response.

Cloud Computing The latest term to describe a grid/utility computing service. Such service is provided in the network. From the perspective of the user, the service is virtualized. In turn, the service provider will most likely use virtualization technologies (virtualized computing, virtualized storage, etc.) to provide the service to the user.

Codec (COmpressor/DECompressor)—The system (hardware, software, or combination of both) used to compress/decompress an audio and/or video file for storage or transmission. Codecs convert data between uncompressed and compressed formats, thereby reducing the bandwidth a clip consumes.

Collocated Satellites Two or more satellites occupying approximately the same geostationary orbital position such that the angular separation between them is effectively zero when viewed from the ground. To a small receiving antenna, the satellites appear to be exactly collocated; in reality, the satellites are kept several kilometers apart in space to avoid collisions. Different operating frequencies and/or polarizations are used.

Colon Hexadecimal Notation The notation used to represent IPv6 addresses. The 128-bit address is divided into eight blocks of 16 bits. Each block is represented as a hexadecimal number and is separated from the next block by means of a colon (:). Inside each block, left zeros placed are removed. An example of an IPv6 unicast address represented in hexadecimal notation is 3FFE:FFFF:2A1D:48C:2AA:3CFF:FE21:81F9.

Compatibility Addresses IPv6 addresses used when IPv6 traffic is sent through an IPv4 infrastructure. Some examples are IPv4 compatible addresses, 6to4 addresses, and ISATAP addresses.

Compressing Zeros Some IPv6 addresses expressed in colon-hexadecimal contain long sequences of zeros. A contiguous sequence of 16-bit blocks set to 0 in the colon-hexadecimal format can be compressed to :: (known as double-colon). The following shows examples of compressing zeros (4):

The link-local address of FE80:0:0:0:2AA:FF:FE9A:4CA2 can be compressed to FE80::2AA:FF:FE9A:4CA2.

The multicast address of FF02:0:0:0:0:0:0:2 can be compressed to FF02::2.

Zero compression can only be used to compress a single contiguous series of 16-bit blocks expressed in colon-hexadecimal notation.

Confidentiality The property that information is not made available or disclosed to unauthorized individuals, entities, or processes.

Constrained Application Protocol (CoAP) CoAP is a simple application layer protocol targeted to simple electronics devices (e.g., IoT/M2M things) to allow them to communicate interactively over the Internet. CoAP is designed for low-power sensors and for actuators that need to be controlled or monitored remotely, using IP/Internet networks.

Continuous Wave In RFID environments, typically a sinusoid at a given frequency, but more generally any interrogator waveform suitable for powering a passive tag without amplitude and/or phase modulation of sufficient magnitude to be interpreted by a tag as transmitted data (7).

Correspondent Node Refers to a node that is communicating with a node that is using mobile IP.

Cover-coding In RFID environments, a method by which an interrogator obscures information that it is transmitting to a tag. To cover-code data or a password, an interrogator first requests a random number from the tag. The interrogator then performs a bit-wise EXOR of the data or password with this random number and transmits the cover-coded (also called ciphertext) string to the tag. The tag uncovers the data or password by performing a bit-wise EXOR of the received cover-coded string with the original random number (7).

DASH7 A long range low-power wireless networking technology, with the following features:

- Range: dynamically adjustable from 10 m to 10 km;
- Power: <1 milliwatt power draw;
- Data rate: dynamically adjustable from 28 Kbps to 200 Kbps;
- Frequency: 433.92 MHz (available worldwide);
- Signal propagation: penetrates walls, concrete, water;
- Real-time locating precision: within 4 m;
- Latency: configurable, but worst case is less than 2 s;
- P2P messaging;
- IPv6 support;
- Security:128-bit AES, public key; and
- Standard: ISO/IEC 18000-7; advanced by the DASH7 Alliance.

DASH7 Alliance The DASH7 Alliance was formed to advance the use of DASH7 wireless data technology by developing extensions to the ISO 18000-7 standard, ensuring interoperability among devices, and educating the market about DASH7 technology. Formed in 2009, the Alliance had more than 20 members at press time. Manufacturers, systems integrators, developers, regulators, academia, and end-users all work together to promote the use of DASH7 technology in a wide array of industries and applications.

Data Encryption Standard (DES) A 64-bit block cipher, symmetric algorithm also known as data encryption algorithm (DEA) by ANSI and DEA-1 by ISO. Widely used for over two decades, adopted in 1976 as FIPS 46 (5).

Data Origin Authentication The corroboration that the source of data received is as claimed.

Datagram Another name for an IP-level packet.

Decoding The decompression of an encoded file for playback or use.

Decoding Time Stamp (DTS) Time stamps are inserted close to the material to which they refer (normally in the PES packet header). They indicate the exact moment where a video frame or an audio frame has to be decoded or presented to the user respectively. These rely on reference time stamps for operation (12).

Default Route The route with a ::/0 prefix. The default route is the route used to obtain the next destination address when there are no other matching routes.

Default Routers List A list of routers that can be used as a default router. The list is populated based on router advertisement messages received that have a non-null router lifetime.

Delay-Tolerant Network (DTN) An architecture being developed by the Delay-Tolerant Networking Research Group (DTNRG), which is a research group chartered as part of the Internet Research Task Force (IRTF). Members of DTNRG are concerned with how to address the architectural and protocol design principles arising from the need to provide interoperable communications with and among extreme and performance-challenged environments where continuous end-to-end connectivity cannot be assumed. Stated another way, one is concerned with interconnecting highly heterogeneous networks together even if end-to-end connectivity may never be available. Examples of such environments include space-craft, military/tactical, some forms of disaster response, underwater, and some forms of ad-hoc sensor/actuator networks. It may also include Internet connectivity in places where performance may suffer such as developing parts of the world (13). This work is also related to DARPA's disruption tolerant networking program.

Delay-tolerant networks make use of store-and-forward techniques within the network in order to compensate for intermittent link connectivity. In the DTN, the fundamental concept is an architecture based on Internet-independent middleware where protocols at all layers are used that best suit the operation within each environment, with a new overlay network protocol (bundle protocol) inserted between the applications and the locally optimized communications stacks. Many applications can benefit from the reliable delivery of messages in a disconnected network. The Internet, in contrast, is a connected network where IPs, most notably transmission control protocol/IP (TCP/IP), are dependent upon (low) latencies of approximately milliseconds. This low latency, coupled with low bit error rates (BERs), allows TCP to reliably transmit and receive acknowledgements for messages traversing the terrestrial Internet. One of the best examples of high latency, high BER links, with intermittent connectivity is that of space communications. One-way trip times, at the speed of light, from the Earth to the moon incur a delay of 1.7 s, while one-way trip times to Mars incur a minimum delay of 8 min. Military applications in the DTN arena are substantial, allowing the retrieval of critical information in mobile battlefield scenarios using only intermittently connected network communications (14).

Denial of Service (DoS) The prevention of authorized access to resources or the delaying of time-critical operations.

Device Lower Layer (DLL) Component of the lower layer in an M2M device.

Digital Signature Data appended to, or a cryptographic transformation of a data unit that allows a recipient of the data unit to prove the source and integrity of the data unit and protect against forgery for example, by the recipient.

Digital Subscriber Line (DSL) A 1990s technology that exploits unused frequencies on copper telephone lines to transmit traffic typically at multi-megabit speeds. DSL can allow voice and high-speed data to be sent simultaneously over the same line. Because the service is "always available," end-users do not need to dial in or wait for call setup. Asymmetrical variations include ADSL, G.lite ADSL (or simply G.lite), VDSL (ITU-T G.993.1), and VDSL2 (ITU-T G.993.2). The standard forms of ADSL (ITU G.992.3, G.992.5, and ANSI T1.413—Issue 2) are all built upon the same technical foundation, discrete multitone (DMT). The suite of ADSL standards facilitates interoperability between all standard forms of ADSL (15).

Digital Subscriber Line Access Multiplexer (DSLAM) Telephone carrier equipment typically residing at the Central Office that terminates multiple DSL lines (usually 96, 192, or 384) and multiplexes the combined output to an ATM, MPLS, or IP uplink. The uplink is typically an OC-3 (155 Mbps) or an OC-12 (622 Mbps).

Distance Vector Routing Protocol A routing protocol in which a router periodically informs its neighbors of topology changes. This is in contrast to link state routing protocols, which require a router to inform all the nodes in a network of topology changes (16).

DNP3 DNP3 is a protocol for transmission of point-to-point data using serial communications. It has been used primarily by utilities, but can also be used in other areas. The DNP3 is specifically developed for interdevice communication involving SCADA RTUs. It is based on the three-layer model contained in the IEC 60870-5 standards.

Domain Name System (DNS) A hierarchical storage system and its associated protocol to store and retrieve information about names and IP addresses.

Double Colon Notation used in compressing continuous series of 0 blocks in IPv6 addresses. For example, the FF02:0:0:0:0:0:0:2 multicast address is expressed as FF02::2.

Dual Stack Architecture A node architecture in which two complete protocols stack implementations exist, one for IPv4 and one for IPv6, each with its own implementation of the transport layer (TCP and UDP).

Dynamic Host Configuration Protocol (DHCP) A configuration protocol that provides IP addresses and other configuration parameters when connected to an IP network.

Dynamic Host Registration A mechanism that informs the network that a host (receiver) is a member of a particular group (otherwise, the network would have to flood rather than multicast the transmissions for each group.) For IP networks, the Internet Group Multicast Protocol (IGMP) serves this purpose.

EDGE (Enhanced Data Rates for Global Evolution) An enhancement of the GSM™ radio access technology to provide faster bit rates for data applications, both circuit and packet switched. As an enhancement of the existing GSM physical layer, EDGE is realized via modifications of the existing layer 1 specifications rather than by separate, stand-alone specifications. Other than providing improved data rates, EDGE is transparent to the service offering at the upper layers, but is an enabler for high-speed circuit switched data (HSCSD) and enhanced GPRS (EGPRS). GPRS can offer a data rate of 115 Kbps, whereas EDGE can increase this to 384 Kbps. This is comparable with the rate for early implementations of wideband code division multiple access (W-CDMA), leading some parties to consider EDGE as a 3G technology rather than 2G (a capability of 384 Kbps allows EDGE systems to meet the ITU's IMT-2000 requirements). EDGE is generally viewed as a bridge between the two generations: a sort of 2.5G (17).

eHealth A term for healthcare practice supported by electronic processes and communication.

Electronic Product Code (EPC) A unique identifier for a physical object, unit load, location, or other identifiable entity playing a role in business operations. EPCs are assigned the following rules designed to ensure uniqueness despite decentralized administration of code space and to accommodate legacy coding schemes in common use. EPCs have multiple representations, including binary forms suitable for use on RFID tags and text forms suitable for data exchange among enterprise information systems.

Encapsulating Security Payload An IPv6 extension header that provides data source authentication, data integrity, and confidentiality.

Encapsulator A network device that receives PDUs (also known as SNDUs) (Ethernet frames or IP datagrams) and formats these for output as a transport stream of TS packets (18).

Encoder A device that converts an audio or video signal to a specific streaming format, for example, MPEG-4 (or MPEG-2). The conversion typically includes compression and generation on an IP packet.

Encoding Converting a file into a compressed format.

Encryption The process of making a message unintelligible for all who do not have the proper key.

Entitlement Access criteria authorizations.

EPCglobal Architecture Framework A collection of interrelated standards ("EPC-global Standards"), together with services operated by EPCglobal, its delegates, and others ("EPC Network Services"), all in service of a common goal of enhancing business flows and computer applications through the use of EPCs.

ESN Electronic serial number.

Ethernet Over an MPLS (EoMPLS) Transport of native Ethernet over an MPLS pseudowire.

ETSI Machine-to-Machine (M2M) Machine-to-machine (M2M) communications is the communication between two or more entities that do not necessarily need any direct human intervention. M2M services intend to automate decision and communication processes. Defined in ETSI TS 102 689 V1.1.1 (2010-08) and ETSI TS 102 690 V1.1.1 (2011-10) (and elsewhere). Basic applications include, but are not limited to, smart meters, eHealth, track and trace, monitoring, transaction, control, home automation, city automation, connected consumers, and automotive (19, 20).

EUI-64 Address 64-bit link-layer address that is used as the basis to generate interface identifiers in IPv6.

eUICC A certified tamper-resistant hardware component, performing the role of a traditional UICC (universal integrated circuit card), which may be soldered into mobile devices, to run the secure network access application (s) and enable the secure changing of subscription identity and other subscription data.

European Telecommunications Standards Institute (ETSI) An independent, non-profit European-focused organization whose mission is to produce telecommunications standards.

Extended Access Barring (EAB) 3GPP-defined capability that extends legacy access control barring (ACB), which can bar all User Equipment (UEs) in a cell.

Extended Unique Identifier (EUI) Link-layer address defined by the Institute of Electrical and Electronic Engineers (IEEE).

Extension Headers Headers placed between the IPv6 header and higher-level protocols headers to provide additional functionalities to IPv6.

Fibre Channel (FC) The dominant storage networking protocol used in the enterprise data center and for (multimedia) content storage. A high-speed storage/networking interface that offers a high performance, large transfer capacity, long cabling distance, system configuration flexibility and scalability, and simplified cabling. The current operating speed is 8 Gbps; the expectation is that a 16 Gbps rate will be achievable by mid-decade (by comparison, 10 Gbps Ethernet is expected to move up to a 40 Gbps or even 100 Gbps rates over the same period).

File Formats Container file formats for various platforms. The more common formats include:

avi (audio video interleave)—A multimedia container file format developed by Microsoft to allow synchronous audio-with-video playback.

.flv—Flash video file format; used to deliver video over the Internet.

.mov—A video publishing file format developed by Apple for use with their QuickTime video players.

.wmv (windows media video)—An audio and video file encoded for use with Windows media player.

Fixed Satellite Service (FSS) A satellite service that (for ITU Region 2 segments covering the majority of the Americas) operates at 14.0–14.5 GHz for the uplink and 11.7–12.2 GHz the downlink. Geostationary satellites are utilized. The service is utilized by television stations/broadcast networks/cable TV systems to distribute signals to affiliates across a wide geographic region, as well as for other traditional telecommunications (voice and data communications) applications. Typical video applications include content distribution from a content-generation center (e.g., studios) to local cable headends. FSS satellites have also been used for direct-to-home (DTH) applications, although Direct Broadcast Satellite (DBS) services at the ku-BSS frequencies (such as those used by DirecTV and Dish Network) are specifically intended for those applications. The term "fixed" is used to imply that the sending station is fixed and the receiving stations are generally (but not always) fixed. This is in contrast to the mobile satellite services (MSSs), which refer to communications satellites intended for use with mobile and portable wireless devices/telephones. MSS-supporting services can be delivered using GEO, medium earth orbit (MEO), or low earth orbit (LEO) satellites.

Flow A series of IP datagrams exchanged between a source and a destination.

Format Prefix Variable number of high-order bits of an IPv6 address that defines an IPv6 address type.

Forward Direction The dominant direction of data transfer over a network path. Data transfer in the forward direction is called "forward transfer." Packets traveling in the forward direction follow the forward path through the IP network (18).

Forward Error Correction (FEC) FEC is a family of well-known simplex error correction techniques that add "coding" bits to the information bits at the transmit end (encoder) that enables the decoder to determine which bits are in error and correct them (up to a limit); for example, R 4/5 FEC means 1 coding bit is added for every 4 information bits (thereby transmitting 5 bits); the more coding bits, the "stronger" the code (requires less transmit power or link quality to get the same performance), but more coding bits mean more bandwidth required. Because satellite transmission can attenuate the signal by up to 200 db, FEC is critical. High coding: R 1/2; low coding: R 7/8. Typical satellite FEC is either convolutional/viterbi with Reed–Solomon or Turbo coding. Typical Turbo codes provide about a 2 dB advantage over conventional codes. 'Viterbi' soft-decision decoding has been the norm (<4.4dB gain). "Turbo coding" has been advanced recently (<6.3dB gain). "Low Density Parity Check" (LDPC) is the newest algorithm (<7.8dB gain).

Fragment A portion of a message sent by a host in an IPv6 datagram. Fragments contain a fragmentation header to allow reassembly at the destination.

Fragmentation Process in which the source device divides a message into some number of smaller messages, termed fragments.

Fragmentation Header An IPv6 extension header that contains information that allows the receiving node to reassemble fragments into the original message.

Frame Rate The rate at which video frames are displayed. The frame rate for movies on film is 24 frames per second (24 fps). Standard NTSC video has a frame rate of 30 fps (actually 60 fields per second). The frame rate of a progressive-scan video format is twice that of an interlaced-scan format. For example, interlaced formats like 480i and 1080i deliver 30 complete frames per second; progressive formats like 480p, 720p and 1080p provide 60 (21).

Full-Rate Asymmetrical DSL (ADSL) Access technology that offers differing upload and download speeds and can be configured to deliver up to six megabits of data per second (6000 Kbps) from the network to the customer that is up to 120 times faster than dialup service and 100 times faster than integrated services digital network (ISDN). ADSL enables voice and high-speed data to be sent simultaneously over the existing telephone line. This type of DSL is the most predominant in commercial use for business and residential customers around the world. Good for general Internet access and for applications where downstream speed is most important, such as video-on-demand. ITU-T Recommendation G.992.1 and ANSI Standard T1.413-1998 specify full-rate ADSL. ITU Recommendation G.992.3 specifies ADSL2 that provides advanced diagnostics, power-saving functions, PSD shaping, and slightly better performance than G.992.1. ITU Recommendation G.992.5 specifies ADSL2Plus that provides the benefits of ADSL2Plus twice the bandwidth so that bit rates as high as 20 Mbps downstream can be achieved on relatively short lines (15).

Fully Qualified Domain Name (FQDN) FQDN gives the full location of a resource within the whole DNS name space. When interpreting the FQDN, one starts at the root and then follows the sequence of domain labels from right to left, going top to bottom within the name space tree. An FQDN includes the top-level domain. For example, www.cnn.com is an FQDN. www is the host, cnn is the second-level domain, and com is the top-level domain. This is in contrast to a partially qualified domain name (PQDN), which does not give the full path to the domain. One can only use a PQDN within the context of a particular parent domain.

Future Network (FN) The ITU-T FN is a network that will be able to provide revolutionary services, capabilities, and facilities that are hard to support using existing network technologies. Also, it is expected that the FN will overcome the limitations of the current networks. The FN includes core technologies that are necessary for constructing future networking infrastructure and application service infrastructure. In 2009, ITU-TSG13 established "Focus Group on Future Networks (FG-FN)" to share the discussion on FNs and ensure global common understanding about FNs with collaboration and harmonization with relevant entities and activities. The FG successfully completed its work in 2010. The FG, by collaborating with worldwide FN communities (e.g., research institutes, forums, academia), aims to

- collect and identify visions of FNs, based on new technologies,
- assess the interactions between FNs and new services,
- familiarize ITU-T and standardization communities with emerging attributes of FNs, and
- encourage collaboration between ITU-T and FN communities.

G.lite ADSL (or Simply G.lite   A standard that was specifically developed to meet the plug-and-play requirements of the consumer market segment. G.lite is a medium bandwidth version of ADSL that allows Internet access at up to 30 times the speed of the fastest 56K analog modems—up to 1.5 Mbps downstream and up to 500 Kbps upstream. G.lite is an International Telecommunications Union (ITU) standard, globally standardized interoperable ADSL system per ITU G.992.2. G.lite has seen comparatively little use, but it did introduce the valuable concept of splitterless installation (15).

Gateway Lower Layer (GLL)   Component of the lower layer in an M2M gateway.

General Packet Radio Service (GPRS)   Packet-switched functionality for GSM, which is essentially circuit switched. GPRS is the essential enabler for always-on data connection for applications such as web browsing and push-to-talk over cellular. GPRS was introduced into the GSM specifications in Release 97, and usability was further approved in Releases 98 and 99. It offers faster data rates than plain GSM by aggregating several GSM time slots into a single bearer, potentially up to eight, giving a theoretical data rate of 171 Kbps. Most operators do not offer such high rates, because obviously if a slot is being used for a GPRS bearer, it is not available for other traffic. Also, not all mobiles are able to aggregate all combinations of slots. The "GPRS class number" indicates the maximum speed capability of a terminal, which might be typically 14 Kbps in the uplink direction and 40 kbit/s in the downlink, comparable with the rates offered by current wireline dial-up modems. Mobile terminals are further classified according to whether or not they can handle simultaneous GSM and GPRS connections: class A = both simultaneously, class B = GPRS connection interrupted during a GSM call, automatically resumed at end of call, class C = manual GSM/GPRS mode switching. Further data rate increases have been achieved with the introduction of EDGE (17).

Geostationary Orbit/Satellite   The orbit of a geosynchronous satellite whose orbit lies in the plane of the earth's equator. A satellite orbiting the earth at such speed that it permanently appears to remain stationary with respect to the earth's surface.

Geosynchronous Object   An object orbiting the earth at the earth's rotational speed and with the same direction of rotation. The object appears at the same position in the sky at a particular time each day, but will not appear stationary if it is not orbiting in the equatorial plane.

GLOB Addressing RFC 2770 recommended that the 233.0.0.0/8 address range be reserved for statically defined addresses by organizations that already have an AS number reserved. The AS number of the domain is embedded into the second and third octets of the 233.0.0.0/8 range. GLOP is a mechanism that allocates multicast addresses to ASs. (GLOP is neither an acronym nor an abbreviation.)

Global Address See aggregatable global unicast address.

GPRS (General Packet Radio Service) A mobile packet data service available to users of GSM. It provides data rates of up to 40–170 Kbps, depending upon device capabilities, network configurations, and system load.

Group-Based Machine-Type Communications (MTC) Feature A group-based MTC feature is an MTC feature that applies to an MTC group. This is a 3GPP concept (22).

Group Identifier Last 112 bits (for predefined multicast addresses) or last 32 bits (for new multicast addresses) of an IPv6 multicast address used to identify a multicast group (RFC2373).

GSM (Global System for Mobile Communications) GSM is a global cellular network standard, but used mostly outside the U.S.

GSM EDGE Radio Access Network (GERAN) GERAN is a radio access network architecture, based on GSM/EDGE radio access technologies. GERAN is the term given to the second-generation digital cellular GSM radio access technology, including its evolutions in the form of EDGE and, for most purposes, the GPRS. The GERAN is harmonized with the UMTS terrestrial radio access network (UTRAN) through a common connectivity to the UMTS core network making it possible to build a combined network for GSM/GPRS and UMTS. GERAN is also the name of the 3GPP™ Technical Specification Group responsible for its development. The Technical Specifications which together comprise a 3GPP system with a GERAN are listed in 3GPP TS 41.101.

HDSL (High Data Rate DSL) A DSL variety created in the late 1980s delivers symmetric service at speeds up to 2.3 Mbps in both directions. Available at 1.5 or 2.3 Mbps, this symmetric fixed rate application does not provide standard telephone service over the same line and is already standardized through ETSI and ITU. Seen as an economical replacement for T1 or E1, it uses one, two, or three twisted copper pairs (15).

HDSL2 (Second-Generation HDSL) A variant of DSL that delivers 1.5 Mbps service each way, supporting voice, data, and video using either ATM (asynchronous transfer mode), private-line service, or frame relay over a single copper pair. This ATIS standard (T1.418) for this symmetric service gives a fixed 1.5 Mbps rate both up and downstream. HDSL2 does not provide standard voice telephone service on the same wire pair. HSDL2 differs from HDSL in that HDSL2 uses one pair of wires to convey 1.5 Mbps, whereas ANSI HDSL uses two wire pairs (15).

HDSL4 A HDSL that is virtually the same as HDSL2 except it achieves about 30% greater distance than HDSL or HDSL2 by using two pairs of wire (thus, four conductors), whereas HDSL2 uses one pair of wires (15).

Hierarchical Storage Management (HSM) A storage system in which new, frequently used data is stored on the fastest, most accessible (and generally more expensive) media (e.g., RAID) and older, less frequently used data is stored on slower (less expensive) media (e.g., tape) (23).

Higher-Level Checksum A checksum based on the IPv6 pseudo-header, used in ICMPv6, TCP, and UDP.

Higher-Level Protocol Protocol that uses IPv6 as transport and is carried as a payload in IPv6, such as ICMPv6, TCP, and UDP.

Home Area Network (HAN) A local area network (LAN) applicable to a residential home. Can be wired or wireless.

Home Network (HN) A communication system designed for the residential environment, in which two or more devices exchange information.

Hop-By-Hop Option Header An IPv6 extension header that contains options that must be processed by all intermediate routers as well as final router.

Host Any node that is not a router.

Host-To-Host Tunnel An IPv6 over IPv4 tunnel where endpoints are hosts.

Host-To-Router Tunnel An IPv6 over IPv4 tunnel in which the tunnel begins at a host and ends at an IPv6/IPv4 router.

HTTP Streaming The default higher-layer protocol for streaming audio and video over the Internet. It involves the simultaneous download and viewing/listening of the file through HTTP (24).

Hypertext Transfer Protocol (HTTP) An application-level, stateless, object-oriented protocol for distributed, collaborative, hypermedia information systems.

ICC Terminal/integrated circuit card

ICMPv6 See Internet control message protocol for IPv6.

IEEE 802.11v 802.11v, wireless network management, is an extension of existing 802.11 Wi-Fi devices first proposed in 2004 to add some networking capabilities to Wi-Fi systems and to address power management issues. 802.11v automatically cutting power to the Wi-Fi chip when it is not being used. Specifically, it provides further extension to base 802.11 power saving, which allows for longer power-off times for 802.11 radios; it enables "wake on WLAN." The access point responds to address resolution protocol (ARP) requests to enable stations to power down for longer periods (25). As of press time, balloting on P802.11v D15.0 had closed; however, an additional recirculation ballot had taken place to address assigned number issues discovered subsequently in industry interoperability testing.

IEEE 802.15.4 IEEE standard for local and metropolitan area networks—Part 15.4: Low-Rate Wireless Personal Area Networks (LR-WPANs). IEEE 802.15.4-conformant devices support a wide range of industrial and commercial applications. The amended MAC sublayer facilitates industrial applications such as process control and factory automation in addition to the MAC behaviors that support the Chinese wireless personal area network (CWPAN) standard.

IEEE 802.15.4j (TG4j) Medical Body Area Networks The purpose of Task Group 4j (TG4j) is to create an amendment to 802.15.4, that defines a physical layer for IEEE 802.15.4 in the 2360 to 2400 MHz band and complies with Federal Communications Commission (FCC) MBAN rules. The amendment may also define modifications to the MAC needed to support this new physical layer. This amendment allows 802.15.4- and MAC-defined changes to be used in the MBAN band (26).

IEEE 802.1ad IEEE 802.1ad (provider bridges) is an amendment to IEEE standard IEEE 802.1Q-1998, intended to develop an architecture and bridge protocols to provide separate instances of the MAC services to multiple independent users of a bridged LAN in a manner that does not require cooperation among the users and requires a minimum of cooperation between the users and the provider of the MAC service. This is a standard version of the Q-in-Q protocol used by Cisco for carrier Ethernet service (11).

IEEE 802.1ah Provider backbone bridges (PBBs) is being formalized by IEEE 802.1ah standards. It allows for layering the Ethernet network into customer and provider domains with complete isolation among their MAC addresses. It defines a B-DA and B-SA to indicate the backbone source and destination address. It also defines B-VID (backbone Virtual LAN (VLAN) ID) and I-SID (service instance VLAN ID).

IEEE 802.1q IEEE 802.1Q was a project in the IEEE 802 standards process to develop a mechanism to allow multiple bridged networks to transparently share the same physical network link without leakage of information between networks (i.e., trunking). IEEE 802.1Q is also the name of the standard issued by this process, and in common usage the name of the encapsulation protocol used to implement this mechanism over Ethernet networks. IEEE 802.1Q also defines the meaning of a virtual LAN or VLAN with respect to the specific conceptual model underpinning bridging at the MAC layer and to the IEEE 802.1D-spanning tree protocol. This protocol allows for individual VLANs to communicate with one another with the use of a layer 3 (network) router (11).

IETF-Constrained RESTful Environments (CoRE) Working Group IETF Working Group that is working on standardization for constrained networks, such as, but not limited to, low-power and lossy networks (LLNs). LLN is class of networks in which both the routers and their interconnects are constrained. LLN routers typically operate with constraints on processing power, memory, and energy (battery power).

IMEI International mobile equipment identity.

IMEISV International mobile equipment identity and software version.

Inclination (Satellite) The angle between the plane of the orbit of a satellite and the earth's equatorial plane. An orbit of a perfectly geostationary satellite has an inclination of 0.

Inclined Orbit An orbit that approximates the GEO but whose plane is tilted slightly with respect to the equatorial plane. The satellite appears to move about its nominal position in a daily "figure-of-eight" motion when viewed from the ground.

Spacecrafts (satellites) are often allowed to drift into an inclined orbit near the end of their nominal lifetime in order to conserve on-board fuel, which would otherwise be used to correct this natural drift caused by the gravitational pull of the sun and moon. North–South maneuvers are not conducted, allowing the orbit to become highly inclined.

Incoming Interface (iif) In protocol-independent multicast-sparse mode (PIM-SM), the iif of a multicast route entry indicates the interface from which multicast data packets are accepted for forwarding. The iif is initialized when the entry is created (27).

Industrial, Scientific, and Medical (ISM) Radio Bands The ISM radio bands are radio bands allocated internationally for the said purpose. The ISM bands are defined by the ITU-R in 5.138, 5.150, and 5.280 of the radio regulations. In the United States, uses of the ISM bands are governed by Part 15 and Part 18 of the FCC rules. There are a number of ISM bands, but the most well known is the one covering the 2400–2500 MHz region (some other bands include allocations a 6.7 MHz, 13.5 MHz, 26.9 MHz, 40.6 MHz, 433 MHz, 902 MHz, and 5725 MHz.)

Infrared Data Association (IrDA®) IrDA is an SIG consisting of about 40 members at press time. The SIG is pursuing a 1 Gbps connectivity link; however, this link only operates over a distance of less than 10 cm. One of the challenges with infrared (IR) signaling is its requirement for line-of-sight (LOS) requirement. Additionally, IrDA is also not very power efficient (power per bit) when compared with radio technologies.

Integrated Services Digital Network DSL (ISDL) A form of DSL that supports symmetric data rates of up to 144 Kbps using existing phone lines. It is unique in that it has the ability to deliver services through a DLC (digital loop carrier: a remote device often placed in newer neighborhoods to simplify the distribution of cable and wiring from the phone company). While DLCs provide a means of simplifying the delivery of traditional voice services to newer neighborhoods, they also provide a unique challenge in delivering DSL into those same neighborhoods. IDSL addresses this market along with ADSL and G.lite as they are implemented directly into those DLCs. IDSL differs from its relative ISDN in that it is an "always-available" service, but capable of using the same terminal adapter, or modem, used for ISDN (15).

Integrity The property that data has not been altered or destroyed in an unauthorized manner.

Interface A node's attachment to a link. A representation of a physical or logical link of a node to a link. An example of a physical interface is a network interface. An example of a logical interface is a tunnel interface.

Interface Identifier Last 64 bits of a unicast or anycast IPv6 address.

Intermediary (in the CoAP Environment) A CoAP endpoint that acts both as a server and as a client toward (possibly via further intermediaries) an origin server. There are two common forms of intermediary: proxy and reverse proxy. In some cases, a single endpoint might act as an origin server, proxy, or reverse proxy, switching behavior based on the nature of each request (28).

Internet-Based TV (IBTV) Video distribution approaches such as Web television, Internet television, and/or user-generated video (UGV).

Internet Control Message Protocol for IPv6 (ICMPv6) Protocol for internet control messages for IPv6. A protocol that provides error messages for the routing and delivery of IPv6 datagrams and information messages for diagnostics, neighbor discovery (ND), multicast receiver discovery, and IPv6 mobility.

Interrogator In RFID environments, a device that modulate/transmit and receive/demodulate a sufficient set of the electrical signals defined in the signaling layer to communicate with conformant tags while conforming to all local radio regulations. A typical interrogator is a passive-backscatter, interrogator-talks-first (ITF), RFID system operating in the 860 MHz–960 MHz frequency range. An interrogator transmits information to a tag by modulating an RF signal in the 860 MHz–960 MHz frequency range. The tag receives both information and operating energy from this RF signal. Tags are passive, meaning that they receive all of their operating energy from the interrogator's RF waveform. An interrogator receives information from a tag by transmitting a continuous-wave (CW) RF signal to the tag; the tag responds by modulating the reflection coefficient of its antenna, thereby backscattering an information signal to the interrogator (7).

Interworking Mechanisms for IPv6 and IPv4 Well-known interworking mechanisms include (29):

- Dual stack: A technique for providing complete support for both protocols—IPv4 and IPv6—in hosts and routers.
- Configured tunneling of IPv6 over IPv4: Manually configured point-to-point tunnels for encapsulating IPv6 packets within IPv4 headers to carry them over an IPv4 routing infrastructures.
- Automatic tunneling of IPv6 over IPv4: Mechanisms for automatically tunneling IPv6 packets over IPv4 networks.
- Translation: Refers to the direct conversion of protocols.

Intra-Site Automatic Tunnel Addressing Protocol (ISATAP) An IPv6 transition technology that provides IPv6 unicast connectivity between devices placed in an IPv4 intranetwork. ISATAP obtains an interface identifier from the IPv4 address (public or private) assigned to the device. This identifier is used for the establishment of automatic tunnels through the IPv4 infrastructure (16).

Intra-Site Automatic Tunnel Addressing Protocol (ISATAP) Address An IPv6 address of the form 64-bit prefix:0:5EFE:w.x.y.z, where w.x.y.z is a public or private IPv4 address allocated to an ISATAP device.

Intra-Site Automatic Tunnel Addressing Protocol (ISATAP) Device A device to which an ISATAP address is assigned to.

Intra-Site Automatic Tunnel Addressing Protocol (ISATAP) Name The name "ISATAP" is resolved by computers with Windows XP or Windows Server 2003 operating system to automatically discover the ISATAP router address for initial configuration.

Intra-Site Automatic Tunnel Addressing Protocol (ISATAP) Router An IPv6/IPv4 router that answers ISATAP node requests and routes traffic to and from ISATAP nodes.

IP Multimedia Subsystem (IMS) IMS is a 3GPP/3GPP2 initiative to define an all IP-based wireless network as an evolution from historically distinct voice, data, signaling, and control network elements.

IP Over Ethernet (IPoE) IP over Ethernet is used in DSL and PON access networks in place of PPPoE.

IP Storage Using IP and gigabit Ethernet to build storage area networks (SANs). Traditional SANs were developed using the FC transport, because it provided gigabit speeds compared to 10 and 100 Mbps Ethernet used to build messaging networks at that time. FC equipment has been costly, and interoperability between different vendors' switches was not completely standardized. Since gigabit Ethernet and IP have become commonplace, IP storage enables familiar network protocols to be used, and IP allows SANs to be extended throughout the world. Variants include:

- Internet FCP (iFCP)
- Metro fiber channel protocol (mFCP)
- Internet small computer system interface (iSCSI)
- Fiber channel over Internet protocol (FCIP)

IP6.arpa The DNS domain created for the IPv6 reverse resolution (RFC 3596). The reverse resolution has the purpose of "reverse mapping" of IPv6 addresses to DNS names.

IPoDWDM Optical Network Carriage of IP packets directly over the optical layer provided by a dense-wavelength division multiplexing optical system.

IPSO Alliance The IPSO Alliance is an advocate for IP networked devices for use in energy, consumer, healthcare, and industrial applications. The objective of the Alliance is not to define technologies or standards, but to document the use of IP-based technologies defined at the standard organizations such as IETF with focus on support by the Alliance of various use cases.

IPv4 Node A node that implements IPv4; it can send and receive IPv4 packets. It can be an IPv4-only node or a dual IPv4/IPv6 node.

IPv4-Compatible IPv6 Address A 0:0:0:0:0:0:w.x.y.z or ::w.x.y.z address, where w.x.y.z is the decimal representation of a public IPv4 address. For example, ::131:107:89:42 is an IPv4-compatible address. IPv6 transition mechanisms no longer use IPv4-compatible address scheme.

IPv4-Mapped IPv6 Address A 0:0:0:0:0:FFFF:w.x.y.z (or ::FFFF:w.x.y.z) address, where w.x.y.z is the IPv4 address of an IPv4-only node. Mapped IPv4 addresses are used to represent an IPv4-only host.

IPv6 in IPv4 See IPv6 over IPv4 tunnel.

IPv6 Node Node that implements IPv6; it can send and receive IPv6 packets. An IPv6 node can be an IPv6-only node or a dual IPv6/IPv4 node.

IPv6 Over IPv4 Tunnel Encapsulating IPv6 packets into an IPv4 datagram and transporting the datagram over an IPv4 infrastructure. In the IPv4 header, the protocol field value is 41.

IPv6 Prefixes The initial bits of an IP address. The number of bits is represented via the prefix-length notation. Prefixes for IPv6 routes and subnet identifiers are expressed in the same way as classless interdomain routing (CIDR) notation for IPv4. For example, 21DA:D3::/48 is a route prefix and 21DA:D3:0:2F3B::/64 is a subnet prefix. IPv4 implementations commonly use a dotted decimal representation of the network prefix known as the subnet mask. A subnet mask is not used in IPv6. Only the prefix-length notation is used (4).

IPv6 Routing Protocol for LLNs (RPL) A mechanism proposed by the IETF to support multipoint-to-point traffic from devices inside LLNs toward a central control point, as well as point-to-multipoint traffic from the central control point to the devices inside the LLN (30).

IPv6 Routing Table Set of routes used to determine the next node address and interface when forwarding IPv6 traffic.

IPv6/IPv4 Node A node that has both IPv4 and IPv6 implementations.

ISA100.11a ISA SP100 standard for wireless industrial networks developed by the International Society of Automation (ISA) to address all aspects of wireless technologies in a plant. The ISA100 Committee addresses wireless manufacturing and control systems in the areas of the: (i) environment in which the wireless technology is deployed; (ii) technology and life cycle for wireless equipment and systems; and (iii) application of wireless technology. The wireless environment includes the definition of wireless, radio frequencies (starting point), vibration, temperature, humidity, EMC, interoperability, coexistence with existing systems, and physical equipment location. ISA100.11a Working Group Charter addresses (31):

- Low-energy consumption devices, with the ability to scale to address large installations
- Wireless infrastructure, interfaces to legacy infrastructure and applications, security, and network management requirements in a functionally scalable manner
- Robustness in the presence of interference found in harsh industrial environments and with legacy systems
- Coexistence with other wireless devices anticipated in the industrial work space
- Interoperability of ISA100 devices

Key A digital code used to encrypt, sign, decrypt, and verify messages and files. A sequence of symbols that controls the operations of encipherment and decipherment.

Key Management Generation, distribution, storage, replacement, and destruction of keys.

Key Pair A public key and its complementary private key. In public-key systems, each user has at least one key pair.

KNX and KNX-RF KNX (administered by the KNX Association) is an OSI-based network communications protocol for intelligent buildings defined in standards CEN EN 50090 and ISO/IEC 14543. KNX is the follow-on standard built on the European Home Systems Protocol (EHS), BatiBUS, and the European Installation Bus (EIB or Instabus). Effectively, KNX uses the communication stack of EIB but augmented with the physical layers and configuration modes BatiBUS and EHS; thus, KNX includes the following PHYs:

- Twisted pair wiring (inherited from the BatiBUS and EIB Instabus standards). This approach uses differential signaling with a signaling speed of 9.6 Kbps. MAC is controlled with the CSMA/CA method;
- Powerline networking (inherited from EIB and EHS);
- Radio (KNX-RF);
- IR; and
- Ethernet (also known as EIBnet/IP or KNXnet/IP).

Layer 2 Layer 2 of the protocol stack. This typically refers to the set of Ethernet protocols that operate below the IP layer of the protocol stack.

Layer 2 Tunneling Protocol (L2TP) Layer 2 tunneling protocol (L2TP) is a tunneling protocol used to support virtual private networks (VPNs).

Layer 3 Layer 3 of the open systems interconnection (OSI) protocol stack. This refers to the IP used for routing in the Internet.

Lifetime in Preferred State Time during which a unicast address, obtained by means of stateless autoconfiguration mechanism, stays in the preferred state. This time is specified by the preferred lifetime field in Routers Advertisement message prefix information option.

Limited Scope Addresses (also known as Administratively Scoped Addresses) The range of addresses from 239.0.0.0 through 239.255.255.255. RFC2365 defines these addresses to be limited to a local group or organization (RFC2365). Routers are required to be configured with packet filters to prevent multicast traffic in this address range from flowing outside of an AS.

Link A communication facility or medium over which nodes can communicate at the link layer, i.e., the layer immediately below IPv6. Examples include Ethernet environments (simple or bridged); PPP links; X.25 Packet Switching, Frame Relay, Cell Relay/ATM; or IPv4.

Link-Local Addresses IP multicast addresses that have been reserved for specific functions. Addresses in the 224.0.0.0 through 224.0.0.255 are reserved to be used by network protocols on a local network segment. Network protocols make use of these addresses for automatic router discovery and to communicate routing information (e.g., OSPF uses 224.0.0.5 and 224.0.0.6 to exchange link state information). IP packets with these addresses are not forwarded by a router; they remain local on a particular LAN segment (they have a time-to-live [TTL] parameter set to 1; even if the TTL is different from 1, they still are not forwarded by the router).

Link State Routing Protocol A routing protocol in which a router informs all the nodes in a network of topology changes. Information exchanged consists of prefixes of networks connected to the router and their associated cost. This is in contrast to distance vector routing protocols that exchange routing table information but only with neighboring nodes.

Link-Layer Identifier A link-layer identifier for an interface. Examples include IEEE 802 addresses for Ethernet or token ring network interfaces and E.164 addresses for ISDN links.

Link-Local Address An IPv6 address having a link-only scope, indicated by the prefix (FE80::/10), which can be used to reach neighboring nodes attached to the same link. Every interface has a link-local address.

Local Address An IPv6 unicast address that is not reachable on IPv6 Internet. Local addresses include "link-local" and "site-local" addresses.

Local Interface Internal interface that allows a node to send packets to itself.

Long-Term Evolution (LTE) (aka 4G) LTE is a project named an "all IP" standard for mobile traffic that will increase the broadband capabilities beyond current 3G mobile technologies. LTE is the 3GPP initiative to evolve the UMTS technology toward a fourth generation (4G.) LTE can be viewed as an architecture framework and a set of ancillary mechanisms that aims at providing seamless IP connectivity between User Equipment (UE) and the packet (IPv4, IPv6) data network without any disruption to the end-users' applications during mobility. In contrast to the circuit-switched model of previous-generation cellular systems, LTE has been designed to support *only* packet-switched services.

Loopback Address The IPv6 address—0:0:0:0:0:0:0:1 or ::1—assigned to the local interface.

Low-Power and Lossy Networks (LLNs) A class of network in which both the routers and their interconnects are constrained. LLN routers typically operate with constraints on processing power, memory, and energy (battery power). Their interconnects are characterized by high loss rates, low data rates, and instability (30).

Lower Layer (LL) Allows DSCL, GSCL, and NSCL components to exchange data on behalf of applications and perform other appropriate communication.

M2M (Machine-to-Machine) Term used to refer to M2M communication, i.e., automated data exchange between machines. ("Machine" may also refer to virtual machines such as software applications.) M2M is an enabler of the Internet of things (IoT).

M2M Area Network Layer Provides the communication between DA/GA components and DSCL/GSCL components.

M2M Service Provider's Domain Domain that includes the network application domain and any standardized systems under the control of the M2M service provider which interact with the M2M service capabilities.

M2M System Comprises network application domain, M2M devices domain, and any interfaces or networks required to connect those entities.

MAC Address A link-layer address for LAN technologies such as Ethernet and token ring. It is also referred to as a physical address, hardware address, or network adapter address.

MAC Header The link-layer header of the IEEE 802.3 standard or Ethernet v2. It consists of a 6B destination address, 6B source address, and 2B type field (see also NPA, LLC) (32).

Machine (Host) A node that cannot send datagrams not created by itself. A machine (host) is both the source and destination of IPv6 traffic and will discard traffic that is not specifically addressed to it.

Machine-to-Machine (M2M) Communication Communication between remotely deployed (generally low-end) devices with specific responsibilities and requiring little or no human intervention, which are all connected to an application server via the mobile network data communications.

Machine-Type Communications (MTC) M2M system communication as described by the 3GPP.

Machine-Type Communications (MTC) Device An MTC device is a UE equipped for MTC, which communicates through a *public land mobile network* (PLMN) with MTC server(s) and/or other MTC device(s).

NOTE: An MTC device might also communicate locally (wirelessly, possibly through a PAN, or hardwired) with other entities which provide the MTC device "raw data" for processing and communication to the MTC server(s) and/or other MTC device(s). This is a 3GPP concept (22).

Machine-Type Communications (MTC) Feature MTC features are network functions to optimize the network for use byM2M applications. This is a 3GPP concept (22).

Machine-Type Communications (MTC) Group An MTC group is a group of MTC devices that share one or more group-based MTC features and that belong to the same MTC subscriber. This is a 3GPP concept (22).

Machine-Type Communications (MTC) Server An MTC server is an entity, which communicates to the PLMN itself, and to MTC devices through the PLMN. The MTC server also has an interface that can be accessed by the MTC user. The MTC server performs services for the MTC user. This is a 3GPP concept (22).

Machine-Type Communications (MTC) User An MTC user uses the service provided by the MTC server. This is a 3GPP concept (22).

Maximum Transmission Unit (MTU) Maximum transmission unit (MTU) refers to the size (in bytes) of the largest packet that a given layer of a communications protocol can pass onward. MTUs are defined at the link layer (frame maximum size) and at the network or Internet layer (maximum IPv6 packet size).

Maximum-Level Aggregation Identifier (aka top-level aggregation identifier— TLA ID). Thirteen-bit field inside the global unicast address reserved for large organizations or ISP by the IANA; hence, it identifies the address range that they have delegated. The TLA scheme has been obsolete by RFC 3587.

M-BUS The M-Bus ("Meter-Bus") is a European standard for remote reading of gas and electric meters; it is also usable for all other types of consumption meters. It is specified as follows:

• EN 13757-2 (physical and link layer)
• EN 13757-3 (application layer)
• Note: the frame layer uses IEC 870 and the network (packet layer) is optional.

A radio variant of M-Bus (wireless M-Bus) is also specified in EN 13757-4.

Media Access Control (MAC) Media access and control of the Ethernet IEEE 802 standard and protocols (18). Its functionalities include the creation of frames and the management of medium sharing and access.

Medical Body Area Network System (MBANS) Low-power radio system used for the transmission of non-voice data to and from medical devices for the purposes of monitoring, diagnosing, and treating patients as prescribed by duly authorized healthcare professionals (33).

MEO satellite A satellite with an earth orbit within the range from a few hundred miles to a few thousand miles above the earth's surface; this orbit is called medium earth orbit, hence MEO. MEO satellites orbit higher than LEO satellites, but lower than geostationary (GEO) satellites.

MEID Mobile equipment identifier.

mHealth A term for eHealth services using mobile phones or cellular networks.

Mobility The ability for the end-user or other mobile entities to communicate and access services irrespective of changes of the location or technical environment.

Motion Picture Expert Group (MPEG) A family of standards used for coding audio-visual information (e.g., movies, video, music) in a digitally compressed format. There are three major MPEG standards: MPEG-1, MPEG-2, and the newer MPEG-4. Both MPG-2 and MPEG-4 are important for IPTV, but the recent trend is in favor of MPEG-4.

MPEG-2 (Motion Picture Experts Group-2) A set of multiplexing/encoding standards specified by the Motion Picture Experts Group (MPEG) and standardized by the International Organization for Standardization (ISO/IEC 113818-1) and ITU-T (H.220).

MPLS VPN A layer 3 virtual IP network specified by RFC2547bis. It used a combination of border gateway protocol (BGP) routing and MPLS forwarding to create a virtual IP network on top of a service provider's physical IP network. MPLS VPN services are replacing frame relay and ATM services (11).

Multicast A methodology and supporting mechanisms, technologies, and standards for distribution of information (including video content) over the Internet. Multicast allows a server to inject a single copy of a given content into the Internet and many receivers (computers, smart phones, Internet-ready TV sets, and so on), but not the entire universe of receivers as would be the case in broadcast, to receive and play the same stream simultaneously.

Multicast Address An address that identifies several interfaces and is used to deliver data from one source to several destinations. That is, an identifier for a set of interfaces typically belonging to different nodes. By means of the multicast routing topology, packets to a multicast address will be delivered to all interfaces identified by that address.

An identifier for a group of nodes. An IP multicast address or group address, as defined in "Host Extensions for IP Multicasting," STD 5, RFC 1112, August 1989, and in "IP Version 6 Addressing Architecture," RFC2373, July 1998. The Internet Assigned Numbers Authority (IANA) controls the assignment of IP multicast addresses. IANA has allocated what has been known as the Class D address space to be utilized for IP multicast. IP multicast group addresses are in the range 224.0.0.0 through 239.255.255.255.

Multicast Address Dynamic Client Allocation Protocol (MADCAP) A protocol defined in RFC2730 that allows hosts to request multicast addresses from multicast address allocation servers. This protocol is part of the IETF Multicast Address Allocation Architecture (34).

Multicast Address Set Claim Protocol (MASC) Protocol defined in RFC2909 that can be used for interdomain multicast address set allocation. MASC is used by a node (typically a router) to claim and allocate one or more address prefixes to that node's domain. While a domain does not necessarily need to allocate an address set for hosts in that domain to be able to allocate group addresses, allocating an address set to the domain does ensure that interdomain group-specific distribution trees will be locally rooted, and that traffic will be sent outside the domain only when and where external receivers exist (35).

Multicast Environment Environment where one system communicates to a select group of other systems.

Multicast Group Set of interfaces listening to a specific multicast address.

Multicast IPv4 Tunnel See 6over4.

Multicast Listener Discovery Protocol (MLDv2) MLDv2 is an MLD protocol that is used by an IPv6 router to discover the presence of multicast listeners on directly attached links, and to discover which multicast addresses are of interest to those neighboring nodes. MLDv2 is designed to be interoperable with MLDv1. MLDv2 adds the ability for a node to report interest in listening to packets with a particular multicast address only from specific source addresses or from all sources except for specific source addresses (36).

The Internet Group Management Protocol (IGMP) (RFC1112, IGMPv2, IGMPv3) allows an IPv4 host to communicate IP multicast group membership information to its neighboring routers; IGMPv3 provides the ability for a host to selectively request or filter traffic from individual sources within a multicast group. MLD defined in RFC2710 (MLDv2) offers similar functionality for IPv6 hosts. MLDv2 provides the analogous "source filtering" functionality of IGMPv3 for IPv6 (37).

Multicast OSPF (MOSPF) Protocol defined in RFC 1584 that provides enhancements to OSPF Version 2 to support IP multicast routing. With MOSPF, an IP multicast packet is routed based both on the packet's source and on its multicast destination (commonly referred to as source/destination routing). As it is routed, the multicast packet follows a shortest path to each multicast destination. During packet forwarding, any commonality of paths is exploited; when multiple hosts belong to a single multicast group, a multicast packet will be replicated only when the paths to the separate hosts diverge.

OSPF, a link-state routing protocol, provides a database describing the AS's topology. A new OSPF link state advertisement has been added describing the location of multicast destinations. A multicast packet's path is then calculated by building a pruned shortest-path tree (SPT) rooted at the packet's IP source. These trees are built on demand, and the results of the calculation are cached for use by subsequent packets (38).

Multicast Payload Forwarding Communication mechanism to forward payload. Almost invariably, this is IP based at the network layer. Typical IP multicast applications make use of user datagram protocol (UDP) at the transport layer; however, TCP can also be used in same applications.

Multicast Routing A mechanism to build distribution trees that define a unique forwarding path between the subnet of the content source and each subnet containing members of the multicast group, specifically, receivers.

Multicast Routing Information Base (MRIB) This is the multicast topology table, which is typically derived from the unicast routing table, or from routing protocols such as MBGP that carry multicast-specific topology information. PIM-DM uses the MRIB to make decisions regarding RPF interfaces (39).

Multicast Scope A range of multicast addresses configured so that traffic sent to these addresses is limited to some subset of the internetwork. Defined in "Administratively Scoped IP Multicast," BCP 23, RFC2365, July 1998.

Multicast Source Discovery Protocol (MSDP) A protocol that allows multiple PIM-SM domains to share information about active sources. The protocol announces active sources to MSDP peers. It is a BGP-like protocol that allows a rendezvous point (RP) to forward source and multicast group information to other RPs (e.g., to support redundant RPs or multidomain applications where each ISP can each have its own RP(s)) (40).

Multichannel audio Audio signal with more than two channels.

Multiprotocol Border Gateway Protocol (MP-BGP) (also referred to by the acronym form MBGP) A protocol that defines multiprotocol extensions to the BGP, the unicast interdomain protocol that supports multicast-specific routing information. MP-BGP augments BGP to enable multicast routing policy and connect multicast topologies within and between BGP ASs. It carries multiple instances of routes for unicast routing as well as multicast routing. Protocol that carries routing information about several protocols, including IP multicast (and also IPv6 and MPLS VPN information, among others). In IP multicast, MP-BGP carries a separate copy of unicast routes. MP-BGP helps establish which links the PIM join messages use, which in turn allows us to control which links the multicast traffic traverses (40).

Name Resolution Procedure to obtain an IP address from a name.

Named Data Networking (NDN) A proposed architecture that moves the communication paradigm from today's focus on "where," i.e., addresses, servers, and hosts, to "what," i.e., the content that users and applications care about. By naming data instead of their location (IP address), NDN transforms data into first-class entities. While the current Internet secures the communication channel or path between two communication points and sometimes the data with encryption, NDN secures the content and provides essential context for security. This approach allows the decoupling of trust in data from trust in hosts and servers, enabling trustworthiness as well as several radically scalable communication mechanisms, for example, automatic caching to optimize bandwidth and the potential to move content along multiple paths to the destination (41). This architecture may be applicable to the IoT.

Near-Field Communication (NFC) A group of standards for devices such as PDAs, smartphones, and tablets that support the establishment of wireless communication when such devices are in immediate proximity of a few inches. These standards encompass communications protocols and data exchange formats; they are based on existing RFID standards including ISO/IEC 14443 and FeliCa (a contactless RFID smart card system developed by Sony, for example utilized in electronic money cards in use in Japan). NFC standards include ISO/IEC 18092, as well as other standards defined by the NFC Forum. NFC standards allow two-way communication between endpoints (earlier generation systems were one-way systems only). Unpowered NFC-based tags can also be read by NFC devices; hence this technology can substitute for earlier one-way systems. Applications of NFC include contactless transactions.

Neighbor Discovery (ND) A set of messages and ICMPv6 processes that fixes the relations between neighbor nodes. ND replaces ARP, ICMP routes discovery, and ICMP redirection messages used in IPv4. It also provides inaccessible neighbor detection.

Neighbor Discovery Options Options in an ND message that show link-layer addresses, information about prefixes, MTU, and routes and configuration information for IPv6 mobility.

Neighbors Nodes connected to the same link.

Neighbors Cache A cache supported by each IPv6 node that stores the IP address of its neighbors on the link, its corresponding link-layer address, and an indication of its accessibility state. Neighbors cache is equivalent to the ARP cache in IPv4.

Network Address Translation-Protocol Translation (NAT-PT) Process performed by a network device on the boundary of an IPv4 and IPv6 network. NAT-PT uses a pool of IPv4 addresses for dynamic assignment to the IPv6 nodes. NAT-PT also allows the multiplexing of multiple sessions on a single IPv4 address via the "port" field.

Network Addresses Translator (NAT) A device that translates IP addresses and port numbers when forwarding packets between a network with private addresses and the Internet.

Network Point of Attachment (NPA) A 6-byte destination address (resembling an IEEE MAC address) within the MPEG-2 transmission network that is used to identify individual receivers or groups of receivers (32).

Network-Attached Storage (NAS) A disk array storage system that is attached directly to a network rather than to the network server (i.e., host attached). It functions as a server in a client/server relationship; has a processor, an operating system, or micro-kernel; and processes file I/O protocols such as SMB and NFS (23).

Next-Generation Network (NGN) According to ITU-T Recommendation Y.2001 (12/2004) "General overview of NGN," an NGN is a packet-based network able to provide Telecommunication Services to users and able to make use of multiple broadband, QoS-enabled transport technologies and in which service-related functions are independent of the underlying transport-related technologies. It enables unfettered access for users to networks and to competing service providers and services of their choice. It supports generalized mobility, which will allow consistent and ubiquitous provision of services to users.

The NGN is characterized by the following fundamental aspects:

- Packet-based transfer
- Separation of control functions among bearer capabilities, call/session, and application/service
- Decoupling of service provision from transport and provision of open interfaces
- Support for a wide range of services, applications, and mechanisms based on service building blocks (including real-time/streaming/non-real-time services and multimedia)
- Broadband capabilities with end-to-end QoS and transparency
- Interworking with legacy networks via open interfaces
- Generalized mobility
- Unfettered access by users to different service providers
- A variety of identification schemes which can be resolved to IP addresses for the purposes of routing in IP networks
- Unified service characteristics for the same service as perceived by the user

- Converged services between fixed and mobile networks
- Independence of service-related functions from underlying transport technologies
- Support of multiple last mile technologies
- Compliant with all regulatory requirements, for example concerning emergency communications and security/privacy.

Next-Level Aggregation Identifier (NLA ID) 24-bit field inside the global unicast aggregatable address that allows the creation of several hierarchical levels of addressing to organize addresses and routing to other ISPs, as well as to identify organization sites. The NLA scheme has been obsolete by RFC 3587.

NIKE+® A proprietary wireless technology developed by Nike and Apple to allow users to monitor their activity levels while exercising. Its power consumption is relatively high, returning only 40 days of battery life from a coin cell. It is a proprietary radio that only works between Nike and Apple devices. Nike+ devices are shipped as a single unit: processor, radio, and sensor (10).

NIT (Network Information Table) MPEG signaling table that contains details of the bearer network used to transmit the MPEG multiplex, including the carrier frequency (PID=10) (12).

Node A device that implements IP.

Node Types Node types in an IPv6 environment include the following (29):

- IPv4-only node: A host or router that implements only IPv4. An IPv4-only node does not understand IPv6. The installed base of IPv4 hosts and routers existing before the transition to IPv6 begins are IPv4-only nodes.
- IPv6/IPv4 node: A host or router that implements both IPv4 and IPv6.
- IPv6-only node: A host or router that implements IPv6 and does not implement IPv4.
- IPv6 node: Any host or router that implements IPv6. IPv6/IPv4 and IPv6-only nodes are both IPv6 nodes.
- IPv4 node: Any host or router that implements IPv4. IPv6/IPv4 and IPv4-only nodes are both IPv4 nodes.

Non-Broadcast Multiple Access (NBMA) A link-layer technology that supports links with more than two nodes, but without allowing the sending of a packet to all nodes on the link (broadcast). Example technologies include X.25 packet-switching service, frame relay service, and cell relay service/ ATM.

Non-Broadcast Networks A network supporting the attachment of more than two stations, but not supporting the delivery of a single physical datagram to multiple destinations (i.e., not supporting data-link multicast). OSPF describes these networks as non-broadcast, multiaccess networks. An example of a non-broadcast network is an X.25 public data network (38).

Non-Multicast router In the context of MOSPF, a router running OSPF Version 2, but not the multicast extensions. These routers do not forward multicast datagrams, but can interoperate with MOSPF routers in the forwarding of unicast packets. Routers running the MOSPF protocol are referred to as either multicast-capable routers or MOSPF routers (38).

Object An object is a model of an entity. An object is characterized by its behavior, and an object is distinct from any other object. An object interacts with its environment including other objects at its interaction points. An object is informally said to perform functions and offer services (an object that performs a function available to other entities and/or objects is said to offer a service). For modeling purposes, these functions and services are specified in terms of the behavior of the object and of its interfaces. An object can perform more than one function and a function can be performed by the cooperation of several objects (42, 43).

Object Storage An emerging storage approach similar to file-based storage except it makes greater use of metadata. It trades the efficiency and performance of block-based storage for easier management and more automation. Object metadata will let content providers and enterprises manage the storage more effectively and apply policies based on the data content, regulatory requirements, ownership of the data, or based on other principles. The metadata can also be used to dynamically store data at the most appropriate service levels (44).

Operating Environment In RFID environments, a region within which an interrogator's RF transmissions are attenuated by less than 90 dB. In free space, the operating environment is a sphere whose radius is approximately 1000 m, with the interrogator located at the center. In a building or other enclosure, the size and shape of the operating environment depends on factors such as the material properties and shape of the building and may be less than 1000 m in certain directions and greater than 1000 m in other direction (7).

Operating Procedure In RFID environments, collectively, the set of functions and commands used by an interrogator to identify and modify tags (also known as the tag-identification layer (7).

Orbit (Satellite) The path described by the center of mass of a satellite in space, subjected to natural forces, principally gravitational attraction, but occasional low-energy corrective forces exerted by a propulsive device in order to achieve and maintain the desired path.

Orbital Plane (Satellite) The plane containing the center of mass of the earth and the velocity vector (direction of motion) of a satellite.

Outgoing Interface (oif) List In PIM-SM, each multicast route entry has an oif list containing the outgoing interfaces to which multicast packets should be forwarded (27).

Packet Protocol data unit (PDU) at network layer. In IPv6, a packet that consists of an IPv6 header and an IPv6 payload.

Parameter Discovery Part of the ND process that allows nodes to learn configuration parameters, including link MTU, and the default hop limit for outgoing packets.

Passive Tag (or Passive Label) In RFID environments, a tag (or label) whose transceiver is powered by the RF field.

Path Determination Procedure to select the route from the routing table for use in forwarding the datagram.

Path MTU Maximum IPv6 packet size that can be sent without using fragmentation between a source and a destination over an IPv6 network route. The route MTU equates with the smallest link MTU for all links in such route.

Path MTU Discovery Process relating to the use of ICMPv6 "Too Big" message to discover the path MTU.

Path Vector A routing protocols approach that involves the exchange of hop information sequences showing the path to follow in a route. For example, BGP-4 exchanges sequences of numbers of ASs.

Peaking Power Plants (also known as peaker plants or peakers) power plants that typically operate only when there is a high peak demand for electric power.

Peer-Entity Authentication The corroboration that a peer entity in an association is the one claimed.

Peer-to-Peer (P2P) Network A distributed system in which all nodes have identical responsibilities and all communication is symmetric. P2P applications rely by design on the interaction between end nodes. The nodes have significant or total independence of central servers. Every participating node acts as both a server and a client. The idea behind P2P is to (1) bring communication to the edges of the network to avoid overloading central servers and (2) harness the great number of underutilized computers and Internet connections in people's homes and offices. This is accomplished by turning every user into a rebroadcaster. The content stream is divided into small parts, and each part is distributed to one user's computer. The participating computers request missing parts from each other and exchange parts to rebuild the whole content. Users can view the content, for example a movie, as if it were sent directly from the content provider (45).

Personal Mobility Mobility for those scenarios where the end-user changes the terminal device used for network access at different locations. The ability of a user to access telecommunication services at any terminal on the basis of a personal identifier and the capability of the network to provide those services delineated in the user's service profile (46).

Phishing Act of acquiring sensitive or personal information such as usernames, date of birth, passwords or credit card details, by masquerading as a trustworthy entity.

Physical Layer In RFID environments, the data coding and modulation waveforms used in interrogator-to-tag and tag-to-interrogator signaling.

PLC (Powerline Communications) PLC (also called powerline communication as a singular term; also called powerline telecommunications [or PLT]) refers to any technology that enables data transfer through powerlines by using advanced modulation technology. Data communication can take place at narrowband or broadband speeds. The technology has been around since the 1950s, but initially only supported narrowband applications for relay management, for example for public lighting. Broadband over PLC only began at the end of the 1990s. PLC is thus a term used to identify technologies, equipments, applications, and services aiming at providing users with communication means over existing "powerlines" (cables transmitting electricity). The term broadband over powerline (BPL) is used to underline the technology capability to address broadband services. As for the term Access PLC, it is used to identify those PLC solutions aiming at providing consumers with broadband services through the external electricity grid, while in-home PLC is used to identify PLC solutions aiming at applications within the home (47).

Point-To-Point Protocol (PPP) Point-to-point network encapsulation method that provides frame delimiters, protocol identification, and integrity services at the bit level.

Point-to-Point Protocol over Ethernet (PPPoE) PPPoE is a network protocol for encapsulating PPP frames in Ethernet frames. It is used mainly with ADSL services. It offers standard PPP features such as authentication, encryption, and compression.

Prefix The initial bits of an IP address. The number of bits is represented via the prefix-length notation.

Prefix length The number of bits in a prefix.

Prefix List A collection of prefixes typically used when creating match conditions, for example, for firewall filters.

Prefix-Length Notation Notation used to represent network prefix length. It uses the "address/prefix length" form, where prefix length indicates the number of bits in the prefix.

Presentation Time Stamp (PTS) Time stamps are inserted close to the material to which they refer (normally in the PES packet header). They indicate the exact moment where a video frame or an audio frame has to be decoded or presented to the user respectively (12).

Privacy The right of individuals to control or influence what information related to them may be collected and stored and by whom and to whom that information may be disclosed.

Private Key Decryption key is often called private key in public-key systems. A private key is also used for signing a message.

Private Security Sector Services and solutions such as but not limited to manned guarding, alarm system integration and monitoring, and cash and valuables handling.

Product Metadata Metadata related to a media file, including product id, category, protecting services, access modes, usage rights, pricing info, scheduling info, maturity rating, addressing, and so on (5).

Protocol Data Unit (PDU) A unit of information associated with a particular protocol. During transmission, the PDU of the N-layer in a protocol suite becomes the payload of the PDU of the N-1 layer.

Proxy (in the CoAP Environment) A "proxy" is an endpoint selected by a client, usually via local configuration rules, to perform requests on behalf of the client, doing any necessary translations. Some translations are minimal, such as for proxy requests for "coap" URIs, whereas other requests might require translation to and from entirely different application-layer protocols (28).

Pseudo-Header Provisional header that is built to calculate the needed checksum for higher layer protocols. IPv6 uses a new pseudo-header format to calculate UDP, TCP, and ICMPv6 checksums.

Pseudo-Periodic Event that is repeated at intervals of various lengths. For example, the routes advertisement sent by an IPv6 router is made at intervals that are calculated between a minimum and a maximum (16).

Pseudowire (PW) Emulation of a native service over a packet-switched network (PSN). The native service may be ATM, frame relay, Ethernet, low-rate TDM, or SONET/SDH, while the PSN may be MPLS, IP (either IPv4 or IPv6), or L2TPv3. The first PW specifications were the Martini draft for ATM PWs, and the TDMoIP draft for transport of E1/T1 over IP. In 2001, the IETF set up the PWE3 Working Group, which was chartered to develop an architecture for service provider edge-to-edge PWs, and service-specific documents detailing the encapsulation techniques. Other standardization forums, including the ITU and the MFA Forum, are also active in producing standards and implementation agreements for PWs (11).

Public Key Encryption key is often called public key in public-key systems. A public key can also be used for verification of signatures (5).

Public-Key Algorithm An algorithm where the key used for encryption is different from the key used for decryption. Furthermore, the private (decryption) key cannot be calculated from the public (encryption) key (5).

Public-Key Infrastructure (PKI) System that provides public-key encryption and digital signature services.

Public-Key Cryptography Standards (PKCS) Set of standards for public-key cryptography from RSA Security Inc. See www.rsasecurity.com (5).

Q-in-Q An enhancement of IEEE 802.1q that allows service providers to create carrier Ethernet VLANs that will preserve the IEEE 802.1q headers used in the internal enterprise VLAN.

Quadrature Amplitude Modulation (QAM) Modulation technique that has been used in Cable TV broadcasting (as well as in other applications).

Quaternary Phase Shift Keying (QPSK) Modulation technique for satellite broadcasting.

Radio Frequency for Consumer Electronics (RF4CE) RF4CE is based on ZigBee and was standardized in 2009 by four consumer electronics companies: Sony, Philips, Panasonic, and Samsung. Two silicon vendors support RF4CE: Texas Instruments and Freescale Semiconductor, Inc. RF4CE's intended use is as a device remote control system, for example for television set-top boxes. The intention is that it overcomes the common problems associated with IR: interoperability, LOS, and limited enhanced features (10).

Rate Adaptive DSL (RADSL) A non-standard version of ADSL. Note that standard ADSL also permits the ADSL modem to adapt speeds of data transfer (15).

Real-Time Streaming Protocol (RTSP) An IETF protocol that is used for continuous (streaming) of audio and video sessions. It provides the control for playing, stopping, and media position control (e.g., fast forward) via bidirectional communication sessions. An application-level protocol for control of the delivery of data with real-time properties. It embodies an extensible framework to enable controlled, on-demand delivery of real-time audio and video data; it uses TCP or/or the user data protocol (UDP), depending on function.

Real-Time Transport Control Protocol (RTCP) (also known as RTP control protocol) An IETF protocol used for signaling, for example, identify and coordinate the reporting of streaming flow information (e.g., lost packets). Control protocol that works in conjunction with RTP to control performance and for diagnostic purposes. RTCP control packets are periodically transmitted by each participant in an RTP session to all other participants.

Real-Time Transport Protocol (RTP) An IETF protocol (a set of commands and processes) that is used to add timing and sequence information to each packet to allow the reassembly of packets to reproduce real-time audio and video information. A UDP-based packet format and set of conventions that provides end-to-end network connectivity functions suitable for applications transmitting real-time data, such as audio, video, and etcetera, over multicast or unicast network services.

RTP provides end-to-end delivery services for data with real-time characteristics, such as interactive audio and video. Those services include payload type identification, sequence numbering, time stamping, and delivery monitoring. Applications typically run RTP on top of UDP to make use of its multiplexing and checksum services; both protocols contribute parts of the transport protocol functionality. However, RTP may be used with other suitable underlying network or transport protocols. RTP supports data transfer to multiple destinations using multicast distribution if provided by the underlying network (48).

Reassembly Procedure to rebuild the original message that had been subject to fragmentation.

Receiver Equipment that processes the signal from a TS multiplex and performs filtering and forwarding of encapsulated PDUs to the network-layer service (or bridging module when operating at the link layer) (32).

Recipient The destination endpoint of a message.

Redirect Procedure included in the ND mechanisms to inform a host about the IPv6 address of another neighbor that is more appropriate as a next hop destination.

Redundant Array of Inexpensive Disks (RAIDs) Also known as "redundant array of independent disks." It is a storage approach (system) that provides high reliability through redundancy. It combines multiple disk drive components into a logical unit, allowing the data to be distributed across the drives in one of a number of ways called "RAID levels."

Reference Time Stamp Time stamp providing the indication of the current time. Reference time stamps are to be found in the PES syntax (ESCR), in the program syntax (SCR), and in the transport packet adaption program clock reference (PCR) field (12).

Representational State Transfer (REST) REST is an architectural style of large-scale networked software that takes advantage of the technologies and protocols of the World Wide Web; it describes how distributed data objects, or resources, can be defined and addressed, stressing the easy exchange of information and scalability (49).

Repudiation Denial by one of the entities involved in a communication of having participated in all or part of the communication.

Request Headers Request headers are used in client requests to communicate information about the client.

Reverse Path Forwarding (RPF) In PIM-SM, RPF is used to select the appropriate incoming interface (iif) for a multicast route entry. RPF is a multicast forwarding mode in which a data packet is accepted for forwarding only if it is received on an interface used to reach the source in unicast (39). The RPF neighbor for an address X is the next-hop router used to forward packets toward X. The RPF interface is the interface to that RPF neighbor. In the common case, this is the next hop used by the unicast routing protocol for sending unicast packets toward X. For example, in cases where unicast and multicast routes are not congruent, it can be different (27).

Reverse Proxy (in the CoAP Environment) A "reverse proxy" is an endpoint that acts as a layer above some other server(s) and satisfies requests on behalf of these, doing any necessary translations. Unlike a proxy, a reverse proxy receives requests as if it was the origin server for the target resource; the requesting client will not be aware that it is communicating with a reverse proxy (28).

Router Node that can forward datagrams not specifically addressed to it. In an IPv6 network, a router is also used to send advertisements related to its presence and node configuration information.

Router Advertisement ND message sent by a router in a pseudo-periodic way or as a router solicitation message response. The advertisement includes, at a minimum, a prefix that can be used by the host to calculate its own unicast IPv6 address following the stateless address configuration procedures.

Router Discovery ND process that allows a node to discover routers connected to a particular link.

Router-Port Group Management Protocol (RGMP) A protocol that constrains IP multicast on switches that have only routers attached.

Routing Loop Undesirable situation in a network where traffic is relayed over a closed loop and never reaches its destination. The TTL field is used to detect such traffic and delete it.

Routing Over Low-Power and Lossy Networks (ROLL) IETF Working Group that has defined application-specific routing requirements for an LLN routing protocol; it has also specified the IPv6 routing protocol for low-power and lossy networks (RPL) (30).

RP-Set In PIM-SM, the RP-Set is a set of RP addresses constructed by the BSR based on candidate-RP advertisements received. The RP-Set information is distributed to all PIM routers in the BSR's PIM domain (27).

Satellite Footprint The geographic area of the earth on which a satellite's direct transmissions can be received by a ground-based station or home dish.

Satellite Systems Satellite communication plays a key role in commercial, TV/media, government, and military communications because of its intrinsic multicast/broadcast capabilities, mobility aspects, global reach, reliability, and ability to quickly support connectivity in open-space and/or hostile environments. Satellite communications is a LOS one-way or two-way radio frequency (RF) transmission system that is comprised of a transmitting station (uplink), a satellite system that acts as a signal regeneration node, and one or more receiving stations (downlink). Satellites can reside in a number of orbits. A geosynchronous (GEO) satellite circles the earth at the earth's rotational speed and with the same direction of rotation, therefore appearing at the same position in the sky at a particular time each day. When the satellite is in the equatorial plane, it appears to be permanently stationary when observed at the earth's surface, so that an antenna pointed to it will not require tracking or (major) positional adjustments at periodic intervals of time (this satellite arrangement is also known as "geostationary"). The GEO is at 35,786 km (22,236 mi) of altitude from the earth's surface. Other orbits include the following: LEOs, MEOs (aka intermediate circular orbits [ICOs]), polar orbits, and highly elliptical orbits (HEOs). LEOs are either elliptical or (more commonly) circular orbits that are at a height of 2000 km or less above the surface of the earth. The advantage of LEOs is that they significantly reduce the propagation delay of the signal. The orbit period at these altitudes varies between 90 min and 2 h, and the maximum time during which a satellite in LEO orbit is above the local horizon for an observer on the earth is up to 20 min. With LEOs, there are long periods during which a given satellite is out of view of a particular ground station; this may be acceptable for some applications, for example, for earth monitoring. Coverage can be extended by deploying more than one satellite and using multiple orbital planes. A complete global coverage system using LEOs requires a large number of satellites (>12+) in multiple orbital planes and in various orbits (50).

Scope For IPv6 addresses, the scope is the portion of the network to which the traffic will be propagated.

Scope ID The scope ID is an identifier for a specific area or scope.

Scope Zone One multicast scope may have several instances, which are known as scope zones or zones, for short. For instance, an organization may have multiple sites. Each site might have its own site-local scope zone, each of which would be an instance of the site-local scope. However, a given interface on a given host would only ever be in at most one instance of a given scope. Messages sent by a host in a site-local scope zones to an address in the site-local scope would be limited to the site-local scope zone containing the host (34).

Scrambling Term used as a word for weaker encryption or controlled distortion of an analog signal. The distortion can be removed by possessing and using the descrambling equipment and proper keys (5).

Scrambling Algorithm An algorithm used in a scrambling (encryption) or descrambling (decryption) process.

Second-Generation VDSL (VDSL2) An ITU Recommendation G.993.2 specifies eight profiles that address a range of applications including up to 100 Mbps symmetric transmission on loops about 100 m long (using a bandwidth of 30 MHz), symmetric bit rates in the 10–30 Mbps range on intermediate-length loops (using a bandwidth of 12 MHz), and asymmetric operation with downstream rates in the range of 10–40 Mbps on loops of lengths ranging from 3 km to 1 km (using a bandwidth of 8.5 MHz). VDSL2 includes most of the advanced feature from ADSL2. The rate/reach performance of VDSL2 is better than VDSL (15).

Security Label The marking bound to a resource (e.g., a data unit) that names or designates the security attributes of that resource.

Security Policy The set of criteria for the provision of security services.

Sender The originating endpoint of a message.

Sensor Network A sensor network is an infrastructure comprised of sensing (measuring), computing, and communication elements that gives the administrator the ability to instrument, observe, and react to events and phenomena in a specified environment. The administrator typically is some civil, government, commercial, or industrial entity. Typically, the connectivity is by wireless means, hence the term wireless sensor network (WSN). The environment can be the physical world, a biological system, or an information technology (IT) framework. Network(ed) sensors systems are seen by observers as an important technology that will experience major deployment in the next few years for a plethora of applications, not the least being homeland security. Typical applications include, but are not limited to, data collection, monitoring, surveillance, and medical telemetry. There are four basic components in a sensor network: (i) an assembly of distributed or localized sensors; (ii) an interconnecting network (usually but not always wireless based); (iii) a central point of information clustering; and (iv) a set of computing resources at the central point (or beyond) to handle data correlation, event-trending, querying, and data mining. In this context, the sensing and computation nodes are considered part of the sensor network; in fact, some of the computing may be done in the network itself. Because of the potentially large quantity of data collected, algorithmic methods for data management play an important role in sensor networks. The computation and communication infrastructure associated with sensor networks is often specific to this environment and rooted in the device- and application-based nature of these networks. For example, unlike most other settings, in-network processing is desirable in sensor networks; furthermore, node power (and/or battery life) is a key design consideration.

Sensors Active devices that measure some variable of the natural or man-made environment (e.g., a building, an assembly line). The technology for sensing and control includes electric and magnetic field sensors; radio-wave frequency sensors; optical-, electro-optic-, and IR-sensors; radars; lasers; location/navigation sensors; seismic and pressure-wave sensors; environmental parameter sensors (e.g., wind, humidity, heat); and biochemical homeland security-oriented sensors. Sensors can be described as "smart" inexpensive devices equipped with multiple on-board sensing elements: they are low-cost, low-power, untethered multifunctional nodes that are logically homed to a central sink node. Sensors are typically internetworked via a series of multihop short-distance low-power wireless links (particularly within a defined "sensor field"); they typically utilize the Internet or some other network for long-haul delivery of information to a point (or points) of final data aggregation and analysis. In general, within the "sensor field," WSNs employ contention-oriented random access channel sharing/transmission techniques that are now incorporated in the IEEE 802 family of standards; indeed, these techniques were developed in the late 1960s and 1970s expressly for wireless (not cabled) environments, and for large sets of dispersed nodes with limited channel-management intelligence. Sensors span several orders of magnitude in physical size; they (or, at least some of their components) range from nanoscopic scale devices to mesoscopic scale devices at one end and from microscopic scale devices to macroscopic scale devices at the other end. Nanoscopic (also known as nanoscale) refers to objects or devices in the order of 1–100 nm in diameter; mesoscopic scale refers to objects between 100 and 10,000 nm in diameter; the microscopic scale ranges from 10 to 1000 μm; and the macroscopic scale is at the millimeter-to-meter range. At the low end of the scale, one finds, among others, biological sensors, small passive microsensors (such as "smart dust"—The *Smart Dust* mote is an autonomous sensing, computing, and communication system that uses the optical visible spectrum for transmission; they are tiny and inexpensive sensors developed by UC Berkeley engineers), and "lab-on-a-chip" assemblies. At the other end of the scale, one finds platforms such as, but not limited to, identity tags; toll collection devices; controllable weather data collection sensors; bioterrorism sensors; radars; and undersea submarine traffic sensors based on sonars. Some refer to the latest generation of sensors, especially the miniaturized ones that are directly embedded in some physical infrastructure, as "microsensors." A sensor network supports any kind of generic sensor; more narrowly, networked microsensors are a subset of the general family of sensor networks. Microsensors with on-board processing and wireless interfaces can be utilized to study and monitor a variety of phenomena and environments at close proximity.

Server The destination endpoint of a request; the originating endpoint of a response.

Service Protection Ensuring that an end-user can only acquire a service, and, by extension, the content contained therein, which they are entitled to receive.

Session Description Protocol (SDP) A media description specification used for describing multimedia sessions for the purposes of session announcement, session invitation, and session initiation.

Session Key A key (normally symmetric) used to encrypt each set of data on a transaction basis. A different session key is used for each communication session. The session key is normally transferred to the receiver using a key exchange mechanism or by encrypting the key under the receiver's public key (5).

Shared Tree A tree that uses a single common root placed at some chosen point in the network. This shared root is called a RP (also called core or center). All sources in the multicast group use the common shared tree. The notation (∗, G) is used to represents the tree. In this case "∗" is a wildcard to mean all sources.

Shortest-Path Tree (SPT) In PIM-SM, it is the SPT that is based on the merged shortest paths from all receivers to the multicast source. This is one of the features that distinguishes PIM-SM from core-based trees (CBT). When appropriate, the use of the SPT provides an optimal distribution network that helps to keep the multicast traffic closer to the minimum required to deliver the information to all members. (51). In PIM-SM, the SPT is the multicast distribution tree created by the merger of all of the shortest paths that connect receivers to the source (as determined by unicast routing) (27).

Singulation Identifying an individual tag in a multiple-tag environment.

Site-Level Aggregation Identifier (SLA ID) 16-bit field in the global unicast address that identifies subnetworks. The SLA ID field is used by an individual organization to create its own local addressing hierarchy and to identify subnets.

Site-Local Address Address identified by the 1111 1110 11 (FEC0::/10) prefix. The scope of these addresses is a local site (of an organization). Site-local addresses are not accessible from other sites and routers should not direct site-local traffic out of a site.

Slotted Random Anticollision In RFID environments, an anticollision algorithm where tags load a random (or pseudo-random) number into a slot counter, decrement this slot counter based on interrogator commands, and reply to the interrogator when their slot counter reaches zero (7).

Smart Energy The term "smart energy" refers to actions and technologies that are used to improve the efficiency of energy consumption.

Smart Grid (SG) An electricity network that can intelligently integrate the actions of all users connected to it—consumers, generators, and those that do both—in order to efficiently deliver sustainable, economic, and secure electricity supplies (as defined by the European Technology Platform for Electricity Networks for the Future).

Smart Ubiquitous Networks (SUNs) ITU-T SUNs are IP-based packet networks that can provide transport and delivery to a wide range of existing and emerging services to people and things. The services provided by the networks can cover aspects such as control, processing, and storage. The networks are smart in the sense that they are knowledgeable, context aware, adaptable, autonomous, and programmable and can instigate services effectively and securely. The networks are ubiquitous in the sense that they allow access anytime, anywhere, through varied access technologies, access devices including end-user devices and human–machine interfaces. Due to emerging trends in Information and Communications Technology (ICT) concerning the extension of communication objects (including not only humans but also machines and objects) and ways of communication, the ITU-T Study Group 13 has proposed a name—SUNs—as a new vision that incorporates current activities and emerging trends. In 2011, it was decided that activities for SUN in the following areas would commence: content awareness, context awareness, programmability, smart resources management, and autonomic network management (52).

Solicited-Node Address IPv6 multicast address used by nodes during the address resolution process. The solicited-node address facilitates efficient querying of network nodes during address resolution. IPv6 uses the neighbor solicitation message to perform address resolution. In IPv4, the ARP request frame is sent to the MAC-level broadcast, disturbing all nodes on the network segment regardless of whether a node is running IPv4. For IPv6, instead of disturbing all IPv6 nodes on the local link by using the local-link scope all-node address, the solicited-node multicast address is used as the neighbor solicitation message destination. The solicited-node multicast address consists of the prefix FF02::1:FF00:0/104 and the last 24-bits of the IPv6 unicast address that is being resolved (16).

Source Tree A tree that has its root at the multicast source and has branches forming a spanning tree over the network to the receivers. The tree uses the shortest path through the network and hence a separate SPT exists for each individual source sending to each group. The notation of (S,G) is used to describe an SPT where S is the IP address of the source and G is the multicast group address.

Source-Specific Multicast (SSM) A form of multicast in which a receiver is required to specify both the network-layer address of the source and the multicast destination address in order to receive the multicast transmission. The 232/8 IPv4 address range is currently allocated for SSM by IANA. In IPv6, the FF3x::/32 range (where "x" is a valid IPv6 multicast scope value) is reserved for SSM semantics, although today SSM allocations are restricted to FF3x::/96 (37).

Sparse-Mode (SM) protocols SM is one mode of operation of a multicast protocol. PIM-SM uses explicit join/prune messages and RPs in place of dense-mode PIM's and DVMRP's broadcast and prune mechanism (27). Multicast routing protocols are designed on the assumption that only few routers in the network will need to distribute multicast traffic for each multicast group. SM protocols start out with an empty distribution tree and add drop-off branches only upon explicit requests from receivers to join the distribution. SM protocols are generally used in WAN environments, where bandwidth considerations are important.

SSM-Aware Host A host that knows the SSM address range and is capable of applying SSM semantics to it (37).

Stateless IP/ICMP Translation (SIIT) An IPv6 transition technique that allows IPv4-only hosts to talk to IPv6-only hosts.

Static Routing Utilization of routes configured manually into a router's routing table.

Static Tunneling Tunneling technique where addresses are manually configured for the tunnel source and destination endpoints.

Storage Infrastructure (typically in the form of appliances) that is used for the permanent or semipermanent online retention of structured (e.g., databases) and unstructured (e.g., business/e-mail files) corporate information. Typically includes (i) a controller that manages incoming and outgoing communications as well as the data steering onto the physical storage medium (e.g., RAIDs, semiconductor memory) and (ii) the physical storage medium itself. The communications mechanism could be a network interface (such as gigabit Ethernet), a channel interface (such as SCSI), or an SAN interface (i.e., FC).

Storage Appliance A storage platform designed to perform a specific task, such as NAS, routers, and virtualization.

Storage Virtualization Software (sub)systems (typically middleware) that abstract the physical and logical storage assets from the host systems.

Stream A flow of a single type of data.

Stream Cipher Algorithms that simply produce a keystream to be XORed with the plaintext. The same keystream is reproduced at the receiver side for decryption (5).

Streaming An approach where a large media file (audio, video, and so on) is partitioned into smaller pieces so it can be viewed or heard immediately; this forgoes having to wait for the whole file to be downloaded first. The process of playing a file while it is still downloading. Streaming technology, also known as streaming media, lets a user view and hear digitized content—video, sound and animation—as it is being downloaded. Using a World Wide Web browser plug-in, streamed sounds and images can arrive within seconds of a user's click (53).

Streaming Media Internet video and/or audio clips that can play directly over the Internet, without needing to be downloaded first onto a computer. Used to view and hear broadcasts, and to interactively play and seek in stored clips (24).

Streaming Protocols Commands, processes, and procedures that can be used to select, set up, start the playing, pausing, recording, and tear down of streaming sessions.

STUB Multicast Routing A mechanism that allows IGMP messages to be forwarded through a non-PIM-enabled router toward a PIM-enabled router.

Stub Network A network having only a single OSPF router attached. A network belonging to an OSPF system is either a transit or a stub network, but never both (38).

Subnet-Router Anycast Address Anycast address that is allocated to router interfaces. Packets sent to the subnet-router anycast address will be delivered to one router on the subnet.

Subnetwork One or more links that use the same 64-bit prefix in IPv6.

Subnetwork Data Unit (SNDU) SNDU is an IPv4 or IPv6 datagram (or other subnetwork packet, e.g., an arp message or bridged Ethernet frame) (18). An encapsulated PDU sent as an MPEG-2 payload unit.

Subscriber A household or business that legally receives and pays for cable or Pay TV services for its own use (not for retransmission).

Suite B security Suite B security is a National Security Agency (NSA) directive that requires that key establishment and authentication algorithms be based on elliptic curve cryptography, and that the encryption algorithm be AES. The United States government has posted the Fact Sheet on NSA Suite B Cryptography that states in part as follows: "To complement the existing policy for the use of the Advanced Encryption Standard (AES) to protect national security systems and information as specified in The National Policy on the use of the Advanced Encryption Standard (AES) to Protect National Security Systems and National Security Information (CNSSP-15), the NSA announced Suite B Cryptography at the 2005 RSA Conference. In addition to the AES, Suite B includes cryptographic algorithms for hashing, digital signatures, and key exchange. Suite B only specifies the cryptographic algorithms to be used ... " The Fact Sheet on Suite B Cryptography requires that key establishment and authentication algorithms be based on elliptic curve cryptography, and that the encryption algorithm be AES. Suite B defines two security levels, of 128 and 192 bits. In particular, Suite B includes (54):

- Encryption: AES—FIPS 197 (with key sizes of 128 and 256 bits)
- Digital signature: Elliptic curve digital signature algorithm (ECDSA)—FIPS 186-2 (using the curves with 256- and 384-bit prime moduli)
- Key exchange: Elliptic curve Diffie–Hellman (ECDH)—NIST Special Publication 800-56A (using the curves with 256- and 384-bit prime moduli)

The 128-bit security level corresponds to an elliptic curve size of 256 bits and AES-128; it also makes use of SHA-256. The 192-bit security level corresponds to an elliptic curve size of 384 bits and AES-256; it also makes use of SHA-384. To accommodate backward compatibility, a Suite B compliant client or server can be configured to accept a cipher suite that is not part of Suite B. Note: Some refer to the two security levels based on the AES key size that is employed instead of the overall security provided by the combination of Suite B algorithms. At the 128-bit security level, an AES key size of 128 bits is utilized; however, at the 192-bit security level, an AES key size of 256 bits is used.

SUNs Smart ubiquitous networks.

Supervisory Control and Data Acquisition (SCADA) A legacy, but widely deployed system used to monitor and control a plant or equipment in industries such as but not limited to energy, oil and gas refining, water and waste control, transportation, and telecommunications. A SCADA system encompasses the transfer of data between a SCADA central host computer and a number of remote terminal units (RTUs) and/or programmable logic controllers (PLCs), and the central host and the operator terminals.

Symmetric DSL (SDSL) A vendor-proprietary version of symmetric DSL that may include bit rates to and from the customer ranging of 128 Kbps to 2.32 Mbps. SDSL is an umbrella term for a number of supplier-specific implementations over a single copper pair providing variable rates of symmetric service. SDSL uses 2B1Q HDSL run on a single pair with an Ethernet interface to the customer. The industry is expected to quickly move toward the higher-performing and standardized G.shdsl technology developed by the ITU with support from T1E1.4 (USA) and ETSI (European Telecommunications Standards Institute) (15).

Symmetric Encryption Type of encryption in which encryption and decryption keys are the same key or can easily be derived from each other. In most cryptographic systems, the decryption key and the encryption keys are identical (5).

Symmetric Flavors DSL Symmetrical variations of DSL that include SDSL, SHDSL, HDSL, HDSL2, and IDSL. The equal speeds make symmetrical DSLs useful for LAN access, video-conferencing, and for locations hosting their own Web sites (15).

Symmetric High-Speed Digital Subscriber Line (SHDSL) A state-of-the-art, industry standard based on ITU Recommendation G.991.2, also known as G.shdsl (2001). SHDSL achieves 20% better loop-reach than older versions of symmetric DSL, it causes much less crosstalk into other transmission systems in the same cable, and multivendor interoperability is facilitated by the standardization of this technology. SHDSL systems may operate at many bit rates, from 192 Kbps to 5.7 Mbps, thereby maximizing the bit rate for each customer. G.shdsl specifies operation via one pair of wires, or for operation on longer loops, two pairs of wire may be used. For example, with two pairs of wire, 1.2 Mbps can be sent over 20,000 feet of 26 AWG wire. SHDSL is best suited to data-only applications that need high upstream bit rates. SHDSL is being deployed primarily for business customers (15).

Tag Air Interface As defined in ISO 19762-3, a conductor-free medium, usually air, between a transponder and a reader/interrogator through which data communication is achieved by means of a modulated inductive or propagated electromagnetic field.

Tag-Identification Layer In RFID environments, collectively, the set of functions and commands used by an interrogator to identify and modify tags (also known as the *operating procedur*) (7).

Telco Traditional telephone company.

Teredo IPv6 transition technology for use when IPv6/IPv4 hosts are located behind an IPv4 network address translator.

Teredo Client Software on an IPv6/IPv4 host allowing it to participate in the Teredo transition technology.

Teredo Relay An IPv6 router that can receive traffic from the IPv6 Internet and forward to a Teredo client.

Teredo Server A node that assists in the provision of IPv6 connectivity to Teredo clients.

Threat A potential violation of security.

Tiered Storage A process for the assignment of different categories of data to different types of storage media. The purpose is to reduce total storage cost and optimize accessibility. In practice, the assignment of data to particular media tends to be an evolutionary and complex activity. Storage categories may be based on a variety of design/architectural factors, including levels of protection required for the application or organization, performance requirements, and frequency of use. Software exists for automatically managing the process based on a company-defined policy. Tiered storage generally introduces more vendors into the environment and interoperability is important.

As an example of tiered storage is as follows: Tier 1 data (e.g., mission-critical files) could be effectively stored on high-quality directly attached storage (DAS) (but relatively expensive) media such as double-parity RAIDs. Tier 2 data (e.g., quarterly financial records) could be stored on media affiliated with an SAN; this media tends to be less expensive than DAS drives, but there may be network latencies associated with the access. Tier 3 data (e.g., e-mail backup files) could be stored on recordable compact discs (CD-Rs) or tapes. (Clearly, there could be more than three tiers, but the management of the multiple tiers becomes fairly complex.)

Another example (in the medical field) is as follows: Real-time medical imaging information may be temporarily stored on DAS disks as a Tier 1, say for a couple of weeks. Recent medical images and patient data may be kept on FC drives (tier 2) for about a year. After that, less frequently accessed images and patient records are stored on AT attachment (ATA) drives (tier-3) for 18 months or more. Tier 4 consists of a tape library for archiving.

Transit Network A network having two or more OSPF routers attached. These networks can forward data traffic that is neither locally originated nor locally destined. In OSPF, with the exception of point-to-point networks and virtual links, the neighborhood of each transit network is described by a network links advertisement (38).

Translation Translation refers to the direct conversion of protocols, for example, between IPv4 and IPv6.

Transport Relay Translator (TRT) TRT partitions the IP layer into two terminated IP legs, one IPv4 and one IPv6. Translation then occurs at the higher layers (16).

Tree Information Base (TIB) This is the collection of state maintained by a PIM router and created by receiving PIM messages and IGMP information from local hosts. The table essentially stores the state of all multicast distribution trees at that router (39).

Tunnel In IPv6 transition context, an IPv6 over IPv4 tunnel.

Tunneling Techniques Tunneling techniques include the following (29):

- IPv6-over-IPv4 tunneling: The technique of encapsulating IPv6 packets within IPv4 so that they can be carried across IPv4 routing infrastructures.
- Configured tunneling: IPv6-over-IPv4 tunneling where the IPv4 tunnel endpoint address is determined by configuration information on the encapsulating

node. The tunnels can be either unidirectional or bidirectional. Bidirectional configured tunnels behave as virtual point-to-point links.

*   Automatic tunneling: Tunneling where the IPv4 tunnel endpoint address is automatically determined, generally being embedded in the IPv6 address. Examples include IPv6-compatible addresses and IPv6 6to4 addresses.

UICC (Universal Integrated Circuit Card) UICC, the smart card used in mobile terminals in GSM and UMTS networks. A UICC typically contain several applications, and the same smart card provides access to both GSM and UMTS networks. The UICC also provides storage (e.g., for a directory). In a GSM network, the UICC contains a subscriber identification module (SIM) application; in a UMTS network it is the USIM (universal subscriber identity module) application. It is a new-generation SIM included in cell phones or laptops using high-speed 3G cellular networks. The UICC smart card typically has of a CPU, ROM, RAM, EEPROM, and I/O circuits.

UMTS Terrestrial Radio Access Network (UTRAN) A collective term for the NodeBs (base stations) and radio network controllers (RNC) that comprise the UTRAN. NodeB is the equivalent to the base transceiver station (BTS) concept used in GSM. The UTRAN allows connectivity between the UE and the core network.

Unicast Address An address that identifies an IPv6 interface and allows network-layer point-to-point communication. It identifies a single interface within the scope of the unicast address type. An identifier for a single interface. A packet sent to a unicast address is delivered to the interface identified by that address. The following list shows the types of IPv6 unicast addresses:

*   Aggregatable global unicast addresses
*   Link-local addresses
*   Site-local addresses
*   Special addresses, including unspecified and loopback addresses
*   Compatibility addresses, including 6to4 addresses

Unicast Environment Environment where one system communicates directly to another system.

Unidirectional Link (UDL) A one-way transmission IP over DVB link, for example, a broadcast satellite link.

Universal Mobile Telecommunications System (UMTS) UMTS is a 3G mobile cellular technology for networks supporting voice and data (IP) based on the GSM standard developed by the 3GPP.

Unspecified Address 0:0:0:0:0:0:0:0 or ::—used to show the absence of any address, equivalent to the IPv4 address 0.0.0.0.

Upstream Interface Interface toward the source of the datagram. Also known as the RPF interface (39).

Upstream Interface (or Router) In CBT, an "upstream" interface (or router) is one that is on the path toward the group's core router with respect to this interface (or router) [BAL199701].

USIM Universal subscriber identity module.

Very High Bit Rate DSL (VDSL) A standard for up to 26 Mbps, over distances up to 50 m on short loops such as from fiber to the curb. In most cases, VDSL lines will be served from neighborhood cabinets that link to a Central Office via optical fiber. VDSL has been introduced in some market to deliver video services over existing phone lines. VDSL can also be configured in symmetric mode (15).

Very Small Aperture Terminal (VSAT) A complete end-user terminal (typically with a small 4–5 ft antenna) that is designed to interact with other terminals in a satellite-delivered data IP-based network, commonly in a "star" configuration through a hub. Contention and/or traffic engineering are typical of these services. Hub or network operator to control the system and present billing based on a data throughput, or other form of usage basis. VSATs are utilized in a variety of remote applications and are designed as low-cost units (say $1500–$3000 depending on application and data rate).

Video Compression The process through which a video file is reduced in size for storing and streaming either on traditional TV systems, IPTV, or IBTV. Performing a digital compression process on a video signal. Compression techniques are used to enable efficient transmission of video signals.

Video Format The file type of a video file. Some of the most well-known formats for digital video include .avi (Microsoft), .mov (Quicktime), .wmv (Windows), and .flv (Flash).

Virtual Infrastructure An infrastructure where there is a dynamic mapping of physical resources to functional service requests, such that the entity requiring service is oblivious to the specific nature of the actual hardware supporting the underlying service.

Virtual Private LAN service (VPLS) VPLS is a way to provide Ethernet-based multipoint-to-multipoint communication over IP/MPLS networks. VPLS allows geographically dispersed sites to share an Ethernet broadcast domain by connecting sites through pseudowires. The technologies that can be used as pseudo-wire can be Ethernet over MPLS, L2TPv3, or even GRE. There are two IETF standards describing VPLS establishment. VPLS requires a full mesh of LSPs which has the n2 scaling problem. H-VPLS helps solve this problem by dividing the virtual LAN into separate hierarchies (11).

Virtualization The abstraction of server, storage, and network resources in order to make them available dynamically for sharing by IT services, both internal to and external to an organization. In combination with other server, storage, and networking capabilities, virtualization offers customers the opportunity to build more efficient IT infrastructures. Virtualization is seen by some as a step on the road to utility computing. An approach that allows several operating systems to run simultaneously on one (large) computer (e.g., IBM's z/VM operating system lets multiple instances of Linux coexist on the same mainframe computer). It is the practice of making resources from diverse devices accessible to a user as if they were a single, larger, homogenous, appear-to-be-locally available resource. Virtualization depends on being able to dynamically shift resources across platforms to match computing demands with available resources: the computing environment can become dynamic, enabling autonomic shifting applications between servers to match demand.

Web Cache A Web cache fills requests from the Web server, stores the requested information locally, and sends the information to the client. The next time the Web cache gets a request for the same information, it simply returns the locally cached data instead of searching over the Internet, thus reducing Internet traffic and response time (23).

Web of Things Technology that aims for direct Web connectivity of things in the IoT context by pushing Web capabilities (e.g., web server) down to devices.

Web Services (WSs) WSs provide standard infrastructure for data exchange between two different distributed applications.

Widget A stand-alone application that can be embedded into a (third party) website by a(ny) user on a page where they have rights of authorship (e.g., a profile on a social media site). A widget is a standardized on-screen representation of a control that may be manipulated by the user. Scroll bars, buttons, and textboxes are all examples of widgets. For example, a "search widget" could be added on a personal website by copying and pasting the embed code into the home page (or some similar action on a Facebook profile). Widgets allow users to turn personal content into dynamic web apps. Traditional web widgets provided functions such as advertising banners and link counters.

Wi-Fi Wi-Fi is a brand originally licensed by the Wi-Fi Alliance to describe the underlying technology of wireless local area networks (WLANs) based on the IEEE 802.11 family of standards, including 802.11a, 802.11b, 802.11g, 802.11n, and 802.11v (55). It was developed to be used for business mobile computing devices, such as laptops, in LANs, but is now increasingly used for additional services, including Internet and voice over IP (VoIP) phone access, gaming, and basic connectivity of consumer electronics such as televisions and DVD players, or digital cameras (11). (Wi-Fi is a trademark of the Wi-Fi Alliance, a commercial organization that certifies the interoperability of specific devices designed to the respective IEEE standard.)

Wildcard (WC) Multicast Route Entry In PIM-SM, wildcard multicast route entries are those entries that may be used to forward packets for any source sending to the specified group. Wildcard bots in the join list of a join/prune message represent either a (∗,G) or (∗,∗,RP) join; in the prune list they represent a (∗,G) prune (27).

Wireless M-BUS The Wireless M-BUS standard (EN 13757-4:2005) specifies communications between water, gas, heat, and electric meters and is becoming widely accepted in Europe for smart metering or AMI applications. Wireless M-BUS is targeted to operate in the 868 MHz band (from 868 MHz to 870 MHz); this band enjoys good trade-offs between RF range and antenna size. Typically, chip manufacturers, for example Texas Instruments, have both single-chip (SoC) and two-chip solutions for wireless M-BUS.

Wireless Sensor Network (WSN) A sensor network is an infrastructure comprised of sensing (measuring), computing, and communication elements that gives the administrator the ability to instrument, observe, and react to events and phenomena in a specified environment. Typically, the connectivity is by wireless means, hence the term WSN (56).

WirelessHART (aka IEC 62591) WirelessHART is a wireless sensor networking technology based on the highway addressable remote transducer protocol (HART). In 2010, WirelessHart was approved by the International Electrotechnical Commission (IEC) as IEC 62591 as a wireless international standard. IEC 62591 entails operation in the 2.4 GHz ISM band using IEEE 802.15.4 standard radios and makes use of a time-synchronized, self-organizing, and self-healing mesh architecture. WirelessHART/IEC 62591 was defined for the requirements of process field device networks. It is a global IEC-approved standard that specifies an interoperable self-organizing mesh technology in which field devices form wireless networks that dynamically mitigate obstacles in the process environment. This architecture creates a cost-effective automation alternative that does not require wiring and other supporting infrastructure (57).

Worldwide Interoperability for Microwave Access (WiMAX) WiMAX is a standards-based technology enabling the delivery of last mile wireless broadband access as an alternative to cable and DSL WiMAX is defined by the WiMAX Forum, formed in June 2001, to promote conformance and interoperability of the IEEE 802.16 standard.

Worldwide Interoperability for Microwave Access (WiMAX) Forum The WiMAX Forum was formed in June 2001 to promote conformance and interoperability of the IEEE 802.16 standard. The WiMAX Forum describes WiMAX as "a standards-based technology enabling the delivery of last mile wireless broadband access as an alternative to cable and DSL."

ZigBee IP (ZIP) The goal of this protocol stack is to extend the use of IP networking into resource-constrained devices over a wide range of low-power link technologies. The effort related to ZIP development has resulted in significant progress to the goal of bringing IPv6 network protocols over 802.15.4 wireless mesh networks to reality. ZIP is a protocol stack based on IETF- and IEEE-defined standards such as 6LoWPAN and IEEE 802.15.4 to be used for the SE 2.0 profile.

ZigBee RF4CE Specification The specialty-use driven ZigBee RF4CE is designed for simple, two-way device-to-device control applications that do not require the full-featured mesh networking capabilities offered by ZigBee 2007. ZigBee RF4CE offers lower memory size requirements, thereby enabling lower cost implementations. The simple device-to-device topology provides easy development and testing, resulting in faster time to market. ZigBee RF4CE provides a multivendor interoperable solution for consumer electronics featuring a simple, robust, and low-cost communication network for two-way wireless connectivity. Through the ZigBee-certified program, the Alliance independently tests platforms implementing this specification and has a list of ZigBee-compliant platforms offering support for ZigBee RF4CE (58).

ZigBee Smart Energy A leading standard for interoperable products that monitor, control, inform, and automate the delivery and use of energy and water. It helps create greener homes by giving consumers the information and automation needed to easily reduce their consumption and save money. ZigBee SE version 1.1, the newest version for product development, adds several important features including dynamic pricing enhancements, tunneling of other protocols, prepayment features, over-the-air updates, and guaranteed backward compatibility with certified ZigBee SE products version 1.0. (58).

ZigBee Specification The core ZigBee specification defines ZigBee's smart, cost-effective, and energy-efficient mesh network based on IEEE 802.15.4. It is a self-configuring, self-healing system of redundant, low-cost, very low-power nodes that enable ZigBee's unique flexibility, mobility, and ease of use. ZigBee is available as two feature sets, ZigBee PRO and ZigBee. Both feature sets define how the ZigBee mesh networks operate. ZigBee PRO, the most widely used specification, is optimized for low-power consumption and to support large networks with thousands of devices (58). (ZigBee is a trademark of the ZigBee Alliance, a commercial organization that certifies the interoperability of specific devices designed to the respective IEEE standard.)

Zone Name A human readable name for a scope zone. An ISO 10646 character string with an RFC 1766 language tag. One zone may have several zone names, each in a different language. For instance, a zone for use within IBM's locations in Switzerland might have the names "IBM Suisse," "IBM Switzerland," "IBM Schweiz," and "IBM Svizzera" with language tags "fr," "en," "de," and "it" (34).

Z-Wave Z-Wave is a wireless ecosystem that aims at supporting connectivity of home electronics, and the user, via remote control. It uses low-power radio waves that easily travel through walls, floors, and cabinets. Z-Wave control can be added to almost any electronic device in the home, even devices that one would not ordinarily think of as "intelligent," such as appliances, window shades, thermostats, smoke alarms, security sensors, and home lighting. Z-Wave operates around 900 MHz (the band used by some cordless telephones but avoids interference with Wi-Fi devices). Z-Wave was developed by Zen-Sys, a Danish startup around 2005; the company was later acquired by Sigma Designs. The Z-Wave Alliance was established in 2005; it is comprised of about 200 industry leaders dedicated to the development and extension of Z-Wave as the key enabling technology for "smart" home and business applications.

REFERENCES

1. 3rd Generation Partnership Project (3GPP) Organization, www.3gpp.org.
2. Third Generation Partnership Project 2 Organization, http://www.3gpp2.org.

3. Bormann C. Getting Started with IPv6 in Low-Power Wireless "Personal Area" Networks (6LoWPAN), Universität Bremen TZI, IETF 6lowpan WG and CoRE WG Co-Chair, IAB Tutorial on Interconnecting Smart Objects with the Internet, Prague, Saturday, 2011-03-26, http://www.iab.org/about/workshops/smartobjects/tutorial.html.

4. Microsoft Corporation, MSDN Library, Internet Protocol, 2004, http://MSDn.microsoft.com.

5. Conax AS. Glossary of Terms, Fred Olsensgate 6, NO-0152 Oslo, Norway.

6. Drake J, Najewicz D, Watts W. Energy Efficiency Comparisons of Wireless Communication Technology Options for Smart Grid Enabled Devices. White Paper, General Electric Company, GE Appliances & Lighting, December 9, 2010.

7. EPCglobal Inc™, EPC™ Radio-Frequency Identity Protocols, Class-1 Generation-2 UHF RFID, Protocol for Communications at 860 MHz–960 MHz, Version 1.0.9, January 2005.

8. Practel, Inc., Role of Wireless ICT in Health Care and Wellness—Standards, Technologies and Markets, May, 2012, Published by Global Information, Inc. (GII), 195 Farmington Avenue, Suite 208 Farmington, CT 06032 USA.

9. Jung N-J, Yang I-K, Park S-W, Lee S-Y. A design of AMI protocols for two way communication in K-AMI. Control, Automation and Systems (ICCAS), Conference Proceedings 2011, 11th International Conference on, Date of Conference: 26–29 Oct. 2011, S/W Center, KEPCO Res. Inst., Daejeon, South Korea, Page(s): 1011–1016.

10. Smith P. Comparing Low-Power Wireless Technologies. Tech Zone, Digikey Online Magazine, Digi-Key Corporation, 701 Brooks Avenue, South Thief River Falls, MN 56701 USA.

11. Cisco. IP NGN Carrier Ethernet Design: Powering the Connected Life in the Zettabyte Era. Cisco Whitepaper, 2007, Cisco Systems, Inc., 170 West Tasman Dr., San Jose, CA 95134, USA.

12. Fairhurst G. MPEG-2 Digital Video, Background to Digital Video, University of Aberdeen, King's College, Dept. of Engineering, Aberdeen, AB24 3FX, UK, January 2001, http://www.erg.abdn.ac.uk/research/future-net/digital-video/mpeg2-trans.html.

13. Delay Tolerant Networking Research Group, http://www.dtnrg.org.

14. Gifford K. Disruption Tolerant Networking for Space Operations (DTN). University of Colorado, Boulder, CO, United States, NASA Research, March 2012, http://www.nasa.gov/mission_pages/station/research/experiments/DTN.html.

15. DSL Forum, DSL Forum, 48377 Fremont Blvd, Suite 117, Fremont, CA 94538, http://www.dslforum.org.

16. IPv6 Portal, http://www.ipv6tf.org/meet/faqs.php.

17. ETSI Documentation, ETSI, 650 Route des Lucioles F-06921 Sophia Antipolis Cedex—FRANCE.

18. Clausen Horst D, Collini-Nocker Bernhard, et al. Simple Encapsulation for Transmission of IP Datagrams over MPEG-2/DVB Networks, Internet Engineering Task Force, draft-unisal-ipdvb-enc-00.txt, May 2003.

19. Machine-to-Machine Communications (M2M); M2M Service Requirements. ETSI TS 102 689 V1.1.1 (2010-08). ETSI, 650 Route des Lucioles F-06921 Sophia Antipolis Cedex—FRANCE.

20. Machine-to-Machine Communications (M2M); Functional Architecture Technical Specification, ETSI TS 102 690 V1.1.1 (2011-10), ETSI, 650 Route des Lucioles F-06921 Sophia Antipolis Cedex—FRANCE.

21. Kindig S. TV and HDTV Glossary. December 02, 2009, Crutchfield, 1 Crutchfield Park, Charlottesville, VA 22911.

22. 3GPP TS 22.368 V10.1.0 (2010-06), Technical Specification, June 2010, 3rd Generation Partnership Project; Technical Specification Group Services and System Aspects; Service requirements for Machine-Type Communications (MTC); Stage 1 (Release 10).

23. SunStar, Storage Glossary of Terms, 900 West Hyde Park Blvd. Inglewood, CA 90302.

24. ReelSEO.com, Online Video Dictionary—Glossary of Online Video Terms, The Online Video Marketer's Guide, 2010.

25. Gast M. Introduction to 802.11v, Trapeze Networks, Interop Presentation, 2008.

26. Krasinski R, Nikolich P, Heile RF. IEEE 802.15.4j Medical Body Area Networks Task Group PAR, IEEE P802.15 Working Group for Wireless Personal Area Networks (WPANs), January18, 2011.

27. Estrin D, Farinacci D, et al. Protocol Independent Multicast-Sparse Mode (PIM-SM): Protocol Specification. RFC2362, June 1998.

28. Shelby Z, Hartke K, Bormann C, Frank B. Constrained Application Protocol (CoAP). CoRE Working Group, March 12, 2012, Internet-Draft, draft-ietf-core-coap-09.

29. Gilligan R, Nordmark E. Transition Mechanisms for IPv6 Hosts and Routers, RFC2893, August 2000.

30. Winter T, editor. ROLL/RPL: IPv6 Routing Protocol for Low power and Lossy Networks, March 2011, draft-ietf-roll-rpl-19.

31. ISA, 67 Alexander Drive, P.O. Box 12277, Research Triangle Park, NC 27709, info@isa.org.

32. Fairhurst G, Montpetit M-J. Address Resolution for IP Datagrams over MPEG-2 Networks, Internet Draft draft-ietf-ipdvb-ar-00.txt, IETF ipdvb, June 2005.

33. ETSI TR 101 557 V1.1.1 (2012-02), Electromagnetic Compatibility and Radio Spectrum Matters (ERM); System Reference Document (SRdoc); Medical Body Area Network Systems (MBANSs) in the 1785 MHz to 2500 MHz range.

34. Hanna S, Patel B, Shah M. Multicast Address Dynamic Client Allocation Protocol (MAD-CAP). RFC2730, December 1999.

35. Radoslavov P, Estrin D, et al. The Multicast Address-Set Claim (MASC) Protocol. RFC2909, September 2000.

36. Vida R, Costa L, editors. Multicast Listener Discovery Version 2 (MLDv2) for IPv6, RFC 3810, June 2004.

37. Holbrook H, Cain B, Haberman B. Using Internet Group Management Protocol Version 3 (IGMPv3) and Multicast Listener Discovery Protocol Version 2 (MLDv2) for Source-Specific Multicast. RFC4604, August 2006.

38. Moy J. Multicast Extensions to OSPF. RFC 1584, March 1994.

39. Adams A, Nicholas J, Siadak W. Protocol Independent Multicast—Dense Mode (PIM-DM): Protocol Specification (Revised). RFC 3973, January 2005.

40. Welcher PJ. The Protocols of IP Multicast, NetCraftsmen White Paper, Chesapeake NetCraftsmen, LLC., 1290 Bay Dale Drive—Suite #312, Arnold, MD 21012.

41. NSF Future Internet Architecture Project, http://www.nets-fia.net.

42. Lee GM, Choi JK, et al. Naming Architecture for Object to Object Communications. HIP Working Group, Internet Draft, March 8, 2010, draft-lee-object-naming-02.txt.

43. ITU-T Y.2002. Overview of Ubiquitous Networking and of its Support in NGN. November 2009.

44. Radding A. SAN of the Future. Essential Guide To Storage Networking, Storage Media Group/SearchStorage.com Whitepaper, March 2010.

45. Sjöberg D. Content Delivery Networks: Ensuring Quality of Experience in Streaming Media Applications. TeliaSonera International Carrier, CDN White Paper, August 14, 2008.

46. Johnson M. ITU-T IPTV Focus Group Proceedings, ITU-T, 2008.

47. PLCforum, http://www.plcforum.org/frame_plc.html.

48. Schulzrinne H, Casner S, et al. RTP: A Transport Protocol for Real-Time Applications, IETF Request for Comments, July 2003.

49. Kay R. Quick Study: Representational State Transfer (REST). ComputerWorld, August 6, 2007.

50. Minoli D. *Satellite Systems Engineering in an IPv6 Environment*. Boca Raton, FL: Francis and Taylor; 2009.

51. Rodbell M. Protocol Independent Multicast—Sparse Mode, CMP COMMs Design, an EE Times Community, 3 June 2007, http://www.comMSDesign.com/main/9811/9811standards.htm.

52. Service Architecture Lab (a leading French research group with a focus on 'Future Services'), http://servicearchitecture.wp.it-sudparis.eu/.

53. California Software Labs, Basic Streaming Technology and RTSP Protocol—A Technical Report, 2002, California Software Labs, 6800 Koll Center Parkway, Suite 100 Pleasanton CA 94566, USA.

54. Salter M, Rescorla E, Housley R. Suite B Profile for Transport Layer Security (TLS). RFC 5430, March 2009.

55. Minoli D. *Hotspot Networks: Wi-Fi for Public Access Locations*. New York, NY: McGraw-Hill; 2002.

56. Minoli D. *Wireless Sensor Networks* (co authored with K. Sohraby and T. Znati). Hoboken, NJ: Wiley; 2007.

57. Emerson Process Management, *IEC 62591 WirelessHART, System Engineering Guide, Revision 2.3*, Emerson Process Management, 2011.

58. ZigBee Alliance, http://www.zigbee.org/.

59. Cisco Systems, Internet Protocol (IP) Multicast Technology Overview, 2007, Cisco Systems, Inc., 170 West Tasman Dr., San Jose, CA 95134, USA.

60. Open IPTV Forum (OIPF), Services and Functions for Release 2 [V1.0]-[2008-10-20], 2008, Open IPTV Forum, 650 Route des Lucioles - Sophia Antipolis, Valbonne, France.

INDEX

Building the Internet of Things with IPv6 and MIPv6: The Evolving World of M2M Communications,
First Edition. Daniel Minoli.
© 2013 John Wiley & Sons, Inc. Published 2013 by John Wiley & Sons, Inc.

Printed and bound by CPI Group (UK) Ltd, Croydon, CR0 4YY

09/06/2025

14685904-0001